Connectedness

An Incomplete Encyclopedia of the Anthropocene

Marianne Krogh (ed.)

con-
nect-
ed-
ness

An Incomplete Encyclopedia of the Anthropocene

Strandberg Publishing

Contents

Foreword: Connectedness is about Sharing
9 Katherine Richardson

Con-nect-ed-ness: An Introduction
12 Marianne Krogh

Abrupt Climate Change
30 Sune Olander Rasmussen

Aesthetics
34 Dehlia Hannah

Agency
36 Tatjana Schneider

Agriculture
40 Sofie Isager Ahl

Air
42 Aerocene

Anthropocene
48 Gaia Vince

Architecture
52 Elke Krasny

Art
56 Line Marie Thorsen

Atmosphere
62 Gernot Böhme

Attachment
64 Emmy Laura Perez Fjalland

Attention
66 Polina Chebotareva
Rasmus Hjortshøj

Bacteria
74 Salla Sariola

Biodiversity
76 Minik Rosing

Body
82 Mwenza Blell

Borders
84 Tiffany Chung

Capitalocene
92 Thomas Hylland Eriksen

Care
94 Joanna Latimer

Chthulucene
100 Donna Haraway

City
104 David Gissen

Client: Earth
108 James Thornton

Climate
112 Bill McKibben

Climate Risk Communities
114 Anders Blok

Coexistence
118 Rosi Braidotti

Connected-ness
122 Josefine Klougart

Corals
126 Nils Bubandt

Creation
128 Liv Sejrbo Lidegaard

Declaration of Rebellion
132 Extinction Rebellion

Declarations of Climate Emergency
136

Denial
138 Simo Køppe

Description
140 April Vannini
Phillip Vannini

Development
144 Gregers Andersen

Dystopia
146 Jesper Just

Earth Ethics
152 J. Baird Callicott

Earthlings
156 Jeff VanderMeer

Ecology
160 Timothy Morton

Energy
162 Kirsten Halsnæs

Environment
166 Cary Wolfe

Explicitation
170 NORRØN

Facts
174 Peter Weibel

Feminism
178 Meike Schalk
Thérèse Kristiansson
Ramia Mazé

Fire
182 Lars Skinnebach

Flood
186 SUPERFLEX

Food
190 Alice Waters

Future
192 Andri Snær Magnason

Garden
198 Hu Fang

Geology
200 Minik Rosing

Geo-Social Classes
204 Nikolaj Schultz

Glaciers
208 Jesper Theilgaard

Global
210 Saskia Sassen

Heatwave
214 Jim Reed

Heritage
218 Ben Dibley

Home
222 lenschow & pihlmann

Imagine
228 Björk

Invisible
230 Rune Bosse

Local
240 Emmy Laura Perez Fjalland

Media
244 Paul Roquet

Migration Flows
246 Thomas Gammeltoft-Hansen

Modernism
250 Asmund Havsteen-Mikkelsen

Moving Earths
254 Bruno Latour
Nikolaj Schultz

Natureculture
266 Flemming Rafn

New Materialism
270 Diana Coole

Next Generation
274 Greta Thunberg

Object-Oriented Ontology
280 Graham Harman

Oil
282 Peter Adolphsen

Over-population
286 Betsy Hartmann

Oxymorons
290 Julius von Bismarck

Pandemic
298 Carsten Jensen

Plantationo-cene
300 Zachary Caple

Plastic
302 Heather Davis

Pollution
304 Frederick Rowe Davis

Posthuman
308 Tomás Saraceno

Power
312 Lars Tønder

Production
314 Sidsel Kjærulff Rasmussen
Till Rickert

Queer
318 Antke Engel

Resilience
324 Aditya Bahadur

Resources
328 Jaime Stapleton
Rikke Luther

Sensitivity
340 Olga Tokarczuk

Soil
350 Vandana Shiva

Sun
352 SPACE10
SachsNottveit

Sustainability
354 Connie Hedegaard

Tenderness
358 Lundgaard & Tranberg Architects

Terraforming
360 Emmy Laura Perez Fjalland

The Sharing Economy
364 Darren Sharp

Time
368 Barbara Adam

Violence
374 Niels Albertsen

Waste
380 Amanda Boetzkes

Water
384 Astrida Neimanis

Weather
388 Astrida Neimanis
Jennifer Mae Hamilton

Wilderness
392 Jason Mark

Window of Opportunity
396 Mike Hulme

World Scientists' Warning to Humanity
400

Xenophobia
404 Georg Metz

410 Notes
414 Index
416 Photo credits

Note for the reader

The alphabetic structure of the book suggests a general reading sequence.

At the top of each contribution is a selection of words, concepts and brief sentences.

Black text marks key words related to the text, while red text offers references to other contributions in the book where you can read more about the given topics.

Each contribution is thus connected to several others, offering an alternative approach to the logic of the alphabet.

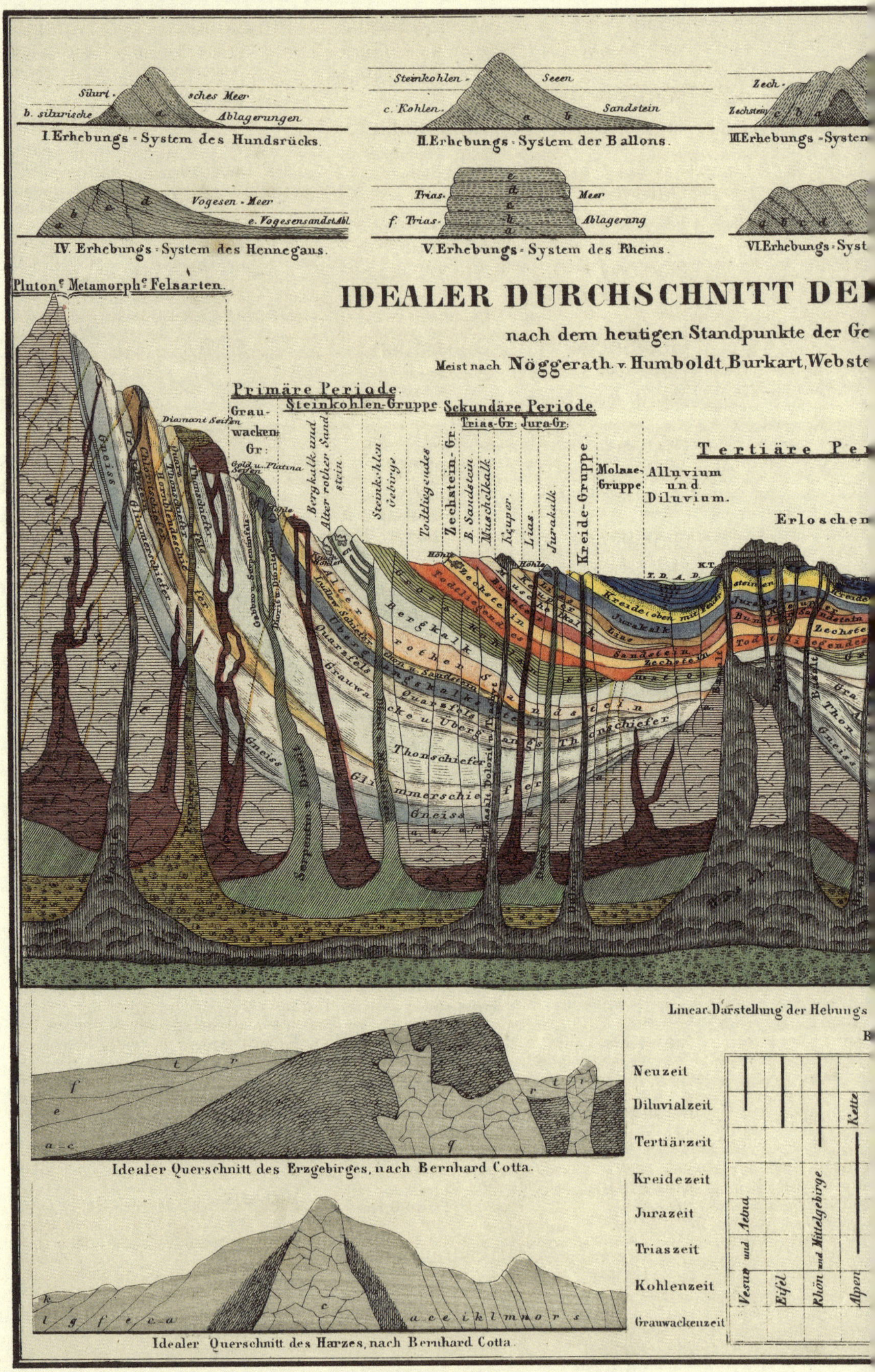

Siluri- sches Meer
b. silurische Ablagerungen
I. Erhebungs-System des Hundsrücks.
Steinkohlen- Seeen
c. Kohlen- Sandstein
II. Erhebungs-System der Ballons.
Zech-
Zechstein
III. Erhebungs-Systen
Vogesen-Meer
e. Vogesensandst. Abl.
IV. Erhebungs-System des Hennegaus.
Trias- Meer
f. Trias- Ablagerung
V. Erhebungs-System des Rheins.
VI. Erhebungs-Syst
Pluton.e Metamorph.e Felsarten.
IDEALER DURCHSCHNITT DE
nach dem heutigen Standpunkte der Ge
Meist nach Nöggerath v. Humboldt, Burkart, Webste
Primäre Periode.
Grau-wacken-Gr.
Steinkohlen-Gruppe
Sekundäre Periode
Trias-Gr. Jura-Gr.
Tertiäre Pe
Molasse-Gruppe
Alluvium und Diluvium.
Erloschen
Diamant Seifen
Gold u. Platina Seifen
Bergkalk und Alter rother Sandstein.
Steinkohlengebirge.
Todtliegendes
Zechstein-Gr.
B. Sandstein
Muschelkalk
Keuper
Lias
Jurakalk
Kreide-Gruppe
Gneiss
Glimmerschiefer
Thonschiefer
Grauwacke
Bergkalk
Quarzfels
Kreide (oben mit Feuerst.)
Jurakalk
Lias
Sandstein
Zechstein
Todtliegendes
Idealer Querschnitt des Erzgebirges, nach Bernhard Cotta.
Idealer Querschnitt des Harzes, nach Bernhard Cotta.
Linear Darstellung der Hebungs
Neuzeit
Diluvialzeit
Tertiärzeit
Kreidezeit
Jurazeit
Triaszeit
Kohlenzeit
Grauwackenzeit
Vesuv und Aetna
Eifel
Rhön und Mittelgebirge
Alpen
Kette

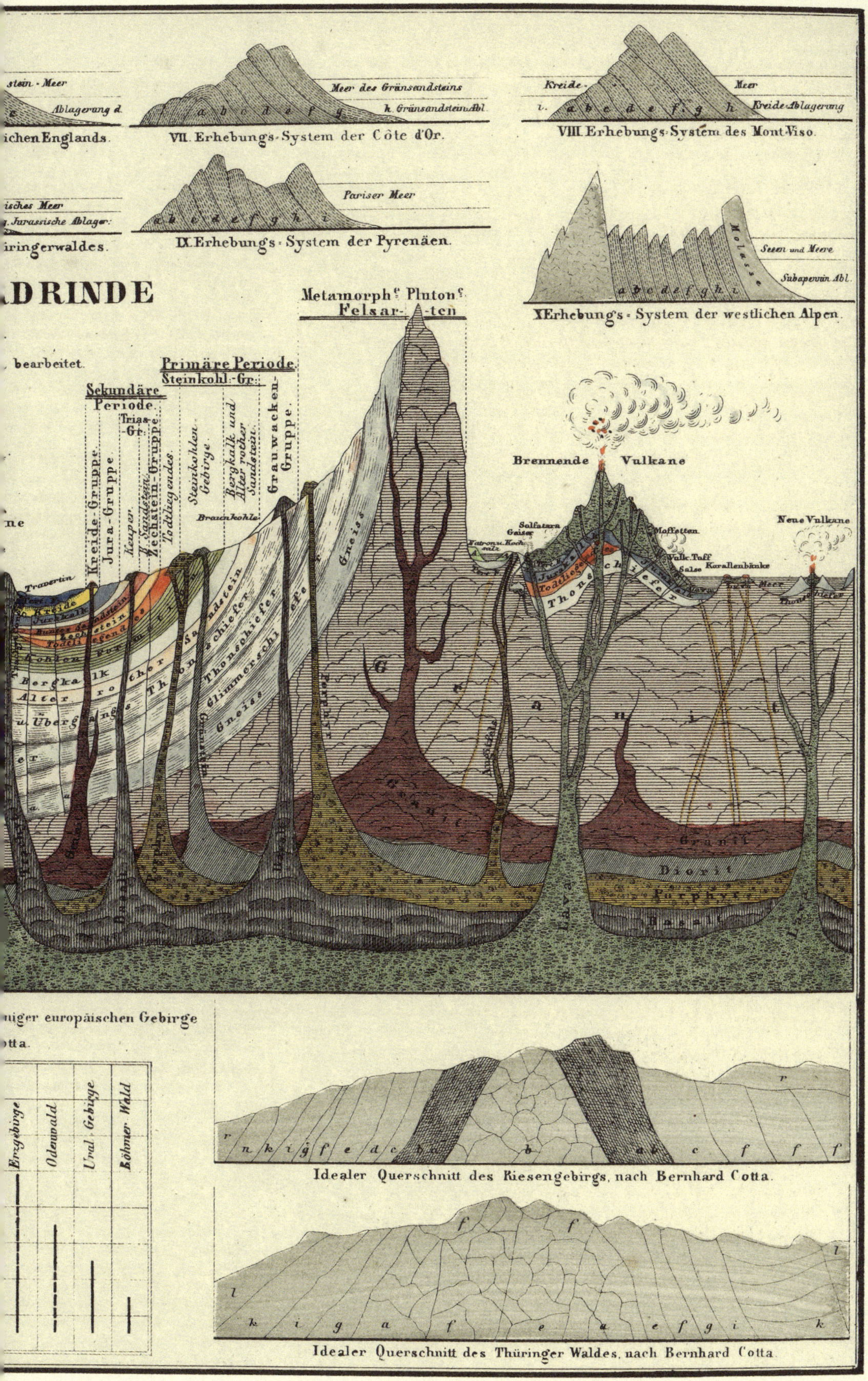
stein - Meer
Ablagerung d.
ichen Englands.
Meer des Grünsandsteins
h. Grünsandstein Abl.
VII. Erhebungs-System der Côte d'Or.
Kreide
Meer
Kreide Ablagerung
VIII. Erhebungs-System des Mont-Viso.
isches Meer
Jurassische Ablager.
ringerwaldes.
Pariser Meer
IX. Erhebungs-System der Pyrenäen.
Seen und Meere
Subapennin Abl.
Molasse
X. Erhebungs-System der westlichen Alpen.
DRINDE
bearbeitet.
Metamorph. Pluton.
Felsarten
Primäre Periode
Steinkohl.-Gr.
Sekundäre Periode
Trias-Gr.
Kreide-Gruppe
Jura-Gruppe
Keuper
Zechstein-Gruppe
Todtliegendes
Steinkohlen Gebirge
Bergkalk und Alter rother Sandstein
Grauwacken-Gruppe
Braunkohle
Brennende Vulkane
Neue Vulkane
Solfatara
Geiser
Natronu. Kochsalz
Moffetten
Vulk. Tuff
Salse
Korallenbänke
Meer
Travertin
Kreide
Bergkalk
Alter rother Sandstein
Thonschiefer
Glimmerschiefer
Gneiss
Granit
Diorit
Porphyr
Basalt
Lava
Jura
Todtliegendes
Thonschiefer
niger europäischen Gebirge
otta.
Erzgebirge
Odenwald
Ural-Gebirge
Böhmer Wald
Idealer Querschnitt des Riesengebirgs, nach Bernhard Cotta.
Idealer Querschnitt des Thüringer Waldes, nach Bernhard Cotta.

previous spread:
A plate from the atlas of Alexander von Humboldt's *Kosmos* illustrating the composition of the Earth's crust via colour-coding. Between 1799 and 1804, Prussian geographer, naturalist and explorer Alexander von Humboldt travelled extensively in Latin America, exploring and describing it for the first time in a manner generally considered to be a modern scientific point of view. His quantitative work on botanical geography laid the foundation for the field of bio-geography.

Connectedness is about Sharing

Foreword

We humans intuitively recognize that we are intimately connected to our own family members, but we are much less conscious of the fact that we are also intimately connected to members of our own species whom we have never met, and to the physical and natural world around us. Humanity's connectedness to the surrounding world was obvious to our earliest ancestors, who, for the first 200,000 years or more after the evolution of modern humans, had no choice but to obtain food and shelter by foraging and hunting in nature. Thus, for most of human history, humans knew that their daily survival was completely dependent on a respect for humanity's *connectedness* with the physical and natural world.

In humanity's most recent history, we have learnt to harness external energy sources and to control our own food production. These innovations removed, at least for much of humanity, the daily reminders that confronted our ancestors regarding the importance of the connectedness between humanity and the global ecosystem of which we are a part. There is an old adage, *out of sight, out of mind*, and, indeed, it fits well when we consider this. Most of us have lost sight of the fact that our societies and their continued development are completely dependent on our connectedness with the Earth and its resources.

Societal development – that is, improving human wellbeing – whether we are talking about poverty, hunger, clothing, shelter, infrastructure or water, comes about through use of the Earth's resources. One can say that these resources are our true currency and that it is these resources, and not money, upon which humanity's prosperity is based. In other words, humanity is still intimately connected to these resources despite the fact that there has been little awareness about this connectedness in recent decades.

Fortunately, there is a growing awareness that respecting the connectedness between different societies and between humanity and the Earth's resources is a prerequisite for continued societal development. Collectively, we are rediscovering the importance of respecting humanity's connectedness with the world around us. This journey of rediscovery may have begun when astronauts on the Apollo Mission sent pictures back from space of the Earth. What impresses us most with these pictures is the fact the Earth is a completely isolated planet. There are no connections between the Earth and any other body in space. Ultimately, that means that when we have used the Earth's resources, we will get no more.

Our connectedness to the Earth implies that further societal development requires careful consideration of how we will share its limited resources among what is soon expected to be a global population of nine to ten billion along with all other living organisms. It is this sharing that connectedness is all about and that all of the contributions in this book, in one way or another, have in focus. Humanity is on a journey in which we are rediscovering just how connected we are with other members of our species and with the world around us. Nothing could be clearer proof of this than the current coronavirus pandemic. The contributions found in this book may help us to discover and understand many other aspects of our global connectedness.

May they enrich and support you
on our common journey!

Katherine Richardson
Professor and the leader of the Sustainability Science Center, University of Copenhagen. Appointed by the UN General Secretary as a member of the Independent Group of Scientists that wrote the 2019 Global Sustainable Development Report.

April, 2020

Con-nect-ed-ness: An Introduction

For a very long time, we have regarded nature as something inherently different from ourselves. We have established societies, languages and mindsets that prevent us from experiencing the world any differently. Hence, we need to develop new languages, new structures and new mindsets to be able to listen to what is 'out there' and sense the answers within ourselves: we are connected, not just to nature, which we are a part of, but to everything around us and to each other. We – you and I, animals, plants, organic and inorganic, systems, artefacts and so forth – not only *share* the space; together we *create* it in a mutual process of emergence where we, as human beings, are not alone in possessing agency while the environment simply reacts. Instead, we co-exist in one coherent, active system where every component has agency and meaning.

Our current production system is designed as if we had inexhaustible resources, as if the earth were one big storeroom. For centuries, we have assigned ourselves a central position as superior beings, able to control our habitat by means of language, reason and consciousness. Precisely because plants and animals lack (human) language and consciousness, we believe we have the right to exploit them for our own needs. Every time we experience a loss of control,

Marianne Krogh (located in Copenhagen, DK) has a PhD in Architectural History and is curator of the exhibition in the Danish Pavilion at the 2021 Venice Architecture Biennale. Her work focuses on the intersection between art and architecture and explores the existential dimensions of spatiality. She also works as an editor at the publishing house Strandberg Publishing in Copenhagen.

←
The exhibition *con-nect-ed-ness* by Lundgaard & Tranberg Architects in the Danish Pavilion is an architectural transformation of the existing spaces. In one of the halls, visitors will experience a suspended canvas sheet hanging from the ceiling. The exhibition reacts with Venice's weather conditions, and the sheet mediates the change of weather through a sensory experience.

we respond with increased control, although that must be regarded a totalitarian impulse that fails to embrace the inherent nature of all living things: to be always in motion.

The result is an obvious imbalance: we are reducing the planet's capacity for binding CO_2, pollution is threatening our fundamental biological survival, biodiversity is plummeting and everything that we once took for granted is becoming increasingly uncertain, including air, water, soil …

Today's world is characterized by a sprawling network of economic, political, geographic, climatic and social connections, systems and structures. These structures are inextricably interrelated, often to such a complex degree that they appear inscrutable and thus difficult to navigate: we are moving in territories we do not fully understand, because we cannot describe them. Before we can act, we therefore have to (re) describe, render explicit, lay bare and reach a common understanding. In the words of the French sociologist and philosopher Bruno Latour, we need to get 'down to earth'. Our lives unfold neither in tiny enclaves, demarcated by the boundaries of the nation state, nor in a space defined by cartographers and satellites. It unfolds in 'the critical zone': a thin membrane around the entire planet, extending from the lowest layer of the atmosphere to a few kilometres into the earth's crust. We need to acknowledge and examine the importance of the hyperlocal within this critical zone in order to understand how the entire planet constitutes one single circuit.

According to modernist values, the future spelt a continuing liberation from all connections and bonds. Free at last! However, the value set is now emerging from a world view defined by circuits and cyclical movements; the future instead revolves around a gradual illumination of all the connections that are needed to preserve our fragile existence. Dependent at last! Responsible! Connected!

Is it too late? Perhaps. However, if we proceed with a humble mindset rather than being driven by an urge to possess and control, and if we begin to approach the earth we inhabit as a living organism that we are all a part of, there is potential for progress. Let us try to move away from trying to predetermine and control everything. Away from assigning value solely based on economic and consumer parameters. Instead, we can assign value according to different criteria: (bio) diversity, change and connectedness. It would be bleak indeed if everything and everybody were the same, and it would be a bleak (and fatal) choice to try to keep the world immutable in form and identity, since life is movement and change. Change is a way of becoming, both for us and for the planet. We are constantly encountering new things – on every scale – and these encounters define

Water connects all life on Earth. Throughout the exhibition in the Danish Pavilion, visitors can encounter water in different stages and atmospheres. By opening ourselves up to the sensory experiences of our connectedness with our surroundings, we also increase our ability to connect to each other.

our becoming, for good and bad. Let us approach these inevitable encounters with care.

There is no doubt that the current times will be crucial for the fate of the planet. The decisions we make now will have consequences far, far into the future. The facts are staggering. One important step towards making a good choice is to describe and understand connectedness, to grasp the notion that all phenomena are connected. A few decades ago, we had to acknowledge and come to terms with the severity of the climate crisis, then the planetary limits of our resources. By now, everyone knows and understands these issues (albeit each in their own way). The current frontier is systems thinking, the acknowledgement that everything is connected.

The modern world is highly specialized, divided into silos, each with its own language and perceptual space, its own logic. We need to relate to all of these specialized areas at once in order to continually vary our vantage point. Granted, that is a challenging task, but the world *is* connected, and we can take a first step by (re) describing it.

An encyclopedia that (re)describes the world

Whether we describe our current era as the Anthropocene or use one of the many other terms that are currently being debated is not the main issue. The key point is that the climate is in a crisis, and that the crisis is a result of the human way of life. That is the general consensus. It is not an ideological point but a fact. Opinion is divided, however, when it comes to determining the root cause of the crisis, who is responsible and how we should proceed. This is where ideology, politics, power and professional perspectives come in, along with whatever else divides and unites individuals and groups.

That diversity is also evident in the present publication. The almost one hundred contributions range from the hopeful to the dystopian, from the critical to the constructive, from the descriptive to the academically complicated and analytical. Opinions differ and sometimes clash. There are voices from the natural sciences, from the humanities, from the arts and from journalism, voices that do not always speak the same language and which may not understand each other. And yet, perhaps it is precisely where we clash, where logic and reason are challenged, that a space may arise where we can experience the many, many different modes of perception that have historically, throughout the modern project, occupied a place at the bottom of the pecking order. As every light casts new shadows, we have to continually shift the projector.

We need to cultivate a different language than the one that has led us astray. In order to speak about the future, we need to examine the past; to speak about science, we need to embrace the perspective of mythology; and to be able to be analytical and holistic at once, we may need to employ the dual perspective of art: zooming in to grasp the big picture and zooming out to grasp the detail.

That is why this book is in the format of an encyclopedia; naturally, we cannot chart all the relevant contemporary debates, nor should we, but we can select some of the concepts that seem relevant right now, each of them related to many of the other concepts in terms of topic, form, emotion, tone, method, history and so forth. Precisely in the same way phenomena naturally interconnect.

The sequence is alphabetic. This avoids hierarchies based on content, voice or mode of expression. Every time we move from one contribution to the next, we shift the projector and thus the shadows.

Most of the contributions are entirely new, and it is the ambition of the book to provide a testimony of the time around 2020. What is our focus? What connects us? What concerns us? What are our hopes? Our capacity for imagination is a wonderful gift.

Upon this book's release, in August 2020, the *con-nect-ed-ness* exhibition was scheduled to be already up and running, welcoming visitors to The Danish Pavilion at the renowned Architecture Biennale in Venice. Sadly, the plans had to be changed because in March 2020 Northern Italy registered an alarming number of people infected with a novel coronavirus that had emerged just weeks earlier in China. To ward off the risk of widespread infection, the Architecture Biennale was thus postponed for a year, to the spring of 2021. Our world is indeed connected.

The exhibition in the Danish Pavilion at the Venice Biennale of Architecture

The occasion for this publication is the *con-nect-ed-ness* exhibition in the Danish Pavilion at the 2020 Venice Biennale of Architecture. The exhibition was designed by Lundgaard & Tranberg Architects, and it offers a weighty contribution to the discussion and reflections addressed in this book. The exhibition could have appeared as a contribution in this publication under the term 'Water' or 'Description' or 'Circuit' or, perhaps, 'Sharing'. Let me tell you about it.

The Danish Pavilion in Giardini Park was constructed in two stages: first, the neoclassical Brummer Hall (named after its architect, Carl Brummer) from 1932; next, the 1960 extension, designed by the architect Peter Koch in 1960 in a humbler, Nordic functionalist style in yellow brick, with smaller rooms. The entrance is placed in the middle; in fact, one can walk straight through the pavilion and out the other side.

As a result, exhibitions often appear to be 'bisected', just as a hierarchy often emerges between the actual exhibition hall and the smaller corridors and niches which are often used to display sketches and small works or simply as storerooms.

However, given the circuit concept, it makes no sense to operate with sharp, hierarchical structures or with an ambition of simply displaying (large or small) objects in the space. If instead of *sharing* the space we *create* it together, it would be an illusion to perceive the 'gap' in between the objects as neutral space or non-space. In a contemporary gaze, which implies a relational and horizontal perspective, it becomes absurd to focus on the individual object or building. Instead, we might ask, what materials were used? How were they sourced and processed? By whom and under what circumstances? How were they transported, and what happens to them after this particular stop on their journey? Where do we stand in this complex network of

Sketch by Lundgaard & Tranberg Architects illustrating the flow of water through the Danish Pavilion during the exhibition.

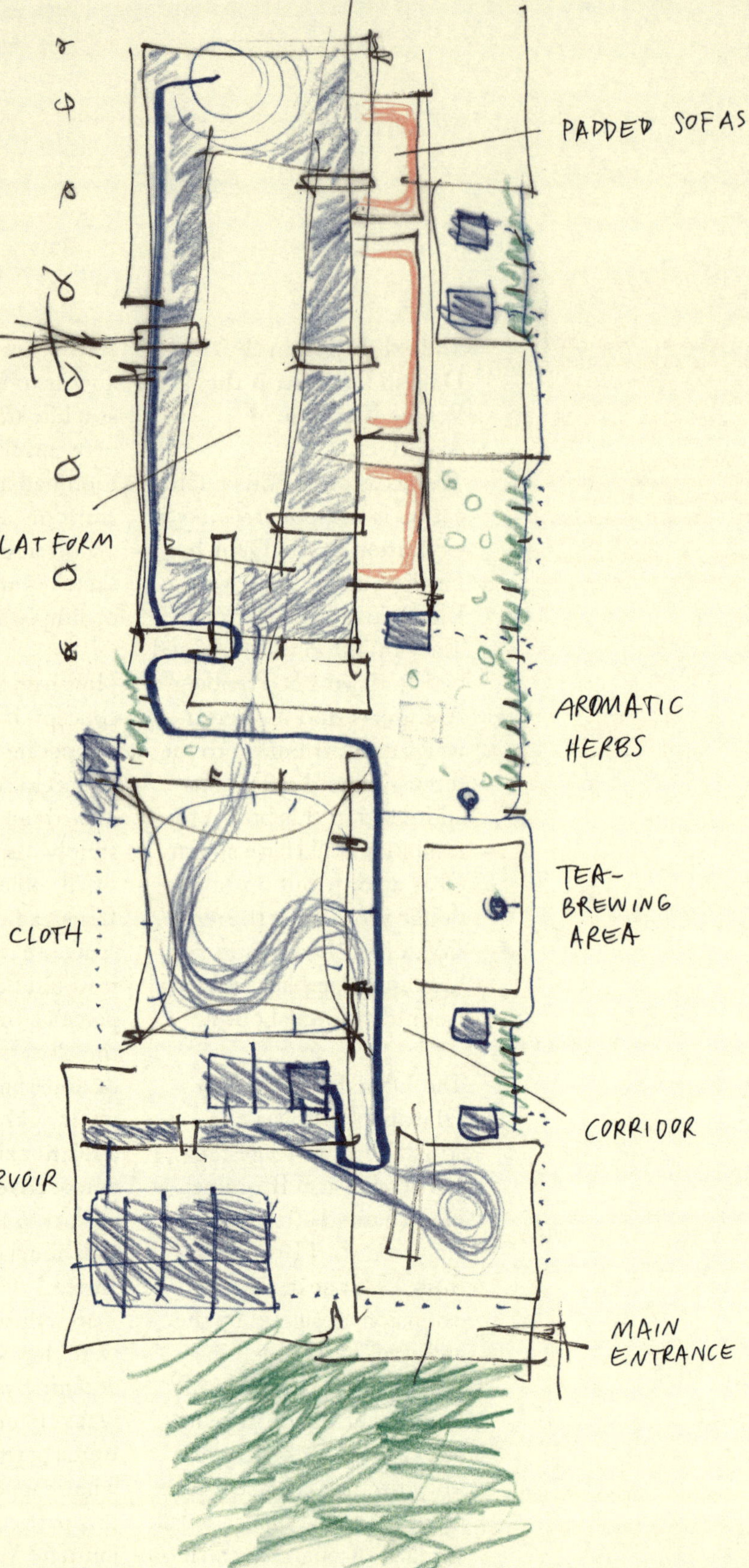

18

The exhibition in the Danish Pavilion includes, among other things, a circulatory system in which the water is in constant motion. Rainwater is collected and led through exposed tanks and pipes that are connected to the weather of Venice and the great circulatory system of the earth.

connections, and how does that affect our relations with the world? The exhibition in the Danish Pavilion thus had to be a total installation, where there is no 'outside' and where everything is connected and imbued with meaning, from the materials to the visitors.

Hence, Lundgaard & Tranberg moved the pavilion entrance to the small gable at the building's north end, so that visitors first move through a planted area enclosing and situating the body and physically framing the initial encounter. From this intimate space, visitors continue into the corridor and niches of the annex, which are on a scale that matches the human body. From here, the proportions gradually grow, until one reaches the larger halls. The pavilion is thus perceived as a succession, with its own flow, intensities, rhythms, producing a melodic ambience that is supplemented by the 'pulse' of water, which can be heard dripping, trickling, splashing from the various rooms as one moves around inside the exhibition space. The exhibition does not shut down when the Biennale closes its doors every day at 18.00; the pulse and the changes continue.

Outside the pavilion, the visitors may notice some water pipes that run along the exterior facades, wind their way around corners and sporadically connect with roof gutters and white water tanks. By the gable entrance, visitors encounter even more pipes: originating in the garden attached to the pavilion, they continue into the entrance corridor and through the building. The pipes are visible, disruptive, playful, and the visitors are able to touch them and even use them as handrails. At the end of the corridor, one can faintly see another water tank. At the same time, water literally runs towards people, washing over the floor and into a corner, where it forms a small lake that people have to jump over. From here, it is sucked into the garden, where one sees the heart of the exhibition: water tanks stacked on top of each other, all interconnected and connected to the roof gutters via pipes. There is also a water-purifying plant and pumps. This is the exhibition's water reservoir, where pipes and hoses are connected into a large circulation network, with main arteries leading into the building and back out again.

The exhibition examines the notion of 'connectedness', articulated by means of water – physically, atmospherically, sensuously and conceptually. The planet's story about the cycle of water and its various states – freezing, melting, flowing, evaporating, falling as precipitation, wholly unaware of the boundaries we have established in the world – is directly connected to the exhibition's story: rainwater is captured, channelled through the pavilion, returned to the reservoir and pumped back out. Along the way, the installation explores water as a phenomenon – atmospheric, lapping, gushing, trickling, dripping and evaporating. You can feel, smell, hear and taste the water through various architectural disciplines, such as scales, relations, condensations, extensions, transitions, materiality, sensations and tectonics. Water flows and finds its own path; meanwhile human beings have found ways to capture and control it, which inevitably subjects it to a political gaze: not everyone has access to clean drinking water, and in some places water is the reserve of a privileged few. Glaciers and polar ice caps are melting, and anticipated sea level rises are being analysed. Rising temperatures are leading to growing precipitation, and floods will become ever more intense, as will droughts. Water is all around us and inside us. It puts us under pressure, it enriches us, and it is the basis of all life.

Connectedness is very much about visualizing connections to be able to address the underlying systems and associations. Hence, the exhibition applies a functional transparency: the components of the circuit – from simple pipes to high-tech purification mechanisms and pumps – are not camouflaged, as they usually are in the sterile space of the white cube, but are instead exposed and used as active elements in the exhibition. Moreover, they are not just visible; they are part of an architectural ambition of revealing, including, embracing and playing with the components that make up our high-tech society, with Lundgaard & Tranberg seemingly aiming to show that these implicit and normally invisible aspects stand in a relationship to us and have the capacity to affect us emotionally.

Following the pipes through the corridor – towards the flow of water on the floor – we are led to a small square hall with skylights. Underneath the ceiling hangs a distended cloth, which captures condensation and lets it slowly drip onto the ground. The distended cloth breaks the light pouring in through the windows above, and we can hear the sound of water dripping on the floor. The room is reflected in the water, which collects on the floor in varying amounts, depending on weather conditions and the amount of water splashing in from further inside the building. The water stages the rhythmic pulse of the room, emphasizing the atmospheric experience where the architecture allows us to sense water against our skin, hear the sound of water dripping, smell how it affects the cloth and see how the room is reflected in the water's surface.

In the middle of the pavilion, where the two very different building volumes meet, so do the visitors. The pipe system splits into two branches, extending into the large neoclassical hall and down towards a veranda enclosed by trellises with aromatic herbs: lemon verbena, mint, sage and chamomile – all plants that grow wild in the local area. The water is led over to the herbs to water them, since, above all, water is life. The visitors are engaged in the activities within the veranda space: picking herbs, boiling water, brewing tea, washing cups and pouring tea together. They can settle down here or take the hot drink with them, as the water moves into the body's circuits and is later carried into the city's.

At the other end of the veranda, we see the water splash out from the main hall and flow into the room with the suspended cloth. If we follow the course of the pipes and climb a ramp, we discover how it is all connected: Lundgaard & Tranberg have transformed the entire floor of the Brummer Hall into a full basin with a large floating platform – like a floor that

In the months ahead of the exhibition, Lundgaard & Tranberg Architects have been testing ideas thoroughly in a 1:20 model of the Danish Pavilion.

has become detached from the load-bearing walls. Via catwalks, the visitors can step onto the floating and slightly unstable floor, which also offers access to the three niches in the hall, where they can relax on padded sofas. At the end wall, the pipes stop, and water gushes into the basin: it is this water level that regularly overflows – depending on weather conditions and human activity – and sends water into the exhibition space, over the floor and back to the reservoir in the garden around the pavilion. The more activity, the more splashing. The actions of the visitors influence the state and dynamics of the water.

The space radiates a subtle sense of 'homeliness'. Every detail is carefully worked out, and people have to make room for and pay attention to, accommodate and relate to each other on a physical level. However, generosity is not the only quality at play: one clearly senses the imbalance that the interaction of the water

Scale model of the exhibition *con-nect-ed-ness*. The largest hall has been transformed into a water basin with a floating floor.

and the destabilizing floor create in the body when one steps onto the floating platform. This gives rise to a sort of duality – inclusive versus insecure – and we have to find our own place and sense of security by trusting and negotiating with each other.

The sensuous experience, the atmospheric quality and the encounter with the water in different states are not distinct from the social and interpersonal experience. They are two sides of the same coin because they spring from the same basis: By opening ourselves up to the sensory experiences of our connectedness with our surroundings, we also increase our ability to connect to each other.

With this exhibition, Lundgaard & Tranberg have created a space that examines how the combination of science, technology and architecture, of facts and experiences can convey issues that are otherwise hard to grasp. As the American anthropologist Anna Tsing points out, alienation occurs when we are separated from what lets us sense that we are alive. The exhibition has no ambition of dictating how we *should* live together, but it does hope to inspire all of us to ask how we *will* live together.

Thank you
Thanks to all the contributors in this book. I have reached out to everyone I thought would best be able to make a clear and concise statement about a particular concept that is relevant to our time, and you all accepted the challenge with sincere interest and dedication. That alone gives cause for hope and confidence.

Thanks also to all the institutions, foundations and collaboration partners that helped make this book and the exhibition in the Danish Pavilion possible: the Danish Arts Foundation's Committee for Architecture Grants and Project Funding, the Danish Ministry of Culture, Realdania and the Danish Architecture Center, Dreyers Fond, the New Carlsberg Foundation, Bestles Fond, Knud Højgaards Fond, Beckett-Fonden, Kvadrat, Mads Nørgaard, Hay, Junckers, Stark, Strandberg Publishing and the many, many people who have brought their professional insight and expertise to bear on the project. Your contributions are deeply appreciated.

My main thanks go to the architects. Lundgaard & Tranberg Architects not only created the most beautiful and engaging exhibition imaginable. They did not just remind us of the potential of architecture in helping us build a sustainable life on this planet. With their profound commitment and creative minds, they have also shown me the potential of the concept of connectedness.

The wells of Venice

In the *con-nect-ed-ness* exhibition in the Danish Pavilion at the Venice Biennale of Architecture, the architects Lundgaard & Tranberg capture rainwater from the roof of the building and run it through a device with a sand filter, where it is purified.

This method has direct references to the way in which Venetians have secured clean drinking water for centuries. Only at the Lido was there access to a limited amount of drinking water via borings, and during the 14th and 15th centuries the city therefore had to develop a special system of wells, resulting in 180 public cisterns and just over 6,000 private ones: through a system of pipes, rainwater was captured from the roofs of the surrounding buildings and then led underneath the yard, where coarser debris, leaves and so forth were filtered out. From here, the water continued into the well pipe through a river-sand filter and could finally be drawn from the well head as cool, clean, tasty drinking water. That method supplied the citizens of Venice for centuries.

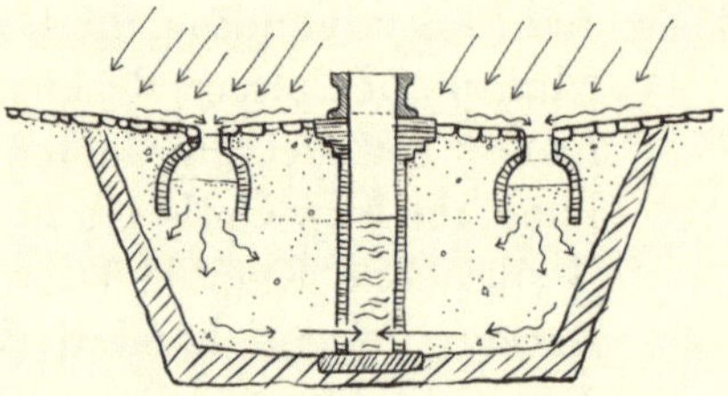

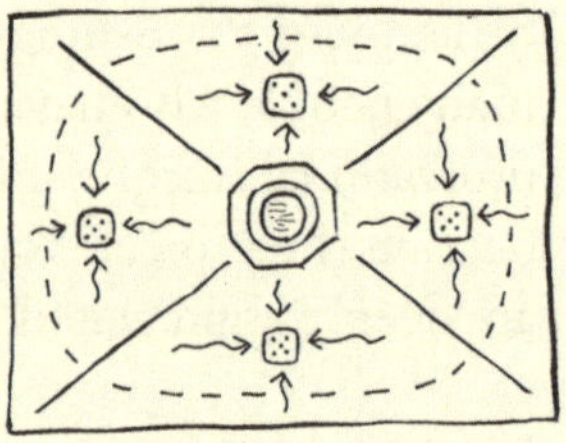

Weather conditions inside and outside the pavilion
Because of its exposed placement in the lagoon, Venice has always been at risk of minor floods, the so-called aqua alta, or tide peaks, caused by climate fluctuations (tides, warm southerly winds and so forth). In recent years, the increase in water levels has been particularly pronounced and damaging, with the construction of the latest airport and the deep fairways for the cruise liners mentioned among the causes. It is also being debated whether global warming has led to more frequent occurrences of extreme precipitation. In any case, the extreme flooding over the past year has been a huge challenge for the fragile city.

The exhibition in the Danish Pavilion, which features a circuit of rainwater captured from the pavilion's roof, is thus directly related to the current fluctuations in the city's weather: after heavy rainfall, water flows through the pavilion at a quicker pace, while times of minimal precipitation will be reflected in a calmer internal circuit of water.

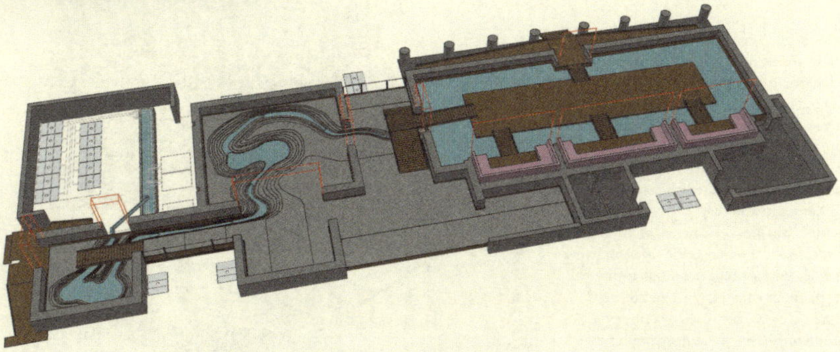

26

Exposure

The clean modernist space – the so-called white cube – is really an illusion, to put it mildly, for behind the clean white surface – floors, walls, ceilings – there is a highly complicated network of pipes, cables, insulation materials and so forth. The hidden systems are like an artificial lung that keeps the built environment alive: water, electricity, ventilation, temperature regulators and other technical installations to make the architecture liveable. As long as we cannot see these features, we also cannot consider them, which means we cannot reflect on our future life on a planet that is in such severe need of new systems. In many cases, the choice is not even up to the architects, who are simply bound by politically determined regulations.

In the exhibition at the Danish Pavilion, the technical aspects are laid bare and made to interact with the architecture, visitors, functions and aesthetics; we are connected to the technological world too, for better and worse.

Tea making
In the Danish Pavilion, tea making is part of the exhibition. Rainwater is led through the building and enters into various constellations with the building's rooms and visitors. Water is the basis of all life, and in the pavilion local herbs are watered by the visible pipe system, the leaves are picked and tea is brewed for the visitors to enjoy. The earth's cycle connects with the exhibition cycle, which connects with the body's cycle, which in turn connects with the city's.

Con-nect-ed-ness is not a contemplative space or a space for consumption where visitors are serviced. Rather, the visitors are involved in making tea, picking leaves from herbs and drinking the tea from recyclable cups.

Ā

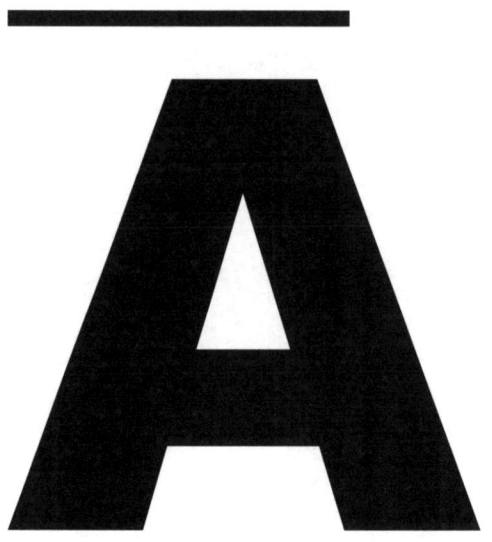

~~a delicious revolution~~ → Food
~~a machine for massifying life~~ → Plantationocene
~~a reflexive force of nature~~ → Aesthetics
~~a world where the mind never works without the body~~ → Creation
Abrupt Climate Change Sune Olander Rasmussen
~~access over ownership~~ → The Sharing Economy
~~action~~ → Next Generation
~~aeronauts~~ → Air
~~aesthetic indifference~~ → Waste
Aesthetics Dehlia Hannah
~~affirming connectedness under conditions of conflict~~ → Queer
Agency Tatjana Schneider
~~agents of disease~~ → Bacteria
Agriculture Sofie Isager Ahl
Air Aerocene
~~airnomads~~ → Air
~~alternative visions of growth~~ → Capitalocene
~~an inhabitor of life itself~~ → Waste
Anthropocene Gaia Vince
~~Anthropocene sensibilities~~ → Art
~~apocalyptic appeal~~ → Overpopulation
~~appropriateness of action~~ → Window of Opportunity
Architecture Elke Krasny
~~architecture as organization~~ → Architecture
~~architecture as style~~ → Architecture
~~architecture's political dimension~~ → Agency
Art Line Marie Thorsen
Atmosphere Gernot Böhme
Attachment Emmy Laura Perez Fjalland
Attention Polina Chebotareva and Rasmus Hjortshøj
~~awareness~~ → Attachment

Abrupt Climate Change

→ Air | → Atmosphere | bipolar seesaw | → Climate | → Geology | glacial-to-interglacial transition | → Glaciers | Greenland and Antarctica | → Heritage | natural archive of snowflakes | reconstructing climate variations | → Time | → Water | → Weather | → World Scientists' Warning to Humanity

Sune Olander Rasmussen (born 1974, located in Copenhagen, DK) is an associate professor at the Niels Bohr Institute, University of Copenhagen. He holds a PhD in Geophysics and works with ice-core research. He is mainly interested in the development of methods for ice-core dating and synchronization, as well as the analysis of climate records from a wide variety of palaeoclimate archives with the aim of understanding the governing mechanisms of past abrupt climate changes.

An ice-core perspective

Snow falls, flake by flake, on the vast, flat, cold and empty surface of the Greenland Ice Sheet. On a clear summer day, some flakes turn back into vapour and escape back into the atmosphere, and winds may move the uppermost snow around, but most of the snow settles and is covered by another layer of snow. Layer by layer, year after year, the snow is gently but relentlessly compressed by the burden of the younger snow. The snow crystals are first rounded and then start to grow together, and meanwhile most of the air between the crystals is squeezed out. Two hundred years after the snow originally settled on the surface, the snow is buried under 58 metres of layers of later snowfall, and the compression has reduced the volume of the original snow to less than a fifth. One cubic metre now weighs 800 kilograms, and in the space between ice crystals, atmospheric air is enclosed and forms tiny bubbles that will remain unaltered as the ice is compressed further and makes its way into the deep, cold interior of the ice sheet. A snowflake falling near the crest of the Greenland Ice Sheet may continue its journey towards the bedrock in ever-thinning layers for hundreds of thousands of years, or it may end up flowing slowly towards the edge of the ice sheet, just to return to the ocean as meltwater or in an iceberg.

For more than half a century, scientists have taken advantage of this natural archive of snowfall. With a method originally conceived by Danish physicist Willi Dansgaard, Danish-Icelandic physicist Sigfús Johnsen, and their colleagues at the University of Copenhagen, Denmark, scientists drill through the kilometre-thick ice sheet and retrieve a cylindrical rod of ice, an ice core, and perform measurements that reveal past climate conditions. Subtle variations in the ratio between the isotopes of the hydrogen and oxygen atoms that make up the ice molecules reflect past atmospheric temperatures around the ice-core site and document climatic changes on all scales: at the surface, the differences between winters and summers are clearly detectable, and half-way to the base of the ice sheet, the isotope-based temperature reconstructions show how the Greenland climate changed from glacial to interglacial conditions 11,700 years ago. Ice sheets are among the cleanest reserves of water on Earth, but still the ice core contains miniscule traces of volcanic eruptions, forest fires, dust storms and other processes that pollute the atmosphere with tiny particles that end up in the snowflakes. While the isotopes of the ice itself reveal past temperatures and the minute impurities in the ice can tell their story, the ice also acts as a sample container for the tiny bubbles of air that were once formed from the ambient air during the transformation of snow to ice. By melting or crushing the ice samples in the laboratory, this air is released and analysed to reveal how the atmosphere's composition has changed across the wide range of climatic conditions of the past. Ice cores from different areas highlight different time periods particularly well, and by piecing these records together and carefully dating the ice by identifying and counting each year's snowfall, scientists have reconstructed climatic variations year by year 60,000 years back through our current interglacial period, the Holocene, and halfway into the glacial. Even when the annual layers are no longer discernible, the ice cores still document climatic changes in outstanding resolution. The longest Greenland records go back 128,000 years, while the cores from Central Antarctica reach even further back and cover many glacial-interglacial cycles due to the very sparse snowfall on the East Antarctic Plateau. When tied together by layers of tiny volcanic glass particles found in several ice cores and variations of methane in the bubbles that are common to all ice cores (because the bubbles were formed from the very same atmosphere), the ice cores form a comprehensive set of records of both greenhouse-gas concentrations and past climate changes as manifested in the high southern and northern latitudes over more than a full glacial cycle.

The records from the Greenland and Antarctic ice cores allow us to place the recent changes in climate and greenhouse-gas concentrations into a perspective that reaches far beyond historical records. Continuous monitoring of the atmospheric composition only commenced about six decades ago, and accurate thermometer measurements go back at best a couple of centuries. Further back, climate-relevant information can be inferred from historical records, which document local and regional climate variations, sometimes with large impact on past societies. The ice cores paint a picture of more radical climate change, with the last major global shift taking place 18,000 to 11,000 years ago, more than twice as far back in time as the oldest written records of any civilization on Earth. To find the ice in the Greenlandic Ice Sheet that originated from snow that fell on the surface 18,000 years ago, we would have to drill to more than a kilometre and a half below the surface, and each annual layer will have thinned to just a centimetre or two. However, the layering is intact, and from the isotope ratios in each layer we can extract an estimate of the temperature in the North Atlantic region. Over the following many thousand years, recorded in more than a hundred metres of Greenland ice core, Earth went from a deep glacial to a mild interglacial climate. In ice of the same age found in Antarctic ice cores, we can see how the temperatures gradually grew over seven millennia in close concert with the CO_2 content of the atmosphere. Although the differences between cores show regional variations, and in particular show that the polar regions warmed more than average, Earth as a whole reacted to small and slow changes in the amount and distribution of energy from the Sun and warmed by somewhere around 6 °C on average. This change was not likely initiated by CO_2, but the ice cores show how CO_2 concentrations rose together with – or were slightly lacking after – the temperature over many thousands of years and was most likely closely tied to temperature via positive feedbacks, involving, among other processes, the exchange of CO_2 between the atmosphere and ocean. The impact was dramatic: the large ice sheet that covered North America all the way down to the Great Lakes melted back and eventually disappeared, and ice caps covering the British Isles, Scandinavia and northern Siberia all decayed and left nothing more than a few mountain glaciers. The global ocean rose on average 120 metres due to the meltwater from these immense amounts of ice, and even today Earth's crust is still adjusting to the removal of the enormous load of the now-vanished ice sheets. Despite the obvious differences to today's situation, the observed climate change since the onset of the Industrial Revolution shares essential features with the glacial-to-interglacial transition: the changes were gradual and relatively smooth in most places, the CO_2 concentration changes were of a similar magnitude, and because the greenhouse-gas concentrations played such a large role, no region on Earth was unaffected.

Drilling a few hundred metres deeper into the Greenland ice, we find repeated evidence of climate change of a radically different nature. During most of the glacial period, which lasted about 100,000 years, Greenland did not experience stable glacial climate conditions for more than a few millennia at a time. Instead, the same pattern of climate change interrupted the cold glacial conditions about 30 times, and although the duration of these interruptions varies widely, they share so many features that they have been given a common label: the Dansgaard-Oeschger events. Each event starts with an abrupt warming of typically around 10–15 °C in Greenland and takes place over a few decades, after which the temperature drops more slowly for a while before returning abruptly to the cold glacial level. The Greenland ice cores do not provide many direct hints about the reason for these extreme changes, but when compared to similar records from Antarctica, a persistent pattern emerges: within a century or two after the abrupt warming sets in over Greenland, Antarctica starts cooling gradually, and conversely Antarctica starts warming slowly after Greenland has returned to its cold state. Records of the ocean circulation from ocean-floor sediment cores show variations that to the best of our knowledge appear contemporaneous with the changes observed in the polar regions, and climate models support that the climate of the hemispheres was coupled via the ocean heat transport. This interpretation is known as the 'bipolar seesaw', as it invokes a seesaw between the North and South Atlantic: When the northward heat transport in the Atlantic is strong, heat is drawn away from the South Atlantic and exported to the high-latitude North Atlantic by oceanic and atmospheric currents, causing Greenland to experience relatively warm conditions while the interior of the Earth's other oceans and the southern hemisphere slowly is losing heat, leading to gradual cooling in and around Antarctica. When the ocean heat transport is relatively weak, the opposite scenario occurs, which again is in full agreement with the ice-core evidence. What causes the ocean circulation to change strength abruptly is still not fully understood, although it seems clear that the amount of fresh water added to the ocean, sea-ice dynamics and variability in both wind and ocean currents play important roles. Greenhouse gases, on the other hand, do not vary enough, and especially not fast enough to play a main role for these changes. While the exact mechanisms behind the changes are still not fully known, it is thus clear that the Dansgaard-Oeschger events represent a different type of climate change than the gradual climate change of the glacial transition and the current warming: the main mechanism of the Dansgaard-Oeschger events was an abrupt change in the redistribution of heat that occurred when the climate system reached a threshold that allowed it to shift from one mode to another.

What is the relevance of Dansgaard-Oeschger events for the current and future climate situation? Although Dansgaard-Oeschger events proper were a glacial phenomenon, they are indirectly relevant to us because they demonstrate a type of variability that has occurred naturally and thus serves as a training ground for climate scientists and the computer models used to describe the most important physical processes in the climate system. They also directly exemplify that when Earth's climate is in a state that is prone to change, it does not take much forcing to initiate a sequence of events that leads to dramatic climate changes, potentially with regionally highly heterogeneous manifestations.

During the Dansgaard-Oeschger events, particularly Greenland and Northern Europe experienced climate change on a scale that would probably have rendered all human adaptation strategies except migration infeasible. It does not seem likely that we will see Dansgaard-Oeschger events in the foreseeable future, but the physical governing mechanisms of the events can also lead to changes on smaller scales, and there are also other elements of the climate system that are able to exhibit abrupt changes and could be triggered by humanity's alterations of Earth's surface and atmospheric composition. I therefore find it is worth considering if just a small increase in the risk of large-scale abrupt climate change is not just as worrying and thus merits just as much action as the gradual and relatively well-understood climate changes that we are already observing and must expect based on projections of future climate.

The iconic 'main dome' of the NEEM ice-core drilling camp on the Greenland ice sheet – here photographed by anthropologist Martin Skrydstrup – was the home of up to 35 scientists and camp staff during the summers of 2007–2011. In 2015, it was moved 465 km on skis from north-west to north-east Greenland and now serves as the hub of the EastGRIP camp. The three floors contain a kitchen, bathroom, work and recreational space, and the field leader's office in the top cupola. The halo in the background is caused by the reflection and refraction in so-called diamond dust, which comprises small ice crystals suspended in the air.

Aesthetics

a reflexive force of nature | → Anthropocene | → Art | double meaning of aesthetics | → Earth Ethics | envision possible futures | → Future | geochronology | → Geology | → Object-Oriented Ontology | → Posthuman

Dehlia Hannah (born 1978, located in Copenhagen, DK, and Berlin, DE) is a philosopher and curator. She holds a PhD in Philosophy from Columbia University and is based in the Department of Chemistry at Aalborg University Copenhagen. Her recent book *A Year without a Winter* (2018) examines contemporary imaginaries of the climate crisis. Her research focuses on aesthetics, philosophy of science and philosophy of nature.

Aesthetics as first philosophy in the Anthropocene
In order to understand the significance of aesthetics to the Anthropocene, one must take account of a double meaning of aesthetics; first, as a science of perception and second, as a branch of value theory. The Anthropocene is posited as the geological time period in which humans are the dominant force on Earth, leaving traces of our activities in the ground, oceans and atmosphere that will be detectable in the rock strata for eons to come. *Detectable to whom, and with what instruments?* one might ask. Geochronology implies an agency of perception for whom material variations are legible as indices of past events. Without assuming that it is necessarily human, one may say that such a sensitive agency is an aesthetic subject in the most basic sense, an entity that can register a change within itself as a reflection of a change within its environs. One who evinces desire or aversion, who interprets such changes and organizes them within an image of the world, enters into a more complex relationship with what she perceives. A world imbued with esteem or utility, with revulsion or regret, is inhabited as a space of meaning: a place.

Only in the Anthropocene does the whole world become a place in this sense. At the hands of an aesthetic subject, geophysical inscriptions become saturated with value. The lasting traces of human use of fire and agriculture, fossil fuels, atomic bombs, plastics; and of the systems of capitalism, colonialism and plantation slavery (all candidates for a golden spike to mark the beginning of the epoch) betray the conflicting agencies gathered under the aegis of Anthropos. In place of the unilateral force of a meteor, or the release of oxygen by cyanobacteria (the first organism capable of photosynthesis), the activities of human beings are varied and uneven, pursued with more or less intention and awareness of consequences. Like every epoch before it, the Anthropocene designates a period of catastrophe for many species of life on the only planet known to sustain it. Yet this is the first time that a geological force hesitates, wonders and asks after itself. British geologists Simon Lewis and Mark Maslin observe, 'We are a geological force of nature, but that power is unlike any other force of nature in that it is reflexive, and can be used, withdrawn or modified.'[1] With the capacity to recognize and modify our behaviours, in order to bring about more desirable effects, comes the capacity for judgement – and here we enter the territory of aesthetics in the second sense.

Insofar as the present condition of Earth's surface and atmosphere is an artefact of the cumulative activities of Anthropos, it becomes an object of normativity on a grand scale. As the primary space of reasoning, *first philosophy* aspires to comprehend the essential nature of things and their ultimate causes. Traditionally (from Aristotle to contemporary analytic philosophy), this pride of place belongs to metaphysics or ontology. In the epoch of humans, we have pushed ourselves forward in the order of causes, not only through the brute force of our actions but also through our reflexivity. Anthropos usurps the position of Nature and God(s) and contemplates in the world the reflection of its own image, the work of its own hand. The Anthropocene names this grandiosity – *signs and dates this world picture* – situating it at once within natural history, the history of science and political history. If metaphysics previously sought a reality transcending time and contingency, it now finds its realm subject to the meddling of a blundering geological force. Once responsibility is justly attributed to (some of) our species, we cannot escape the implication that we must evaluate the fruit of our labours and improve upon them (through restraint and more careful creative action). This is an ethical, a political and a technical project, but it is ultimately an agenda for aesthetics.

Aesthetics as first philosophy investigates our capacity to sense, imagine and comprehend the myriad ecological catastrophes of the Anthropocene, attending not only to the 'arts of noticing'[2] but also to the will to ignorance, denial and selective vision.[3] It attends to the nexus of the aesthetic with the ethical and the political, envisioning the environmental conditions of possibility of a just society, in which humans and other creatures do not merely survive but flourish. Just as aesthetics relates, in its familiar historical sense, to the creation and evaluation of works of art, architecture and design, it must be deployed in the Anthropocene to envision possible futures that would overcome the myriad violations of nature that we countenance today. If there is a widespread turn towards the arts in critical discussions of the Anthropocene, this is perhaps because they offer provocations to hone our aesthetic judgement and creative practices for deployment on a much larger scale: that of continents, oceans, worlds. In what styles may Anthropocene futures be crafted? Will the ages to come resemble prelapsarian visions of nature? What intentional actions will future geologists be able to detect in the rock strata?

Works cited:

Lewis, Simon L., and Mark A. Maslin. 2015. 'Defining the Anthropocene'. *Nature*, 519 (7542), March 12.

Lewis, Simon, and Mark Maslin. 2018. *The Human Planet: How We Created the Anthropocene*. London: Penguin.

Norgaard, Kari Marie. 2011. *Living in Denial: Climate Change, Emotions and Everyday Life*. Cambridge, MA: MIT Press.

Tsing, Anna Lowenhaupt. 2015. *The Mushroom at the End of the World: On the Possibility of Life in Capitalist Ruins*. Princeton: Princeton University Press.

Agency

→ Architecture | architecture's political dimension | → Capitalocene | → Care | → Declaration of Rebellion | → Denial | new form of commons | playground for capital | → Power | → Queer | reflexive position | response-ability | → The Sharing Economy | → Violence

What is architecture? What do architects do? For many, the answers to those two seemingly straightforward questions are, still, easy enough. Architects are people who design buildings. Sometimes smaller. Sometimes bigger. Sometimes more complex spatial situations. This is – despite a considerable amount of noise to the otherwise – what students of architecture learn in school and what, upon completion of their university training, most continue with in architectural offices. Architecture then, in turn, is the stuff that architects do. It's the sum of those smaller parts. Not much to those questions, you could say. Why even bother asking?

Well, those questions are here, right at the beginning of this text, because nothing, really, is ever that simple. And the same goes for this discipline, this field, this practice, this profession.

Architecture.

Innocent this word appears. But it is not. For this field, from which it emerges and of which it is part, is, in fact, a tangle: a bunch of controversies, ambitions, desires. It is woven into this complex mesh of challenges and interdependencies.
It occupies different, sometimes contradicting parts within a myriad of networks, which are, in themselves, composed of a multitude of other networks. It is made up and inhabited by stuff: people and ideologies, technologies and regulations, materials and matter. And, of course, it is charged with power. It speaks of money and the possibility to make lots of money – not necessarily as architects (but sometimes this, too). It is this entanglement of buildings with capital that make things as murky as can be – as buildings have come to stand for safe investments, often even before they've been built and inhabited. They mean, you could say, big bucks. And it is those systems and mechanisms, then, that more often than not drive and define architecture, turning architects and their skills into instruments for the realization of ever more wealth for the already privileged.

Tatjana Schneider (born 1974, located in Braunschweig, DE) is Chair of the Institute for History and Theory of Architecture and the City at the Technical University of Braunschweig, Germany. Focusing on expanding the theoretical and practical scope of dominant architectural debates and discourses, her work is concerned with the questioning of normative ways of thinking, producing and consuming space and the making of other (urban) imaginaries.

At the moment, still, most architects are happy to play along. They do this despite a growing body of knowledge and heaps upon heaps of observations that point to the violent nature and the exploitative practices of these processes. For to understand buildings as licences to print money, as cash cows, means disregarding the consequences of those ways by which profits will be made – including forced displacement disguised as progress or the ravaging of the planet and its fragile ecosystem for short-term gains.

'This has nothing to do with architecture and architects,' you might say. To which I'd say, 'Wrong!'

'Don't be silly. There's nothing, nothing at all, that architecture and architects can do,' you continue. 'Well', I respond, 'you couldn't be more wrong.'

By denying architecture's political dimension, which the negation of entanglement amounts to, the discipline and its protagonists have willingly, consciously, sometimes deliberately submitted themselves to being designers of pretty surfaces at best, shifting focus away from or even ignoring those powerful forces of appropriation – which appear to have the production of space in such a tight grip. But that is no reason to continue with this ever so comfortable business-as-usual attitude. Instead, architecture and architects need to get their act together here and now – not just because the ever-accelerating climate crisis (that we are already in the midst of) and its consequences on Gaia calls for a complete overhaul and requalification of *our* terms and practice of engagement.

'Come to think of it that way, okay', you say. 'But what's your point exactly? Isn't this old hat? Many, many practices exist that do not put their head in the sand and, as you say, got their act together a long time ago. What's more, aren't those projects, groups and collectives growing in number, too?'

And, of course, the answer to this is, 'Yes. This is true. In many respects, it's old hat. We cannot speak of a denial per se and should shy away from being so indifferent to the multitude of practices that exist and have existed for a long time. But, that's not my point,' I say.

What I want to call attention to here is that, of course, we could talk about those practices and projects of recent years that have begun to make visible, analyse and sometimes also resist and transform those processes and practices that have contributed to turning architecture into a playground for capital. Yes, those practices are important, not only because they tell tales of how other modes of engagement can point to different ways of making futures. They also talk of how taking seriously architecture's responsibilities for the many (and not just the few) can lead to environments that are less exploitative, less violent. They show how defining architecture through a much broader scope of spatial engagement – in which a building is no longer the focal point for interventions – can break the cycle of appropriation by those who see architecture simply as something to make money with. Yes, there are many such examples that have taken things into their own hands. Many more, also, than meet the eye when scanning books, journals or magazines of recent years. So, of course, it would be easy to leave behind those normative practices and architects I've been ranting about – who don't seem to be getting the urgency of 'other ways of doing'[1] – and focus on the things that activate those ever so hostile environments and transform them into different beings.

This, exactly this, would be the space of agency. It is a space that not only makes visible, documents and analyses those normative understandings of the production of space. Instead, it uses knowledges generated from those more investigative processes to propose and make spaces and environments where responsibility to and for all takes centre stage and where, through processes of care and different ways of organizing, this entanglement of social, economic and ecological levels is more than just an afterthought. In this – let's call it – *alternate* space, we could celebrate those successes, their acquired and hard-fought-for powers. We could celebrate the impact such contributions have had and, along with others who do just that, idolize or even iconize them as harbingers for change for a better world or as promises of a more emancipatory form of urban practice: the neighbourhood-run experimental garden, the artist-cum-civic-society-controlled regeneration processes, the tiny housing projects that manage to preserve, sometimes freeze, their current state of existence.

But this isn't the finish line, right?! Especially when looked at through the lenses of those more recent social movements that have built around Fridays for Future and Extinction Rebellion, this self-styled new civil society that co-produces a garden here and a house there has considerable limitations that all too frequently are either completely ineffectual or, worse, reinforce, as Harvard-based professor of urban theory Neil Brenner once put it, the 'tight control over the production and appropriation of urban space'.[2] We now see quite clearly how those practices that attempt to develop new forms of commons often do so on an extremely insular scale. And recurrently, they remain, in fact, just that: insular. This is not to say that these practices are impotent or powerless. But pausing reflection, stopping critical interrogation, being content with what's been achieved and comforting one another within our bubble of difference? No, this cannot be the aim of such types of praxis that attempt to shift focus, attempt to alter the ways in which we can think about anything, really: from housing standards and (shared) mobility to that which limits the resources we should have access to.

Understanding the limits to one's capabilities is necessary here to develop and define one's (spatial) agency; for only a reflexive position, one that is aware not only of the possibilities but also about the challenges along the way, can help define the necessary openings for further interventions, further approximations to this *other* world. But, I see very little of this, neither within the field of architecture proper nor within this bubble of other urban practices that have been emerging in recent years. Indeed, what seems to be lacking, really lacking, is a much more rigid investigation of architecture's response-abilities, capabilities and possibilities to foster agencies. There is nothing of that sort. Agreements on even the most basic of actions that address our climate emergency are shied away from on the political stage. It's simply not something to win elections with – despite the day-on-day worsening state of affairs. So, we continue to act as if there were no tomorrow. We continue to exploit the planet and start wars over access to resources. We continue to consume beyond our fair share. We continue to make up practices that reproduce the systems that go on to abuse, ill-treat and manipulate processes that could produce change. We continue to not take seriously the crushing climate science, to talk away the existence-threatening changes as glitches in a system that will sort them out despite mounting evidence to the contrary – with architects and architecture right bang in the middle of it.

This is where the notion of agency enters the stage again. This time, more prominently, but without wanting to put too much stress on the term. If, as British sociologist Anthony Giddens writes, agency 'depends on the capability of the individual to "make a difference" to a pre-existing state of affairs or course of events',[3] it is important not just to state agency but to understand how and where exactly difference can be made. Recognizing and acting upon one's individual possibilities for action is crucial – the (localized) impact this may have has been mentioned. However, what seems to be even more pertinent in our times of crisis is to pay attention to those examples of practice where people meet and solidarize around globally shared issues and concerns that address, in the widest sense, (climate) equity and where individual agency becomes shared to advance those causes of common, of societal, concern. It is exactly those examples that deserve more discussion and attention. Why? Well, sticking band-aids on the gaping wounds, those Mortal-Engine-sized track marks that said violent forms of production have been carving into our landscapes globally, is no longer an option.

Don't say: 'Just let me go out to buy a life-size pack of band-aids.'

Do say: 'I'm going to solidarize with others and work with networks that fight all violent forms of the production and reproduction of space.'

Works cited:

Brenner, Neil. 2013. 'Open City or The Right to The City?' *Topos*, 85, pp. 42–45.

Giddens, Anthony. 1984. *The Constitution of Society: Outline of the Theory of Structuration*. Berkeley: University of California Press

Schneider, Tatjana, and Jeremy Till. 2009. 'Beyond Discourse: Notes on Spatial Agency'. *Footprint*, 4.

Agriculture

→ Biodiversity | → Creation | → Energy | liquid carbon pathway | poetry | regeneration | → Soil | → Sun

---

Regeneration comes from the Latin *regeneratus*, 'being born again', from *re-*, 'again', and *generare*, 'to create or bring forth'. In biology, regeneration is described as the biological process by which living organisms replace lost cells, tissue or body parts. The term is also used, as an adjective, to describe a new farming practice.

Regenerative agriculture has been called an agricultural revolution. Billions of tonnes of carbon dioxide have been released into the atmosphere, in part as a by-product of the food production practices that also deplete our soil. Regenerative agriculture actively seeks to bind CO_2 in the soil, increasing its humus content and improving the so-called liquid carbon pathway – a term coined by the Australian soil ecologist Christine Jones and used to describe the process by which atmospheric carbon dioxide is converted into soil humus. She calls the farmers who practice regenerative methods 'light farmers', because a key aspect of their approach is to optimize photosynthesis. Plants use energy from the sun to transform atmospheric carbon dioxide into organic matter and oxygen:

$$6\,CO_2 + 6\,H_2O \xrightarrow{\text{LIGHT}} C_6H_{12}O_6 + 6\,O_2$$

Ninety-eight per cent of the plant consists of nutrients that it receives from the sky. The last two per cent come from ash in the soil. Perhaps our crops are not of the earth at all but of the sky.

The French philosopher Simone Weil wrote in her book *The Need for Roots* (1949) that for farmers, everything should be centred around the cycle of sunlight: how it is drawn into the plants and retained in them by the action of chlorophyll, how it is then concentrated in seeds and fruits, and enters into human beings in the form of food and drink to nourish the muscles that in turn prepare the soil. Everything connected with science can be situated around this cycle, she writes, because energy is at the heart of everything – and if farmers had a deeper understanding of this, it would permeate their labour with poetry. It was clear to Weil that industrialized farming led to a detachment from the earth – and from their labour – that made it impossible for farmers to sense the holistic impact of their own involvement.

Sofie Isager Ahl (born 1988, located in Copenhagen, DK) is a writer, translator and PhD fellow at the Department of Anthropology at Copenhagen University. She has translated the work of American anthropologist Eduardo Kohn and Chinese–American poet Mei-Mei Berssenbrugge into Danish. Her first book is called *Naboplanter* (Companion Plants) (2018).

Poetry comes from Greek *poiein*, 'to create'. A poetic practice is one that not only sustains or perpetuates the world but actively creates it. Brings something from non-being into being. In regenerative farming, the chemical properties of the plants and the soil are at the heart of the farmers' labour when they are challenged, on a daily basis, to engage as meaningfully as possible in this cycle of light. Their labour is aimed at facilitating the path of the light through the plants and into the soil, awakening the micro-life that surrounds the plant, illuminating it, evoking it. Such a farming practice is one that engages with the underlying generative process.

Legend has it that agriculture was invented in Eleusis as a gift to humankind from the Greek goddess Demeter. Her daughter Persephone was picking flowers when she was abducted by Hades, King of the Underworld. The ground gaped open, and he stole her away from the world. Demeter went out in search of her. She came to a well by Eleusis, where she sat down to grieve. No one could console her. Every one of the Olympian gods was sent her way, but to no avail. However, one day, when the old crone Baubo came along and performed a grotesque and outrageous dance, Demeter began to laugh.

Demeter's laughter was liberating. Out of sorrow sprang a light, a laughter, sudden and unexpected. Out of darkness grow the shoots. Every year, we are surprised: the absurdity, the creativity of it all. Demeter was granted four months a year with her daughter. And thus, Persephone has become an image of our crops, the corn, the life force rising out of the ground. We see her disappear; we see the bare soil. We sense her absence – daughter of the goddess of agriculture, Queen of the Underworld. And there, in the deep, she is resurrected, as an image of spiritual regeneration: virgin birth.

Agriculture is ancient, and so are the stories surrounding it. The myths are a form of knowledge that has been passed down for generations. From one mother to another, Demeter and her daughter. I imagine how the work being carried out today might appear to those who come after us. How the outlines of the people working might look like archetypes to their hazy gaze. Wonder what light might shine through.

Perhaps it will one day be said that the fields lay grey and barren. A dry earth, flattened. Life had begun to disappear. The calamities came. Drought, lack of feed, floods. The pollinators died, and the beetles, the animals in the ground.

Perhaps it will one day be told that they began to talk about the light. They built up carbon in the soil. They practiced surface composting, spread lactic acid bacteria and humus preparations. They stopped ploughing altogether. They harrowed and sowed. They barely touched the ground, disturbed the soil as little as possible. They practiced binding the nutrients to the fields. And their actions were given new names. Their labour was no longer the same.

Earthworms, ground beetles, springtails. Many with each spit of the spade. Life began to return. And so did the light. They prayed for Demeter to laugh. They thought she was gone; they gathered and grieved. They sat with their faces in their hands when, one day, someone began to dance through the fields, then two, then three. And the laughter was restored.

aeronauts | airnomads | breathing | → Coexistence | → Energy | → Imagine | planetary rhythms | → Pollution | post-fossil fuel era | → Sun | the multi-species many | the rivers of the atmosphere

Aerocene Manifesto: Aeronauts Unite!

Towards a new epoch, free from borders, free from fossil fuels

Aerocene Community

Air has no end or beginning
– it poses no artificial separation of areas.
Air inter- and intra-connects everything and everyone;
it flows through, in and around.
Air and the energy of the Sun cannot be dominated by
any one particular geopolitical power.
Air thus embodies the opportunity to rethink sociality, political
logic and causality and upturn fossil fuelled mentalities.

Aerocene (founded and initiated by artist Tomás Saraceno in 2015, located around the world) is an interdisciplinary artistic community that seeks to reactivate a common imaginary for an ethical collaboration with the atmosphere and the environment, in an envisioned era free from borders, free from fossil fuels. Aerocene's activities manifest primarily in the circulation of aerosolar sculptures that become buoyant only by the heat of the sun.

While fossil fuel–based industries continue their attempts to colonize other planets, the air – this common interface of terrestrial life – continues to be compromised: carbon emissions pervade the air, particulate matter accumulates in our lungs while electromagnetic radiation envelops the Earth, dictating the tempo of surveillance capitalism. This control held by the few enacts the suffering of the multi-species many in the current era of ecological crisis. A different epoch is needed, one which radically upturns fossil narratives of materiality and re-examines the inscribed notions of property and properties, human and inhuman, of production and subjection. How would breathing feel in a post-fossil fuel era? How can we challenge the dominance of dispossessing geopolitical forces and overcome the extractive approach to Earth and the wealth of life it provides for? Together, we call for this new epoch, which has been named the Aerocene.

Aerocene is a proposal – a scene in, on, for and with the air – towards a reciprocal alliance with the elements capable of restoring the air to a commonwealth of life.

Aerocene imagines *space* as a commons, a physical and imaginative place subtracted from corporate control and government surveillance.

Aerocene promotes de-securitized free access to the atmosphere, through new tools and relational practices emerging from communities attempting to move the Earth's masses towards a post-fossil fuel era.

The launch pad towards this new epoch is an aerosolar balloon, a Do It Together (DIT) entrance to the aerial, whose only (non-) engine is the wealth of energy gifted by the Sun. Once inflated with air and heated by the Sun, it elevates into the air, becoming a flying sculpture that rises without the use of fossil fuels, helium, hydrogen, solar panels, batteries or burners. In floating without carbon emissions, these aerosolar journeys speculate on the kinds of nomadic sociopolitical structures that may emerge if we could navigate the rivers of the atmosphere. This is to become *airnomads*, to move from *Homo economicus* to *Homo flotantis*: who attunes to planetary rhythms, conscious of living with other humans and non-humans, and floats with the ocean of air, uprooting dominant geocentric logics, in a move towards embodying an ever more entangled relationship with the atmosphere and the cosmos.

In bearing the consequences of the fossil-capital regime's material practice of extraction, the atmosphere has become a highly stressed zone of the commonly composed terrestrial world. Aerodynamics, in constant movement and transformation, inherently entails complex spatial, temporal, sociopolitical and ecological processes and today embodies the unequal relations of power projected upwards from the land. Hegemonic modes of re-/production in the midst of the Capitalocene, along with human mobility and organization within the web of life, have enacted the breach of atmospheric pollution thresholds, with CO_2 emissions now exceeding more than 400 ppm (parts per million). This corruption of the air is the trigger for state shifts in the Earth's systems, critical changes already under way, with planetary temperatures increasing and multifold inequalities proliferating in an age of resurgent nationalism and geopolitical instability.

What are the rites of passage, the corridors we need to open, in order to restore the right to drift and breathe? How can we overcome the paradox of decisions made by the few simultaneously forcing and inhibiting the mobility and breathability of the multi-species many? Aerocene calls for an interplanetary ecology of practices which could reconnect with elemental sources of energy and the strata borne from the Sun and other planets, rising upwards towards an era of renewed symbiotic relations and sensitivities within life's entanglements.

top and middle:
Becoming Aerosolar, free flight, from Germany to Poland, 2015
Aerial photography, lifted only by the sun, free from fossil fuels. Courtesy of the Aerocene Foundation. Photography by aerial camera, 2015. Licensed under CC BY-SA 4.0 by the Aerocene Foundation.

bottom:
Aerocene Gemini, free flight, Schönfelde, Germany, 2016
Still of a glitch taken from an aerial recording, lifted only by the sun, free from fossil fuels. Courtesy of the Aerocene Foundation. Photography by aerial camera, 2016. Licensed under CC BY-SA 4.0 by the Aerocene Foundation.

previous spread: Aerocene, launches at White Sands (NM, United States), 2015
The launches in White Sands and the symposium 'Space without Rockets', initiated by Tomás Saraceno, were organized together with curators Rob La Frenais and Kerry Doyle for the exhibition *Territory of the Imagination* at the Rubin Center for the Visual Arts. Courtesy of the Aerocene Foundation. Licensed under CC BY-SA 4.0 by the Aerocene Foundation.

Tomás Saraceno
Aerocene 5.2 m, 2015
Courtesy of the artist; Andersen's, Copenhagen; Ruth Benzacar, Buenos Aires; Tanya Bonakdar Gallery, New York/Los Angeles; Pinksummer contemporary art, Genoa; Esther Schipper, Berlin.

Aerocene, launches at White Sands (NM, United States), 2015
Courtesy of the Aerocene Foundation. Licensed under CC BY-SA 4.0 by the Aerocene Foundation.

Tomás Saraceno
Untitled (Iceland Series), 2008
Courtesy of the artist; Andersen's, Copenhagen; Ruth Benzacar, Buenos Aires; Tanya Bonakdar Gallery, New York/ Los Angeles; Pinksummer contemporary art, Genoa; Esther Schipper, Berlin.

Tomás Saraceno
Aerocene – Cloud Cities, 2015
Digital collage
Courtesy of the artist and the Aerocene Foundation.

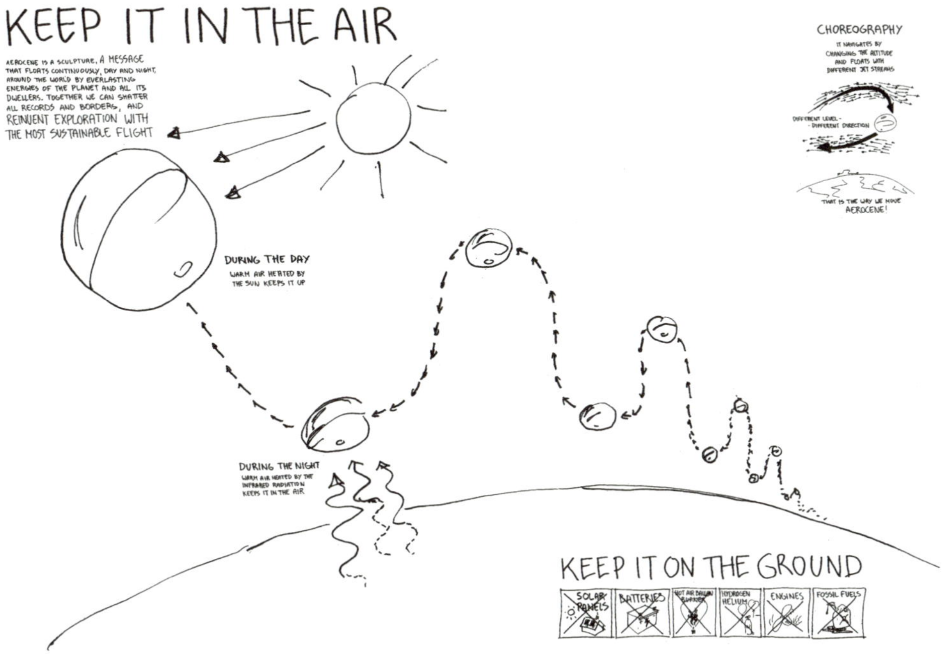

Aerocene: Around the World Free from Fossil Fuels, 2015
Sketch by Tomás Saraceno for *Aerocene Newspaper* on the occasion of the United Nations Climate Change Conference COP21, 2015
Courtesy of the artist and the Aerocene Foundation. Licensed under CC BY-SA 4.0 by the Aerocene Foundation.

We suggest a model for a landscape that harnesses and balances our relationship with the unlimited potential of the Sun. This realization requires a thermodynamic leap of imagination, just like during an eclipse, when only in the absence of light do we become aware of our scale in the shadow of the cosmos.

Researchers in industrial and social ecology refer to 'socio-metabolic regimes' to define the epochal shifts in energetic relationships between humans and their environment, establishing a strict correlation between it and specific sets of social values. They argue that two of the main kinds of these regimes have been solar-based, the ones of hunter-gatherer societies and those of agrarian. Despite the existence of societies that still embody such relationships with the Sun – together with all the other species and life forms – they and the conditions for today's civilizational infrastructures are threatened by the domination of the current socio-metabolic regime, the one based on fossil fuels, powering the Capitalocene. This raises the urgency to rethink modes of being and co-existence with the planet and all the species we share it with.

What could be the fourth socio-metabolic regime? What are our varying response-abilities within the current crises of our social, mental and environmental ecologies under capitalism? What would be the new set of values necessary to drift us from the shadow sun of fossil capital, returning our sociopolitically captured senses to the Earth and the elements, rather than the imaginaries of the global and national?

It may be through a rearticulation of our relationship with the Sun, air and cosmos that we open the boundaries of the Earth, to inhabit space with renewed interplanetary sensitivity, for this world and all others – free from borders, free from fossil fuels. Aeronauts, unite!

Anthropocene

→ Agency | → Climate | → Declaration of Rebellion | → Future | geology of humanity | growing protests | → Heritage | the Age of Humans

We imagine our future by projecting forward our experience of the past, updating and changing bits to reflect our present. But what about when the pace of change is so great that we are going somewhere radically different – how then do we imagine our future?

We are creating a new world, you and I, and it's different from anything that's gone before. The changes humans have made in recent decades are on such a scale that they have altered our world beyond anything it has experienced in its 4.5 billion-year history. Our influence is no longer confined to a local area or even a region – it's global, and so profound that it is pushing the planet into a new era that geologists are calling the Anthropocene, the Age of Humans.

Millions of years from now, a strip in the accumulated layers of rock on Earth's surface will reveal our human fingerprint just as we can see evidence of dinosaurs in rocks of the Jurassic, or the explosion of life that marks the Cambrian. Our influence will show up as changes in the chemistry of the oceans, the loss of forests and the growth of deserts, the damming of rivers and the retreat of glaciers. The fossil records will show the extinctions of various animals and the abundance of domesticates, the chemical fingerprint of artificial materials such as aluminium drinks cans and plastic carrier bags, and the footprint of projects like a mine in the oil sands of Alberta, Canada, which moves twice as much earth every year than flows down all the rivers in the world in that time. Under average Holocene conditions, each year around 10 billion tonnes of sediment makes its way from the mountains to the oceans via rivers and glaciers. Humans now shift around double that every year through mining projects and other extractions for building materials.

Gaia Vince (located in London, UK) is a science writer, broadcaster and author interested in the interplay between humans and the planetary environment. In 2015, she became the first woman to win the Royal Society Science Book of the Year prize for her debut, *Adventures in the Anthropocene* (2014). Her latest book, *Transcendence* (2019), explores human cultural evolution.

In the Anthropocene, humanity has become a geophysical force on a par with the earth-shattering asteroids and planet-cloaking volcanoes that defined past eras. Earth is now a human planet. We decide whether a forest stands or is razed, whether pandas survive or become extinct, how and where a river flows, even the temperature of the atmosphere. We are now the most populous big animal on Earth, and the next in line are the animals we have created through breeding to feed and serve us – just 3% of all the land vertebrates are wild creatures. Four-tenths of the planet's land surface is used to grow our food. Most of the world's fresh water is controlled by us – rivers have been rerouted and dammed, with more than three times as much freshwater now in reservoirs than in rivers and lakes, irrevocably altering siltation patterns. Some 75% of the globe's terrestrial ecology has been modified by humans – deforestation alone fells 80,000 km^2 a year. It is an extraordinary time. In the tropics, coral reefs are disappearing, ice is melting at the poles and the oceans are becoming empty of fish because of us. Entire islands are vanishing under rising seas, just as naked new land appears in the Arctic.

Our human world

No part of this planet is untouched by human influence – we have transcended natural cycles, altered the physical, chemical and biological processes of the planet, created a geology of humanity. We have the power to heat the planet further or to cool it right down, to eliminate species and to engineer entirely new ones. We have shifted our own evolutionary pathway with medical advances that save those who would naturally die in infancy. We have surmounted the limitations that restrict other species by creating artificial environments and external sources of energy. In changing the Earth, we have been able to live longer and healthier, in greater numbers than ever before. However, humans are still of nature, we breathe air, drink water and eat protein. We rely on the planet to provide everything – all our materials, fuels, food and clothes – and to clean our air, recycle our water and manage our waste. Our growing population and the way we live in this new human world are making us more demanding than ever of our planet's resources and processes, reducing its ability to meet our needs.

We have always altered ecosystems to serve our needs and presumably will continue to do so. We have improved the planet for our survival in a number of ways, including by staving off the next ice age, but we have also made it worse. Some of those negative consequences we can overcome through technological advances or migration or other adaptations. Others we will need to reverse, some others we will need to learn to live with.

And while science may be able to identify biophysical issues, it cannot tell us how to react – that is for society to decide. Humans are no longer just another animal; we have specifically human rights that are expected to be achieved through development, including access to sanitation and electricity – even the Internet. Delivering social justice and protecting the environment are closely linked; how poor people get richer will strongly shape the Anthropocene.

A cultural species

The enormous impacts we're having on our living planet in the Anthropocene are a direct consequence of the immense social changes we're undergoing – changes to how we live as a species. We now support a massive global population of more than 7.5 billion people, but we have not simply multiplied the number of small hunter-gatherer communities. More than half of the world's people now live in cities – artificial constructs, which act as giant factories consuming the planet's plants, animals, water and mineral resources.

As a species, we're incredibly culturally diverse, and the Anthropocene is affecting us in different ways. We are at a crossroads; we don't know what is going to happen in the Anthropocene – it could be good, even better. But we need to think differently and globally, to take ownership of the planet.

The last time we passed a geological boundary some 12,000 years ago, we were a pretty insignificant species, struggling to survive in a world where so many of our cousins, including *Homo neanderthalensis*, had failed to make it. The global warming event at the end of the last ice age, which marks the epochal crossover from the Pleistocene into the Holocene, was the making of us.

As our planet heated up, ice melted and the tropics became wetter. People began taking advantage of the new conditions: grasses proliferated, and those with nutritional seeds, like wheat and barley, could be farmed. Around the world, people began settling in larger communities and processing food rather than simply hunting and gathering. This stability led to the development of culture and civilizations – our species became more populous and so successful that we spread across six continents.

We have always made some local impact on the natural world we live in, but sometime within the last couple of generations, our scope changed. The Industrial Revolution increased our ability to 'own' nature and, in the years after the First World War, saw a great acceleration in human activity: human beings became so influential that we are altering the Earth's very geology on a global scale. The greenhouse gases we emit are warming the atmosphere, and the laws of physics dictate the resulting climate change. Humans triggered this physics, and that is why it is the human system that must be targeted if we are to do something about it. That means addressing our societal systems, including populism, consumption and globalized hard-to govern markets, as well as the energy infrastructure and technologies that emit those gases … None of this is easy. Nobody deserves climate change; nobody planned this. It is not a punishment; it's not happening because humans are fundamentally bad. It is a consequence of yesterday's society, just as tomorrow will be a consequence of today's.

Making our future

It's a brave person who attempts to peer into the future and tries to decipher meaning in its endless landscapes. Yet to give ourselves the best chance of thriving tomorrow, we must prepare and plan today. That requires understanding this new world we are making and imagining what our changes will mean for us as interconnected human societies dependent on natural ecosystems.

Our activities today affect this future world, making it easier or more difficult to survive, more or less equitable, more or less wild … In other words, as we peer further into the future, little is certain. The most reliable projections are demographic: we can predict roughly how many people will be alive in 2050. This is useful because it is the planet's human population that is driving the environmental changes we are experiencing. Crucially, though, it is not simply the number of people that is important but where and how these people live. Currently, just a small, wealthy percentage of the global population is having by far the greatest influence. Towards the end of the century, however, predicting even numbers of people will become hazier: estimates range from 9 billion to 12 billion. The global population may well peak before 2100 and decline. We simply don't know.

Happily, the present is much more knowable, and we have never had so many tools to help us, including highly proficient atmospheric modelling systems, satellite monitoring tools, ocean circulation probes, global demographic data, landscape surveying technologies and accurate sensors. We can now see the changes we are making in real time as we make them – and from a planetary perspective. Using airborne LiDAR surveying, we can see chlorophyll forming in the leaf cells of individual trees in the Amazon rainforest as they take up carbon dioxide, just as satellite images reveal the path of a churning hurricane as it approaches the islands of the Caribbean. Satellites chart the hourly change in temperature of the planet's surface and also of the troposphere (the bottom part of our atmosphere), ice cores reveal the carbon dioxide content of Earth's past atmospheres and ocean sampling shows us the accumulation of new pollutants in our waterways.

The environmental problems we face are local as well as planetary, and systemic. They are caused by all of us, but the effects are not felt equally by all, nor are all people equally implicated. This is a mixture of physical, chemical, biological and social change that all interact and feed back to each other to cause changes in our planetary and human systems – which are themselves intimately interconnected. Trying to understand how our impacts in one area, such as river extraction, affect another, such as food provision, is a complex task. But that's what new collaborations of scientists, sociologists, economists, ecologists and others are trying to do. And while our problematic practices in one area can impact many other areas, the good news is that so can our restorative ones: improving biodiversity in a wetland ecosystem can also reduce water pollution and soil erosion and protect farmlands against storm damage, for instance.

To some extent we are all pawns, riders of humanity's seemingly unstoppable tsunami. But that is to miss our individual agency as voters, consumers, gardeners, parents and witnesses. In 2020, we can no longer claim we are unaware of environmental change – it is shown everywhere across our media. So too are the growing protests demanding change. Every day, our little and big choices ripple across society and are multiplied and added into the greater wave. We have the power to change the social justice systems underlying our broad environmental changes – and this power also extends to managing their impacts on us. We live in our own small local environment that we can ourselves defile, restore or enhance. It is a part of the bigger whole, just as we are part of a bigger humanity.

Archi-tecture

architecture as organization | architecture as style | → Care | → Explicitation | → Modernism | perspective of care | → Violence

Dr **Elke Krasny** (born 1965, located in Vienna, AT) is a professor at the Academy of Fine Arts Vienna. She focuses on architecture, urbanism and art that addressed and addresses ecology, economy, labour, memory and feminisms. Together with Angelika Fitz, she introduced the notion of critical care through architecture in the age of climate-change catastrophe. They co-edited *Critical Care: Architecture and Urbanism for a Broken Planet* (2019).

On defining architecture

Why is yet another definition of architecture needed? Why should we work on a new entry on architecture in the general lexicon? Why, at this point in time, should all those professionally concerned with the production, reflection and dissemination of architecture worry about a new definition of architecture in the architectural lexicon? The following essay uses these questions of definition to think through a number of issues as they concern concrete historical power relations, epistemic power and the relationship between architecture, environmental interdependence and human/nonhuman entanglements. While definitions are largely perceived as definitive and lasting as they capture the fundamental character of something, I suggest to work with defining here as a generative process that opens up prospective horizons of critically needed change *in*, *for*, *with* and *through* architecture.

Let me first turn to the dictionary entry on architecture. The online free dictionary provides us with the following ones: Architecture is 'the art and science of designing and erecting buildings'. Architecture is 'buildings and other large structures'. Architecture is 'a style and method of design and construction'. Architecture is the 'orderly arrangement of parts; structure'. And finally, architecture is 'any of various disciplines concerned with the design or organization of complex systems'.[1] While the first three are concerned with architecture proper, the latter two mobilize broader concepts not necessarily connected to erecting physical buildings but rather to the organization of systems in general. Connecting more closely to each other the understanding of architecture as buildings and the understanding of architecture as organization will be useful for our purpose to arrive at generatively producing a new definition for architecture in light of living on a broken planet.

Definitive architecture

Even though the dictionary entry speaks of architecture as buildings in general, which would include the built environment in its entirety, Architecture, as commonly held, is much more narrowly defined to refer to significant buildings designed by architects. Therefore it is useful to distinguish Architecture written with capital A from architecture – that is, all kinds of buildings.

Architecture with capital A refers to a specific class of buildings that accrue value over time and form part of a cultural heritage, which the United Nations defines as 'physical artifacts and intangible attributes of a group or society that are inherited from past generations, maintained in the present and bestowed for the benefit of future generations'.[2] Even though examples of so-called vernacular, traditional, mundane or informal architecture have been included in the notion of cultural heritage, Architectural legacy continues to be most commonly understood as Architectural masterpieces. The masterpiece remains the organizing principle through which the modern canonical history of Architecture is being established. Masterpieces are linked to style. They are the definitive expression of a specific style. Therefore, when thinking about the definition of architecture, we also have to think about definitive architecture, the class of architecture that expresses a specific paradigm as it comes to define Architecture. Stylistic analysis is concerned with defining masterpieces, with analysing what makes these masterpieces definitive as they define the Architectural canon which constitutes Architectural heritage and legacy. In historical terms, architectural history originated as stylistics. When architectural history was established as an academic discipline and a field of study in its own right in the 19th century, it was a sub-discipline of art history. The German term for stylistics is *Stilkunde*. This term is instructive to understand how style relates to the archives of regimes of power knowledge. *Stil*, the first part of this composite word, translates into 'style'. *Kunde*, the second part, means 'knowledge and teachings'. The word originated in the Netherlands and was adopted from Dutch by the German language in the course of the 17th century. Architectural history as *Stilkunde*, therefore, is the disciplinary knowledge and the teachings of style. History practiced as stylistics operating with the idea of the masterpiece established definitive Architecture, which continues to govern the notion of how Architecture is being defined. Therefore, definitive – that is, distinct and authoritative – masterpieces continue to determine what is defined as Architecture and what is merely architecture.

Style defines Architecture, discursively. When thinking of definitive Architecture linked to style as it continues to be taught in architectural history and is disseminated in tourist guidebooks or architectural guides, overlapping exclusions of gender, sexualities and race continue to define which masterpieces are considered more definitive than others. Therefore, the canonical history of Architecture is still marked by Eurocentric, male-centric and white-centric hierarchies. Unsettling the politics that define how definitive Architecture is being recognized and being made canonical is important for critical future work based on the premise of avoiding the masculinist masterpiece trap. Style defines Architecture, physically. Therefore it is important to draw attention to the fact that style is as much made out of bricks, mortar, glass or steel as it is discursively constructed. Style relies on economies and resources, on building materials. Even if the use of specific materials, such as stone, brick, glass or steel, are considered relevant to expressing a specific style, issues of resource extractivism or conditions of labour characteristic to the production regimes connected to specific building materials are rarely touched upon in Architectural history. In order for there to be a move towards a critically generative process of defining architecture by way of bringing ethical and political concerns into view that will ultimately allow for defining architecture differently, it is necessary to move towards an approach that does not stop short of including resource politics connected to building materials – connected to style – in the discursive-epistemological construction of the physical existence of Architecture/architecture.

Style is deeply connected to the systems of value characteristic to specific periods. Periodization through style as a way of distinguishing different types of architecture from each other locates architecture not only in place but also in time. From the Egyptian Pyramids to the Guangzhou Opera House, from the super-blocks of Red Vienna Housing, the Bauhaus Masters' Houses in Dessau to Lina Bo Bardi's Glass House, buildings represent the Architecture of their time. Such buildings are not only definitive Architecture but more broadly definitive to the period which gave rise to them. Such buildings are the physical expression of hegemonic cultural value systems. They are the material representation of the powers at work. Buildings like the ones mentioned above of course not only emerge from creative labour, historically linked to the idea of creative genius gendered white and male, but much rather have to be understood as the result of complexly interrelated and interdependent political and economic processes. Political powers and markets define Architecture. In turn, Architecture powerfully represents the political regimes and the economic conditions that made the access to land, access to resources for the production of building materials, and provision of labour for construction possible.

Defining architecture for catastrophic times

Let me return to the question again that I raised at the beginning: Why is yet another definition of architecture needed? Critical scholarship has examined the gendered, racialized and sexualized exclusions from writing Architectural history – that is, from defining what Architecture is. I have introduced the notion of defining as a generative process. Such an approach links defining to temporality. Therefore it is necessary not only to critically examine the political and material power and the epistemic power defining Architecture but to raise the question of when. When is architecture defined? And how can such a generative process of defining architecture concern not just history and theory but also the future of architecture? When does defining architecture make a difference? And why is this crucial today?

Today, we have no time to lose. We live, as Belgian philosopher Isabelle Stengers has written, in 'catastrophic times'.[3] Other names that have been suggested for our era with its fossil addiction, its unprecedented pace of species extinction and its rapidly accelerating climate catastrophe include the term 'Anthropocene', introduced by biologist Eugene F. Stoermer and atmospheric chemist Paul Crutzen, and the term 'Capitalocene', used among others by environmental historian Jason W. Moore. The Anthropocene understands humankind as a geological force that has made a mark, a mark that carries its originator, the Greek word *ánthrōpos*, 'man', in its name. Many thinkers, scholars and activists, among them Anna Tsing, Donna Haraway, McKenzie Wark and Vandana Shiva, are critically engaging with the notions behind this term. They are by no means disputing the realities of climate catastrophe and ecocide, but they are disputing the Anthropocene since it conceals the unevenly distributed responsibility of humans across the globe and it continues to place humankind, and in particular the notion of subject as it was developed with Enlightenment Man, above nature. This notion of the subject was fully aligned with the modern formation of the architect as it was defined through the systematic architectural education developed during the Enlightenment period.

Man above nature is fundamentally linked to the idea of modern Architecture.

Modern architecture was largely based on the blank slate ideology, which corresponds to the *terra nullius* ideology of settler colonialism. Therefore, modern Architecture can be understood as the representative expression of capitalism and coloniality, as the capitalist-colonial regime transformed land into commodity, and nature into a resource to be extracted from. Modern Architecture takes centre stage in the politics of land and resources. Building as if nature did not exist, building as if nature was a view to be consumed, building as if nature was a resource to be extracted from is among the defining features of modern Architecture. Therefore, Architecture was profoundly entangled with the violence of modernity. Emancipatory claims of transparency linked to steel and glass are deeply enmeshed with industrialized, standardized, Fordist production regimes. Modern Architecture was not a mere reflection of capitalism and coloniality but one of its driving forces. Architecture was part of defining the modern project. Modern Architecture rested on the premise of building the better future. With this modernity in ruins and, even worse, with contemporary iconic Architecture turbulently accelerating the dark sides of capitalism and coloniality, we are left with shifting the question of defining architecture differently to the ethical obligation and the political task of defining architecture differently. This needs to be done so that architecture can play a part in restoring futurity – that is, the very possibility of there being a future in the future.

Defining architecture differently needs to link architecture understood as design and construction to architecture understood as the organization of complexity. Moving the conceptual premise for architecture closer to an understanding of being part of building the environment, not outside or vis-á-vis nature but in the midst of naturecultures, to use Donna Haraway's term,[4] will be central to defining architecture differently. Letting go of the masterpiece ideology of Architecture will evenly be central to shifting architecture to organizing complexity. The underlying premise for defining architecture differently, architecture response-able in and for catastrophic times, is a perspective of care. Following the definition provided by political theorist Joan Tronto together with Berenice Fisher as early as 1990, caring 'includes everything that we do to maintain, to continue, and to repair our "world" so that we can live as well as possible'.[5] They write that 'our world includes our bodies, our selves, and our environment, all of which we seek to interweave in a complex, life-sustaining web'.[6] Caring always starts from the given and takes it into account. Rooted in a perspective of care, architecture starts from the given. Today, the given means our catastrophic times require a radical shift from anthropocenic, fossil-addicted Architecture to caring, low-carbon architecture. This much needed process of defining architecture differently is based on the relational concept of care as being response-able to humans and nonhumans alike. Defining architecture for our catastrophic times is the task at hand that connects organizing complexity to care-fully designing and constructing buildings for futurity.

Works cited:

Fisher, B., and J. Tronto. 1990. 'Towards a Feminist Theory of Care'. In E. Abdel and M. Nelson, eds. *Circles of Care: Work and Identity in Women's Lives*, pp. 35–62. Albany: State University of New York Press.

Free Dictionary. 2019. 'Architecture'. https://www.thefreedictionary.com/architecture. Accessed 20 December 2019.

Haraway, Donna J. 2003. *The Companion Species Manifesto: Dogs, People, and Significant Otherness*. Chicago: Prickly Paradigm Press.
Stengers, Isabelle. 2015. *In Catastrophic Times: Resisting the Coming Barbarism*. S.l.: Open Humanities Press.

UNESCO. 2019. 'Cultural Heritage'. http://www.unesco.org/new/fileadmin/MULTIMEDIA/FIELD/Dakar/pdf/CULTURALHERITAGE.pdf. Accessed 20 December 2019.

Architect Yasmeen Lari revives traditional Pakistani clay-and-bamboo construction methods to develop flood-resistant homes and community facilities. Barefoot Entrepreneurs pass on their building skills in a snowball system. Over 40,000 flood-resilient homes have been built in the last few years with a minimum of financial means.

→ Aesthetics | → Anthropocene | Anthropocene sensibilities | → Ecology | → Environment | → Moving Earths | 'ordinary' aesthetic experiences of ecologies

Line Marie Thorsen (born 1985, located in Denmark and Japan) is currently a postdoc with the Independent Research Fund Denmark, based at Osaka University, Japan, and Aarhus University, Denmark. She holds a PhD in Art History and Anthropology from Aarhus University and has carried out research on artists committed to climate change and ecological crises in East Asia since 2015. In 2017, she curated the exhibition Moving Plants at Rønnebæksholm in Denmark and edited a book of the same name.

Art in the Anthropocene, at the margins and in the everyday

What does it mean and entail to approach the Anthropocene from the vantage point of art-making? What kind of arts proceed from, and are needed for, living in the Anthropocene? And how may 'we' need to recalibrate notions of art and of which arts matter in this new planetary epoch? I will be attending to these questions in this article, but to get at them, a bit of (art) history is needed first. While artists are now increasingly addressing the specificities of anthropogenically induced changes in climate, geology, ecology and much else besides, the topic of humans and/in nature is far from new in arts. In a certain way, art has always fundamentally been about relaying the human experience of being in, part of and dependent on 'the environment'. That is, of being a live creature in and because of environmental conditions, as American pragmatist philosopher John Dewey put it in his book *Art and Experience* from 1934.[1]

Yet even though this may be true in one sense, a *particular* category of art often referred to as 'eco-art' and 'environmental art' came into being from the 1960s onwards, referring to the fact that this category – 'the environment' – became the explicit stake of the art practices involved. Owing to emerging environmentalism, spurred by books like *Silent Spring*,[2] this period marks a moment where concern for the environment as something humans are part of and owe responsibility towards becomes an explicit topic of political and artistic discussion and practice. Departing in North America, art historian Barbara Matilsky argues that an emerging awareness of 'fragile ecologies' turned artists onto 'nature and began interpreting its life-generating forces to create radically new kinds of art'.[3] In other words, artists became explicitly attentive to the way humans and nature affect each other for better and worse and began experimenting with new forms of art capable of attending to this: Hans Haacke planted seeds and grew grass in gallery spaces (*Grass Grows*, 1967–1969, and *Bowery Seeds*, 1970), Alan Sonfist created small-scale parks featuring precolonial plants in New York City (*Time Landscapes*, 1965–1968), Anna Mendieta literally inscribed her body in rocky, muddy, mossy and flowering landscapes (the *Silueta* series, 1973–1980), and

Joseph Beuys had 7,000 oak trees planted for documenta 7 in Kassel (*7000 Oaks*, 1982).

At this point in time, artists, like most others, developed this from a somewhat new awareness of the natural environment as a subject of human exploitation, and so most art practices departed in an assumed separation between nature and culture, resulting in an idealist conception of a primordial Nature (capital N) to be saved from Man's cultural domination.[4] This is a notion of nature-culture relations which enjoyed much attention in the following decades, until the entrance of what we may call 'Anthropocene sensibilities'. While the strive for cultural domination of nature is still a key point of concern, the realization that human activity is a force of planet-transforming scale on par with nature's geophysical powers means that the separation between nature and culture is no longer (nor has it ever been) viable.

In the Anthropocene, the experience of being a live creature is dramatized in specific ways. The relationship may have always been dramatic, but the Anthropocene skews the experience from one of humans at the mercy of 'natural forces' to one of being dangerously entangled with and co-producers of those devastating forces. At the same time, however, we become aware that there is no singular humanity and culture to hold accountable. It is certainly human and cultural practices that have spun the entirety of earthlings into the Anthropocene, but not all humans and cultures are equally accountable. This triple awareness of nature-culture entanglement, and dispersed and unequal responsibility with a global reach, marks a shift in art practices as well.[5]

American art theorist T.J. Demos traces a shift in which artists have become more attentive to the 'global Other' and thus to the unequal environments people inhabit across localities and regions of the world. He also identifies a change in attention from a 'Nature-versus-Culture' frame and into something closer to 'naturecultures' – that is, an acknowledgement of the situated entanglements at work in human and nonhuman ecologies and their various globalized encounters.[6]

Also, newer generations of eco-artists attentive to Anthropocene issues, like Henrik Håkansson, Tue Greenfort, Tomás Saraceno, Ursula Biemann, Subhankar Banerjee, Amy Balkin, Roni Horn and Olafur Eliasson, are insisting on a kind of 'autonomy' in art via the specific modes of engagement afforded by *aesthetic* practices while simultaneously articulating a wide range of social engagements, cross-disciplinary collaboration and critical projects. Here, art as political, social and material *as well as* aesthetic practice is seen to offer particular approaches to articulations of concerns that other forms of engagements, such as activism, cannot.[7]

The Anthropocene has thus effectuated new – or shifted – engagements from art and aesthetics in more recent eco-art history and has spurred a great variety of interdisciplinary commitments. 'The Anthropocene' is a fairly new notion in common academic and mainstream discussions, yet its popularity and spread has been so fast that we have already, for some time, been discussing its merits, failures and terminologically more precise alternatives.[8] While the term originates in geological discussions on stratigraphy, the Anthropocene has had a rich life outside of strictly geological discussions, not least in art practices and exhibitions.

Indeed, while strictly speaking a geological term, the Anthropocene gains much of its impetus from arts, humanistic and social science collaborations and thus shapes up as a popular notion for planetary troubles very much *as* an interdisciplinary notion. This involves some ironies not lost on French philosopher Bruno Latour, who remarks that the geological subcommittee tasked with gathering proof for an Anthropocene epoch in geological terms 'is so badly funded that they had to rely on the "*Haus der Kultur der Welt*" in Berlin to pay for their meeting ... Artists financing geologists to decide upon the name of the *Zeitgeist*! You have to recognize that the Anthropocene is a strange animal.'[9]

As Latour hints, the Haus der Kulturen der Welt has indeed become a centre for Anthropocene arts, embodied in their 'Anthropocene Project' from 2013 to 2014[10] along with their online 'Anthropocene Curriculum'. But they have certainly not been alone. Other high-profile Anthropocene-inflected exhibitions include, for instance, *Anthropocene Monument* (2014) at Les Abattoirs, Toulouse; *Welcome to the Anthropocene: The Earth in our Hands* (2014–2016), a collaboration between the Rachel Carson Center at Ludwig-Maximilians-Universität and Deutsches Museum, Munich; and the travelling exhibition *Anthropocene* (2018–2019), showing the collaborative *Anthropocene Project* by Nicholas de Pencier, Edward Burtynsky and Jennifer Baichwal at The National Gallery of Canada, Ottawa, and the Art Gallery of Ontario, Toronto.

Apart from these explicit titular examples, several exhibitions have utilized the momentum of the Anthropocene as a way of qualifying related foci such as 'gardens', 'multispecies living', 'art- science collaborations', 'nature' or 'landscapes'.[11] Here, however, it is important to reintroduce the question of cultural diversity in the face of Anthropocene issues. If there is no single humanity or culture, then the arts responding to Anthropocene issues are equally diverse. This means that to see and appreciate the arts that grapple with the Anthropocene, we have to also let go of this term.

There are *also* numerous exhibitions, art projects and practices dedicated to the implications of the Anthropocene, climate change and their multifarious ecological crises that just never use or invoke any of these (arguably) 'Western-dominated' buzzwords. This is true within Europe and North America, but this is especially true outside of Euro-America. To get at such art practices, I will now, finally, turn towards East Asia. Here, as arguably most places, a great variety of artists are indeed dedicated to Anthropocene issues, without ever using the term. Instead, many are committed to art forms which have become somewhat marginalized as compared to the more dominant modes of Euro-American art history: art made with significance to everyday life and 'ordinary' aesthetic experiences of ecologies rather than galleries and grand planetary scales. Such art can take many forms and can include work such as that by Yukiko Iwatani from Japan, for instance. Iwatani is a sculptor of sorts, who crafts small sculptural beings from weeds and inconspicuous plants native to the areas she exhibits in. Through a long process of getting to know the plants and their communities, Iwatani

reshapes them into new forms, in dialogue with the plants themselves and with their environments. In doing so, the plants may become noticeable and better cared for by their immediate human guardians.

It can also take the form of artists turning themselves into permacultural and 'natural' farmers.[12] In long-term commitments, artists like the Hong Kong Farmers and Sense Art Studio at the Echigo-Tsumari Art Triennale, or Itoshima Art Farm in Fukuoka, Japan, learn how to cultivate foods in ecologically sustainable ways, but also how to cultivate relations built on solidarity with the conventional farmers – and, indeed, how to practice art from the margins in ways that align it with everyday life and attachments to local ecologies. Thinkers and philosophers like Shunsuke Tsurumi and Yuriko Saito from Japan and American John Dewey have variously theorized such art practices as 'marginal art' and pertaining to everyday aesthetic experience.[13] This strand of research and theorizing argues that both art and aesthetic sensibilities are and have always been plural and that the things and experiences referenced as 'art' and 'aesthetics' in dominant modes of ('Western') scholarship actually only encompass a limited sub-set of those more broad-based practices and histories rightly pertaining to these cultural repertoires. In the Anthropocene, such a broader notion of art,

Yukiko Iwatani
Phytolacca Decandra, 2015
Plant matter
5 × 10 × 6.5 cm

aesthetics and the way they come to matter in local settings and variations becomes key. The Anthropocene, like climatic changes, nature and culture, is not *one* thing: Scandinavia is and will be experiencing a different Anthropocene than East Asia. For the same reason, artists also approach these phenomena on variable terms. To see and learn from art in a time in which we desperately need to rethink our ways of living, it may then serve us well to forget about the Anthropocene as a guiding term, in favour of carefully noticing the sprawl of arts that help us imagine other modes of living on and with the Earth.

Yukiko Iwatani
Pennisetum Alopecuroides and Japanese Hare Hair, 2015
Plant matter and animal hair
8 × 14 × 11 cm

Yukiko Iwatani
Circaea Mollis Sieb. et Zucc. and Japanese Hare Hair, 2015
Plant matter and animal hair
3 × 3 × 3 cm

Works cited:

Carson, Rachel. 1962. *Silent Spring*. London: Penguin.

Demos, T.J. 2010. 'The Politics of Sustainability: Art and Ecology'. In *Radical Nature: Art and Architecture for a Changing Planet 1969–2009*. Edited by Francesco Manacorda, Graham Sheffield, Kate Bush and Jonathan Porritt, pp. 16–30. Cologne: Walther König.

Demos, T.J. 2018. 'The Arts of Living at the End of the World'. In *Eco-Visionaries: Art, Architecture, and New Media after the Anthropocene*. Edited by Pedro Gadanho, Museu de Arte, Arquitectura e Tecnologia, Bildmuseet, HeK, and LABoral Centro de Arte y Creación Industrial. Berlin: Hatje Cantz Verlag.

Dewey, John. 2005. *Art as Experience*. New York: Berkley Publishing Group.

Fukuoka, Masanobu. 1993. *The Natural Way of Farming: The Theory and Practice of Green Philosophy*. Translated by Frederic P. Metreaud. Madras: Bookventure.

Gan, Elaine, Steven Lam and Sarah Lookofsky. 2014. 'Kunsthal Aarhus: DUMP! Multispecies Making and Unmaking'. https://kunsthalaarhus.dk/en/Exhibitions/Dump-Multispecies-Making-And-Unmaking-2015. Accessed 17 January 2020.

Haraway, Donna. 2015. 'Anthropocene, Capitalocene, Plantationocene, Chthulucene: Making Kin'. *Environmental Humanities*, 6, pp. 159–165.

Haraway, Donna, Noboru Ishikawa, Scott F. Gilbert, Kenneth Olwig, Anna L. Tsing and Nils Bubandt. 2015. 'Anthropologists Are Talking – About the Anthropocene'. *Ethnos*, 81 (3), pp. 535–564. https://doi.org/10.1080/00141844.2015.1105838. Accessed 17 January 2020.

Klingan, Katrin, Ashkan Sepahvand, Christoph Rosol and Bernd M. Scherer, eds. 2015. *Textures of the Anthropocene: Grain, Vapor, Ray*. Cambridge, MA: MIT Press.

Latour, Bruno. 2014. 'Anthropology at the Time of the Anthropocene – a Personal View of What Is to Be Studied'. Distinguished Lecture presented at the American Association of Anthropologists, December, Washington, DC.

Malm, Andreas, and Alf Hornborg. 2014. 'The Geology of Mankind? A Critique of the Anthropocene Narrative'. *The Anthropocene Review*, 1 (1), pp. 62–69. https://doi.org/10.1177/2053019613516291. Accessed 17 January 2020.

Matilsky, Barbara C. 1992. *Fragile Ecologies: Contemporary Artists' Interpretations and Solutions*. New York: Rizzoli International for Queens Museum of Art.

Saito, Yuriko. 2007. *Everyday Aesthetics*. Oxford and New York: Oxford University Press.

Saito, Yuriko. 2017. *Aesthetics of the Familiar: Everyday Life and World-Making*. Oxford: Oxford University Press.

Thorsen, Line Marie. 2019. *On the Margins of Eco-Art: Aesthetics, Plants and Environmental Imaginations in East Asia*. PhD thesis: Aarhus University, Denmark.

Vandsø, Anette, Erlend G. Høyersten, Anne Mette Thomsen and Jakob Vengberg Sevel, eds. 2017. *The Garden: End of Times, Beginning of Times*. London: Koenig Books.

鶴見 (Tsurumi), 俊輔 (Shunsuke). 1967. 限界芸術論 (Genkai Geijutsuron). 東京: 筑摩書房 (Tokyo: Chikuma Shobō).

Atmosphere

→ Aesthetics | → Attention | bodily feeling | → Environment | environmental aesthetics | mood | → Natureculture

On the Concept of Atmospheres

In 1989, I introduced the concept of atmosphere in the context of environmental aesthetics.[1] The latter was part of my criticism of ecology. The science of ecology stemming from Ernst Haeckel (19th century) at that time was presented as a means to cope with the problems we humans amassed living in a certain environment. Yet we are not mere natural agencies. In the environment concerned, our behaviour is politically, economically and juridically patterned according to certain norms. To give an example: our environment may be natural, but it is cut into parcels and treated as property. Thus the proposition of my former working group was to introduce concepts stemming from humanities into the science of our environment. This led us to the paradoxical claim of a social-natural science (*Soziale Naturwissenschaft*[2]). Part of this was my turn to aesthetics: what was missing in the contemporary ecology, seen as a science of environment, was our aesthetic relation to that environment.

We appreciate our environment through the bodily feeling of it: the environment is beautiful, pleasant and even good if we feel well in that environment. We feel where we are – in the sense of in what sort of environment. From here came the main thesis: through our bodily feeling we are aware of what sort of environment we are actually in.

This is the place where the concept of atmosphere comes in: atmospheres are conceived as something mediating objective facts of the environment with our subjective feeling of them. An example is smell: well, a bad smell may be an indicator of the air surrounding us being toxic, but it does not have to be that way. Proof is in the case of a nice smell: we may encounter a wonderful smell in a park, but the pleasure of it, though triggering our vitality, does not mean that this smell has any physiological effect.

The environmental facts, from lightning to sounds, from colours to forms, from the qualities of air to the movement of it – i.e. winds – are producing a certain mood of the space concerned, be it nature or built environment. A space with a certain mood carrying it: that is an atmosphere.

Dr **Gernot Böhme** (born 1937, located in Darmstadt, DE) is a retired professor of philosophy from the Technical University of Darmstadt and is director of the private Institute for Practicing Philosophy. Most recent publications in English are *Atmospheric Architectures: The Aesthetics of Felt Spaces* (2017) and *Critique of Aesthetic Capitalism* (2017).

We may learn a lot about the connection of environmental facts of a space and the mood we are feeling by studying this relation from the perspective of production aesthetics, i.e. the practices to produce a certain mood in a given space.

Works cited:

Böhme, Gernot. (1989) 1999. *Für eine* ökologische *Naturästhetik*, 3rd edn. Frankfurt/M.: Suhrkamp. Polish edition Warsaw: Oficyna Naukowa, 2002.

Böhme, Gernot, and Engelbert Schramm, eds. 1985. *Soziale Naturwissenschaft: Wege zur Erweiterung der* Ökologie. Frankfurt/M.: Fischer.

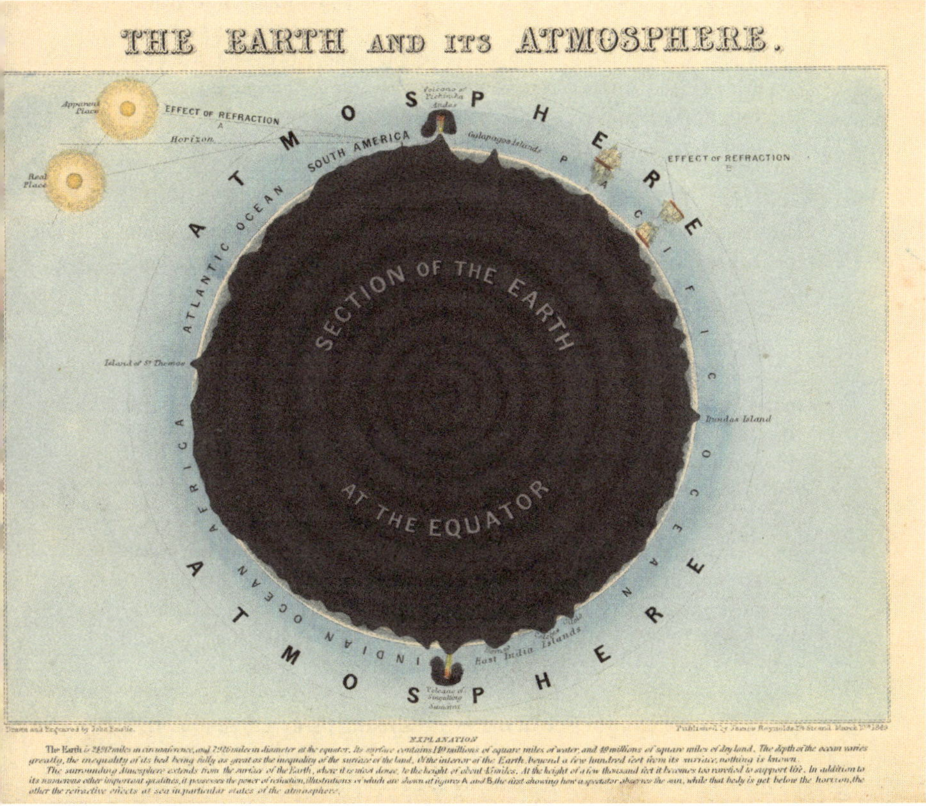

One of a set of twelve hand-coloured astronomical prints with an explanatory card. The prints are contained in a brown striped portfolio with blue marbled paper along the spine, embossed with gold lettering on the front, reading 'Astronomical Diagrams'. These cards were first issued by the British publisher James Reynolds in 1846, although he and other publishers continued to produce them throughout the second half of the 19th century. They responded to a perceived market for popular science products and were intended for informal learning within the home. They could be bought in sets or singly and, at a price of 1 shilling, were affordable to middle-class audiences.

Antony Gormley
Blind Light, 2007
Fluorescent light, water, ultrasonic humidifiers, toughened low-iron glass and aluminium
320 × 978.5 × 856.5 cm
Installation view, Hayward Gallery, London

Attachment

→ Aesthetics | → Attention | awareness | → Care | → Chthulucene | → Connectedness | embodied stories | → Feminism | reparative practice | response-ability

Emmy Laura Perez Fjalland (born 1987, located in Copenhagen, DK) is a postdoctoral researcher at the Institute of Architecture, Urbanism and Landscape, at The Royal Danish Academy of Fine Arts in Copenhagen. She works with environmental humanities and explores the connections between critical thinking (feminist materialist and speculative realist traditions) and the current dialogues of environmental doom, more-than-human ontologies and ecological practices.

As a thing, 'attachment' refers to matters that we add on to something else. Something we connect something else with. It can refer to a tool that you can fix onto a machine to make it do another job; it can be the act of joining one thing to another, or a thing that joins two things together. Attachments hold links, connections, details. Details matter, and how they are attached matters. Attachments can be materials, matters, components, and they seem to make the relationality – a stickiness that can be done and undone – of this world's becomings and beings tangible and visible. Attachments hold a stickiness because they can stick with what they are attached to, and each of these attachments are most likely stuck together by manifold other attachments. Each with a sticky story, together they create new stories. A story or an article is made up by different matters, meanings, figures such as data, references, witches, critters, sites, tools, scales. These are materials, beings, practices and becomings of themselves, but as attachments to each other (as they *become attached, are attached, want to become attached*) they create new stories (of science, of arts, of becomings, of landscaping) in significant ways.

Attachments might then be material, biological, social, cultural, organic (to mention just a few), and the creations of the attachments as the connections – 'attaching' – seem both fragile and pliable. Attaching is a delicate, sensitive *practice* that can be cut off, broken, obstinate, remade, readjusted, slow. Attachment can also refer to a short time spent working with an organization such as a university, hospital, school, government or the armed forces. This kind of attachment holds a kind of being-with-organization, not just something someone does but rather a becoming-with-an-organization. It is an active doing and being. Attachment is a matter, material and practice, and they may tell us stories of a layered attached world made of attachments and practices of attaching, connections between someone(s), something(s). Human, organic, non-organic. For making better accounts of the manifold and more than human world-making practices always around us, becoming aware of the attachments themselves and their constructions, histories, the practices of privilege, of oppression, might help 'us'. Help us with attempts to build knowledges, sciences, technologies and stories about lives and world-makings that continue, that stick – unending, cyclical stories moving beyond the so-called Anthropocene.

Thinking of attachment alongside the looming ecological and environmental changes, a 'dis-attachment' (or disconnection, dichotomy) between so-called cultures and natures is often argued to be part of the extinction, crisis and emergency. A modernist science. Becoming *aware* of the troubles might increase attachment, which in this understanding holds a dangerous potential of romanticizing the attachment itself and moralizing it as something that would 'naturally' lead to something 'good'. This is a rational thought, a logical logic. Becoming *aware of attachments* may be experienced as fulfilling, enchanting, regenerative, a kind of belonging, and comforting, but it may also feel uncomfortable, even abrasive, incarcerating, demanding, dooming. The American political theorist and philosopher Jane Bennett, whose work has been significant within the so-called material turn in humanities and social sciences, depicts how the stories of disattachment – the significant story about modernity as dead, alienated and disenchanted – blocks our minds and imaginations.[1] We have never been disconnected, disattached, and we might never have been Modern (as Latour once wrote).[2] From this line of thinking, there is much more to the story of alienation and disattachment between so-called culture and nature. Becoming aware (as a curious and speculative art of [re]search) of attachments directs one's attentions and nurtures one's sensibilities towards the more-than-human worlds. It might become attaching. One might become aware of significant trees, bushes, compost piles, critters, cats, carrots, bacteria, sourdoughs, pigeons, bed bugs. The practice invites us into the attachments of and between the human, the more than human organic and in-organic physical worlds and world-making practices. And how they attach, are detaching, becoming attached. These must be the *arts of attaching*, *stories of stickiness*. Becoming aware might propel a kind of ethical awareness that could resituate humans in ecological terms and non-humans within ethical terms.[3] The potential enchanted moments of this becoming aware of the attachments might even propel an ethical laudable generosity and sensibility that according to Jane Bennett involves humans and more-than-humans.[4] It is sustained 'by periodic bouts of being enamored [enchanted] with existence, and that it is too hard to love a disenchanted world. Affective fascination with a world thought to be worthy of it may help to ward off the existential resentment that plagues mortals'.[5]

Attachment also refers to a belief in and support for an idea or a set of values, or to a strong feeling of affection for somebody/something. Attachment as emotional, feeling. As love is not only adorable, attachment and attaching can be a burden; it may feel as an incarceration. And there is no direct logical connection as becoming aware + attachment = doing a 'good' thing. In some environmentalist projects with an apocalyptic tone, this seems likely to be the idea – that the information of loss will decrease the non-environmentalist behaviour. Becoming aware as in seeing, sensing, tasting, smelling might draw us into the worlds of Earth-others. It might bring some attention to *where* we are, *who* we are and who we are *with*, and help us make better accounts of the world(s) we live with. What we might do with this knowledge, and what kinds of politics and ethics might come out of this kind of knowledge is still up for exploration – yet we might find that we too are of Earth, just among other critters. Not above. Not separated. Yet significant and powerful. We are attached, we are contaminated, connected, related. Organs, lungs, bacteria, water, blood, carrots, intestines, stardust, faeces. Becoming aware of the attachments and attachings should not to be confused with an innocent, peaceful practice; becoming aware and becoming attached can be heavy, guilty, pleasing, dirty, troublesome, releasing, joyful and painful. It might be like carrying a burden, something that is thrust upon you. And it can be more than that.

A kind of ethical generosity and sensitivity could open up the politics for human and more-than-human 'response-abilities' or abilities to respond – and enhance chances of living on. Response-ability is not understood ethically as a normative, individual behavioural responsibility nor as a higher guiding moral principle for how much humans can hurt 'nature' – such as the scale of the use of chemicals, colonizing seeds, advancing breeding techniques, optimum modification of feed, tolerable stable standards. Response-abilities are about exploring ethical responses that are situated, practical and embodied, that are attachments, attached and sticky. A *were, who, with*. Building knowledge about response-abilities can come from becoming aware and exploring the attachments of human worlds, more-than-human organic worlds and physical, non-organic worlds. An embodied (sticky) knowledge practice that might open up time and space for alternative Earth habitation, a practice that might bring new tactile experiences, sensuous moments and stories relating to the spaces and beings we move through and with every day. These might be a bit transformative and make us (humans) experience things differently, *make us sense* the world differently, and this might develop how we talk about the world, how we *make sense of* the world and how we act with(in) 'it'. Becoming aware of the more-than-human sites, situations, collaborations, contaminations – attachments – can be viewed as small gestures, small invitations into a post-anthropocentric world, which might cultivate response-abilities. We are all responsible, but in very different ways.[6] What politics could come from the sciences, technologies and stories that attach and detach attaching or detaching attachments?

Works cited:

Bennett, Jane. 2001. *The Enchantment of Modern Life*. Princeton: Princeton University Press.

Gibson, Katherine, Deborah Bird Rose and Ruth Fincher, eds. 2015. *Manifesto for Living in the Anthropocene*. New York: Punctum.

Haraway, Donna J. 2016. *Staying with the Trouble: Making Kin in the Chthulucene.* Durham, NC: Duke University Press Books.

Latour, Bruno. 2014. 'Anthropology at the Time of the Anthropocene – a Personal View of What Is to Be Studied'. Distinguished Lecture presented at the American Association of Anthropologists, Washington, December.

Attention

→ Aesthetics | → Care | critical sensitivity | deep attention | entanglements | → Explicitation | framing | hybrids | hyper attention

Agger Tange, the isthmus north of the Thyborøn Channel, on the west coast of Denmark, is a wild nature reserve and the southernmost point of Thy National Park. Harboøre Tange, the southern isthmus, is an urban centre expanding from Thyborøn harbour city. At first sight, the two sides of the Thyborøn Channel seem like complete opposites.

A long thin road sears through the middle of the nature reserve, leading our attention to green lowlands exposed to the sea waves, currents and erosion on each side. This isthmus seems wild, untouched and untamed.

A long road also sears through the middle of Thyborøn. To the left and right of this road are urban formations – industry, windmills, houses, parking. The sea and its forces are out of sight. This urban centre feels much like any other provincial city anywhere in the world. Here, the wild forces that feel so present on the other side of the channel are out of sight.

After spending some time in and becoming more sensitive to the surroundings, the two sides of the channel surprisingly acquire an uncanny similarity. What seemed urban is also wild, and what seemed wild is also tamed. It becomes apparent that the two curated landscapes are actually one complex, entangled territory of human activity and natural processes.

In fact, the two sides of the Thyborøn Channel once formed a continuous isthmus. A storm in the 19th century punctured a hole through the narrow land and created a connection between the sea and the fjord. This connection was advantageous for the growing industry, and it has since been maintained and fortified.

Today, sand from excavations of the seabed to deepen the channel for larger ships to enter the harbour and enlarge the industry is used to feed the coastline on Harboøre

66 **Polina Chebotareva** (born 1989, located in Copenhagen, DK) holds an MSc in Psychology and is currently finishing her PhD in Architecture. Polina links architectural research with psychology to create spatial design with an impact on perception and human relations. She specializes in drawing attention to overlooked qualities of everyday surroundings. Polina is the founder of the design studio Between Architecture & People (BAP Projects).

Rasmus Hjortshøj (born 1979, located in Copenhagen, DK) is a Danish architect and founder of COAST – Collective Architecture Studio. In his PhD, Rasmus uses architectural photography to represent the entanglement of society and nature in coastal territories of the Anthropocene. He explores how territorial hybrids, emerging through the entanglement of cultural and natural processes, may be aesthetically framed and discussed to inform future coastal planning.

Tange to maintain beaches and infrastructure. Meanwhile, similar coastal protection on Agger Tange maintains and enlarges bird habitats following the Ramsar Convention on Wetlands of International Importance. The two sides of the channel are like mirrored hybrids of the Anthropocene.

These hybrids, composed of entanglements between human activity and geophysical forces, and between international law and wildlife habitats, question where the urban begins and the wild ends. Such hybrids are a defining feature of the Anthropocene. However, this complexity escapes our attention in the curated everyday landscapes.

Agger Tange with its dynamic natural processes embedded in a rigid frame of coastal protection and international conventions.

The Anthropocene is characterized by a certain perceptual blindness. People are insensitive to the connections between their actions and global ecosystems. Although most people know that human activity impacts the climate, in the everyday it is difficult to focus on singular occurrences and feel a personal connection to this issue. This blindness often leads to disengagement. Drawing people's attention to the entangled conditions of the Anthropocene might stimulate a new sensitivity and engagement.

Attention, according to the Merriam-Webster dictionary, is the act of applying the mind to something and a condition of readiness for such attention involving a selective narrowing or focusing of consciousness and receptivity. Furthermore, it is defined as a consideration with a view to action and a sympathetic consideration of the needs and wants of others.

In other words, attention is closely linked to conscious action and care. Such attention is often referred to as deep attention. Deep attention fixates things from the surroundings in one's focus and thereby helps to uncover the details beyond the surface. The attention that a person gives to another thing can be considered an ethical act of decision-making. Being attentive to something involves a consideration of the other's vulnerability and the responsibility that one has towards it. Care is at the root of deep attention.

Our everyday life, however, is dominated by another type of attention – hyper attention, also referred to as inattention. Information overflow characterizes the urban experience. From to-do lists and music in one's headphones to traffic lights, event posters, shopfronts and other people. We briefly attend to the multitude of stimuli from different agents that compete to make us look their way. We attend so briefly to the stimuli that the things do not enter our conscious focus or consideration. Yet they still affect our actions.

Our attention, one can say, is often exploited by commercial, political and other agents. The so-called attention economy employs mechanisms to effectively manage our limited attention span. Things that matter most to certain agents are strategically brought into focus without making people aware of the mechanisms mediating their attention. And, perhaps as a result, the Anthropocene hybrids remain overlooked.

Territorial hybrid on Thyborøn Tange, curated as urban but with active natural processes.

Bringing the hybrids into focus demands a critical sensitivity to the mediated surroundings and an intention to focus on and keep difficult things in one's consciousness long enough for consideration and care to arise.

Such sensitivity and intention may be fostered through artistic framing. The arts have a long history of drawing people's attention to certain phenomena through composition and framing. The photograph in particular can fixate our attention on elements from our everyday surroundings that we overlook. And a framing of seemingly unrelated phenomena brings their entanglement into focus.

Returning back to the two sides of the Thyborøn Channel, framed with the attention of the architectural photographer Rasmus Hjortshøj, we can attend to the Anthropocene hybrids.

The two isthmuses are similar in plan but are composed of landforms that seem to be created by different processes – the urban and the geophysical. The landform at the northernmost tip of Harboøre Tange has a clearly visible coastal fortification and infrastructure, which is representative of the Thyborøn urban area. The second landform, on Agger Tange, seems to be formed by sea currents and dynamic sea sediment deposits; its coastal protection is barely visible – something that is representative of Thy National Park. By applying a similar geometric composition to the wild and the urban side of the channel, Rasmus Hjortshøj exposes the entangled territory beneath the curated surface landscapes.

Framed by industry and human-made landscape formations, this urban area on Thyborøn Tange is experienced as a tamed and a stable typology. However, the natural processes visible during tidal flux challenge this notion of stability.

following spread:
Agger Tange in the background, Thyborøn Tange in the foreground.

Territorial hybrid on Agger Tange, curated as natural but with stabilizing urban interventions.

The coastal protection, in different forms on both of the two sides, maintains the channel in its current shape. Traces of the tide and habitats of the seabed are exposed on the empty coast of Agger and the industrial port of Thyborøn. Sand dunes, formed by wind on one side and by excavator on the other, are overtaken by the same vegetation.

The aesthetic of a desaturated colour palette connecting all elements of the composition does not overwhelm the viewer with a sublime quality or sharp contrast. The subtle framing seeks to stimulate a new sensitivity to familiar places rather than to pass judgement.

Beyond the photograph, the new sensitivity stimulates considering the relation between architecture and the environment with a focus on and care for the entanglement between the wild and the urban. It is possible that a felt connection can be established between our local actions and global ecosystems. We might ediscover the territories beneath our everyday landscapes.

B

Bacteria Salla Sariola

~~banality of environmental horror~~ → Plastic

~~becoming-rock~~ → Heritage

~~becoming-with~~ → Feminism

~~beyond the human~~ → Wilderness

Biodiversity Minik Rosing

~~bio-geochemical cycles~~ → Geology

~~biosphere~~ → Geology

~~bipolar seesaw~~ → Abrupt Climate Change

~~bodily feeling~~ → Atmosphere

Body Mwenza Blell

~~border patrols~~ → Borders

Borders Tiffany Chung

~~breathing~~ → Air

~~bridging~~ → Resilience

~~butterfly effect~~ → Sensitivity

Bacteria

agents of disease | → Body | → Corals | entanglements | microbes and privilege | → Pollution | → Posthuman | relationality | → Resilience | → Sustainability | temporal becoming

The discovery of bacteria with a magnifying glass, microscope and culturing methods quickly went from amazement to eradication. Bacteria were identified as the long-sought-after agents of disease. The possibility to treat and protect against widespread human disease was a life-changing contribution of Western science and medicine. But this view of bacteria has had consequences.

In public health, bacteria were deemed as dirty and dangerous disease-producing contagions, easily spread from one person to another. Such has been the fear of these microbes that ever since antibiotics were discovered in 1928 by German physician Paul Ehrlich, antibiotics became an essential tool in what was assumed as being good for human health, the elimination of bacteria. Now, antibiotics against bacterial infections are used world over, prescribed by doctors, nurses and traditional medical practitioners, as well as bought over the counter and shared between patients themselves. Reliance on antibiotics to treat infections as well as preventing potential infections during major operations has made modern medicine what it is today.

Antibiotics are not restricted to humans; they are also fed to animals 'prophylactically' to prevent bacteria-borne diseases and to promote growth. Livestock, often kept indoors in confined quarters and fed 'unnatural' foods, are prone to infectious disease. The extensive use of antibiotics for humans and animals has caused these antibiotics to become much less effective, leading to antimicrobial resistance, the ability of a microbe to survive the effects of antibiotics that used to be able to kill it.

The ability of bacteria to become resistant to antibiotics is of major concern to healthcare as it means that the 'magic bullets' of modern medicine no longer work. There are very few new antibiotics in the pipeline, and interventions to cut down antibiotic use are dependent on several surrounding factors. How different organizations and countries are able to implement programmes against antimicrobial resistance depends on public and international investments in healthcare, functioning healthcare systems, the availability of probiotics and alternative livelihood options for those working in animal husbandry, technical know-how, and other cultural priorities and abilities. In short, there are no simple alternatives for antibiotics. Moreover, to build post-antibiotic worlds will require changes in drug regulatory systems, rethinking industrial farming, investments in the filtration of waste waters, overall development in low-income countries and other such measures that are concerned more with prevention than treatment.

The second consequence of viewing microbes solely as pernicious disease-causing entities is that it prevents seeing microbes as important factors promoting normal health. Thus, while these changes in dealing with drug-resistant microbes are urgent and inevitable, underlying them is a broader need for rethinking human relationships to microbes. Throughout her career, Lynn Margulis, an American biologist, proposed a different, symbiotic relationship between humans and microbes, underscoring an interactive approach to living and non-living entities. Margulis advocated for a systemic approach to life made of complex processes where no organism was independent,

Salla Sariola (located in Helsinki, FI) is a researcher in sociology at the University of Helsinki. Her current research on the social study of microbes includes fermentation, composting, and exploring changing scientific practices of microbiota and antimicrobial resistance in India, Benin and Finland. She is the author of *Research as Development: Biomedical Research, Ethics and Collaboration in Sri Lanka* (2019).

self-driven or self-contained. Together with British scientist James Lovelock, she coined the Gaia hypothesis, in which planet Earth is made of multiple co-evolving ecological interactions across all scales.[1] In this emergent dynamism, the emphasis is placed on relationality, temporal becoming and entanglement.

New research since the 2000s has supported Margulis's systemic and symbiotic thinking. Metagenomic methods, which sequence numerous genomes simultaneously, show that microbes are everywhere in unforeseen quantities – living inside and outside our bodies. Only about a tenth of microbes are pathogenic (potentially causing disease), and our environments (water, air, soil etc.) are teeming with helpful and benign as well as yet unidentified bacteria. These can keep potentially pathogenic bacteria in check if a balance is maintained. Recent work on microbiota is starting to show that the perception of microbes as dangerous is a limited view and that bacteria play important roles in sustaining life from gut health to environmental ecologies.

For example, human guts carry bacteria that, among others functions, communicate with the endocrine system, nervous system and immune system, enabling the absorption of essential nutrients, and work to maintain our health and well-being. It has been claimed that even our emotions may be regulated by bacterial communication! The gut is connected to the brain through the vagus nerve, which transmits messages concerning mood, satiety and other 'gut feelings' between the two. The bacteria appear to transmit information from the gut to the brain through this channel. New research also shows that, contrary to what has been assumed, over-cleanliness is in fact detrimental to health: a lack of microbes in maintained, urban environments is associated with higher risks of asthma, allergies and autoimmune diseases. Communities living outside modern infrastructures have many more types of gut microbes than those of Western populations and have significantly fewer non-communicable diseases. It appears, then, that internal microbes have crucially supportive functions in human health.

The commensality of microbes is not restricted to human gut functions. Our environmental supplies of oxygen and usable nitrogen are regulated through bacterial symbioses with plants. A recent consensus report on microbes underscored this by stating that tackling climate change will depend on humanity's relationship with microbes.[2] Much is unknown. Global warming creates favourable conditions for microbes to grow and infections to spread, while the melting of ice masses and permafrost allows the entry of new microbes and microorganism into the earth's systems with unpredictable results.

The complexity of human-microbe relations is manifested in how publics across the world respond to present microbial changes. On the one hand, those people in low- and middle-income countries, especially those who are living in rapidly urbanizing areas without sufficient sanitation infrastructure, are seeing more persistent infections. Particularly children under the age of five are still at high risk of infectious diseases. On the other hand, in more prosperous countries, people are intentionally experimenting with microbes and harnessing them for everyday use. Such experiments include bokashi composting, where lactobacilli are used to pickle food waste for rapid composting; pox parties, where parents bring children together with the intention of purposefully contaminating children with common childhood illnesses for 'naturally' induced immunity; and fermenting foods and drinks (sauerkraut, sourdough, kimchi, kombucha, kefir, etc.) for better gut health and overall well-being. Such examples show that the ability to live, and play, with microbes is aligned with access and opportunities, social inequalities and privilege. Whether bacteria present a risk or an opportunity is connected to other biosocial factors, and the dynamics of infrastructures and power. But as in the case of the hygiene hypothesis, who the winners and losers are is not always entirely foreseeable. Microbes are multiple and complex and spark awe for their ubiquitousness and unruliness. Margulis thought that bacteria 'did it all', and there was not much left for so-called higher order biological entities to do or invent.[3] In sum, bacteria provide a lot of food for thought for different areas of sciences, social theory, arts, biomedicine and health. Dominant views about microbes are changing, through various communities and disciplines, slowly shifting from being defined simply as pathogens towards relationality and symbiosis. The survival of *Homo sapiens* may rely on not only our own ingenuity but how well we get along with our bacteria.

I would like to thank and acknowledge Scott Gilbert for his overwhelmingly generous comments on this manuscript.

Works cited:

Haraway, Donna J. 2016. *Staying with the Trouble: Making Kin in the Chthulucene*. Durham, NC: Duke University Press Books.

Margulis, Lynn. 1998. *The Symbiotic Planet*. London: Weidenfeld and Nicholson.

MacFadden, Derek. R., Sarah F. McGough, David Fisman, Mauricio Santillana and John S. Brownstein. 2018. 'Antibiotic Resistance Increases with Local Temperature'. *Nature Climate Change*, 8, pp. 510–514. doi:10.1038/s41558-018-0161-6. Accessed 15 January 2020.

Biodiversity

→ Connectedness | → Corals | → Declaration of Rebellion | → Declarations of Climate Emergency | desire | dominion over nature | ecosystem diversity | → Environment | geochemical and geophysical cycles | humans as a component of ecosystems | → Imagine | → Sustainability | within species diversity

As Prussian naturalist Alexander von Humboldt climbed mountains, paddled rivers and slashed tracks through rainforests, he realized that life is a unifying phenomenon, shared by all species of animals and plants. From 1799 to 1804, he ventured on a journey through South and Meso-America with no particular objective other than to study nature. Without a specific plan, he was free to observe with an open mind, follow the paths his curiosity inspired and spend as much time as he needed to document and understand any subject that intrigued him on his way.

In the tradition of the naturalists of his time, Humboldt collected and described thousands of specimens of the flora, fauna and geology along his route and placed them into a systematic taxonomy of plants, animals, minerals and rocks. This, in its own right, was a major achievement. However, the most astonishing and transformative aspect of Humboldt's work was his realization that every living thing participates in geochemical and geophysical cycles. All forms of life represent equal and mutually dependent component parts of ecosystems and thus individually rely on the well-being of all other species. Humboldt was the first person to explicitly formulate the fundamental importance of biological diversity for the functioning of Earth, and thus for human society.

Most religions teach some level of moral obligation towards other living species. They tend to rank Earth's living species in a hierarchy, partition them into kingdoms and propose a purpose for all other organisms – in short, what use they are to us. The view that humans were fundamentally different to and better than animals was incorporated into European science as it developed during the Enlightenment, and it is still the common starting point in modern societies. We still feel entitled to dominion over nature. We don't really accept that preservation of nature, or our failure to preserve it in its broadest sense and biological diversity in particular, will determine our own fate. The term 'biodiversity' is used to encompass the vast variety of life on our planet. Flourishing biodiversity is the foundation for functional societies that sustain our wellbeing and, not to put too fine a point on it, our very survival as a species.

Minik Rosing (born 1957, located in Copenhagen, DK) is a professor at GLOBE Institute and a geologist working on the influence of life on the geological evolution of Earth's continents, oceans and climate. His work is mainly based on field research in his native Greenland. He was curator of the Danish Pavilion at the 2012 Architecture Biennale in Venice, thematizing the harmonious development of Greenland in a rapidly changing world.

We wrongly believe that ecosystems are isolated phenomena that can be observed from the outside and exploited for our purposes. Most people have convinced themselves that the intention to protect and preserve ecosystems is rather like collecting or conserving antiques, of hobby value. To preserve something that has pleasant decorative or sentimental value but does not really matter. But we humans are a component of ecosystems, and if these systems deteriorate, we will go down with them.

In Darwin's understanding of life's evolution on Earth, life has enjoyed an ongoing ever-branching trend towards higher complexity and greater diversity, as illustrated in Haeckel's analogy to a tree from 1879 (*Evolution of Man*). We now tend to compare the lineages of present life to a web – a complex interconnectedness between everything living.

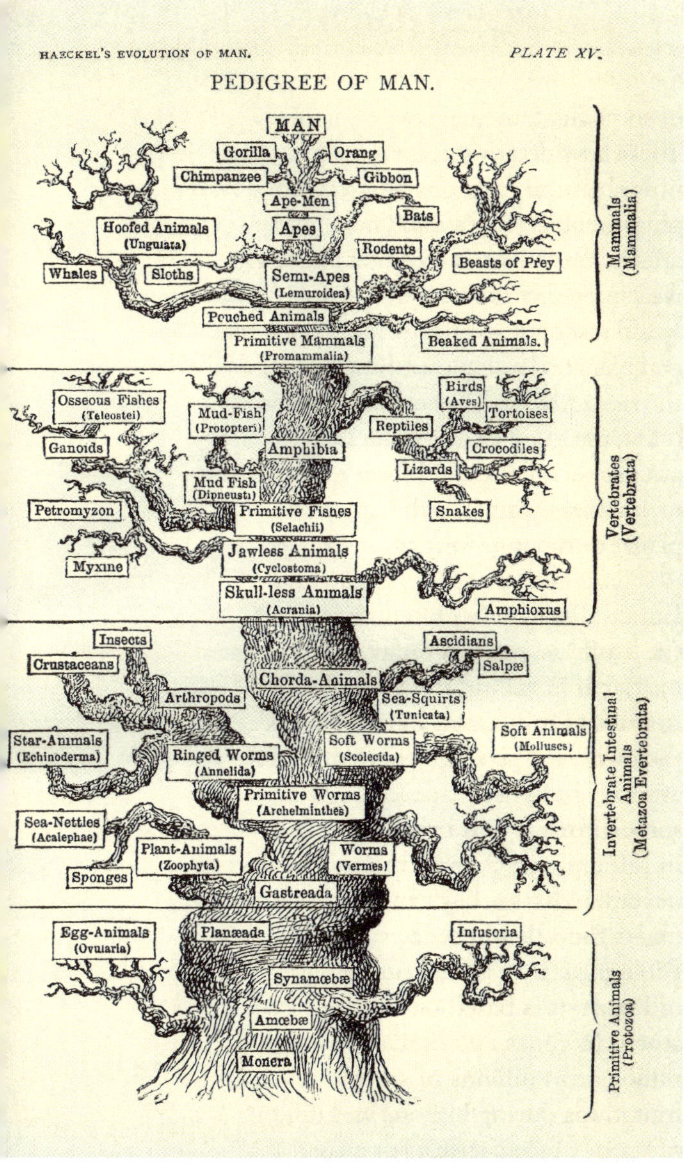

Despite Humboldt's early insight into ecosystems – the connectedness of all living species to one another and to the physical Earth – 19th- and 20th-century biology developed along the conveniently hierarchical view of life. But British geologist Charles Darwin was clearly inspired by Humboldt's idea of connectedness within the biosphere. He explored the concept in his own way – that is, by realizing that every extant species was derived from one common ancestor through evolution.

In 1879, the German naturalist Ernst Haeckel produced a tree of life as a metaphor for evolution as the basis of biological diversity. Biologists spent most of their time on mapping the tree and naming the species – the outermost little twigs defining the perimeter of the tree crown; that is, the taxonomy of present-day life – but they neglected to explore the interactions within and between Earth's ecosystems.

In recent years, there has been more emphasis on understanding the functionality of the tree itself. We now realize that all the leaves and twigs on the tree interact, and none of them would function outside of the realm of the tree. Still, what inspired Humboldt, Darwin and Haeckel was the incomprehensible and unfathomable flutter of life that surrounds us in the sea, on land and in the air: biodiversity.
The vast variety of life – biodiversity – can be defined in several ways. There is the straightforward diversity of species, like dragonflies, celery and elephants. But there is also the genetic diversity within a single species, such as the many variations in height, eye, skin and hair colour, and the ability to digest lactose or to react fatally to nuts, for

example, that we see within our own species, even within our own families. This *within species diversity* is important for keeping the population dynamic and being able to withstand changes in the environment. Diversity can also be expressed as diversity of ecosystems – the same species may take on different roles in different ecosystems and express different parts of their genetic heritage in different environments.

We are facing a consortium of inevitable crises. They are each rooted in our appropriation of resources and our impact on the natural environment. As Humboldt observed so long ago, there exists an intimate relationship between Earth's climate and its life. The trees in the rainforest are responsible for the rain, while the rain sustains the trees in a delicate balance, which may break down if disturbed. A minor human intervention may tip the balance and turn a luscious green rainforest, teaming with life of all sorts, into a scorched desert, barren of life and with no return ticket to its paradisiacal past.

We are already observing an alarming rise in the number of species on the brink of extinction or already lost forever. Extinction of a species is easy to communicate as a problem, and there are large and powerful grassroots organizations that do important and commendable work to preserve threatened species. However, the other two aspects of biodiversity, within species diversity and ecosystem diversity, are also under great strain and suffer great losses. These phenomena are more diffuse, not easily observable and difficult to communicate but constitute the true core of the biodiversity crisis.

It has long been known that the physical world operates within the constraints

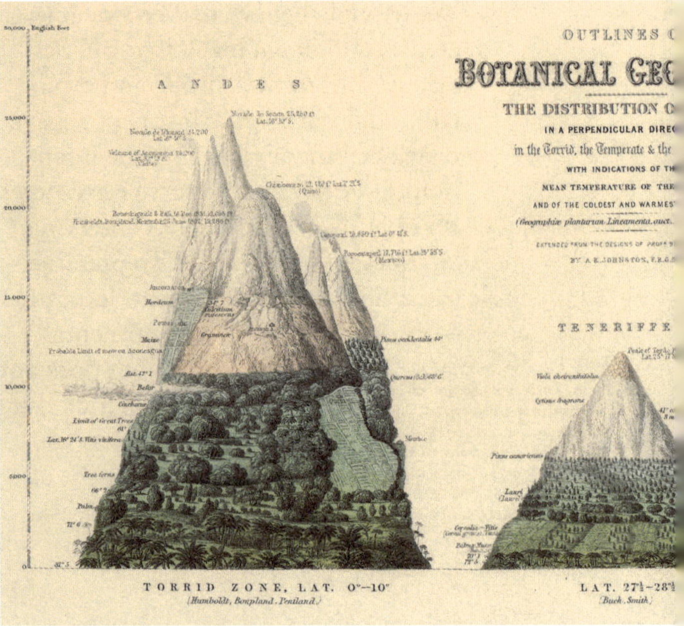

of some fundamental laws of nature. These laws determine, for example, how chemical reactions progress, how physical objects move and how heat affects substances. If we know the laws, we can predict how the non-living world responds to change and how stars and planets develop over time. Given the same physical and chemical environment, the same minerals, rocks and atmospheric gasses will form regardless of when and where in the universe a planet or moon is formed.

Because Earth is a closed system, all the 'stuff' we possess today will remain on Earth in the future. We will not run out of mineral resources because they will still be somewhere on Earth after we have used them. It may take some effort to find them again, but, in principle, geological resources can never be lost, as they can form again under the rule of the laws of nature. Biological diversity is completely different. It is based on information, stored in genes and derived through billions and billions of stochastic mutations during billions and billions of years. Once a species or a part of

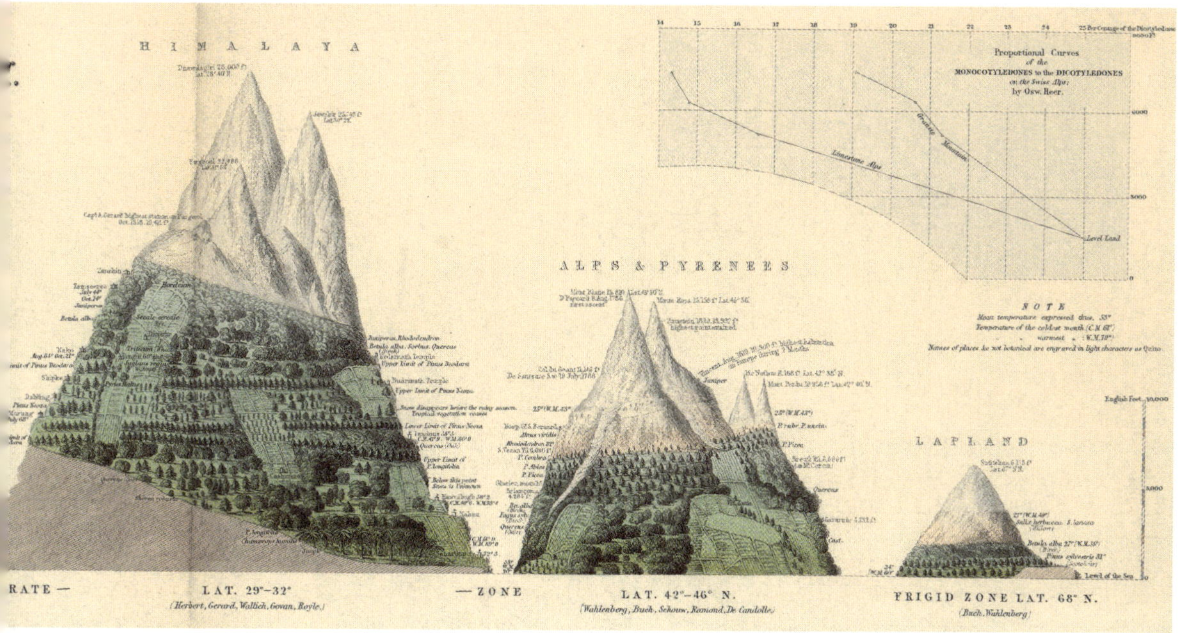

Alexander von Humboldt introduced the concept of bio-geography and showed how similar climatic conditions support comparable eco-systems across the globe. During a daring ascent of the volcano Chimborázo in Equador, the highest mountain known in his time, Humboldt mapped the distribution of plant species and their ecosystems on the volcano and explained them through climate zonation. He introduced the notion that biodiversity responds to climate and, consequently, that climate may change if the eco-system in a region is perturbed and that ecosystems change if climate is perturbed.

the common within-species gene pool of an organism is lost, it can never be reconstructed, and Earth will forever be a poorer and less habitable home for us and all our fellow living relatives.

Although our impact on nature often takes place through the application of technology, technology is not the root cause of our problems. Human impact on climate and environment are all governed by sociological processes. The extent and type of agriculture, fisheries, forestry, transportation and cultural activities such as fashion, communication, gastronomy and entertainment are not just governed by fundamental needs. We do not appropriate what we need but what we desire. We are blessed with a love for music, colour, structure, taste and fragrance, most of which are derived from and dependent on global biological diversity. Our quest for beauty possesses a treat to the biological diversity through our appropriation of natural resources but can just as well derive from activities that strengthen and revitalize the natural environment. The way we fulfil our quest for beauty and cultural stimulation is a matter of choice, which in turn is guided by cultural trends. It takes only imagination to shift destructive fashions to constructive ones.

This is why arts and all the other things we do with other people are the most powerful agents to preserve a liveable world. Nothing can change humanity's basic need, but arts can change our desires, which are the source of most of our impact on Earth's environment and biological diversity.

following spread:
In 1807, Alexander von Humboldt and his travel companion Aimé Bonpland published this synthesis of their observation from their 1799–1804 journey through tropical America. The print is 61 × 91.4 cm and shows the distribution of plants in relation to altitude on the volcano Chimborázo, with notes in the side tables on gravity, temperature, blueness of the sky and any other observations of Nature they made. The *Naturgemälde* is the first of its kind and meant to illustrate Humboldt's realization that all phenomena in nature are connected.

Schönberger und Turpin, gest. von Bouquet, die Schrift von L. Aubert, gedruckt von Langlois

Geographie der Pfla

ein Naturge

auf Beobachtungen und Messungen, welche vom 10.ten Grade nörd

von ALEXANDER VON

-TER	… durch den höchsten und niedrigsten Stand des Thermometers ausgedrückt	… NATUR des LUFTKREISES	… SCHNEES, nach Verschiedenheit der Geographischen Breite.	… nach der HÖHE IHRES WOHNORTS	… WASSERS nach Verschiedenheit der Höhen
6500				Kein organischer Stoff an den Erdboden geheftet.	Siedhitze zu 77°,0. (61°,6. R.) Bar. 0,320m
6000 5500	Zu wenig besuchte Regionen, um ihre Temperatur genau zu kennen. Die mittlere Wärme scheint unter dem Eispunkte zu seyn. Doch sieht man auf 5403 M. Höhe das Th. noch bisweilen 17°,8.	Die Sauerstoffmenge scheint in der obern Luftregion eben so groß als in der Ebene zu seyn; aber die Nähe der Vulcane kann auf den hohen Gipfeln der Andes die chemische Mischung des Luftkreises modificiren.	Die Luft, welche man aus dem Schneewasser entbindet, enthält 0,287 Sauerstoff.	Der Condor der Anden. Einige Fliegen und Sphinxe, wahrscheinlich durch senkrechte Luftströme emporgehoben.	Siedhitze zu 81°,0. (64°,8. R.) Bar. 0,367m
5000 4500	Von -7°,5 bis 18°,7. Mittlere Temperatur 3°,7. (3° R.) Es schneit bis 4100 M.		Schneegrenze unter dem Äquator und unter 5° nördl. und südl. Breite auf 4800 M. (2464 T.) Höhe. Oscillation kaum 80 M. Schneegrenze unter 20° nördlicher Breite 4600 M. (2361 T.). Oscillation im Winter bis 3800 M.	Heerden von Vicuna, Alpaca u. Huanaco. Einige Bären. Condor. Falken. Caprimulgus. Keine Fische in den Seen.	Siedhitze zu 84°,7. (67°,7. R.) Bar. 0,418m
4000 3500	Von 0 bis 20°. Mittlere Temperatur 9°. (7°,2. R.) Viel Hagel, selbst bisweilen Nachts.	Der Wasserstoff, welcher in der Atmosphäre vorhanden ist, beträgt weniger als zwei tausend Theile. Die Luft, in 7000 M. Höhe gesammlet, ist nicht wasserstoffreicher als die der Ebenen.	Ewiger Schnee unter 35° nördl. Breite auf 3500 M. (1800 T.) Höhe. Ewiger Schnee unter 40° Breite auf 3100 M. (1600 T.) Höhe.	Lamas, verwildert am westlichen Abfall des Chimborazo. Der kleine Bär mit weißer Stirn. Große Hirsche. Der kleine Löwe. Einige Colibris. Kein Pulex penetrans.	Siedhitze zu 88°,1. (70°,5. R.) Bar. 0,474m
3000 2500	Von 1°,2 bis 25°,7. Mittlere Temperatur 18°,7. (15° R.) Viel Hagel und tiefe Nebel.		Schneegrenze unter 45° nördl. Breite 2500 M. (1282 T.). In den Pyrenäen zu 2440 M., in den Schweizer Alpen auf isolirten Bergen 2700 M.; aber auf Gipfeln, deren Höhe 3100 M. übersteigt, zu 2530 M. Im Ganzen ist das Phänomen der Schneelinie veränderlicher in den nördlichen Ländern als unter dem Äquator.	Viverra mapurito. Felis tigrina. Große Hirsche. Palamedea bispinosa. Menge von Enten und Tauchern. Viele Läuse (Pediculus humanus).	Siedhitze zu 91°,3. (73°,0. R.) Bar. 0,536m
2000 1500	Von 12°,5 bis 36. Mittlere Temperatur 21°,2. (17° R.) Wenig Hagel, aber häufiger Nebel.	Die atmosphärische Luft besteht aus 0,210 Sauerstoff, 0,787 Stickstoff und ohngefähr 0,003 Kohlensäure?. Der Sauerstoffgehalt der Atmosphäre scheint nicht um 0,001 zu wechseln.		Kleine Hirsche (Cervus mexicanus). Tapir. Sus tajassu. Felis pardalis. Einige Affen (Aluaten). Trupiale (Oriolus). Coluber coccin. Keine Boa, kein Crocodil. Viele Niguas (Pulex penetrans) auf Menschen, Hunden und Affen.	Siedhitze zu 94°,3. (75°,3. R.) Bar. 0,605m
1000 500	Von 16°,5 bis 38°,4. Mittlere Temperatur 25°,3. (20°,2 R.) Kein Hagel. Der Sand oft bis 52° erhitzt		Es schneit unter dem Äquator in 4100 M. (2100 T.) Höhe, in Neu-Spanien unter 19° nördl. Breite bis 1800 M.	Affen (Sapajous und Aluaten). Jaguar (Felis onça). Schwarzer Tiger. Löwe (Felis concolor). Cavia capibara. Faulthier. Ameisenbär. Cervus mexicanus. Armadille. Aptenodytes. Crax. Ampelis. Boa. Crocodil. Lamentin. Elater noctilucus. Mosquito. (Oestrus humanus.)	Siedhitze zu 97°,1. (77°,7. R.) Bar. 0,679m
0	Die Wärme der Meeresfläche ist unter dem Äquator, fern von Strömungen, 28°; aber in 400 M. Tiefe ist die Wärme nur 7°,6. Die Temperatur des festen Erdkörpers scheint 22°,3.		Schneegrenze unter 75° Breite.	Im Innern der Erde unbeschriebene Dermestes-Arten, welche sich von den unterirdischen Pflanzen ernähren.	Siedhitze zu 100°. (80° R.) Bar. 0,762m

der

Die Nat… Ganzen un… Höhe über… zelnen Th… man eine… Schichtun… ge eines p… ziehungek… ben diese… schwierig… über die… der Äquat… Nahe a… ben einan… der Welt,… gedehntes… südlicher… auf dem… ge von me… Höhe; doc… gegen den… noch sch… dem 19° n… nördl. Bre… 4700 M. (… M. (2800 T.)… rial-Ebene… tlichen Ab… dem Ama… silianisch… sind in 7… 70 M. bis… fläche er.… Alle Ge… der Erdob… den sich u… mengedrä… und ihre… zen dieser… mäßigten… glimmera… Feldspath… körnige;… schiefer u… genseitig… Flözgebir… zwei Gyps… mazion er… Grünstein… Perlstein-… blematisc… auf dem… dillera in… einzelt —… weisen die… der entfer… Merkwü… rikanisch… ungeheur… schichten… über der M… ropa steht… und 470… all unbe… deskette i… höher als… sten Gr… hen bis zu… hornblend… che einig… schen Feu… selben n… Sandstein… zu einer H… Das Steink… det sich… dem Meer… Bogota au… mit Flözsc… salz bede… finden sich… hoch (in E… Auf den G… man, in 2… ten-Knoch… Cuenca ist… zion, west… M. mächtig… Die Ande… brennende… 37 bis 40… liegen. Die… de Lava a… stein- und P… stein und v… ge Wasser… Letten, in… melodus (…

…en in den Tropen-Ländern;

…de der Anden,

…bis zum 10.ten Grade südlicher Breite angestellt worden sind, in den Jahren …

…BOLDT und A. G. BONPLAND.

Body

→ Bacteria | → Environment | environmental justice | → Feminism | fertility | human rights | microbes | → Overpopulation | → Plastic | → Pollution | → Resilience | → Violence

Whose body do we mean when we use the term body?

The term used in the singular on its own like this indicates a missing assumed modifier: human, the *anthropo* in Anthropocene.

When we see this word, do we imagine a chalk outline on the sidewalk? Do we imagine the drowned body of an asylum seeker?
Do we imagine an anatomical diagram?
Do we imagine Da Vinci's Vitruvian Man?
Does the body we imagine have a vulva?

Generic bodies in text and image are often white and male (with cisnormative muscularity) even though most bodies in existence are not like that.

We've got an issue with bodies to address now that we find ourselves living in the Anthropocene. There are some things that have to be brought together and sorted through. One is the body as understood via social theory, which lacks materiality and includes so much potential possibility that it can be shaped in so many ways. The other is the body as represented in biology, which is material and part of the animal kingdom.

Dr **Mwenza Blell** (born 1979, located in Newcastle-upon-Tyne, UK) is a biosocial anthropologist who explores the impact of social inequality on bodies, taking seriously people's own interpretations and experiences of their biological processes in relation to biomedical and bioscientific understandings. She has conducted ethnographic research on four continents. Her latest research centres on health systems, data science and reproductive justice.

In the Anthropocene, the materiality of bodies becomes impossible to ignore for more and more people, even for those who never liked science. The global environmental crisis prompts us to think about what our bodies cannot withstand in terms of our environment, about the fragility that is a result of our survival being dependent on being within a relatively narrow range of temperatures, breathing a particular balance of nitrogen to oxygen, experiencing a limited range of air pressures, eating non-toxic food and water and the fact that we must let our guard down and sleep from time to time.

Such things are already well established because bodies have been a subject of study for a long time. Can we avoid the reductionism and essentialism that have characterized much past human biology whilst gaining a more detailed understanding of bodily vulnerabilities in a world that is changing? Our bodies have always been open, responsive to, co-constituted by and in feedback-loop ecological relationships with environments of all kinds (social, biotic, built). Those effects are made ever more visible now, in the Anthropocene, when we can see macro-level effects on the world (polar ice caps melting, sea levels rising) and effects on living bodies and human lives (climate migration, deaths from severe weather incidents); these are the effect of the actions of ourselves and our industrial ancestors. Like our anaerobic bacterial ancestors of the Paleoproterozoic era, we are destroying our world. It is not uniquely human to cause ecological catastrophe in this way. Maybe we take after these ancestors more than we might think at first glance?

Our lives are still entwined with those of microbes, of course. Despite the fact we have acted so combatively against microbial life by popularizing antimicrobial hand gels and have entered into an arms race with increasingly virulent anti-biotic resistant microbes, we need microbes inside and on the surface of our bodies in order to survive. Indeed, we have never been without them. Life on earth so often is comprised of combinations of life forms in fact. Nearly every single example of plant, fungus and animal on earth relies on microbial life within it (mitochondria) to survive. Human genomes contain countless sections of microbial DNA, and, whether calculated by cell count or by biomass, a large proportion of each human body is microbial cells. What are the implications of a closer look at the materiality of our bodies, giving attention to who (else) lives in, on and alongside our bodies? Whose survival matters most? Can our survival be separated?

Environmental justice and reproductive justice have deep interconnections. The term reproductive justice combines reproductive rights and social justice into a single concept that includes the human right to personal bodily autonomy, freedom from sexual violence, the right to choose whether to have children or not, to have equal access to safe abortion, affordable contraceptives and comprehensive sex education, and the right to parent the children one has in safe and sustainable communities. The connection between environmental and reproductive justice exists, for one, because ecofascists use and have used Malthusian eugenic logics to counter reproductive justice arguments. It is also the case that some environmentalists see human reproduction as being in conflict with the reproduction of other life forms on earth and think the rights of other life forms need greater consideration. We also know that environmental damage threatens those already struggling for reproductive justice because of global structural inequalities. Reprotoxic exposures, both occupational and environmental, whether from chemicals in plastics or lead, are a threat to poor people more than wealthy ones. This is because wealthier people can make 'healthy' consumer choices and avoid toxic products. They live in less polluted environments and have fewer harmful occupational exposures compared to, for example, slum dwellers in the Global South, who may engage in waste picking for a living and have to drink polluted water. What is more, in the case of a problem, the wealthy can pay for the reproductive services they need from IVF doctors and labs, from gamete donors and even from gestational surrogates.

The threat that reprotoxicity represents awakens fears in many people. Increasingly in the past decades, moral panics have been whipped up about changes to reptile and amphibian genital morphology and behaviour reportedly due to hormones from oral contraceptives excreted in urine entering waterways via sewage systems. These arise entangled with sexism, homophobia and transphobia but speak to the varied political potentials as a result of fear of environmental degradation. How can we take action about these reproductive justice concerns without undermining the rights of LGBT people and straight cis women?

Attention to bodily difference (without sexist, racist or other forms of essentialism) can help us to see the environmental justice perspective on bodies and the Anthropocene. Who benefits more from this catastrophe and who suffers more? Can we separate understandings of suffering from oppressive normativities and moralizing that sometimes lurk in biomedical and 'healthy living' discourses? What would have to change to be able to mobilize to protect the bodies that are most vulnerable?

Borders

→ Abrupt Climate Change | border patrols | → Flood | → Future | → Home | memories | migration | → Migration Flows | refugees | → Resources | → Water | → Xenophobia

Tiffany Chung (born 1969, located in Houston, US) is internationally noted for her research-based installations and cartographic works that examine conflict, migration, urban transformation and environmental impact in relation to the history of specific places. She has exhibited in numerous biennials and museums including the 56th Venice Biennale, 21st Sydney Biennale, Smithsonian American Art Museum, MoMA and the Nobel Peace Center.

Water Memories

If water has memories, it will remember what I remember, even in fragments. 1978 / New Economic Zone / Sông Cửu Long / Mekong River / nine tributaries / brown water / leaping silver fish / tropic migrations / floodplains. Every afternoon, a child sits on the windowsill of her new home, far away from the home of her childhood. Her Siamese fighting fish swims in a jar next to her; both stare at the rising brown sea out there, beyond the hospital's fence. A beautiful, frail woman walks between rooms – her white coat flows in the hall filled with the smell of antiseptic disinfectant liquid. In the coming days, which feel like fleeting moments, the brown sea keeps rising, swallowing the windowsill / hospital yard / gate / fence / muddy village road / river.

On one of the afternoons, the child, her younger sister and another little girl take the boat out to the brown sea / relieving themselves / balancing / boat floating / sister drowning. In the water's memories, Uncle Khá, the hospital's pharmacist, wades and leaps like a dolphin in the water to the drowning girl's rescue.

The brown water swallows what it can and continues to rise. People are no longer walking. The water remembers the movements of boats in and between rooms, and to the brown sea. Memories of water stay with the girl between her sleeping and waking hours, for many years to come. Bed on bricks / bed on bed / straw mat / sleeping on water / dreaming / waking up / Mom's long black hair / floating in the room.

1980 / Saigon in the wee hours / darkness / crowded bus / vomiting / Mekong / river ferry. The girl and her little sister step down from the bus, walking into the misty fog. Auntie cô Năm / country home / Mom / crying / us / waving / off we go.

Mekong River / narrow long boat / people / coconut ladles / plastic ladles / bailing out water. The girl and her sister let go of their floating flip-flops and follow people wading towards a big boat. The water embodies sleepless nights and watches people's shadows submerging in darkness. The boat departs from Cửa Đại river mouth, finding its way to international waters. People without shadows / laying / sitting / hanging on the edges / relieving themselves / vomiting / fainting / time passing.

Suddenly the girl hears gunshots. Shadowless people push one another towards the fish compartment. Please get off my chest / out of breath / little sister / pleading / in darkness / bottom of the boat. The night feels heavier with the lack of oxygen. In between breathless breaths is the sound of jewellery and watches being dropped into a tin can. Bodies frozen / souls restless / mouths muzzled. Border patrols wait until all valuables are stripped off in the blackness of the night and airtight compartment. Suddenly, silence breaks into bodies rushing to emerge from the bottom, hurriedly inhaling a gulp of fresh air before being pushed onto the border-patrol boat, spirits spiralling downward into the bottomless pit of despair.

The end of one journey is the beginning of the next.

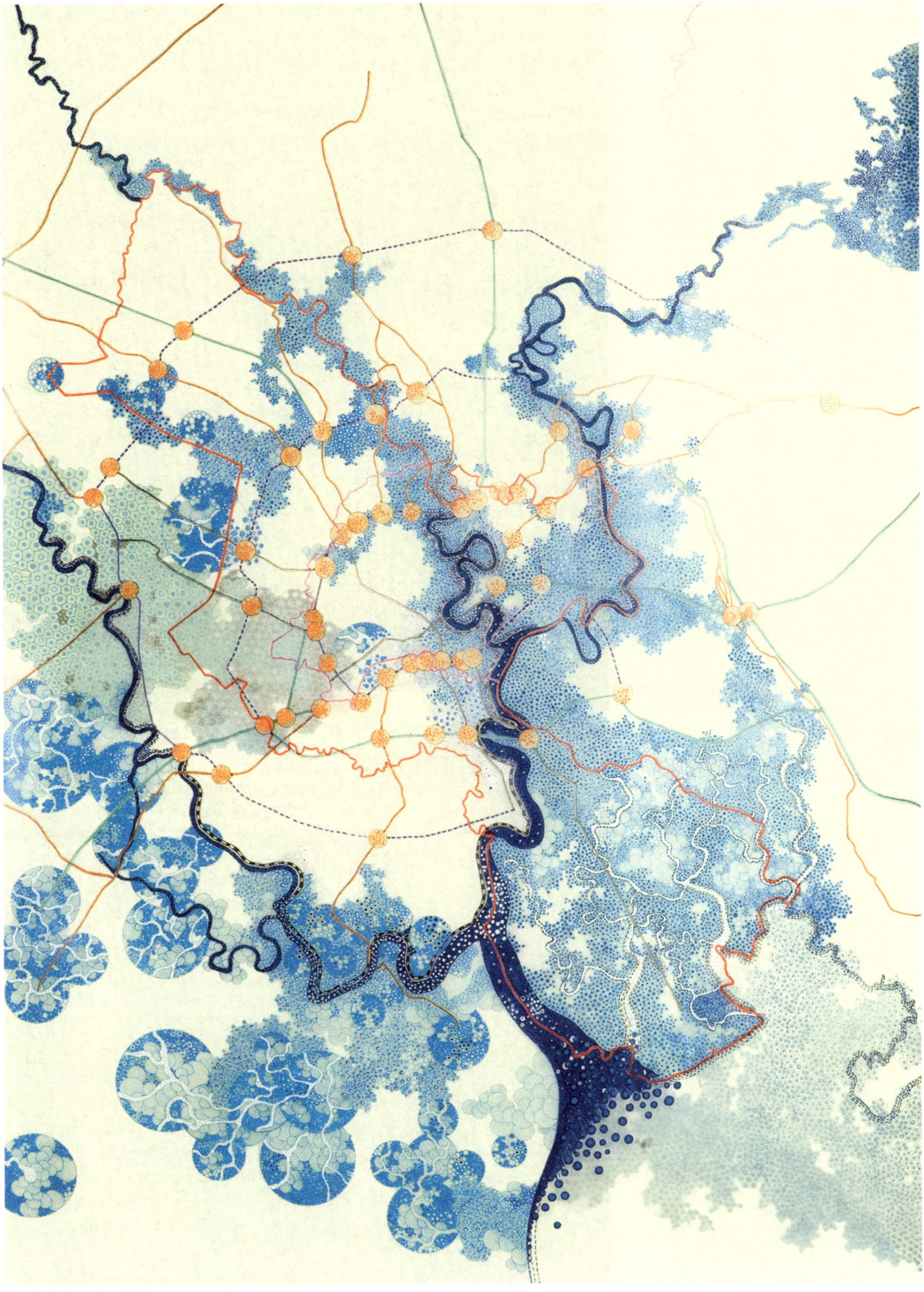

Tiffany Chung
one giant great flood 2050, 2010
Micro pigment ink, oil and
Copic marker on vellum
and paper
110 × 70 cm

Tiffany Chung
stored in a jar: monsoon, drowning fish, colour of water, and the floating world,
2010–2011
Mixed-media installation (Plexiglass, wood veneer, plastic, aluminium, paint, steel cable, foam, copper wire, etc.)
Dimension of installation: 600 × 360 cm; houseboat dimensions variable
Commissioned by the 2011 Singapore Biennale

Tiffany Chung
up and down the river – migrations of the fish, 2010
Embroidery, beads, metal grommets and buttons on canvas
108 × 183 cm

The sea embraces those who dive into it, leaving the imprints of their bodies in the water's memories for years to come. Schools of fish migrate upstream and downstream the Mekong, decades after decades. The water's memories of those soulless bodies travel with the fish in search of home.

But it seems increasingly challenging for the fish to migrate and for the Mekong tributaries' waters to flow seamlessly, even with age-old established patterns and memories. From two upstream and five midstream hydropower dams built in the 1970s, there are 56 existing hydropower infrastructures in the Mekong River Basin now – with an additional 31 dams under construction, 74 planned and 23 proposed ones. The continuing hydropower development will further aggravate poverty in the region. Dams alter the flow of water and, with sudden fluctuations in water levels, disrupt fish migration and spawning. Constricting water flows also means trapping the nutrient-rich sediment needed to fertilize rice paddies, to feed the fish and to replenish rich alluvial soil in preventing deltas from sinking and from saltwater intrusion. Reservoirs cannot replace the natural habitats essential to many of the more than 500 aquatic species native to the Mekong River. Floods that occurred with dams and with sea-level rise due to climate change will exacerbate the negative impacts of such stagnant ecosystems. In the Lower Mekong Basin alone, memories of water, fish migrations and over 60 million people depend on the river as their lifeblood: food supply, health, income, culture and identity. Such lives and memories are struggling to exist, as the river itself struggles to embody the physical and spiritual home for those fighting for survival, as well as for the lives and memories that have been lost at sea during the post-1975 epic refugee exodus. Further into the world, chronic flood projections in Climate Central's October 2019 study warn that rising seas could affect all and erase some coastal cities by 2050 – southern Vietnam could disappear under the sea with Saigon, while Shanghai, Dhaka, Bangkok, Mumbai and Jakarta are also imperilled. Land currently home to 300 million people could fall below the high-tide line in 30 years. Together with political and armed conflicts, climate and economic crises have produced and will continue to produce refugees. Redefining the term 'refugee' constituted by the 1951 Convention and 1967 Protocol Relating to the Status of Refugees is not a hypothetical question or suggestion. The future is now.

C

~~capital as the ultimate crop~~ → Plantationocene

~~capitalism~~ → Capitalocene

Capitalocene Thomas Hylland Eriksen

Care Joanna Latimer

~~caring for conflicts~~ → Queer

~~changing our 'minds-eye'~~ → Window of Opportunity

~~chemicals~~ → Pollution

~~children of Mother Earth~~ → Geology

Chthulucene Donna Haraway

~~citizen of the planet~~ → Pandemic

City David Gissen

~~class~~ → Geo-Social Classes

Client: Earth James Thornton

Climate Bill McKibben

~~climate change targets~~ → Declarations of Climate Emergency

~~climate justice~~ → Next Generation

Climate Risk Communities Anders Blok

~~CO_2~~ → Climate → Energy → Production

Coexistence Rosi Braidotti

~~cognitive dissonance~~ → Facts

~~collective actions~~ → Climate Risk Communities

~~colonialism~~ → Terraforming

~~communities~~ → Climate Risk Communities

~~compost~~ → Chthulucene

Connectedness Josefine Klougart

~~consumption~~ → Capitalocene

Corals Nils Bubandt

~~cosmological turn~~ → Moving Earths

Creation Liv Sejrbo Lidegaard

~~critical sensitivity~~ → Attention

~~critical zones~~ → Moving Earths

~~curiosity~~ → Terraforming

~~cycles~~ → Water

Capitalocene

alternative visions of growth | → Anthropocene | capitalism | → Climate | consumption | → Development | → Ecology | economic growth | global middle class | → Modernism | nodes in an ecology | → Oil

Thomas Hylland Eriksen (born 1962, located in Oslo, NO) is a professor of social anthropology at the University of Oslo and the author of many books including *Overheating: An Anthropology of Accelerated Change* (2016), *Boomtown: Runaway Globalisation on the Queensland Coast* (2018) and, co-edited with R. Ramtohul, *The Mauritian Paradox* (2018), with M. Jakoubek, *Ethnic Groups and Boundaries Today* (2019) and, with A. Stensrud, *Climate, Capitalism and Communities* (2019).

I have struggled with this term for some time, in the same way as you might bicker with a friend over trifles or grow lovingly impatient with an undisciplined dog. It seems to promise too much, yet the term takes issue with the more established concept of the Anthropocene in a way that calls for serious consideration. For the problems and ailments of the overheated planet are not really caused by *anthropos*, people as such, but by people behaving in a particular way. The planet is running a high fever because so many of us are fuelled by greed, propped up by a societal formation demanding continuous growth in production and consumption, supported by technological advances fed by scientific endeavours funded by that very same system – a world system which is oblivious of the cost to the planetary ecology, indifferent to the long-term effects of ruthless resource exploitation, a master creator of wealth and inequality. Paraphrasing Irish playwright Oscar Wilde, it is a system that knows the price of everything but the value of nothing.[1]

Capitalism has been a blessing and a curse. The first to fully understand how it simultaneously unleashed productive forces leading to human progress and created a world callously exploiting people and mindlessly draining the world of its accumulated wealth was Karl Marx, writing in London at the height of the Victorian era. He predicted, as a card-carrying member of the evolutionist club dominating intellectual life in his time (and, ironically, in capitalist ideology), that the system would eventually be superseded by something more just and humane. This did not come about. To the extent that capitalism was dethroned in the following century, it was replaced by far more oppressive social systems with no ecological sensitivity whatsoever.

Now, when it is necessary to propose anew alternatives to capitalism, it is for reasons other than those articulated by Marx and his followers. Although inequality remains a global problem, and working conditions bordering on slavery are widespread in some parts of the world, capitalism has proved more flexible, and much more popular among ordinary working people, than what seemed likely to left-wing Victorians. On a planetary level, things are going rather well for the time being, seen from the myopic, short-term perspective of the human species. Not for everybody, but for many. The global middle classes are swelling. Life expectancy has almost doubled since Marx was born. Nutrition, sanitation, entertainment options and life opportunities in general have improved, and not just in the richest countries. People have more leisure time, fewer go to bed hungry, child labour and child mortality have declined. Through electronic media, we are connected in ways unimaginable a few generations ago. These and other developments have taken place in, and courtesy of, the capitalist economic system, albeit tweaked and mitigated by states limiting the scope of market forces and offering services which cannot be ensured through the mechanisms of supply and demand.

The main problem of capitalism in the Anthropocene does not consist in its cruelty to people, its creation of hierarchies and wealth disparities or its production of misery on a large scale. In fact, on these and other criteria it performs better than its alternatives, be they feudalism, theocracies or state socialism. The problem lies in its being inherently and necessarily destructive by basing its existence and flourishing on economic growth as a necessity and the availability of cheap energy as fuel for its engines.

It was the marriage of the steam engine with coal that marked the onset of the Anthropocene, fanned into world domination by economic practices explained and encouraged by the likes of British political economist David Ricardo, who taught that a comparative advantage exists when it is cheaper to produce and sell a product in location A rather than location B. To Ricardo's global mind, the whole world was a single bazaar, if somewhat sprawling, so if it was cheaper to grow and transport bananas to Britain from Dominica than from Madeira, one should. The logic of the comparative advantage stimulates competition and increased efficiency in production, ultimately turning the world into a single place and its people into runners on a treadmill.

Fast forward to our time. The containerization of sea transport has, since its feeble beginnings in the 1960s, resulted in an accelerated globalization of trade through enormously reduced costs and increased efficiency. Without the container ship, the Chinese economic miracle would have been impossible. The growth in world trade has been massive, from USD 2 trillion in 1980 to USD 20 trillion in 2019. This relies on a parallel growth in the production of manufactured goods and is, at the end of the day, about consumption. It has enabled Norwegians to buy tonnes of clothing that they will wear once or twice, Africans to get online with affordable smartphones, South Americans to have more than one pair of sneakers.

But all this comes at a cost, and one is often reminded, these days, of the old countercultural quip about standing at the edge of a cliff, being about to take a long step forward.

For two centuries, the availability of cheap and abundant energy was a blessing for humanity. It has now turned into a curse. We are undermining the very conditions of our existence by bringing plants and animals into extinction, filling the seas with plastic waste, razing rainforests for soya and scrublands for mining, eating more than our fill of beef and chicken (more than 60 billion birds a year), flying on weekend trips to fight boredom, watching Netflix for similar reasons, and innumerable other comfortable, increasingly frictionless activities that make us, the global middle classes, full and complacent but simultaneously drains our planet of its life-sustaining capabilities.

This is not a problem caused by humanity as such but by the inner logic of capitalism, which demands expansion, growth and the extraction of anything that can be valued in euros or dollars, whether it is human labour or human leisure, biotopes that can be converted into productive sites, that can generate wealth for the fictitious owners, whose right it has never been to own the future of other living creatures, human or not.

The truth is that our wealth, our growth, our prosperity and the fanning out of lives worth living, which is a fact often touted as proof that we are on the right track, depend on the destruction of ecosystems and futures. The facts are undeniable. Insects dying, dead whales filled with plastic, burning rainforests, the loss of 60% of the world's wild mammals since 1970; the coalmine is buzzing with canaries.

It was through his familiarity with the dismal living conditions of the new industrial working class that Friedrich Engels wrote his most damning tract about capitalism.[2] Today, at the height of the Anthropocene or Capitalocene, the evidence is no less tangible for anyone who cares to look, leading to the inevitable conclusion that there is a pressing need for new models of society. Humanity has to move beyond the contradictions of the Capitalocene, but we should be able to do so without relinquishing the achievements of modernity. This is not a time for embracing new age cosmologies, romanticizing indigenous worlds as a model for humanity *tout court*, glorifying irrationality and anti-scientific ideas as a counterpoint to a science and its technologies which are guilty as charged. In order to move forward, what is needed is an alternative vision of progress founded in a modernity which has learned from its mistakes yet remains committed to the ideals put forward from the Enlightenment onwards. A refurbished view of development which has transcended the limitations inherent in the Capitalocene sees the economy not as a means to enrich already absurdly wealthy people even more but as an integrated part of a way of life where the objective is to satisfy fundamental human needs and desires, which are not about gadgets, trips and status symbols but about satisfying and enduring relationships to other people and our surroundings. We will learn to see ourselves not as the masters of the universe but as nodes in an ecology on which we gratefully depend. Labellers may feel free to speak of it as decentralist ecosocialism. I rest contented imploring us to slow down, scale down and cool down. We will then have transcended the limitations and the catastrophic potentialities of the Capitalocene without losing our common sense.

Works cited:

Wilde, Oscar. (1893) 2000. 'Lady Windemere's Fan'. In *The Plays of Oscar Wilde*. Hertfordshire: Wordsworth Editions Limited.

Engels, Friedrich. (1845) 1987. *The Condition of the English Working Class*. Harmondsworth: Penguin Classics.

Care

→ Bacteria | → Capitalocene | → Chthulucene | → Client: Earth | → Connectedness | dividuals | extraction | facing Gaia | human-non-human material relations | (hu)Mans | kin | mantra of growth | → Moving Earths | → Sensitivity | → Waste | → Water

Joanna Latimer (born 1954, located in York, UK) is Professor of Sociology, Science & Technology and director of the Science & Technology Studies Unit (SATSU) at the University of York. She has published many articles and books, including *The Conduct of Care* (2000), *(Un)knowing Bodies* (2009), *The Gene, the Clinic and the Family* (2013) and *Intimate Entanglements* (2019). She was awarded the 2014 FSHI annual book prize. She is currently writing up her study of ageing and biology, *Naturecultures at the Limits to Life*.

Social scientists, among others, write about how we live in times in which the mantra of growth has come to dominate many societies. So much so that a need to care and cherish things, persons and practices are traduced by having their value extracted solely in terms of their potential to create profit and wealth. Following the 'logic of the market' leads to modes of organizing for growth that fuse production and consumption directly to the generation of capital. This results not only in societies overlooking their complex interconnections to disposal in terms of wealth and waste. The current fixation on globalization has also led some writers to describe the times we are living in not as the Anthropocene but more specifically as the Capitalocene.[1]

This figuring of everything as resources in the Capitalocene is not so much a logic as it represents what French philosopher and social theorist Michel Foucault might call an 'attitude',[2] or relation to the world. This is because capitalism today institutes particular relations between human advancement and technoscience. For instance, Martin Heidegger, the German philosopher, suggests how technologies more and more institute people and the 'natural' environment as 'standing reserves'[3] available for extraction and exploitation, the stuff of mines. In a different tradition, the British philosopher Alfred North Whitehead describes the bifurcation of Nature, in which the mind of the human is set apart from the materiality of the world in a subject-object divide, overlooking how human beings are interactants that are deeply entangled with other interactants, as equally entangled parts.[4] Whatever the merits of these different explanations, what is nonetheless observable is the way in which some (hu)Mans appear to stand outside the plane of the action – she or he is not of the same stuff of the world; these (hu)Mans configure themselves as standing outside and able to dominate the world and all those Others that they, explicitly or implicitly, cast as less-than-human.

Pressing an ethics of more-than-human worlds, American philosopher of science Donna Haraway argues that the devaluing relation between the (hu)Man and Others cannot continue:

> Cheapening nature cannot work much longer to sustain extraction and production in and of the contemporary world because most of the reserves of the earth have been drained, burned, depleted, poisoned, exterminated, and otherwise exhausted.
>
> Donna Haraway, 2015, p. 160.

The ravaged earth that Haraway evokes is French sociologist and philosopher Bruno Latour's Gaia.[5] Gaia here represents the entangled, more-than-human assemblages, multiplicities and multitudes that make up earth and that now incorporate in their fabrics and processes the effects of (hu)Man's carelessness. Gaia, ravaged and angry, has risen up and turned on all that dwell on the planet – through the elementally devastating effects of global warming and climate changes, including extinctions and refuge-lessness,[6] as well as abundances.[7] Gaia is speaking truth to (hu)Man's destructive power:

> As Latour reminds us, the Earth system (Gaia) is both nurturing and destructive. She is not indifferent because

she is so clearly affected by human behaviour. But She has aims that directly produce human insecurity and civilizational collapse. She is simultaneously '… too fragile to play the calming role of old nature, too unconcerned by our destiny to be a Mother, too unable to be propitiated by deals and sacrifices to be a Goddess.'

Cameron Harrington, 2017.

Latour exhorts us to *face* Gaia.[8] *The Prophecy*, an ongoing global project featuring a series of so far 13 photographs of composed assemblages set in different African landscapes, cityscapes and seascapes by the Beninese-Belgian artist Fabrice Monteiro, seems to me to be facing Gaia.

Some of the images evoke a sense of Gaia rising. She is Black, She is Africa. In these images Black Gaia rises like a goddess: partially composed of the waste together with symbols of Africa and its heritage. She is magnified and magnificent, towering over, or rising up from, the ruins. Fabrice's work enacts how the history of the extraction of Africa's value – for example, in the form of mining for minerals and the buying and selling of slaves – as well as the more contemporary forms of globalization that are modernizing African life – such as the advance of industrialization and digitalized communication – assembles bodies, machines, infrastructures and networks through which Africa's value can be capitalized. His art reminds us how the Anthropocene is built upon, and preys upon, intersectional inequities and inequalities: through the rendering of most humans as less-than-human. Fabrice noted in a personal email to me how 'anthropocenic problems are indissociable from a colonial way of inhabiting the world that has been the norm for the last 5 centuries.'[9] He makes his African goddess the epitome of all the more-than-human and less-than-human connections and entanglements which co-constitute the Capitalocene and which specific relations between (hu) Mans and the constitution of less-than-human Others has produced. What the images emphasize is that the Capitalocene has relied upon the rendering of Others (animals, some human beings, the soil, the air, water, the land) as less-than-human – that there are moral economies of techno-scientific production and fabricated ecologies always at work that rely upon the elevation of some over others. These are relations of asymmetry and power. But he is also enacting something that both Latour and Haraway advocate, collaboration with non-human others:

'Moral economies […] are integral to science: to its sources of inspiration, its choice of subject matter and procedures, its sifting of evidence, and its standards of explanation.'
Lorraine Daston, 1995, p. 5.

> Bacteria and fungi abound to give us metaphors; but, metaphors aside (good luck with that!), we have a mammalian job to do, with our biotic and abiotic sym-poietic collaborators, co-laborers. We need to make kin sym-chthonically, sym-poetically. Who and whatever we are, we need to make-with – become-with, compose-with – the earth-bound (thanks for that term, Bruno Latour-in-anglophone-mode).

Donna Haraway, 2015, p. 161.

The Canadian organization studies scholar Beth Dempster contrasts sympoiesis and autopoiesis emphasizing how sympoietic systems, from the Greek words for 'collective' and 'production', are not closed but 'organizationally ajar'.[10] They are 'characterized by cooperative, amorphous qualities', and 'interactions among components

Fabrice Monteiro
Untitled #8, 2015
Colour inkjet print on baryta paper
Courtesy of Fabrice Monteiro, Galerie Magnin-A

Since 1998, the use of monofilament or multi-mono-filament nylon nets has been prohibited by Article 30 of the Fisheries Code, yet their import is authorized by the Commercial Code. Decomposing only after 500 years, these nets allow nothing to pass through. They are abandoned or lost upon the reefs and wrecks of the sea floor, creating an ecological disaster. Thousands of tonnes of lost nets choke marine life, causing our fish to disappear.

Fabrice Monteiro
Untitled #11 / Ogun 2016
Colour inkjet print on baryta paper
Courtesy of Fabrice Monteiro, Galerie Magnin-A

Agbogbloshie, in the heart of Accra (Ghana) is host to one of the largest electronic waste dumps in Africa. In this area, the poorest classes of Accra have been spending years dismantling, recovering, weighing and reselling parts and metals extracted from the scrapped devices and from the heaps of electronic waste. The main issue is the burning of electronic cables to extract the copper contained in it. The process, often performed by youths, produces highly toxic smoke.

and the self-organizing capabilities of a system are recognized as the defining qualities'.[11] I want to suggest Fabrice's art performs sym-poietic collaboration and composition with non-human others – not bacteria and fungi but the *materials* of Capitalocene's 'ruins'.[12] More specifically, the images and the compositions they record invert Capitalocene's relations because they enact care for what is being ruined. They do this by performing Africa's dignity, power and beauty and thereby invoking hope: hope that what has almost been lost, the magnificence of Africa, can be revived. We can see similar effects in other continents, not least in Brazil, elegiacally recorded in the work of artist Miguel Rio Branco, housed in the gallery dedicated to him at Inhotim. This work, at the same time as it connects gendered and racialized violence, poverty and the ravaging of the land to Brazil's history of slavery and colonialism, evokes the immanent dynamism and power of peoples and places.

Some critics think that ecological balance can be reset through changing the political economic ordering of things from growth to degrowth and 'a designed reduction of total energy and material use to realign society with planetary limits, while improving people's lives and distributing resources fairly. It is an economic model that recognizes that the route to greater welfare for all is not one of more extraction and expansion, but of more sharing and co-operation.'[13]

The problem with this imaginary is the word 'all'. As important as a changing economic model is, it is not, as Belgian philosopher Isabelle Stengers suggests, enough to think of change as just for and about the human.[14] And that 'all' does not take into account those humans who have little choice or who are offered opportunities to improve their lot through selling their labour as a part of their leader's deals. In addition, it is not that (hu)Man needs just to be less materialistic; rather, as Spanish social studies of science scholars Blanca Callén Moreu and Daniel López Gómez argue,[15] it is the way of thinking about human-non-human material relations that needs to shift, including the importance of paying more attention to life with objects by emphasizing the affect required to attach to, and detach from, some materials rather than others. To put it bluntly, as Greta Thunberg and Extinction Rebellion have iterated, and as Fabrice Monteiro's photographs help reveal, the Anthropocene is best understood, in its widest sense, as a *crisis of care*. This epithet is usually preserved for the crisis of care in terms of the economic and personal costs

Fabrice Monteiro
Untitled #1, 2013
Colour inkjet print on baryta paper
Courtesy of Fabrice Monteiro, Galerie Magnin-A

Located 30 km from Dakar (Senegal), Mbeubeuss is an unauthorized landfill site, where each day, 350 rubbish trucks dump an estimated 1,300 tonnes of household waste, from Dakar and its environs. It is an ecological bomb: since its creation in 1968, the landfill has been growing and increasingly gaining ground, polluting surrounding waters, soils and the environment. But Mbeubeuss is also a source of income for about 1,800 people who work in and earn their living from the site.

of an ageing population, but I want to broaden out the crisis of care to encompass the complexities and entanglements in which the Anthropocene thrives.

The British anthropologist Marilyn Strathern's work (juxtaposing Melanesian ways of world-making with those of Euro-Americans) can help us here. Strathern stresses a different way of thinking about kin: kin requires recognition of our selves not just as individuals – those sovereign subjects of Cartesian dualistic thinking excited by cultures of consumption and incited to choose among this and that in their ever-desiring to be more complete. Rather, she invites us to reimagine ourselves as 'dividuals', whose being depends upon many different others.[16] Haraway stretches this way of thinking to remembering that we are always and forever becoming-with and are dependent upon many different Others as no more or less than sym-compounds.

Within this potent framing of things, what Strathern aptly calls naturecultures,[17] care becomes a matter of shifting relations to a sensibility and an ethics of 'more-than-human'. This is to say, moving from anthropocentric relations which elevate human exceptionalism, including competition, domination and extraction of resources – from our individuating each other, and from our treating the earth as an endless, super-abundant resource to be mined – to understandings of relations in which kin and kindness extend and incorporate all that makes it possible to live, to make worlds together with non-human others.[18] Donna Haraway describes this widening of how we should look at the present epoch as the Chthulucene:

> One way to live and die well as mortal critters in the Chthulucene is to join forces to reconstitute refuges, to make possible partial and robust biological-cultural-political-technological recuperation and recomposition, which must include mourning irreversible losses. Thom van Dooren and Vinciane Despret taught me that. There are so many losses already, and there will be many more. Renewed generative flourishing cannot grow from myths of immortality or failure to become-with the dead and the extinct.

Donna Haraway, 2015, pp. 160–161.

Within this imaginary of the Chthulucene, soil, air, water, biotic, human and other animals, even minerals themselves are co-labourers. Hence we need ways to let the non-human speak not as less-than-human but as collaborators; they must be heard:

'Tigergrowl', Extinction Rebellion, Waterloo Bridge, London, 15 April 2019.

'Grandfather', Extinction Rebellion, Waterloo Bridge, London, 15 April 2019.

> Water has a role and a responsibility to fulfil, just as people do. We do not have the right to interfere with water's duties to the rest of Creation. Indigenous knowledge tells us that water is the blood of Mother Earth and that water itself is considered a living entity with just as much right to live as we have.
>
> Cameron Harrington, 2017, pp. 38–38.

Social movements such as Extinction Rebellion as well as activists like Greta Thunberg, with the growing movement of striking school pupils across the world, have helped enact how to care, specifically in terms of shifting both attachments and sensibilities, by *doing* and *making* worlds together differently. So, it is not simply perspectives on production, consumption and their all-but-forgotten relations to disposal that need to change, as important as these are, but also our sense of *attachment* and *detachment*.[19] Attaching and detaching from different things and different others with care means garnering a sense of with whom we are intimately entangled[20] – a sense of with whom and with what we are connected across vast tracts of time-space, to make a world, a life. As we drink Brazilian coffee, we become intimately entangled in Brazilian geopolitics; we become connected to the people whose labour turns Brazilian coffee beans into wealth for the few, to the ruptured soil that produces the coffee plants that is or isn't treated with care.

Through this reimagining of the sympoietic relations that attachments compose, we can understand how human and the more-than-human can become-with each other in more fruitful and generative ways. This is not to collapse differences in some kind of mulch (apologies to compost lovers!) but to preserve a sense of being alongside[21] each-otherness in partial and intermittent connection, and in ways that do not divide into hierarchical moral economies of division and exploitation that also characterize much of the biosciences, as at the same time as they preserve and respect difference.

Works cited:

Daston, Lorraine. 1995. 'The Moral Economy of Science'. *Osiris*, 10, pp. 2–24. https://www.jstor.org/stable/301910. Accessed 8 May 2019.

Dempster, Beth. 2000. 'Sympoietic and Autopoietic Systems: A New Distinction for Self-Organizing Systems'. In *Proceedings of the World Congress of the Systems Sciences and ISSS 2000*, ed. J.K. Allen and J. Wilby. Presented at the International Society for Systems Studies Annual Conference, July, Toronto, Canada.

Callén Moreu, Blanca, and Daniel López Gómez. 2019. 'Intimate with Your Junk! A Waste Management Experiment for a Material World'. *The Sociological Review*, 62 (2), pp. 318–339.

Foucault, Michel. 1984. 'What is Enlightenment?' In Paul Rabinow, ed. *The Foucault Reader*, pp. 32–50. New York: Pantheon Books.

Giraud, Eva, Eleanor Hadley Kershaw, Richard Helliwell and Gregory Hollin. 'Abundance in the Anthropocene'. *The Sociological Review*, 62 (2), pp. 357–373.

Harper, Phineas. 2019. 'The Architecture of Degrowth'. *Dazeen*. https://www.dezeen.com/2019/09/25/oslo-architecture-triennale-architecture-degrowth-phineas-harper/. Accessed 9 January 2020.

Haraway, Donna. 2015.

'Anthropocene, Capitalocene, Plantationocene, Chthulucene: Making Kin'. *Environmental Humanities*, 6, pp. 159–165.

Harrington, Cameron. 2017. 'Posthuman Security and Care in the Anthropocene'. *E-International Relations*. https://www.e-ir.info/2017/10/10/posthuman-security-and-care-in-the-anthropocene/. Accessed 15 January 2020.

Heidegger, Martin. 1996. 'The Question Concerning Technology'. In David F. Krell, ed. *Martin Heidegger: Basic Writings*. Revised and expanded edition. London: Routledge.

Latimer, Joanna. 2013. 'Being Alongside: Rethinking Relations amongst Different Kinds'. *Theory, Culture & Society*, 30, 7/8, pp. 77–104.

Latimer, Joanna. 2019. 'Science under Siege: Being alongside the Life Sciences, Giving Science Life. *The Sociological Review*, 62 (2), pp. 264–286.

Latimer, Joanna, and Daniel López Gómez. 2019. 'Introduction: Affects, More-Than-Human Intimacies and the Politics of Relations in Science and Technology'. *The Sociological Review*, 67 (2), pp. 247–263.

Latour, Bruno. 2013. 'Facing Gaia: Six Lectures on the Political Theology of Nature'. Gifford Lectures, 18–28 February.

Munro, Rolland. 1996. 'The Consumption View of Self: Extension, Exchange and Identity'. In Stephen Edgell, Kevin Hetherington and Alan Warde, eds. *Consumption Matters*. Sociological Review monograph series, no. 44, pp. 248–273. Oxford: Blackwell Publisher.

Meulemans, Germain. 2019. 'Wormy Collaborations in Practices of Soil Construction'. *Theory, Culture & Society*, pp. 93–122. First published online 7 July. https://doi.org/10.1177/0263276419851857. Accessed 15 January 2020.

Puig de la Bellacasa, Maria. 2019. 'Re-Animating Soils: Transforming Human–Soil Affections through Science, Culture and Community'. *The Sociological Review*, 62 (2), pp. 391–407.

Stengers, I. 2015. *In Catastrophic Times: Resisting the Coming Barbarism*. S.l.: Open Humanities Press.

Strathern, Marilyn. 1980. 'No Nature, No Culture: The Hagen Case'. In Carol MacCormack and Marilyn Strathern, eds. *Nature, Culture and Gender*, pp. 174–222. Cambridge: Cambridge University Press.

Strathern, Marilyn. 1988. *The Gender of the Gift: Problems with Women and Problems with Society in Melanesia*. Oakland: University of California Press.

Strathern, Marilyn. 1991. *Partial Connections*. Lanham: Rowman and Littlefield.

Tsing, Anna Lowenhaupt. 2015. *The Mushroom at the End of the World: On the Possibility of Life in Capitalist Ruins*. Princeton: Princeton University Press.

Whitehead, Alfred North. 1920. 'Theories of the Bifurcation of Nature'. In *The Concept of Nature*, pp. 26–48. Cambridge: Cambridge University Press.

Chthulu-cene

→ Anthropocene | → Capitalocene | → Coexistence | compost | → Corals | → Earthlings | humus | → New Materialism | ongoingness | → Plantationocene | stay with the trouble | sympoietic

We are not posthuman; we are compost. We are not homo; we are humus. We are terran; we are earthlings; we are many; we are indeterminate. We bleed into each other in chaotic fluid extravagance. We eat our own snakey tails in sympoietic whorls to generate polymorphic ongoingness; we are enmeshed with the ouroboroi of diverse interlaced netherworlds. We are chthonic, of and for the earth, of and for its unfinished times. We live and die in its ruins. We tunnel in the ruins to germinate in the seams. We can be resurgent yet. There may still be time. Composting is so hot.

Sticker made by artists Beth Stephens and Annie Sprinkle with Kern Toy Design, www.sexecology.org.

The outrages meriting names like Anthropocene or Capitalocene are about socioecologically, historically situated human beings (not humankind all the time everywhere) destroying places and times of refuge for people and other critters. The Anthropocene and the Capitalocene designate double death, the killing of the conditions of ongoingness.[1] These are appropriately ugly names for unprecedentedly destructive webs of systemic processes. Their consequences, their materialities are already etched into the rocks, airs, waters and flesh of terrans, in chemical and nuclear signatures, in heat-trapping gasses, in hot acid seas. Capitalocene is one of those necessary but insufficient words that pop into one's mouth unbidden. Unhappy with the false and arrogant humanist universalism of the Anthropocene, I started lecturing about the historical extractionism and extinctionism of the Capitalocene (and of the Plantationocene, that name for processes for making wealth through radical simplification, rooted in global transportations of peoples, plants, animals and microbes and in slavery, colonialism, heteronormative familialism, racism and other forced systems of production and reproduction, all of which made the great accelerations of the Capitalocene possible). But no one invents terms like Capitalocene *de novo*; notice how many people propose similar important terms at the same

The very useful notion of the great acceleration for dating the ugly thing called the Anthropocene dates to 2004, in an attempt to describe graphically the growth curves of natural and social systems from 1750 to the present. Like all such global aggregates, the data mask vast and diverse inequalities and also threaten to mystify the sympoietic natural-technical processes for making such inequalities and ontological homogenizations. Still, the striking shared inflection points around 1950 of so many heterogeneous exponential growth curves (human population, species extinctions, use of paper, carbon emissions, metals extraction, industrial animal production, forced and free human migrations, etc. etc.) cry out for the situated historical analysis of webbed processes, and not for enthralled appeals to the mathematics of exponential growth curves as if they described natural laws and necessary directions of time.

Donna Haraway (born 1944, located in Santa Cruz, US), from the University of California, works in the fields of feminist science and technology and multispecies studies. Her works include *Staying with the Trouble* (2016), *Manifestly Haraway* (2016), *When Species Meet* (2008), *Companion Species Manifesto* (2003), *Modest_Witness@Second_Millennium* (1994), *Simians, Cyborgs, and Women* (1991), *Primate Visions* (1992), *Crystals, Fabrics, and Fields* (1976), *Story Telling for Earthly Survival* (film by F. Terravova, 2016) and, with Adele Clarke, *Making Kin Not Population* (2018).

time. We lust for names to designate a shared, intolerable and flatly unnecessary condition. The established disorder is not necessary; how many times and in how many ways must we learn to notice this fact? Not only was 'my' Capitalocene part of a cat's cradle game of invention, as always, but Jason Moore had already developed compelling arguments to think with. Moore himself first heard the term 'Capitalocene' in 2009 in a seminar in Lund, Sweden, when then graduate student Andreas Malm proposed it. In an urgent historical conjuncture, words to think with pop out all at once from many bubbling cauldrons because we all feel the need for better net bags to collect up the stuff crying out for attention.[2]

Scott Gilbert pointed out that the Anthropocene (and Plantationocene) should be considered a boundary event like the K-Pg boundary, not an epoch. As far as I know, the conversation cited is the first place the term Plantationocene appeared (p. 22).

However, the Anthropocene and Capitalocene are perhaps really more boundary events than epochs, like the K-Pg boundary between the Cretaceous and the Paleogene.[3] The Anthropocene and Capitalocene mark severe discontinuities; what comes after will not be like what came before. The scale of destruction wreaked in the Anthropocene, in the Capitalocene, has consequences. There will be no *status quo ante*. Loss is real and ongoing. Mourning is required, and it is and will be hard. The boundary that is the Anthropocene/Capitalocene means many things, including that immense, irreversible and unequally borne destruction is really in train, not only for the 11 billion or so people who will be on earth near the end of the 21st century but for myriads of other critters too. (The incomprehensible but sober number of around 11 billion people will only hold if current worldwide birth rates of human babies remain low; if they rise again, all bets are off. Anti-racist, anti-imperialist feminists stopped talking about this; shame on us.) The edge of extinction is not just a metaphor; system collapse is not a thriller. Ask any refugee of any species. Our job is to make the Anthropocene and Capitalocene as short and thin as possible and to cultivate with each other in every way imaginable epochs to come that can replenish refuge.[4]

Right now, the earth is full of refugees, human and not, without refuge. 'Chthulucene' is a simple word. It is a compound of two Greek roots (*khthôn* and *kainos*) that together name a kind of time-place for learning to stay with the trouble of living and dying in response-ability on a damaged earth. Kainos means now, a time of beginnings, a time for ongoing, for freshness. Nothing in kainos must mean conventional pasts, presents or futures. Thick times have many shapes; arrows entangle, double back on themselves, proliferate and lead astray; times are bumptious materialities. Besides all that, there is nothing in times of beginnings that insists on wiping out what has come before or, indeed, wiping out what comes after. Kainos can be full of inheritances, of remembering, and full of comings, of nurturing what might still be, as well as noticing what still is. Resonating in sympoietic complexity, kainos plucks the threads of thick, ongoing presence, with stringy hyphae infusing all sorts of temporalities and materialities. Chthonic ones are beings of the earth, both ancient and up to the minute. Chthonic ones are replete with tentacles, feelers, digits, cords, whiptails, spider legs and very unruly hair. Chthonic ones romp in multi-critter humus but have little patience with sky-gazing Anthropos. Chthonic ones are monsters in the best sense; they demonstrate and perform the material meaningfulness of earth processes and critters. They also demonstrate and perform consequences. Chthonic ones are not safe; they have no truck with ideologues; they belong to no one; they writhe and luxuriate in manifold forms and manifold names in all the airs, waters and places of the earth. They make and unmake; they are made and unmade. They are who are; they are what are. They do not do 'I' very well; they are sympoietic, not autopoietic. No wonder the world's great monotheisms in both religious and secular guises have tried again and again to exterminate the chthonic ones. The scandals of times called the Anthropocene and the Capitalocene are the latest and most dangerous of these exterminating forces, these Singularities dealing out double death. Living with and dying with each other potently in the Chthulucene can be a fierce reply to the dictates of both Anthropos and Capital in the exterminationist times of the Moderns. It turns out that the chthonic ones are not dead; they writhe and slither within all of earth. Like Medusa, they are mortal and on the move. Like the octopuses, squid and cuttlefish appreciated in fifth-century BCE Greece, the chthonic ones are critters of aporia. They secrete the inky darkest night; they are artisans of disguise; they are relentlessly polymorphic; they entangle the world in their numerous tube-feet-lined, stinger-endowed tentacles.[5] The chthonic ones are spiders of the sea; they are predators; they are not exterminators.

The Titan goddess Metis is of an earlier, more tangled age than Zeus and his siblings. Despite efforts to build her into Olympiad genealogies by marrying her to Zeus, in my stories of the Chthulucene Metis remains true to her earth-wide tentacular kin.

We need a name for the dynamic ongoing sym-chthonic forces and powers of which people as humus are a part, within which ongoingness is at stake. Ongoingness is not futurism; ongoingness is full of continuities, discontinuities and surprises. Maybe, but only maybe, and only with intense commitment and collaborative work and play with other earthlings, flourishing for rich multi-species assemblages that include human people will be possible. I am calling all this the Chthulucene – past, present and to come. These real and possible time-spaces are not named after SF writer H. P. Lovecraft's misogynist racial-nightmare monster Cthulhu (note the spelling difference) but rather after the diverse earth-wide tentacular powers and forces and collected things with names like Naga, Gaia, Tangaroa (burst from waterfull Papa), Terra, Haniyasu-hime, Spider Woman, Pachamama, Oya, Gorgo, Raven, A'akuluujjusi and many many more. 'My' Chthulucene, even burdened with its problematic Greek-ish tendrils, entangles myriad temporalities and spatialities and myriad intra-active entities-in-assemblages – including the more-than-human, other-than-human, inhuman and human-as-humus. Even rendered in an English-language text like this one, Naga, Gaia, Tangaroa, Medusa, Spider Woman and all their kin are some of the many thousand names proper to a vein of SF that Lovecraft could not have imagined or embraced – namely the webs of speculative fabulation, speculative feminism, science fiction and scientific fact, so far.[6]

'Os Mil Nomes de Gaia/the Thousand Names of Gaia' was the generative international conference organized by Eduardo Viveiros de Castro, Déborah Danowski and their collaborators in 2014 in Rio de Janeiro. For all the videos from 'Os Mil Nomes de Gaia', see https://www.youtube.com/c/osmilnomesdegaia/videos.

We need ugly words like Anthropocene and Capitalocene to do needed critique; we need the snakey no-name/thousand-name ones for actual living and dying as earthlings. It matters which stories tell stories, which concepts think concepts. Mathematically, visually and narratively, it matters which figures figure figures, which systems systematize systems.[7]

Works cited:

Bird Rose, Deborah. 2006. 'What if the Angel of History Were a Dog?'. *Cultural Studies Review*, 12 (1).

Detienne, Marcel, and Jean-Pierre Vernant. 1974. *Les ruses de l'intelligence: la métis des Grecs.* Paris: Flammarion et Cie.

Haraway, Donna. 2014. 'Entrevista'. https://www.youtube.com/watch?v= lx0oxUHOlA821, August 2014. Accessed 19 November 2019.

Haraway, Donna J. 2016. *Staying with the Trouble: Making Kin in the Chthulucene.* Durham, NC: Duke University Press Books.

Haraway, Donna, Noboru Ishikawa, Scott F. Gilbert, Kenneth Olwig, Anna L. Tsing and Nils Bubandt. 2015. 'Anthropologist Are Talking – About the Anthropocene'. *Ethnos*, 81 (3), pp. 535-564. https://doi.org/10.1080/00141844.2015.1105838. Accessed 17 January 2020.

Moore, Jason. 2013. 'Anthropocene, Capitalocene, and the Myth of Industrialization'. https://jasonwmoore.wordpress.com/2013/06/16/anthropocene-capitalocene-the-myth-of-industrialization/, 16 June. Accessed 19 November 2019.

Moore, Jason. 2016. 'The Capitalocene, Part 1: On the Nature and Origins of Our Ecological Crisis'. http://www.jasonwmoore.com/uploads/The_ Capitalocene_ Part_I _June_2014.pdf, 2015. Accessed 15 March 2016.

Steffen, Will, Wendy Broadgate, Lisa Deutsch, Owen Gaffney and Cornelia Ludwig. 2015. 'The Trajectory of the Anthropocene: The Great Acceleration'. *The Anthropocene Review*, 2 (1).

Tsing, Anna Lowenhaupt. 2015. *The Mushroom at the End of the World: On the Possibility of Life in Capitalist Ruins.* Princeton: Princeton University Press.

City

→ Air | exhaust of industrialization | → Explicitation | → Heatwave | → Modernism | → Pollution | subnature | → Sun | urban darkness

David Gissen (born 1969, located in New York City, US) is the author of the books *Subnature* and *Manhattan Atmospheres* and numerous essays on the history and theory of 19th- and 20th-century architecture, urbanism and environmental history. He is currently Eero Saarinen Visiting Professor of Design and Visiting Professor of Architecture History at the Yale School of Architecture.

Architects often imagine the city as a space set *against* nature and that it must be understood in dialogue with this non-human realm. We can see this point of view from the 15th-century drawings of cities juxtaposed against a surrounding landscape to contemporary ecological projects that attempt to remake the city based on natural processes. In addition to this vision of the city, we can also understand the city as a space where forms of nature are generated and produced. The city is not just set within nature, containing it or consuming it, but is a space of bio-physical and environmental production itself.

Of all the forms of nature produced by the city, I have been committed to charting a form of nature particular to modern urbanization and that I call 'subnature'. Subnature (sub, as in that which is below nature) comprises those forms of environmental and material conditions, flora and fauna deemed lesser and undesirable but undeniably an aspect of the urban experience. Subnatures include the dust, gas and exhaust of industrialization and automobility, the leaks and flooding of burst water mains, and the piles of rubble and weeds that appear in the city's interstices and demolition sites, among many other examples. Subnatures are another way of describing what economists label the 'externalities' or unwanted products of urbanization. The city produces countless externalities, including poverty, corruption and homelessness. But subnature describes those externalities that take on the physical position often occupied by more normative forms of nature. They become the matter produced by the city and often the disturbing material setting for urban lives.

A hallmark of many enlightened, modernist visions of the city is the elimination of subnature from the physical experience of the city. The great urban reform projects of the 19th and 20th centuries were often examinations and transformations of the city's dominant subnatures – fetid water, lightless interiors and stagnant air. Such qualities were charted, objectified and, in many cases, eliminated from sectors of several cities. Twentieth-century reformist mantras such as 'Sun, light and air' or 'Light, air, greenery' drove the reconstruction of urban space and the elimination of the subnatural as an integral aspect of the urban experience. These mantras demanded that municipalities replace subnature with another more healthful urbanized nature. This often took the form of an architecture bringing sunshine to the city with light and airy spaces often set among urban parks and greenery.

A hundred years later, architects and urbanists have arrived at a new reckoning with subnature. Today, we must also understand that subnature has the capacity to be folded into liberatory visions of a future city, just like the nature that was to replace it. Such a statement will likely appear flippant in light of the history of urban disease, poverty and environmental degradation. The subnatures of the historic and contemporary city remain dangerous threats to our respiratory, circulatory and neurological systems. But a few subnatures and subnatural qualities can be rethought and refashioned into far less menacing aspects of the urban experience.

For example, consider something as common as the historical and contemporary experience of urban darkness: one of the modern city's

The City Builds an Urban Sun, 1900–2000

The first collective drawing – *The City Builds an Urban Sun, 1900–2000* – shows more than ten canonical architecture and urban designs. Each project shown here is by an architect or planner who sought to remake urban space by introducing more sun and light into the city. The projects are shown in tandem with those aspects of urban architecture despised by their architects. For example, Charles Garnier's Cité Industrielle is shown in comparison to the dreary industrial towns he despised; The 'Dumb-Bell Tenement' of Lower New York is set among the pre-law lightless tenements of the 19th century; Le Corbusier's Plan Voisin is shown adjacent to the dense historicist Parisian context that he hated; Bruno Taut's Stadtkrone is shown in another dense industrial city; Hugh Ferriss's Set-Back Skyscraper can be seen among multiple versions of the Equitable Building, whose dark shadows inspired his drawing of light entering the skyscraper city; and the top of the Chrysler Building is contrasted with less sparkly tower tops. The drawing also includes the United Nations Building, Ralph Knowles's Solar Envelope Concept, I.M. Pei's Louvre Pyramid, and Kevin Roche's Dendur Room at The Metropolitan Museum of Art.

The City Reconstructs Darkness, 2000–2100

The second collective drawing – *The City Reconstructs Darkness, 2000–2100* – represents the ways that we might reclaim darkness for the future city in an era of climate change and increasing solar-heat gain in cities. Here, each of the above modernist and late-modernist efforts to increase sun and light in the city is subverted and challenged. These modern and late-modern buildings become the background for a new set of proposals for the city. The proposals in the second drawing introduce increased shade and shadow by returning historical density and medieval street profiles to the city, resurrecting the urban underground and by simply turning stepped modernist forms upside down!

Instructors David Gissen and Surry Schlabs. Drawings by Yale Architecture students Yue Geng, Gabe Gutierrez Huerta, Srinivas Narayan Karthikeyan, Shiqi Li, Andrew Economos Miller, Kelsey Rico, Qizhen Tang, Adam Thibodeaux, Alper Turan, Hongyu Wang, Daniel Whitcombe.

most pervasive forms of subnature was darkness. Modern and, in particular, capitalistic forms of urbanization produced enormous amounts of lightless streetscapes and darkened interior spaces. The two cities where I live, New York and Vienna, both have a history of urban governments waging battles against the darkness produced by modern urbanization in the 19th and early 20th centuries. In both cities, rampant speculation and development deprived inhabitants of access to sunlight. In New York and Vienna, lightless basements became homes to countless people, preyed upon by the champions of a brutal real-estate economy. In New York, real-estate speculators became alarmed at how easily unregulated commercial skyscraper building could cover a block in dark shadows.

In response, reformist architects and urbanists attempted to eliminate the above qualities through the development of new zoning codes or the redesign of entire areas of the city. The former work includes the redesign of codes governing sunlight and air in tenements and the shaping of the profiles of skyscraper construction. The latter work includes the creation of park-like settings for housing and with often cruciform or crystalline architectural forms. Both efforts are part of the radiant aesthetics of modernity where space is 'solarized', exposed to intense levels of sunlight. The solarization of the city and the construction of radiant forms include efforts to increase exposure to the sun as well as the aesthetics of radiance and luminosity – from the gilt domes of the Secessionist architecture of Vienna to the glittering top of New York's Chrysler Building.

In contrast to the above history, contemporary architects and urbanists are exploring how the city might produce *more* darkness, but as a positive aspect of the city. This is primarily a response to increasing spring and summer heat and a populace's struggles with this increasingly warmer climate. Dark spaces, which were often associated with environments that impaired people, might ironically offer those who are most vulnerable to heat an alternative, modernized environment. In a recent meeting with municipal officials in Vienna, my students and I listened to a planner describe how his team is looking at pre-modern streetscapes, which typically have a more narrow and shady quality. Such spaces seem critical to the ability of the city to protect the elderly, disabled people and young children from the increasingly brutal late-spring and summer sun.

We can extend and intensify these efforts by looking more closely at those spaces railed against by many modern architects – the profiles of medieval streets, the character of baroque cellars and the generally more dark and gloomy urban character of the former city. Some architects have drawn inspiration from the aesthetics of medieval spaces before and have examined pre-modern forms of shade in countless projects. But to draw inspiration from medieval spaces' bio-physical qualities, to embrace darkness as a positive component or visionary quality of a future city is more provocative. In any event, urban reformers of a hundred years ago have done much of this work for us, because these were precisely the conditions they documented so that they could eliminate them.

To imagine something like darkness having a pronounced and positive role in the future architectural environment of the city challenges many of the ethical and liberatory promises attributed to the vitalistic and radiant aesthetics of modernity. This for me is the essential aspect of subnature. We cannot easily proclaim it as a future, desirable aspect of the city; one must always contend with it as a material and historic burden. To imagine subnature in our futures is less an evolution of the urban ideal and more about the dismantling of the often singular, socio-natural ideals of the past. It marks the introduction of a more thorough understanding of the urban production of nature. And it brings a more complex politics into this urban production process and its histories.

Client: Earth

→ Care | → Declaration of Rebellion | → Denial | → Earth Ethics | ecological civilization | → Imagine | → Next Generation | → Pollution | using law | voice of science | voice of the Earth | voice of the people | → World Scientists' Warning to Humanity

When we connect with the Earth, it becomes many things to us. Our Mother, the place we make our home, the locus of our struggles, the arena for our battles, the womb in which we create, the nest in which we celebrate love.

For me, it is also my client. As a lawyer, I devote myself to serving the Earth and all who dwell upon her. As a Buddhist, I've taken a vow to save all sentient beings. These two are the same for me.

A lawyer must interview their client. You must ask her what she needs, help assess her problems and try to find a pragmatic path to solutions.

When the Earth is your client, how do you interview her? It starts with the science. The Earth speaks to us in the grammar of science. We listen. Then we take what the science is saying about climate, ocean acidification, the effect of air pollution on children's lungs, and all the rest. We let science set where the goal needs to be. What is a good result for the climate, the ocean, a child's lungs?

With the goal in mind, we craft policy that captures the core of the science. Then go to the legislature and work to embody that policy in a system of rules that is fair, open and transparent. Rules which, if followed, will move society to the desired goal.

Once the law is in place, it must be implemented correctly. Those whose behaviour the law would change – for example, fossil fuel or chemical companies – will lobby hard to make sure the law is not properly implemented. So we must be vigilant and require that the government ministries charged with implementing the law actually do so.

Inevitably there will be gaps. Often, even when there are good laws, they are not enforced. In wealthy Europe, for example, air pollution causes early deaths for some 600,000 people every year. So citizens must take the law into their own hands, and enforce it.

We are therefore working with groups of citizens all over Europe to enforce air-quality law, and winning. In Germany,

James Thornton (born 1954, located in London, UK) is the founding CEO of ClientEarth. He is also a member of the bars of New York, California and the Supreme Court of the United States. Using corporate law to address the climate crisis, ClientEarth is developing a truly global reach. It works with investors to move markets towards renewable energy, stops coal-fired power plants and uses the courts to force governments to clean the air.

home of the diesel engine, we have got courts to ban diesel in the centres of Stuttgart, Düsseldorf, Munich, Berlin. The Bavarian environment minister has refused to obey the German court order, and so the European Court of Justice has recently instructed the German court to consider putting the minister in jail.

If government ministers start going to jail for not respecting the Earth and the environmental rights of people, our client will have more of a chance.

Over the last 30 years that I have been using law in these ways, three important things have happened.

The first is not good news: the problems have grown and accelerated.

The second is good news. When I stood up as a young man and argued that we needed to make fundamental changes in the way we lived on the planet, I was often dismissed as a dreamer. 'There are no ways of doing what you want,' people would tell me.

Now, solutions are all around us. We know how to generate clean energy, cheaper in much of the world than fossil fuel energy. We are building electric cars to be powered by clean energy. We are close to making affordable hydrogen from renewable energy, and hydrogen is a clean fuel that can push fossil fuel out of the heaviest industries. We know how to grow our food in ways that regenerate soil, eliminate poisons from our diet and sequester carbon. We can make meat substitutes that meat eaters like and can buy in hamburger chains. Soon we will affordably make 'clean meat' in labs, actual animal tissue grown by bacteria from sugar and water in pharmaceutical vats. This will lead to the end of the industrial farming of animals. It will also remove the pressure to cut down the rainforest for pasture and soybeans.

Solutions are upon us. But incumbent industries are locked into mental inertia. Electric utilities that use coal, for example, are loath to change. Companies that build coal plants plan hundreds more. The same is true in farming, chemicals, plastics and so on. Here is where citizens using law come in again.

Think of those incumbent industries as dragons blocking the road of our transition. Citizens using the sharp sword of the law can slay those dragons. And so we and others stop new coal plants and close existing ones in Europe and America. In a new effort, we will work with groups all over Asia to block the construction of new coal plants and try to ensure that the millions who need electricity gain it from clean sources.

The third change is also good news. Citizens everywhere are waking up to the fact that the Earth needs their help. We see millions of children going on climate strikes. We see polls around the world showing that people are demanding change. This demand needs to increase.

When the demand is loud enough, politicians, many of them now living in the same alienated state as coal companies and denying that the increasing fires and floods around the world are climate-related, will see they need to act.

When they understand they must act, lawyers for the Earth are needed again. Who will help take the people's aspirations and translate them into a new system of stronger rules to ensure that human civilization thrives long into the future? Eco-lawyers will help the voice of the people; the voice of science and the voice of the Earth have a strong say in producing the new sets of needed rules.

One of the new sets of needed rules will be about money. 'Follow the money' is good advice when it comes to the health of the planet. A leading economist has calculated that it will take around 90 trillion dollars in investment by 2035 to build the new clean infrastructure we need. Most of that will have to be private investment.

So is private investment moving fast enough? No, and without changes in the rules it won't. Some salutary changes have happened already. We worked to get the UK pension rules changed so that pension fund managers now have to assess the climate risk to their investments. This should lead to more climate-friendly investments. The Bank of England will require banks to stress-test their portfolios for climate, looking out decades ahead.

Much more needs to be done though. I am interested in what changes to the rules we need so that smart corporate leaders can move in the right direction. What changes need to be made so that a CEO can walk into the boardroom with a plan to reach carbon neutrality by 2030? Right now, CEOs are getting fired for such leadership. What new rules will get them applauded, not shot down? This is a crucial area for further work.

Raising our eyes from the rulebooks, let's talk about story. People are storytelling animals more than rational animals. So what story about our future civilization do we want to tell? Environmentalists like me have not been good at envisioning a positive future. We've focused on everything that is wrong. While the problems are important, focusing only on the negative disempowers people. We need to be excited about the future not depressed.

So let us also dream.

Let us dream of an ecological civilization. We created an agricultural civilization 10,000 years ago and an industrial civilization a couple of hundred years ago. Now we need another turn of the wheel.

Let's dream of a civilization in which we generate clean energy, have regenerative agriculture, clean industry and economic theory that lead to outcomes good for the planet and its people, in which there are clean air and water, fish in the sea, rainforests undisturbed and protected by native peoples, and a system of enforceable rules to guarantee all this.

It would be an ecological civilization. One I'd like to live in, one that would cope with the changes that are coming and cannot be avoided while preventing catastrophe. One in which, as Pink Floyd frontman David Gilmour memorably said, 'guitars can be played and songs can be sung.'

Tweet sent by @davidgilmour on 19 June 2019.

I was nurturing this dream for decades. Then I went to China, to work with their Supreme Court, their federal prosecutors and the environment ministry. I found they have a similar dream. And they are working on it in a concerted way. Hundreds of their best people are designing the theory and practice of it. And they call it ecological civilization.

It gives me hope that the world's biggest polluter is now working hard to shift their direction of travel. They want a future of living harmlessly on the planet. They have set up environmental courts with over 3,000 specialized judges. In 2018–2019, the Chinese prosecutors initiated around 100,000 environmental enforcement cases. They recognize the problems, and they are looking for solutions. Personally, I will do everything I can to help them.

We need to empower everyone to work for the Earth. Each of us can do so. Each of us can nurture a positive vision, and let our love flow forward, into the civilization we want to see, bring our children into and are prepared to fight for. If we all fight for it, starting at home, in our neighbourhood, at our workplace and at the ballot box, we will certainly win.

Climate

→ Atmosphere | CO_2 | → Declaration of Rebellion | → Fire | → Flood | from background to main drama | → Future | → Oil | → Power | shift the zeitgeist | → Time | → Weather

Climate: The usual condition of the planet – the temperature, humidity, rainfall, wind and so forth at a given location over a period of time. In the human past, this has always been more or less in the background: we lived our lives against a stable climatic backdrop, which is a crucial reason civilizations could emerge over the last ten thousand years. The weather changed daily, but underlying it was an essential predictability. If you grew corn in a certain field, the odds were very good your great-granddaughter would be able to do likewise. This happy state of affairs began to shift ever so slightly in the 18th century, as humans began to burn measurable amounts of coal, and then gas and oil. When these fuels are burnt, the combustion process mixes the carbon atoms they contain with oxygen atoms from the air to form carbon dioxide, and the structure of this molecule has an unusual property: it traps heat near the planet that would otherwise radiate back out into space. This has always been a good thing: without some CO_2 in the atmosphere, we would live on a very cold planet. But a 50% increase in two centuries is unprecedented in the geological record,

Bill McKibben (born 1960, located in Vermont, US) wrote the first book on climate change for a general audience, *The End of Nature* (1989), and founded 350.org, the first planet-wide grassroots climate campaign.

and it has brought us to a place where, as a result, temperatures have begun to rise steadily and rapidly. July 2019 was the hottest month ever recorded on our planet, and the heat has given rise to floods, fire and famine; the Arctic has lost most of its sea ice. Note, however, the biggest changes: the climate is no longer in the background but is increasingly the main drama. And the predictability that has always marked our physical world is now a thing of the past. We are still in the early days of this phenomenon; on current trajectories of fossil fuel burning, however, we will likely see at least a tripling of the heat we've caused so far.

Climate: In political and cultural terms, the mood of the moment. Given the rapid heating now underway, the crucial question is whether humans can muster movements large and savvy enough to interfere with the political power of the fossil fuel industry and quickly cease the combustion of hydrocarbons. By dramatically dropping the price and increasing the efficiency of solar and wind power, engineers have given us an opening, but we will need to move more quickly than at present to exploit it. The point, therefore, of growing movements like Extinction Rebellion or Fridays for the Future or 350.org is to change that mood – to shift the zeitgeist.

Another way of saying this is that our ability to stabilize the physical climate rests on our ability to destabilize the political climate. And quickly.

Climate Risk Communities

collective actions | communities | → Connectedness | → Declaration of Rebellion | inter-urban climate networks | → Resilience | → The Sharing Economy | unequal interconnectedness | world risk society diagnosis | → World Scientists' Warning to Humanity

Sociopolitically speaking, anthropogenic climate change is ambivalent and conflictual. As it threatens to undermine conditions of life for humans and nonhumans across the world, and to release new resource wars and mass migrations, climatic threats are *also* generating new conditions for solidarity and commonality beyond national boundaries. Such at least is the vision with which German sociologist Ulrich Beck coined the concept of climate risk communities.[1] This concept is crucial if we are serious about searching for common ground across difference in the era of the Anthropocene.

Already in the mid 1990s, Beck argued that in world risk society, the distinction between nature and culture was rapidly losing all foundation, alongside distinctions between local and global, 'them' and 'us'.[2] Transboundary risks like ozone depletion, nuclear radiation, agricultural chemicals and global warming was un- and remaking relations and heralding a cosmopolitan era of unequal, planetary interconnectedness. When 15 years later geologists would debate the Anthropocene as a new epoch in the Earth's history, one in which 'humanity' had attained planet-transforming powers, Beck would be forgiven for suggesting that, finally, the natural sciences were catching up with the social sciences![3]

Beck was not alone, of course, in sensing the serious sociopolitical upheavals underway in the wake of ecological disruptions. Writing in parallel, French anthropologist Bruno Latour similarly deployed the ozone hole debacle, made of chemical and political reactions, to herald the end of the modernist belief in Nature, capital N, as a purified ontological domain knowable and controllable by the techno-sciences.[4] Allied to this, American feminist philosopher of science Donna Haraway invoked the world's multiform biological agencies in her call for less omnipotent and more situated ways of knowing natureculture relations.[5] Such a project would feed, she argued, from cross-cutting conversations spanning the radical heterogeneity of life across the planet, with no Eurocentric God's-eye view to guarantee the outcome.

Amidst this landscape of important interlocutors – of which many more deserve attention – Beck's world risk society diagnosis stands out for its sustained insistence on linking global environmental risks to the exploration of a world being rewritten in its most fundamental sociopolitical coordinates. Foremost amongst these is the very question of belonging and community. Whereas early, or 'first' modern, industrial societies were shaped by what Irish political scientist Benedict Anderson dubbed the imagined community of the nation state, public life today is shaped by risky affiliations and interconnectedness that criss-cross any stabilized sense of the near and the far away.[6] To capture this new Anthropocene condition, Beck engaged in theorizing and exploring the planet-spanning conditions and effects of new climate risk communities.

I myself had the enormous privilege of partaking in this particular conceptual moment, situated as it was in collective attempts to study and compare diverse climate riskscapes in East Asia and Europe as well as their unequal forms of entanglement. Formally, we defined climate risk communities as 'new transnational constellations of social actors, arising from common experiences of mediated climatic threats, organized

Anders Blok (born 1978, located in Copenhagen, DK) is Associate Professor of Sociology at the University of Copenhagen. He has published widely within science and technology studies (STS), urban studies, environmental sociology and social theory. He is co-author, with Torben Jensen, of *Bruno Latour: Hybrid Thoughts in a Hybrid World* (2011) and co-editor, with Ignacio Farías, of *Urban Cosmopolitics* (2016).

around pragmatic reasoning of causal relations and responsibilities, and thereby *potentially* enabling collective action, cosmopolitical decision-making and international norm generation'.[7] Transnational climate activism fits this definition, as do new inter-urban climate networks and eco-technological innovation alliances, sitting alongside the more unbounded ways in which science, politics, economy and everyday life now all reorients towards anticipated threats to humankind.

Note the term 'potentially', however: the rise of new climate risk communities to facilitate ambitious forms of so-called green transitions towards more sustainable societies is held up here, in Beck's wider thinking, as *one* amongst other, perhaps more plausible and certainly less benign, future possibilities. To Beck, tensions over (un-)sustainability act as the endemic Janus face of world risk society as a state of perpetual unrest, one in which society's power institutions are forever on democratic trial for their ability to learn, self-correct and become accountable to the risky futures they themselves have begotten. History here is open-ended, and Beck's own conceptual efforts, akin to a practice of hope, meant to push the playing field ever so slightly away from threatening probabilities and towards new possibilities.

Unlike popular stereotypes of the 'Western intellectual' broadcasting his framework to the rest of the world, true to form Beck acted in these cross-continental settings more like a dialogical-cosmopolitan thinker out to learn from diverse experiences of a world at risk.[8] Such curiosity is foreshadowed in his work through the crucial distinction between cosmopolitanism and cosmopolitization. Whereas the Western-philosophical tradition from the Stoics to Kant and Arendt has concerned itself mostly with cosmopolitanism as a normative ideal of world citizenship, cosmopolitization is what unfolds in the unwanted and sometimes unseen globalized social tensions set in train by climatic and other global risks. Such tensions unfold in the vernacular of everyday life, undercut existing national jurisdictions and intensify transnational hybridity through new geographies of unequal interconnectedness.

After all, much like a sociopolitical version of a Freudian return of the repressed, the 'side effects' borne via accumulated carbon emissions carry the subliminal message that what happens when I turn on my electric toothbrush in Copenhagen is tied in indirect but consequential ways to intensified flooding events, draughts and famines in places like Surat in North-West India (two cities where I myself have done climate-related fieldwork). More generally, Beck was adamant in pointing out how anthropogenic climate change exacerbates and intensifies globalized socio-natural inequalities, in that risks are generated predominantly in the Global North yet initially impact the hardest in already vulnerable regions of the Global South. Even *this* conflictual process is sociopolitically ambivalent, however, in that it *also* serves to spur various activist-political negotiations regarding calls for global climate justice.[9]

My own work deals primarily with questions of *urban* climate politics, a domain in which the notion of cosmopolitan risk community immediately resonates with important, real-world tendencies. Most importantly, over the past 15–20 years, cities of all hues and sizes have banded together in still more voluntary intra- and interregional climate and sustainability networks, sharing know-how and cooperatively setting new norms of sustainable urbanism. The 94 privileged and powerful world cities banded together in the C40 network – including the likes of New York, Tokyo, London and Singapore – have successfully accrued world public-political attention to themselves for their largely technology-driven efforts to reduce what remain disproportionally large carbon footprints. In stark eco-ideological contrast, yet in similarly cooperative ways, networks of smaller Transition Towns have mushroomed across Europe and beyond.

Increasingly across the northern hemisphere, cities reframe post-industrial waterfronts into transnational showcases for 'advanced' forms of 21st-century eco-urbanism. On the ground, however, professional, political-economic and public-activist groups route and translate climate risk communities in place- and history-specific ways.[10] In Rotterdam, for instance, water professionals in engineering, architecture and urban planning are busy positioning themselves as the climate adaptation capital of the world, deploying new water-sensitive designs also along postcolonial routes as part of development assistance in South-East Asia (Fig. 1).[11] In Yokohama, by contrast, a good spread of corporate Japan, from Nissan to Panasonic, is teaming up in public-private partnership visions of Asian-style smart eco-urbanism, routed mainly to the vast and fast-growing market of Chinese urban development. Meanwhile in Seoul-Incheon, government is reacting to popular disconcertment with nuclear power following the Fukushima Daiichi disaster in Japan in 2011 by tying public solar-power investments to the promise of a post-nuclear-power future.

Fig. 1. Network of Rotterdam-based climate adaptation initiatives, deploying web hyperlinks to illustrate the existence of a far-flung climate risk community. Governmental and research organizations dominate the community. The Delta Conference and Alliance has participants from 18 countries, including Vietnam, Indonesia and Myanmar. The C40 platform is visible in the periphery.

Prior to his premature death in 2015, Beck himself acted as a public intellectual on the part of concerned cosmopolitan publics inside those political-institutional learning processes that followed in the wake of Fukushima Daiichi and led to what became the German energy transition (*Energiewende*). As such, he set a demanding example of engaged and dialogical scholarship for others to follow as the socio-cultural sciences turn to grapple with the new exigencies of the Anthropocene. Nowadays, such efforts tend to exert themselves in new materialist reckonings with earthly processes, in eco-Marxist revisions of the history of capitalist exploitation of cheap nature since the 16th century, and via the (re-)appearance in collective history of a ticklish Gaia as planetary subject likely out for revenge.[12]

These conceptual efforts valuably push and pull at the world risk society diagnosis, opening new avenues for thinking beyond Beck's vision. Even so, the notion of climate risk communities usefully reminds us that, in the threat-filled landscapes of the Anthropocene, questions of commonality and belonging – as well as of conflict and confrontation – will exert themselves at neither the local, the national, nor some unified global scale. Rather, they will continue to play out in processes of risky and collective translation among senses of place and senses of planet[13] and in attempts to confront and diplomatically mediate across diverse visions of their trans-local, cosmopolitan alignment for more viable and liveable futures.

Works cited:

Anderson, Benedict. 1983. *Imagined Communities: Reflections on the Origin and Spread of Nationalism*. London: Verso.

Beck, Ulrich. 1999. *World Risk Society*. London: Wiley.

Beck, Ulrich. 2010. 'Remapping Social Inequalities in an Age of Climate Change: For a Cosmopolitan Renewal of Sociology'. *Global Networks*, 10 (2), pp. 165–181.

Beck, Ulrich, Anders Blok, David Tyfield and Joy Y. Zhang. 2013. 'Cosmopolitan Communities of Climate Risk: Conceptual and Empirical Suggestions for a New Research Agenda'. *Global Networks*, 13 (1), pp. 1–21.

Blok, Anders. 2015. 'Towards Cosmopolitan Middle-Range Theorizing: A Metamorphosis in the Practice of Social Theory?' *Current Sociology*, 63 (1), pp. 110–114.

Blok, Anders. 2019. 'Climate Riskscapes in World Port Cities: Situating Urban-Cosmopolitan Risk Communities via Ulrich Beck's Comparative Tactics'. *Global Networks*, https://doi.org/10.1111/glob.12258. Accessed 3 December 2019.

Blok, Anders, and Casper B. Jensen. 2019. 'The Anthropocene Event in Social Theory: On Ways of Problematizing Nonhuman Materiality Differently'. *The Sociological Review*, 67 (6), pp. 1195–1211.

Haraway, Donna. 1991. *Simians, Cyborgs, and Women: The Reinvention of Nature*. New York: Routledge.

Heise, Ursula K. 2008. *Sense of Place and Sense of Planet: The Environmental Imagination of the Global*. Oxford: Oxford University Press.

Latour, Bruno. 1993. *We Have Never Been Modern*. Cambridge, MA: Harvard University Press.

Co-existence

→ Chthulucene | → Corals | → Creation | defamiliarize our mental habits | → Environment | → Feminism | → New Materialism | → Object-Oriented Ontology | → Posthuman | → Power | → Queer | the freedom to affect and be affected by others | → Violence | 'we' are neither One, nor the Same

That humans should learn to coexist with non-humans of both the organic (animals, plants, the planet as a whole) and the inorganic (technological networks, algorithms etc.) kind is by now a point of consensus. This realization is framed by the posthuman predicament,[1] defined as the convergence of posthumanism on the one hand and post-anthropocentrism on the other. The former criticizes the universal humanist claim that 'Man' is the measure of *all* things, while the latter targets species hierarchy and anthropocentric exceptionalism. The two critical axes overlap and are often used interchangeably in general debates, but they do not necessarily follow from each other. You can be critical of Western humanism and remain perfectly anthropocentric, or critique anthropocentrism but reassert humanistic values. By stressing their convergence, I mean to respect their specificity, both in terms of genealogies and practical implications, but also avoid segregating their respective perspectives and knowledge claims.

The posthuman convergence is not a future utopia or dystopia, but a feature of our historicity:[2] the simultaneous occurrence of the Fourth Industrial Revolution[3] and the Sixth Extinction.[4] Their convergence dissolves a number of traditional social distinctions between growth and decline and also lifts conceptual divides between nature and culture, human life (bios) and non-human life (zoe), thus expanding our understanding of the multiple ecologies we partake of. The separation of the human from all other species is crucial to Western philosophy and its project of modernity. Our culture tends to define the human/Man mostly by what he is not – that is to say, through dualistic oppositions which aim to confirm that he is not a woman/LBGTQ+/animal/indigenous/vegetable/mineral. These oppositional patterns oppose Man to a range of sexualized, racialized and naturalized 'others' that are excluded from the rights and entitlements of humanity. Defined by negation of the devalorized others, Man institutes an exclusionary vision of the human as the thinking being par excellence, the master of an exceptionally intelligent species – *Homo sapiens* – that deserves to be the dominant culture. The gender is no coincidence, as this is also a patriarchal power structure.

A credible argument for coexistence, collaboration, community and collective action, stressing transversal interconnections, therefore, must confront this particular vision of the human within the fraught landscape of the posthuman convergence. But how does one embrace the non-human agents and entities as integral elements of one's activity of thinking and producing knowledge? There is a substantive difference between accepting the structural interdependence among species and actually treating the non-humans as equal fellows and knowledge collaborators. I want to argue, however, that this is precisely the qualitative challenge of the posthuman convergence: we need to defamiliarize our mental habits and learn to think differently about what 'we' are in the process of becoming as heterogeneous subject assemblages.

Mindful that 'human' is not a neutral term but one that polices access to powers, entitlements, rights, social visibility and a sense of belonging, I argue for a critical posthuman stance that moves beyond dominant humanism and Eurocentric anthropocentrism and the hierarchies they uphold. This confronts us with a fundamental tension: 'we' may well

Rosi Braidotti (born 1954, located in Utrecht, NL) is Distinguished University Professor at Utrecht University. Her publications deal with continental philosophy, gender and feminist theories, and contemporary humanities from a posthumanist angle. Key publications include *Nomadic Subjects* (1994), *Nomadic Theory* (2011), *The Posthuman* (2013) and *Posthuman Knowledge* (2019).

be together in confronting the threats and challenges of our times, however 'we' are neither One, nor the Same. We are rather positioned differently in terms of power, entitlement and access to the very ecologies – environmental, social, technological and affective – that define us.[5] Therefore, 'WE' are not a homogeneous, unitary notion but a complex and diverse one, reflecting the multiple differences and tensions that compose 'us'.

This grounded approach is not relativism but rather the awareness of embedded and embodied materially located positions. Theoretically, it can be rendered through a number of different methods – for instance, the multidirectional or nomadic feminist politics of locations,[6] conjoined with the neo-materialist politics of immanence.[7] Both of these can be set in dialogue with much older indigenous epistemologies,[8] which are revived today by decolonial critiques in terms of their perspectivism.[9] These methods emphasize transversal connections across species and entities and function on a multiplicity of scales, layers and locations to account for contemporary posthuman subjects and the knowledge they produce.

This asserts the diversity of zoe – non-human life – in a non-hierarchical manner that acknowledges the differential intelligence of matter and the respective degrees of ability and creativity of all organisms. Living systems, which I redefine as zoe-geo-techno entities, are thus thought of as partners in knowledge production, which means that thinking and knowing are not the prerogative of humans alone but are the stuff of the world.[10] The world is defined by the coexistence of multiple organic species, computational networks and technological artefacts alongside each other. Zoe-geo-techno transversal entities allow us to think across previously segregated species, categories and domains.

The transversal, zoe-geo-techno-mediated subject formations of our times call for new grounding. My philosophical proposal in order to ground coexistence in a process ontology that allows for both dynamic flows and ethical accountability is to adopt neo-materialist immanence, coupled with feminist and anti-racist politics of locations. This approach rests on a vital, embedded and embodied, affective and relational understanding of living entities, including humans. Let me explain.

Vital neo-materialism refers to the concept that matter, the world and humans themselves are not dualistic entities structured according to principles of internal or external opposition but rather materially embedded subjects-in-process circulating within webs of shared relations. Following contemporary Spinozism,[11] all entities are variations on a common matter. This translates into a nature-culture continuum, which is best expressed by Australian philosopher Genevieve Lloyd's assertion that we are all 'part of nature', in so far as nature has become nature-cultural and that it is technologically mediated.[12] Matter is defined as one, intelligent and self-organizing, and it is driven by the ontological desire to express a fundamental freedom to endure in its existence. To be alive means to enjoy the freedom to go on becoming, within a differential materially embedded process ontology, aware that we differ from each other all the more as we co-define ourselves within the same living matter.

Ontological relationality is of the essence. Each individuated entity is the expression of a common core, which is the freedom to affect and be affected by others. The motor of individuation is an entity's relational capacity and the ability to grow with and become alongside others. This kind of immanence also supports a democratic move towards a kind of ontological pacifism, driven by affirmative ethics, which implies the rejection of negativity, antagonism and of violent dialectical oppositions. The understanding of living matter as a symbiotic and collaborative system of co-dependence supports an ethics that rests on an ethology of forces – that is to say, qualitative degrees of relational interconnections across different entities as variations within a common matter. This produces a displacement of anthropocentric and unitary visions of human subjects and their moral value systems. It also prioritizes affirmation and joyful interdependence over negativity and confrontation. Ethics as relational forces makes qualitative distinctions within the continuum of self-organizing vital systems, of the environmental, technological, psychic and social kinds.[13]

This avoids both naturalistic foundationalism and social constructivism in favour of transversal relationality. A subject thus defined does not coincide with liberal individualism but is rather a haecceity – which means an event of complex singularities or intensities, an immanent degree of power as *potentia*.[14] Subjectivity is both post-personal and pre-individual and fully immersed in the conditions that one is trying to understand and modify, if not overturn.

Posthuman thought therefore needs to fulfil the multiple requirements of a process ontology, along thematic, methodological and conceptual lines. Thematically, it involves the inclusion of non-anthropomorphic objects of study, including networked technological apparatus and big data sets. Methodologically, it rests on transversal and post-constructivist approaches. Conceptually, it supports interrelations and cross-hybridization, overcoming the denaturalized vision of a social order somehow disconnected from its environmental and organic foundations. It enacts a set of zoe-geo-techno mediations that entail qualitative shifts of perspective. This has practical implications as well. It is crucial, for instance, to see the links between the greenhouse effect, the depletion of biodiversity and the worsening global status of women and LBGTQ+, racism, xenophobia, populism and frantic consumerism and not stop at any fragmented portions of these realities.

The neo-materialist expressivist method expresses the embodied and embedded materialist nature of the subject and a non-antagonistic, trustful relationship to 'Life', living systems and to lived experience. It also expresses the dynamic interaction of differences outside dialectical oppositions, as modulations of the same matter, in a multilayered and multidirectional relational manner. This post-constructivist method stresses the need to account for processes and for a change of scale, to unveil power relations in the multiple specific locations, and discursive and social perspectives. A post-constructivist, transversal method facilitates links to animality, to algorithmic systems, to planetary organism, on equal but rhizomic terms that involve territories, geologies, ecologies and technologies of survival.

This expressivist, post-constructivist approach also foregrounds issues of power and entitlement, as opposed to the standardized corporate sound bites about the social and moral responsibility of institutions, including the university. The posthuman convergence raises questions that have less to do with morality – that is to say, conventions – than with ethics – that is to say, ethology of forces and power. Morality deals with rules and protocols, while ethics, in the affirmative neo-materialist mode, interrogates power as both the negative sense of entrapment (*potestas*) and the positive one of empowerment (*potentia*). The moralization of public debates on all the key issues like climate change is a trait of neoliberal governance, and it avoids serious analyses of power. It is all the more misleading as cognitive capitalism[15] is primarily responsible for the immoral and unjust monetarization of all that lives and the privatization of knowledge production. Advanced capitalism also produces an opportunistic displacement of anthropocentrism, in so far as it profits from the knowledge about the genetic and algorithmic codes of multiple living systems, organic and inorganic, and capitalizes on all species, human and non-human alike. This is alternatively known as 'bio-piracy',[16] or 'life as surplus'.[17]

Posthuman affirmative ethics is the alternative to the ruthless exploitation of Life in advanced capitalism. It is a praxis of the collective construction of affirmative relational values and projects to sustain the construction of alternative posthuman subject positions. Affirmative ethics does not reinstate the normative system based on humanistic and anthropocentric premises but rather foregrounds relational ethics, so as to honour our multiple ecologies and address the complexity of the posthuman convergence. Affirmation is not a psychological disposition but an ethological one: it is the ability to open up to others and take in – and take on – more of the world, whereas negativity is a decrease in the same ability. Affirmative ethics embraces non-human agents and devises forms of solidarity, justice, care and democratic debate and dissent, in a transnational, cross-species transversal manner.

In this regard, posthuman subjects are a work-in-progress: they emerge as both a critical and a creative project within the posthuman convergence along posthumanist and post-anthropocentric axes. Their heterogeneity pre-empts any predetermined outcome: what they may become is a matter of relational alliances and on-going material practices, as they are capable of different things, forces and speeds. This is not relativism but rather immanent neo-materialism and situated perspectivism.

Coexistence defined with affirmative ethics stresses collaboration while avoiding hasty reconstructions of 'Humanity'.[18] The focus remains on the differential materially embedded and embodied locations and perspectives. 'We' – the subjects of the posthuman convergence – are confronted by painful contradictions: we are electronically interlinked, but also divided and fragmented by social inequalities, economic disparities and xenophobic suspicions. Humanity is recreated as a reactive, vulnerable category bonded in fear but remains fractured by new and old power differences.

I resist the abstract idea of a 'new' pan-humanity, bonded in shared anxiety about survival and extinction and the recompositions of corporate neo-humanism and its opportunistic moralistic rhetoric. I propose instead embedded and embodied, relational and affective cartographies of the new power relations that are emerging from the current geo-political and post-anthropocentric world order. Class, race, gender and sexual orientation, age and able-bodiedness are more than ever significant markers of human 'normality'. Accordingly, we need environmentalisms of the poor[19] and posthuman visions from those who were considered less-than-human.[20]

Yet, considering the global reach of the problems we are facing in the posthuman convergence, it is the case that 'we' are indeed in *this* anthropocenic crisis together. Such awareness must not conceal or flatten out the power differentials that sustain the collective subject ('we') and its endeavour (*this*). It may be more useful to work toward multiple actualizations of new transversal alliances, communities and planes of composition of the new humans: many ways of developing affirmative posthuman forms of coexistence together.

Works cited:

Alaimo, Stacy. 2010. *Bodily Natures: Science, Environment, and the Material Self.* Bloomington: Indiana University Press.

Braidotti, Rosi. 2011. *Nomadic Subjects: Embodiment and Sexual Difference in Contemporary Feminist Theory*. New York: Columbia University Press.

Braidotti, Rosi. 2013. *The Posthuman*. Cambridge, UK: Polity.

Braidotti, Rosi. 2017. 'Posthuman, All Too Human'. *The 2017 Tanner Lectures on Human Values*. Utah: Whitney Humanities Center, Yale University and the Tanner Foundation.

Braidotti, Rosi. 2019a. *Posthuman Knowledge.* Cambridge, UK: Polity.

Braidotti, Rosi, and Simone Bignall, eds. 2018. *Posthuman Ecologies.* London: Rowman & Littlefield International.

Braidotti, Rosi, and Maria Hlavajova, eds. 2018. *Posthuman Glossary*. London: Bloomsbury Academic.

Cooper, Melinda. 2008. *Life as Surplus: Biotechnology and Capitalism in the Neoliberal Era.* Seattle: University of Washington Press.

Deleuze, Gilles. 1988. *Spinoza: Practical Philosophy*. San Francisco: City Lights Books.

Deleuze, Gilles. 2003. *Pure Immanence: Essays on a Life.* New York: Zone Books.

Deleuze, Gilles, and Félix Guattari. 1994. *What is Philosophy?* New York: Columbia University Press.

Descola, Philippe. 2009. 'Human Natures'. *Social Anthropology*, 17 (2), pp. 145–157.

Descola, Philippe. 2013. *Beyond Nature and Culture.* Chicago: University of Chicago Press.

Gatens, Moira, and Genevieve Lloyd. 1999. *Collective Imaginings*. New York: Routledge.

Guattari, Félix. 2000. *The Three Ecologies*. London: Athlone Press.

Hayles, N. Katherine. 1999. *How We Became Posthuman: Virtual Bodies in Cybernetics, Literature and Informatics.* Chicago: University of Chicago Press.

Kolbert, Elizabeth. 2014. *The Sixth Extinction*. New York: Henry Holt Company.

Lloyd, Genevieve. 1994. *Part of Nature: Self-Knowledge in Spinoza's Ethics.* Ithaca: Cornell University Press.

Moulier-Boutang, Yann. 2012. *Cognitive Capitalism.* Cambridge, UK: Polity.

Nixon, Rob. 2011. *Slow Violence and the Environmentalism of the Poor.* Cambridge, MA: Harvard University Press.

Schwab, Klaus. 2015. 'The Fourth Industrial Revolution'. *Foreign Affairs*, 12 December.

Shiva, Vandana. 1997. *Biopiracy: The Plunder of Nature and Knowledge.* Boston: South End Press.

Viveiros de Castro, Eduardo. 1998. 'Cosmological Deixis and Amerindian Perspectivism'. *The Journal of the Royal Anthropological Institute,* 4 (3), pp. 469–488.

Viveiros de Castro, Eduardo. 2009. *Cannibal Metaphysics: For a Post-structural Anthropology.* Minneapolis: Univocal Publishing.

Whyte, Kyle P. 2016. 'Is It Colonial déjà vu? Indigenous People and Climate Injustice'. In Joni Adamson, Michael Davis and Hsinya Huang, eds. *Humanities for the Environment: Integrating Knowledges, Forging new Constellations of Practice*, pp. 88–104. Abingdon-on-Thames: Earthscan Publications.

Further reading:

Braidotti, Rosi. 2002. *Metamorphoses: Towards a Materialist Theory of Becoming*. Cambridge, UK: Polity.

Braidotti, Rosi. 2006. *Transpositions: On Nomadic Ethics*. Cambridge, UK: Polity.

Braidotti, Rosi. 2016a. 'The Contested Posthumanities'. In Rosi Braidotti and Paul Gilroy, eds. *Contesting Humanities*. London: Bloomsbury Academic.

Braidotti, Rosi. 2016b. 'The Critical Posthumanities; Or, Is Medianatures to Naturecultures as Zoe is to Bios?' *Cultural Politics*, 12 (3), pp. 380–390.

Braidotti, Rosi. 2019b. 'A Theoretical Framework for the Critical Posthumanities'. *Theory, Culture & Society*, 36 (6). First published online in 2018. https://doi.org/10.1177/0263276418771486. Accessed 21 January 2020.

Connectedness

→ Body | collective repression | → Creation | → Home | → Imagine | nature's attempts at understanding itself | nature's vibrant energy | → New Materialism | → Sensitivity | the concrete | the myth of economic growth | tipping points | to be vulnerable and powerful | → Window of Opportunity | → World Scientists' Warning to Humanity

Josefine Klougart (born 1985, located in Copenhagen, DK) is a novelist, who graduated from Forfatterskolen (The National School of Creative Writing) in Copenhagen in 2011. She studied art history and comparative literature at Aarhus University and held a guest professorship at the University of Bern in 2017. She is co-founder of and editor at the Danish publishing house Forlaget Gladiator and is the author of six published novels, with the 2016 *New Forest* as the most recent release. Klougart's books have been translated into 15 languages.

I remember the warmth, how it rises up through my thin nylon trousers from the horse underneath me, as I ride under the trees in the fringe of the wood because the rain has begun. I am a child, 11 years old, maybe 12, as I wait there, sitting on the horse in the fringe, listening to the rain falling on yellow and red and green leaves. I ride through the wood, the shower passes, a greyish white flank opens up in the sky. And that is when everything seems to become connected, the heat from the horse's body, the scent of the pine trees and the wet earth and the sun that suddenly breaks through somewhere over the sea, and the sun, the sun suddenly sends its long ribbons of light in between the tree trunks, causing the water in the air to sparkle as we come out on the other side, where the landscape slants, and the horse begins its descent, gingerly picking its way down the slope, sort of braiding the air in front of itself. The horse brings one front leg forward and then in front of the other, again and again, the hooves slipping a few centimetres until they grip the soil, and I sense my own body, sense how it grows heavy and soft and almost becomes one with the animal in a way that, for a moment, a few seconds or minutes, makes it impossible for me to say whether it is my hoof or the horse's, impossible to determine where my body ends and the horse's begins, what is the forest's breathing and what is mine.

In the course of our lives, there are moments when the world speaks to us with particular intensity. A profound connectedness reveals itself to us; the concrete world, nature, reminds us of something we had forgotten we knew. Thus, today I can look out at the trees, all yellow and red and luminous, and at the same time, equally clearly, see another afternoon, another autumn, on a day when the trees had the same colour and the air was similarly dense and heavy with rain. We lean into nature and have a sense of being connected to it. We sense that we are alive and engaged in a constant exchange with all living things, nature around us, other people, everything, really, even other ages and other spaces that are otherwise invisible to us, sensing them as present, pulsating, breathing alongside us. What we sense is that being human, above all, means being part of nature's vibrant energy – being nature, simply. The particular part of nature that is able to ride a horse and sense how the two move together as one body, sense that the rain falls more softly from the leaves than out in the open and – at the same time – perceive itself as the one perceiving this, now. It is a sense of unity that lasts for a moment, and as long as it lasts we sense, instinctively, wordlessly, the greater whole that we are a part of. That sense, the sense of connectedness with nature, also contains an awareness of the fundamental human condition: we experience unity and we experience ourselves having this experience, experience how we are thrown off and are left standing alone in what remains, but with the memory and the knowledge that the connectedness may reveal itself to us again.

Poetry and literature are full of these types of experiences, moments of epiphany. As when Virginia Woolf writes in 'A Sketch of the Past', 'If life has a base that it stands upon, if it is a bowl that one fills and fills and fills – then my bowl without a doubt stands upon this memory. It is of lying half asleep, half awake, in a bed in the nursery at St Ives. It is of hearing the waves breaking, one, two, one, two, and sending a splash of water over the beach; and then breaking, one, two, one, two, behind a yellow blind. It is of hearing the blind draw its little acorn across the floor as the wind blew the blind out. It is of lying and hearing this splash and seeing this light, and feeling, it is almost impossible that I should be here; of feeling the purest ecstasy I can conceive.'[1] W.B. Yeats writes about similar experiences, like the ones that create a hierarchy of recollected images that a poet must test his or her poetry against: 'The final test of the value of any work of art to our particular needs, is when we place it in the hierarchy of those recollections which are our standards and our beacons. At the head of mine are a certain night scene long ago, when I heard the wind blowing in a bed of reeds by the border of a little lake, a Japanese picture of cranes flying through a blue sky, and a line or two out of Homer.' And Matthew Arnold speaks of poetry's '"touchstones", high points of imaginative experience – "those recollections which are our standards and our beacons"'.[2] And when William Faulkner writes about how a single picture, the picture of a girl sitting in muddy drawers in a pear tree, can be the single point from which an entire novel grows,[3] that refers exactly to that poetic power, the inherent intensity of the moment, the perceived, recollected or constructed moment. This is not an exalted experience, it is not religious, it exists in the concrete world and does not point out of this world to something *beyond*; it always points *into the concrete*, to the depth of what exists *here*, and which we have access to when we are able to lean into the world and experience it with the full force and sensitivity of our consciousness.

Much has changed since that day in the forest. I am different, the world is different, the horse is long dead and gone, taken to the butcher in Tved, the stable almost lost in a thicket of brambles and stinging nettles, as tall as a man, in the back of my parents' garden; the wood has been felled, and there is no shelter for the rain, which every year washes sand and stones down through the ravine, and new sand is trucked in to preserve the path to the right of it. However, the image of the forest that day, the sunlight extending in ribbons in between the tree trunks, the sensation of the horse's movements that are transmitted to my body and somehow become mine, the feeling of being able to reach out and be one with something that has existed long before me and which is going to be there long after I am gone – it is as clear to me now as it was then, this sense of connectedness.

We live in a time when it is almost impossible to write about the sense of connectedness to nature without also writing about how we, at least in our part of the world, appear to have forgotten that connection. We live in a collective repression of the fundamental fact that we are not separate from nature, that it is not possible to maintain a distinction between human beings here and nature out there. We are not only part of the same cycle; we are nature. As the Danish poet Inger Christensen points out, poetry, philosophy, mathematics and science – everything that makes up our culture – represent different forms of perception and understanding: different ways in which humankind strives to grasp nature and the world.[4] And since humankind itself is nature, all of this, our entire proud cultural history, is really nature's attempts at understanding itself.[5] Culture and science do not mark a distinction between humankind and nature but an intimate connection. When we speak, we are nature speaking; when we think, we are nature thinking; when we subdue nature out there, we are nature subduing something inside ourselves.

Over the past century, we have had a huge impact on our planet; we are facing climate changes that threaten to destroy our own living conditions and those of most other species. We have created an economy that requires us to consume and produce, to keep the wheels spinning. A globalized economy with internal dynamics and power structures of such an inscrutable nature that they seem completely abstract to most of us and de facto makes it impossible for us to understand what is happening and take action. It is difficult to hold on to the perception of something delicately vibrant, difficult to recall something we only glimpsed. We have assigned the experience of connectedness and the euphoria Woolf speaks of to the private sphere – to art, rave parties, meditation and religious contexts. We have created a hierarchy where the concrete sensuous experiences need to be elevated to an abstract level, ideally to the rational faculty of consciousness, to have any value at all. Everything has to be translated, elevated to symbolic order – and thus we empty the world, without hardly noticing it. We reap nature's resources and forget to give something back; we deplete the world and forget that we are really depleting ourselves. And then we are left standing there, like suspicious little fantasists who fail to believe our own eyes when we see nature begin to change because it answers us in a language we do not understand, operates on a scale that is abstract to people who only believe in what they can grasp, who are suspicious of their own feelings and who fail to make connections – not only with nature but also with their own tender, sensitive experiences with reflection and action.

Whatever the case may be, it is remarkable that as a species we seem incapable of responding to the existential threat we are facing. Thirty years have passed since James Hansen, head of the American NASA Goddard Institute, warned against the consequences of the continued use of fossil fuels. We have had three decades to wean ourselves off coal, oil and gas and have basically made no progress; on the contrary. Our forests are going up in flames, the ice is melting and the level of CO_2 in the atmosphere is as high as it was more than three million years ago, when water levels were 10–20 metres higher. Scientists tell us there is still time but also that it will take a rapid and pervasive transformation of our society.

It is difficult to find any indications that society is taking this message to heart. Our chance of stopping catastrophic climate change is growing increasingly theoretical. Our leaders simply do not take the action we know is necessary. Scientists have documented that if we do not begin a radical decarbonization of our societies now, nature's positive feedback mechanisms will lead to irreversible temperature rises. We do not know exactly where the so-called tipping points are – the points of no return – but we do know that they are close, and that by the time we find the precise answer, it will be too late.

That is why the United Nations' goal of keeping temperature increases under 1.5 °C is important, and that is why we cannot simply pin our hope on new technologies that have yet to be developed. As the American writer and futurologist Alex Steffen puts it, 'Winning slowly is basically the same thing as losing outright.'[6] We need to take radical action and we need to do it now.

In our part of the world, we still believe in the Enlightenment ideal that knowledge is power, but in practice it almost seems that the opposite is true: power is knowledge, since power creates the knowledge it needs in order to persist. 'Every society clings to a myth by which it lives. Ours is the myth of economic growth,' writes the British economist Tim Jackson in his report *Prosperity Without Growth*.[7] Jackson was economics commissioner on the UK Sustainable Development Commission. He was put on ice after describing how continued economic growth was incompatible with sustainable development.

There seems to be a broad consensus that economic growth is necessary, that economic growth is the answer to our problems. Hardly anyone addresses the fact that economic growth implies a growing consumption of resources and energy. That our investments in renewable energy are undermined by a growing demand for power. In the essay 'Why Growth Can't Be Green',[8] the English anthropologist Jason Hickel reviews three large-scale recent studies that seek to analyse what it takes to combine economic growth with sustainable development. The conclusion is clear: economic growth and resource consumption are related. Regardless how optimistic and, within the current system, unrealistic conditions the scientists feed into their scenarios – a global tax on resources, a tax on CO_2, great leaps in technological development and so forth – continued economic growth will require increased resource consumption. Today, we are already using many more resources than the planet is able to regenerate; continued economic growth is only going to make it worse.

'We are a part of nature, but we are also that unique part of nature that is able to consider nature and thus ourselves,' writes Inger Christensen.[9] We are a part of vibrant life, we breathe like trees, our bodies are energy, we are engaged in a constant exchange with the world around us. We are also the part of nature that, given our reflective consciousness, should be able to change our actions, now that we know that the course we are on is going to destroy the basis of our society.

That just has not happened yet. The system is strong, and we do not have much time. No one knows whether humankind will be able to act in time to stop the destructive forces, or whether we are bound into such abstract hierarchies of power and economic systems that the freedom to think is not going to transition into the freedom to act before it is too late. 'I believe we are losing the race. Climate change is running faster than we are,' said the UN secretary-general António Guterres in January 2019.[10]

We can only hope that our experience of powerlessness, our fear that it is already too late, will drive us to act and to make fundamental systemic changes rather than mere local and individual ones. I do not believe the answers to the crisis can come primarily from individuals, as *political consumers*. And I do not believe we can limit the climate changes within the required timespan without abandoning the notion of continued economic growth in favour of a goal of securing the basic needs of every person on the planet – with the requisite care for nature, which we are not only dependent on but a part of.

It may seem sentimental, here, on the verge of disaster, to point to our experiences of connectedness with nature as part of the answer as to how we can turn the trend and succeed in fundamentally changing society and economic policies. It might seem like a return to Romantic ideas, and to some degree maybe it is, but this is not about religious sentiments; it is not even about dogmatism. I believe these experiences are an important source of empowerment, a power that we can also use to achieve change – on an individual basis and in society. Precisely how that transfer of energy is going to take place I don't know. In fact, there is a great deal that I don't know but would like to explore and examine: this story contains so much doubt and so many mysteries. One of them is the mystery of life itself, what it is about and what it means to be human. To me, this mystery has to do with science as well as with my recollection of that rainy autumn day and many other days, a night on a mountain in Switzerland as well, a summer morning when I was seven and searched my parents' garden only to discover I was entirely on my own. Another mystery is how to effect political change, how to build a new and fairer, green and, perhaps, circular economy and sustainable production. Those are mysteries that we will need to address, individually and together, a little at a time, proceeding with insistence, calm and great energy.

One place to start might be to take the anxiety seriously that many of us feel in our bodies and which we tend to soothe or run away from instead of leaning into it and examining it. When WHO, the World Health Organization, points to depression as the next major epidemic, an epidemic that affects the privileged Western world in particular, might this not be related to the fact that we are destroying the basis of the continued existence of civilization? Perhaps the depression afflicting society, at least from a broader perspective, is an indication of a culture that is in mourning over having lost a connection to something vital.

By attributing value to our experiences of connectedness, by taking them seriously as an opportunity to sense and understand what it means to be human, we are also leaving ourselves open to acknowledging our vulnerability and the need to mobilize much more energy in the effort to transform our societies and economies – so that we give more than we take and share what we have much more equitably.

What I am speaking about here is also a necessary defence of the concrete, of what we can perceive, sense, see and point to. With our bodies, first of all, but also with art and science. We need to reach out with everything we have and everything we are. We need to use the power that lies in our sense of connectedness as a source of action. The sun falls through the trees in the city's parks, suburban hedges bloom in June, their heavy perfume enveloping the girl sitting on the warm paving stones, drawing with a white stone. And the boy who just discovered a snail on the Christianshavn Embankments in Copenhagen. Little moments like that arise all the time. With practice, we can learn to recognize the full breadth and depth of the world – and of nature and humankind. We have to dare to sense what we are up against, dare to mourn what we have lost. We have to insist on really seeing the life – the rich and diverse life – we are reshaping so radically. That is about looking at graphs and reports, about temperature increases and nature's self-intensifying processes, but it is also about the tangible experience of kicking a boot heel into the ice on a frosty January morning to give the animals access to water, scooping out the ice with your hands and then tucking them back into your pockets, fingering the bits of twine and kernels there. It is about sensing the anxiety inside you when you stand under a wild apple tree in June and realize there is not a single insect to be heard buzzing amongst the black branches and white blossoms, sensing the grief this brings. It is about the feeling of holding something immensely valuable in your hands while also being in the grips of something bigger. To be vulnerable and powerful at the same time, a child's hand, a tiny ripple in the sea and an entire world, stepping under a tree when it begins to rain, the way you did as a child, one autumn day long ago. The sound of the waves, the scent of ammonia in the stable, a cat snoozing in a sunbeam, a child waking up in a courtyard and a mother
getting
up.

I thank Lars Borking for our inspiring conversations and help with researching the scientific aspects of the text.

Works cited:

Christensen, Inger. 2000. *Hemmelighedstilstanden.* Copenhagen: Gyldendal.

Stein, Jean. 1956. 'The Art of Fiction'. *Paris Review*, 4 (12), Spring, pp. 28–52.

Haugland, Anne Gry. 2013. 'Digtets Natur'. *Kvant*, 4, December.

Heaney, Seamus. 1980. *Preoccupations: Selected Prose, 1968–1978.* New York: Farrar, Strauss and Giroux.

Hickel, Jason. 2018. 'Why Growth Can't Be Green'. https://www.jasonhickel.org/blog/2018/9/14/why-growth-cant-be-green, 14 September. Accessed 28 January 2020.

Jackson, Tim. 2009. *Prosperity without Growth? Foundations for the Economy of Tomorrow*, London: Sustainable Development Commission. https://www.growthintransition.eu/wp-content/uploads/prosperity_without_growth_report.pdf. Accessed 30 January 2020.

Steffen, Alex. 2017. 'The Last Decade'. https://thenearlynow.com/the-last-decade-and-you-489a5375fbe8. Accessed 28 January 2020.

WEF 2019. World Economic Forum. 'António Guterres: Read the UN Secretary-General's Davos Speech in Full'. https://www.weforum.org/agenda/2019/01/these-are-the-global-priorities-and-risks-for-the-future-according-to-antonio-guterres/, 24 January. Accessed 28 January 2020.

Woolf, Virginia. 1985. 'A Sketch of the Past' (1939). In *Moments of Being*, 2nd edition, pp. 64–65. San Diego: Harvest Book.

Corals

→ Biodiversity | → Capitalocene | → Chthulucene | → Coexistence | → Earthlings | ecosystem extinction | → Invisible | many Anthropocenes | multispecies individuals | → Posthuman | symbiosis | → Water

'Coral reefs will be the first, but certainly not the last, major ecosystem to succumb to the Anthropocene – the new geological epoch now emerging.'

Roger Bradbury, 2012.

Catastrophe

Corals are in the midst of a global crisis, affected by a toxic human-made cocktail of overfishing, agricultural runoffs, coastal development and climate change. By some predictions, tropical coral reefs will no longer constitute functional ecosystems by 2050 as a direct effect of human changes to their environment. Species extinction is one thing, ecosystem extinction is another, like the difference between murder and genocide. Thirty out of thirty-four phyla of animal life exist on coral reefs. In the spectre of coral reef mega-death, the abstract hyper-object of the Anthropocene is made concrete to experience, a terrible ghost come to life.

'Coral, which is like a stone, is red in color and rounded like a root, and it grows in the sea.'

Earle Caley and John F. Richards, 1956, p. 53. Quote from Theophrastus, Greek philosopher (372–287 BCE).

Wonder

Corals are ghost-like. To the ancient Greeks, corals failed to fit into neat categories. Aristotle, like his student Theophrastus, saw them as half plant, half stone: alive yet dead. Greek myth had it that coral had soaked up the blood of Medusa's decapitated head, giving it the capacity to turn hard when exposed to air. This power also gave red coral amulets the ability to protect children against witchcraft and the evil eye. By the 14th century, red coral was associated with piety, the Christ Child and the promise of Resurrection.

'Zoophyta: Composite animals efflorescing like vegetables'.

Charles Linné, 1806, p. 9. Swedish botanist Charles Linné was also known as Carl von Linnaeus.

Multispecies entanglements

Corals are multispecies individuals: dense associations of animal and plant that come to life because of each other. Between five and fifty million algae cells (called zooxanthellae) crowd inside every square centimetre of the skin of the polyp animal in scleractian corals. Modern microbiology calls this symbiosis, suggesting that evolution proceeds by multispecies association. Evolutionary individualism, as imagined by Darwinism and neo-Darwinism, has come under fire by this insight provided by coral multispecies individualism. So have classical evolutionary views of isolated species and kingdoms of life. But early modern scientists already imagined that animals and plants could sometimes be entangled in each other. During the Renaissance, the existence of zoophytes, composites of animal and vegetable life, was testimony to the wondrous power of God. The legendary vegetable lamb of Tartary was one example of this multispecies entanglement of animal and plant. Corals were another.

Nils Bubandt (born 1964, located in Denmark) is Professor of Anthropology at Aarhus University and currently engaged in a project about corals and the end of the world in Papua, Indonesia. He is co-editor-in-chief of the journal *Ethnos* and editor, with A. Tsing, H. Swanson and E. Gan, of an anthology on the more-than-human Anthropocene, entitled *Arts of Living on a Damaged Planet* (2017).

'About a quarter of all marine species may be found on coral reefs, even though this habitat occupies only an estimated 1 or 2 per cent of the area of the earth.'

Charles Sheppard, 2014, p. 65.

Abundance

Symbiosis, evolution by association, is the secret behind the incredible fecundity of tropical coral reefs. Coral reefs are the most productive of all ecosystems, in spite of the fact that they generally exist in nutrient-poor environments. A quarter of a million described species inhabit tropical coral reefs. Maybe three times as many species still await scientific discovery. Corals are the rain forests of the sea. And like forests, they are abundantly peopled, by nonhumans and humans.

'Encountering the sheer not-us, more-than-human worlding of the coral reefs, with their requirements for ongoing living and dying of their myriad critters, is also to encounter the knowledge that at least 250 million human beings today depend directly on the ongoing integrity of these holobiomes.'

Donna Haraway, 2016, p. 56.

Banal Evil

The humans who depend on coral reefs live muted lives, and yet there are many. The livelihood of a quarter of a billion people is directly tied to the coral reefs they inhabit. Most of these people live in the Global South. Distributed in nations that used to be colonies of European empires, these people face one of the many cruel banal evils of the Anthropocene. Historically, the inhabitants of coral reef worlds have contributed the least to the great industrial acceleration since the Second World War that has sent the world tumbling into the Anthropocene, and yet it is they who are now facing the most dramatic of its consequences first. There is not one Anthropocene; there are many.

'When we see an advertisement that links a picture of a tropical island to the word *paradise*, the longings that are kindled in us have a chain of transmission that stretches back to Daniel Defoe and Jean-Jacques Rousseau: the flight that will transport us to the island is merely an ember in that fire.'

Amitav Ghosh, 2016, p. 10.

Petrologics

Dreams are the real fuel of the Great Acceleration, not petroleum products. Climate change is driven by dreams: dreams of new things, dreams of faraway places, dreams of experiencing more. Capitalism is a dream economy: the production and fulfilment of dreams that have been condensed from colonial history, fiction and philosophy. Nature is one such condensed dream. And tourism, one of the industries that cater to this dream by promising holidays in natural and untouched places, is booming. Take dive tourism. In the late 1980s, there were two million certified PADI scuba divers worldwide. Today, 27 million have become certified through PADI alone. Many of these divers dream of marvelling at the wonders of the tropical coral reef, knowing full well that the flight that takes them there will accelerate its disappearance. Such is the cognitive dissonance of the Anthropocene.

Works cited:

Bradbury, Roger. 2012. 'A World Without Coral Reefs'. *The New York Times*, 13 July 2012. http://www.nytimes.com/2012/07/14/opinion/a-world-without-coral-reefs.html. Accessed 9 January 2020.

Caley, Earle, and John F. Richards. 1956. *Theophrastus: On Stones Introduction, Greek Text, English Translation and Commentary*. Original written in the fourth century. Columbus, OH: The Ohio State University.

Ghosh, Amitav. 2016. *The Great Derangement: Climate Change and the Unthinkable*. Chicago and London: Chicago University Press.

Haraway, Donna J. 2016. *Staying with the Trouble: Making Kin in the Chthulucene*. Durham, NC: Duke University Press Books.

Linné, Charles. 1806. *A General System of Nature Through the Three Grand Kingdoms of Animals, Vegetable, and Minerals: Animal Kingdom*. Vol. 4: *Worms*. London: Lackington, Allen and Co.

Sheppard, Charles. 2014. *Coral Reefs: A Very Short Introduction*. Oxford: Oxford University Press.

Further reading:

Bowen, James. 2015. *The Coral Reef Era: From Discovery to Decline: A History of Scientific Investigation from 1600 to the Anthropocene Epoch*. Cham: Springer.

Braverman, Irus. 2018. *Coral Whisperers: Scientists on the Brink*. Berkeley: University of California Press.

Davidson, Osha Gray. 1998. *The Enchanted Braid: Coming to Terms with Nature on the Coral Reef*. New York: John Wiley & Son.

McCalman, Iain. 2013. *The Reef. A Passionate History. The Great Barrier Reef from Captain Cook to Climate Change*. New York: Farrar, Straus and Giroux.

Creation

a world where the mind never works without the body → Body → Ecology → Feminism → Imagine → New Materialism prehistoric futuristic world → Queer

I want to show my daughter how to make things. She loves sawing, she loves things that connect, to be able to split things up, take them apart and reassemble them in new ways; I want LEGO, but not LEGO. I imagine all kinds of different materials: bamboo, tissue, metal, fibres, linen, crystals. That these parts are also what the world of adults is made of. We bake a cake. She licks the spoon, as I did when I was a kid. I am not afraid of salmonella. I want her to know how to shoot a bow, to be able to survive, in this world, and in some prehistoric world that has taken up almost all the space in my imagination lately.

It is at the same time ancient and futuristic. It is a fantasy. It is a complicated and sophisticated world, mysterious and unpredictable. A human world, full of things and mythologies. But much more physical than the one we live in now. A world where the mind never works without the body. A world where big mammals and big forests still exist. And I wonder, the prehistoric people, were they afraid?

I am not afraid when she gets a cold, I am not afraid if she eats dirt, or snails, or drinks from the puddles, I am not afraid that she'll hurt herself with a fork or fall off the chair she has climbed up on or choke on an olive stone. I am afraid she will come to hate her own body, that she will feel powerless, that she will never learn to sing and dance properly; I am afraid she will think of how she looks instead of how she feels, that she will feel that she shouldn't take up too much space, that she shouldn't be too loud or too corny. I am afraid that she will learn that she shouldn't be the one that reaches out; I am afraid she will learn that the most important thing she can do is to be desired by men.

I want her to move freely in her body, to be active, to have desires, to dare, try and fail – in other words, to learn, to have friends, in all kind of shapes, to love them. I want her to know that it is what is inside her that will make people love her, not her looks. I am afraid of all this, because it suddenly became clear that I'm only beginning to learn it myself.

What I want is a world that we can interact with, made of objects that fit into each other, that can be combined in billions of different ways, that fit into our hands, and tools that are never too far away, like pots and pans and cooking spoons. Knots. To wind and rewind, robes to connect, assemble and loosen again. What is it we want to build? Labyrinths, shelters, hiding places, hubs, obstacle courses, places for plants to grow, small tubes to send secret messages by, ways to remember, small things that can move by themselves and be sent astray.

She finds a lint roller and begins to roll everything. It causes a weird mix of joy and shame in me. The joy comes from the way she looks at the world, her enthusiasm about the lint roller that makes me see it again, its hidden potential as a thing. The shame comes from the feeling that a lint roller is what this world has to offer her, her strong and wild and daring mind and body.

She's not very interested in toys. She's interested in what I do, what other grown-ups do, tools, language, books, phones, and suddenly the toys look perverse to me; they become a symbol of how

Liv Sejrbo Lidegaard (born 1986, located in Copenhagen, DK) is a writer and has published two books of poetry, *Fælleden* (The Common) (2015) and *Vi er her* (We Are Here) (2018), which investigate the nature, communities and ethics of the Anthropocene. Graduated from the Swedish writers school Litterär Gestaltning (MFA in Literary Composition), she also holds an MA in Comparative Literature from the University of Copenhagen.

little we have to do in this world, how imagination and creation has been isolated and disarmed, in the reign of children, their playing, and the ones who can't stop playing, who will not give this sphere up, will become artists and continue dreaming and thinking – this is regarded as an interesting and weird and maybe entertaining thing.

I sit in a café, and I watch other mammas pass by in the street. I sit with my laptop. My child is with her father; she is still so little, not even a year. I look at the mothers passing by. I sit here to work again, to write, to be a person, that thinks, longs and has a job, and I feel that it is a huge privilege. I feel bad for them, as they walk by; they look very pale, very stressed and very tired at the same time. I feel guilty, like I have abandoned them. I move away from their situation as quickly as I can, maternity leave scared the shit out of me. They walk the streets. Everybody will tell them this is what joy is, this is the most important thing they can do. But what is there, actually, for them to do?

My daughter has picked all the tomatoes, while still green, from the tomato plant that I planted in early spring. It has grown monstrous over the past week; I have fed it two litres of water every day, and still it wants more, more earth, more space and light! She accompanies each pick with a small scream of delight. It grows in all directions, as if its mission was to overgrow the whole place.

This prehistoric futuristic world, of materials that I can interact with, that I can teach my child how to interact with, that I dream of: the baby makes it so clear that our surroundings are made, mostly, for comfort, or to look at. Things are not for touching. They will break, they will become dirty. Keep your dirty little fingers away from my books. It is like when we take a walk in the forest. We can look at it and visit it, but we do not know how to live in it, how to interact with it, how to understand or read it. Or when we walk alongside a field. Those places are not made for us to inhabit. The only thing we can do there is move along.

The field is at once completely fixated and completely alienated. It is dead. To be alive is to appear and then disappear, then appear again in a new form. This is the way of the physical world, molecules, water, leaves. I understand it as a material thing rather than a question of belief. An atom disappears in one place and appears in another simultaneously. Our history goes in so many different directions at the same time.

So how did the prehistoric people arrange themselves? What would a day be like? Making pots in clay, painting animals and gods, sewing beads onto a vest, keeping a fire alive. Gathering the right herbs. Following trails. Resting in a nest. It was properly a very risky thing to have a child, a task for the whole tribe. And I guess the children made the adults laugh sometimes. And that the mother and the child were seldom left alone.

Nothing disappears, it just becomes something else, quickly or slowly, brutally or softly; there is no point of fixation. This is at once the catastrophe and the hope of our time. We cannot settle in an alienated world. To inhabit the earth is to find ways to interact with it that are not destructive but creative. I search for these ways to interact with my surroundings everywhere, in art, in children, in books, in the countryside, in the parliament, the playing of light, the changes to come, as a possibility to reconnect to the material world, and free our everyday life.

D

~~dark rain~~ → Garden

~~darkest hour~~ → Declaration of Rebellion

Declaration of Rebellion Extinction Rebellion

Declarations of Climate Emergency

~~deep attention~~ → Attention

~~defamiliarize our mental habits~~ → Coexistence

~~dehumanization~~ → Xenophobia

Denial Simo Køppe

Description April and Phillip Vannini

~~desire~~ → Biodiversity

~~destruction of all we hold dear~~ → Declaration of Rebellion

Development Gregers Andersen

~~difference~~ → Environment

~~direct impact on the future~~ → Future

~~diversity~~ → Resilience

~~dividuals~~ → Care

~~dominion over nature~~ → Biodiversity

~~double meaning of aesthetics~~ → Aesthetics

~~doxacracy~~ → Facts

~~drought~~ → Glaciers

~~duty to act~~ → Declaration of Rebellion

~~dynamic processes of becoming~~ → New Materialism

Dystopia Jesper Just

Declaration of Rebellion

act on behalf of life | → Air | → Biodiversity | → Climate | darkest hour | destruction of all we hold dear | duty to act | → Future | mass extinction | restore dutiful democracy

Extinction Rebellion (founded 2018, located in London, UK) is an international movement that uses non-violent civil disobedience in an attempt to halt mass extinction and minimize the risk of social collapse. All those wishing to adhere to their principles and values are welcome.

DECLARATION OF REBELLION

"To love truth for truth's sake is the principal part of human perfection in this world, and the seed-plot of all other virtues"

John Locke

We hold the following to be true:

This is our darkest hour.

Humanity finds itself embroiled in an event unprecedented in its history. One which, unless immediately addressed, will catapult us further into the destruction of all we hold dear: this nation, its peoples, our ecosystems and the future of generations to come.

The science is clear – we are in the sixth mass extinction event and we will face catastrophe if we do not act swiftly and robustly.

Biodiversity is being annihilated around the world. Our seas are poisoned, acidic and rising. Flooding and desertification will render vast tracts of land uninhabitable and lead to mass migration.

Our air is so toxic that the United Kingdom is breaking the law. It harms the unborn whilst causing tens of thousands to die. The breakdown of our climate has begun. There will be more wildfires, unpredictable super storms, increasing famine and untold drought as food supplies and fresh water disappear.

The ecological crises that are impacting upon this nation, and indeed this planet and its wildlife can no longer be ignored, denied nor go unanswered by any beings of sound rational thought, ethical conscience, moral concern, or spiritual belief.

In accordance with these values, the virtues of truth and the weight of scientific evidence, we declare it our duty to act on behalf of the security and well-being of our children, our communities and the future of the planet itself.

We, in alignment with our consciences and our reasoning, declare ourselves in rebellion against our Government and the corrupted, inept institutions that threaten our future.

The wilful complicity displayed by our government has shattered meaningful democracy and cast aside the common interest in favour of short-term gain and private profits.

When Government and the law fail to provide any assurance of adequate protection, as well as security for its people's well-being and the nation's future, it becomes the right of its citizens to seek redress in order to restore dutiful democracy and to secure the solutions needed to avert catastrophe and protect the future. It becomes not only our right, it becomes our sacred duty to rebel.

We hereby declare the bonds of the social contract to be null and void, which the government has rendered invalid by its continuing failure to act appropriately. We call upon every principled and peaceful citizen to rise with us.

We demand to be heard, to apply informed solutions to these ecological crises and to create a national assembly by which to initiate those solutions needed to change our present cataclysmic course.

We refuse to bequeath a dying planet to future generations by failing to act now.

We act in peace, with ferocious love of these lands in our hearts. We act on behalf of life.

extinction rebellion

Search Extinction Rebellion / Follow us on social media for updates and events

Please sign-up with MissionLifeForce.org | Aligning the force of law with the force of life

Extinction symbol courtesy of www.extinctionsymbol.info

In solidarity with all beings already affected by the ecological crisis

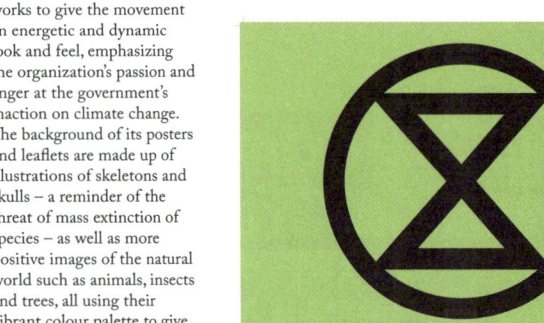

The bold black logo and typeface with colourful graphics works to give the movement an energetic and dynamic look and feel, emphasizing the organization's passion and anger at the government's inaction on climate change. The background of its posters and leaflets are made up of illustrations of skeletons and skulls – a reminder of the threat of mass extinction of species – as well as more positive images of the natural world such as animals, insects and trees, all using their vibrant colour palette to give a positive edge.

OR LIFE

extinction rebellion

ATHY

extinction rebellion

POLITICS

extinction rebellion

E TRUTH

extinction rebellion

IOLENT

extinction rebellion

Declarations of Climate Emergency

→ Biodiversity | → Client: Earth | climate change targets | emergency | global warming | political action | → Weather

Observations from the editor
A Declaration of Climate Emergency is a document, passed by a governing body, that deliberately states such an emergency, calling on political, crisis action to reverse global warming and often containing specific targets from the 2018 IPCC report. Declarations vary in their level of commitment and detail and are used, often symbolically, to voice the gravity of climate change and demand a change of discourse and action towards climate change to deal with these destructive, continuous processes.

The first Declaration of Climate Emergency petition was launched in Australia in April 2016, and as of March 2020 eleven countries have made a formal binding Declaration of Climate Emergency: Argentina, Austria, Bangladesh, Canada, France, Gibraltar, Ireland, Italy, Maldives, Malta and Spain as well as the European Union as a whole (according to Cedemia).[1] In November 2019, the European Parliament declared a climate and environmental emergency in Europe and across the globe.

As the declarations are often symbolic, they are objects of great discussion. On the one hand, they can be vehicles for action as they raise questions of what to do next; however, they simultaneously face the threat of potentially being left as hollow statements.

Not included in Cedemia's list of *binding* declarations is the United Kingdom, which famously became the first country to declare a National State of Climate Emergency on 1 May 2019, when the House of Commons motioned:

That this House declares an environment and climate emergency following the finding of the Intergovernmental Panel on Climate Change that to avoid more than 1.5 °C rise in global warming, global emissions would need to fall by around 45 per cent from 2010 levels by 2030, reaching net zero by around 2050; recognises the devastating impact that the volatile and extreme weather will have on UK food production, water availability, public health and through flooding and wildfire damage; notes that the UK is currently missing almost all of its biodiversity targets, with an alarming trend in species decline, and that cuts of 50 per cent to the funding of Natural England are counter-productive to tackling those problems; calls on the Government to increase the ambition of the UK's climate change targets under the Climate Change Act 2008 to achieve net zero emissions before 2050, to increase support for and set ambitious, short-term targets for the roll-out of renewable and low carbon energy and transport, and to move swiftly to capture economic opportunities and green jobs in the low carbon economy while managing risks for workers and communities currently reliant on carbon intensive sectors; and further calls on the Government to lay before the House within the next six months urgent proposals to restore the UK's natural environment and to deliver a circular, zero waste economy.[2]

Works cited:

Cedemia. 2019. 'ICEF – Governments emergency declaration spreadsheet'. *Climate Emergency Declarations.* https://www.cedamia.org/global/. Accessed 20 November 2019.

Corbyn, Jeremy, Rebecca Long Bailey, Sue Hayman, Barry Gardiner, Valerie Vaz and Nicholas Brown. 2019. 'Environment and Climate Change'. *Publications & Records, House of Commons Session 2017–19, Business for Wednesday 01 May 2019.* https://publications.parliament.uk/pa/cm201719/cmagenda/ob190501.htm#_idTextAnchor005. Accessed 20 November 2019.

Denial

→ Facts | insidious anxiety | → Oxymorons | populism | suspicion | → World Scientists' Warning to Humanity | → Xenophobia

In our daily lives, we are often faced with conflicting choices about what to think and how to act. In choosing one option over another, the key is usually whether our perceptions ultimately match reality – the reality of our own needs and desires as well as the reality of the conditions that the world imposes on our choices and actions. In interactions with others, we often form ideas about the other's intentions, desires and motives and tend to use these constructions of the other person to justify our own actions. In this way, we construct connections between actions, statements, political decisions and so forth and their justifications. We may be firmly convinced we understand the more or less hidden motivations underlying other people's actions.

Denials are a particular way of relating to opinions or actions and their justification. When we deny a connection that others find fairly obvious, we do so because we have constructed a set of causes that do not appear to be particularly likely. So why do we do it? In part because we seek to defend attitudes that are important to us and which sometimes even serve to define our identity. Thus we deny obvious truths because they threaten values and aspects of our life that we are not prepared to give up.

Simo Køppe (born 1951, located in Copenhagen, DK) is a professor in the theory and history of psychology. He holds a dr.med. (medicine), a PhD in biology and an exam.art. in psycholinguistics.

From a standard psychological point of view, denial is often an indirect confirmation of the opposite – for example, in the form of a self-negating verbal statement. One typical example is Richard Nixon's 'I am not a crook', which hardly served to turn public sentiment in his favour.

In the slightly narrower context of psychotherapy, denial is an often unconscious way to shore up repression – usually in the form of an affectively charged negation of the therapist's interpretation: 'No, it has nothing whatsoever to do with my relationship with my father.'

In a contemporary context, the term is frequently used in the climate debate, although it may seem peculiar to deny the climate crisis, since 97–98% of all scientists who have dealt with the issue are convinced that the potentially lethal damage to our climate is human-made. Such denial may have many different explanations – from deeply personal issues to political or ideological structures. Some relate fairly specifically to the climate crisis, while others can be generalized to common psychological reactions or conditions in society.

One of the most common reasons for denying the climate crisis is the belief in a technological fix: 'Sure, the climate may be moving in an unfortunate direction, but the engineers will fix it.' This rationale illustrates one of the main functions of denial: dampening the insidious anxiety that is so widespread, also among children and youth.

Many discussions revolve around personal initiatives – for example, to reduce CO_2 emissions. Here, denial may be a reaction to changes in one's own living conditions. It is convenient to use denial to defend one's often unnecessary overconsumption and one's potentially necessary, more radical changes in personal transportation, diet, housing and so forth.

Denial may take the form of casting doubt about scientific findings. That comes in many variants – from exaggerating the relatively few natural explanations of climate change (sunspots, for example) to toning down the evidence: 'Yes, but it's only a small share of the scientific findings that suggest there's a crisis.'

Others deny scientific findings by positing conspiracy theories – from claiming that individual scientists are choosing to focus on the climate crisis because it helps them get funding to speculating that they are on the payroll of companies that have an economic interest in attacking the extraction of fossil fuels, for example.

Some of these types of denial may be seen as a reflection of general political populism, which casts aspersions on all types of authorities – including science, which is regarded as an opinion like any other, where you can simply choose to favour another view.

Ultimately, denial is always the denial of truth. In most cases, it is a truth we defend against by turning it into a matter of opinion. That comes close to delegitimizing the very notion of truth, which is problematic.

Description

→ Connectedness → Creation Eurocentric Anthropocene → Explicitation → Garden → Geology → Heritage land as a commodity → Soil the power of sharing stories

There is a place on this island where a large sandstone rock looks out to the Salish Sea with a pensive look on its human-like facial shape. A recent exhibit at the Gabriola Island Museum created with the collaboration of Coast Salish Hul'qumi'num-speaking Snuneymuxw Elders teaches us that the rock's name is Xuwtluqs. Its face is that of a greedy old man that Xe:els the Transformer turned into stone and placed there. It is a rock with the formidable power of changing the direction of the wind. If the right words are spoken, the winds will change propitiously. But if the wrong words are spoken or loud noises are made in its proximity, the winds will change to gale force.

This information was gathered from Snuneymuxw Elders and is presented in an exhibit featured at the Gabriola Island Museum.

English-language maps call this island Gabriola and place it a few kilometres east of Vancouver Island and a few kilometres west of Vancouver. We write from here, as two settler colonial dwellers whose ancestors hail from multiple parts of Europe. We write as islanders, as ethnographers, as inhabitants of a place rich with stories that can teach us about our connections to the Land and the Anthropocene.

Ethnographers gather knowledge through the stories that people bequeath them. American anthropologist Clifford Geertz called what ethnographers do 'thick description'.[1] In generating thick description, ethnographers provide knowledge about a cultural context and interpret meanings within such context. Thick descriptions are stories richly vivid in detail, evocative in a way that shows knowledge more than it tells it, in a way that provokes understanding rather than a definitive explanation.

Thick description is old business. Since time immemorial, Indigenous peoples around the world have passed on their knowledge across generations through stories rich with inductive meaning, rich with moral and practical information about their place in the world. It is with the stories shared by the First Nations who have inhabited this island that we want to begin our description of what the Anthropocene is. These descriptions reveal lessons that have been erased, never understood or maybe completely forgotten – due to the ethnocentrism typical of settler-colonialism.

April Vannini (born 1976, located in Gabriola Island, CA) received her PhD from the European Graduate School in Media and Communication and teaches at Royal Roads University in Victoria in the School of Communication and Culture as an associate faculty member.

Phillip Vannini (born 1974, located in Gabriola Island, CA) is Canada Research Chair in Public Ethnography and a professor at the School of Communication and Culture at Royal Roads University, Victoria, CA. He is author/editor of 15 books and producer/director of three documentary films, including the latest, *A Time for Making* (2018), filmed on Gabriola Island, where he resides.

The same museum exhibit says that the First Ancestors dropped from the sky at the beginning of the world. Immediately, they set out to transform the world by clearing it of dangerous creatures and settling the original villages. Then the Creator Xe:els arrived. Xe:els too was a transformer, and he is the one who made things as they are today. He transformed the First Ancestors into deer, into cedar trees, into rocks. Xe:els taught the Hul'qumi'num people about the values of respect and reciprocity, about sharing the obligations owed to this world.

The Snuneymuxw Nation system of morality towards the Land is based on the principle that the Land is owed respect because its inhabitants all descend from the same First Ancestors.[2] Humans and non-humans are all related because they are all transformations of the Creator and all kin: all subjects of the making of this Land. Snuneymuxw stories tell about how Ancestors made extensive use of these territories, through hunting, fishing grounds, and the picking of camas root and berries. Stories speak about the clam beds, the hunting grounds and the fish weirs that have been held in common across generations. These stories indirectly point to something else too: the Anthropocene is a colonial creation wrapped in Western epistemologies that conceptualize Land as a commodity and nature as separate from culture.

Scholars of the Anthropocene alert us to the fact that *our* epoch is marked by the active role in which *we* are transforming the planet. This, critics of the Anthropocene tell us, shows that *our* connection to the planet *we* inhabit has never been understood or has been forgotten by *us*. Their critique awakens *us* to the realization that the earth's resources are owed respect. They teach *us* that nature is not outside of the human sphere; they teach *us* that we are connected. Anthropocene scholars instruct *us* about life as balance, as reciprocity, as a web. Environmental activists armed with data on climate change direct *our* attention to the fact that ecosystems are interconnected, to the fact that humans and non-humans are in constant processes of co-creation. All of this is now an emergency, a crisis, material for news and scientific discovery. But *for whom* is this new? Who is this '*we*', this '*us*' in this discourse? Certainly not the Indigenous peoples around the world, people for whom kinship and connectedness are the fundamental ontological and epistemological cornerstones of their entire way of life, people who have known about the business of interconnection for time immemorial, people whose knowledge about kinship has long been silenced.

Critical Indigenous Canadian scholars Heather Davis and Zoe Todd (Métis) rightly argue that discussions over the Anthropocene are invariably Eurocentric. In their view, the Anthropocene dates back to the onset of the colonial and imperial project of the 17th century. Their view 'calls for the consideration of Indigenous philosophies and processes of Indigenous self-governance as a necessary political corrective'.[3] We agree with their view. We have to look no further than the oral stories about the island now called Gabriola and the Salish Sea to learn about our colonial place in this Land, about our role as settler-colonial transformers, about the respect and reciprocity demanded of our kinship with this place, with the animals, plants and rocks living here. That is the power of stories, the power of descriptive knowledge.

Contemporary stories from this Land
Ethnographic description demands we connect with each other, that we learn from one another. Description demands we ask, listen and pay respect to each other's knowledge, to each other's stories. The accumulation of these stories, old and new, generates mutual knowledge. Xuwtluqs is perhaps the first historical transformer of the weather and the climate of this island. More recent transformations can be just as vivid. As a way of learning more about the Anthropocene, we asked three of our fellow islanders to share some of their stories about how they connect with the place where we live.

Steve is a geologist, one of our neighbours. He goes to the earth to look for stories. 'Rural life often requires digging: digging beds for vegetables, holes for planting trees, creating a pond, finding clay to line the pond, digging a grave for a loved animal,' he tells us. Steve likes digging, and he's always curious to discover what's hidden underground. At times, he sees evidence of the glaciers that scraped across British Columbia; other times, he notices how part of the land his family occupies 'was once covered by a post-glacial lake – one that had a thriving population of diatomaceous algae'. As a geologist, he is aware that chunks of charcoal in the mix are evidence that there were wildfires back then. 'What I find beneath the surface here', he tells us, 'takes us back about 12,000 years (the lake sediments) and about 25,000 years (the glacial sediments), and around 70 million years (sandstone and shale with fossils from a tropical environment).' But there are modern stories too. There was a roofing business operating near his property, and so he often comes across shingle, nails, bits of machinery. And he even finds occasional signs that a market garden once operated here. 'It all makes me wonder: how will the Anthropocene show up in the geological record of this region?' Steve asks. His answer is profoundly revealing:

Looking around, while taking a break from digging, I started comparing the number of Western red cedars [*Thuja plicata*] to the more common conifers. These cherished and magnificent trees – that sustained the Coast Salish people for millennia – represent a small fraction of the forest at this location, and it's clear that they are struggling. In fact, over the past decade almost one quarter of the cedars on this piece of land have either died, and are now little more than standing skeletons, or have become visibly stressed, with whole branches a deep orange – probably because of climate-change-related drought. Sadly, Western red cedar will not likely have much of a presence in the Anthropocene fossil record of this region, or perhaps anywhere.

Roger is another islander, and also a poet, a writer and a professor of literature. When we speak about climate change, he reveals to us, he is sometimes 'haunted by a nagging fear of being overwhelmed by the ocean'. It's a feeling that was first stirred in him as a boy, in a series of dreams about tsunamis. As island dwellers, we know very well that today's rising sea levels, storms, hurricanes and other 'catastrophic weather events' can turn nightmares into reality. But these aren't external threats, Roger reflects; these are forces that reveal our connection with this island, its seas, its murmurs and its shakings. These lives are 'always already inside us, lodged in the dream of progress, returning now as our collective nightmare'. His poem 'Tsunami' reveals this in descriptive detail.

Reich suggests that sexuality
is a 'base' productive force.
We understand this immediately
when we consider the fact that
the 1973 tidal wave disaster film
Nihon Chinbotsu ('Submersion of Japan')
yielded USD12,000,000 in profit.

When I was a child the waves
also came from the East
darkening the horizon
in an ominous liquid pewter
silver plumes brushing against
an undulant sky. Now
the whitecaps surge against
the shores of an island
where many years ago we
had buried on the beach
the remains of a dream.
It is not true
that the sea reflects
the sky but rather that
the sky reflects the sea.
Thus, catastrophic weather
originates in depths of
humanity, not the stars
while the ocean – a 'base'
productive force – keeps
piling wreckage upon
wreckage before our feet.

Poems, stories from the earth, descriptive details about our kinship, and our connections have the power not so much to counter 'big data' but to provide a different kind of knowledge, the kind of knowledge that 'slows things down', as Susan might put it. A retired school teacher and librarian, Susan still visits the island's elementary school's young pupils. She reads books to them. A dozen years ago, a little boy in grade two told her, 'I love it when you read to us because it slows things down.' That's what description does. That's what stories do.

Though retired, Susan still spends time at the school. She sees the power of slowing down when children play outside, away from human infrastructure, in grassy grounds 'where their eyes, ears and bodies can connect with surroundings that have natural gradients of light and sound, and where their bodies can expand, relax and knowingly or otherwise connect with the earth'. But she also sees a different power, the shiny appeal of expensive computers, TV screens and digital technologies that in one way or another end up removing children from the environment outside, the same ground where 'all of their senses are awakened' every time they can go and play and just be on this island.

We are indebted to Steve Earle, Roger Farr and Susan Yates for sharing their stories and knowledge with us.

Coming to terms with the Anthropocene, Susan explains to us, means 'finding the human key to the inhuman world around us, connecting the individual with their community, the known to the unknown, and connecting the present to the past and the future'. It's really a simple story in the end, whether we make those connections with children, with adults, with Ancestors or with our world. And that, she tells us, means sharing stories, 'and not just any stories, the best stories our ancestors and storytellers have to offer.'

Description is a simple word. To *de* – 'down' in Latin – *scribe* – 'write' in Latin – doesn't just mean 'writing down', however. It means passing down, sharing, gifting knowledge about a context and about meanings from which we can all learn. To describe the Anthropocene means gathering stories, the best stories Ancestors and our neighbours have to share about this common world. Stories about what's hidden underground, about the waves of the seas and the ripples in the sky, about what children can learn by connecting to the world, and about what we can all learn by connecting to Coast Salish Ancestors and all relations with this Land.

Works cited:

Davis, Heather, and Zoe Todd. 2017. 'On the Importance of a Date, or Decolonizing the Anthropocene.' *ACME*, 16 (4), pp. 761–780.

Geertz, Clifford. 1973. 'Thick Description: Toward an Interpretive Theory of Culture'. In *The Interpretation of Cultures*, pp. 3–36. New York: Basic Books.

Struggling Western Red Cedar.

Develop-
ment

→ Dystopia | → Modernism | new global paradigm | progress | → Resources | utopia | → Violence

The present was seen as an uncomfortable dead spot, an inconvenient moment to be endured in order to access the safety of hindsight. It was this fear of the present and the desire to fast-forward into a utopian future that forced the world to shift into reverse and move backwards faster than it ever had advanced.

Martine McDonagh, 2012, p. 157.

Coming from the sinister future world of the post-apocalyptic cli-fi novel *I Have Waited, And You Have Come* (2012) and aimed at the present psychology of Western modernity, these words lay bare the 'split identity' of development in the Anthropocene. As this description indirectly warns its readers, the chase for continuous progress, for more and more rapid modernization through economic growth and technological advances, may thus very well be a 'highway' to the very opposite, to a world where human civilization will fall into decline rather than experience further improvements.

Development in the Anthropocene tends in this sense to activate two, contrasting imaginative paths, one leading to utopia, the other to dystopia. On the path to utopia, the Anthropocene is not imagined to represent a radical break with the past. Rather the path from the past to the future is imagined to be linear, in the sense that human progress is seen as an inevitable consequence of time passing. The story here goes that technological evolution prompted by perpetual economic growth will eventually bring solutions to the climate crisis and other ecological perils paving the way for a 'great Anthropocene'.[1] Conversely, the imagination of the Anthropocene as a path to dystopia departs from a very different understanding of history. Herein the accelerating – albeit uneven – modernization of human civilization has only been possible because of a more and more destructive extraction and consumption of natural 'resources'. Hence as this extraction and consumption have rapidly increased so have the dangers of collapsing ecosystems and

Gregers Andersen (born 1981, located in Stockholm, SE) is a postdoctoral researcher in environmental humanities at the Department of English, Stockholm University. He is the author of the monograph *Climate Fiction and Cultural Analysis* (2019) and several journal articles on how literature, film and philosophy contribute to the understanding of life in the Anthropocene.

uncontrollable global warming. As the scientific recognition of the Anthropocene makes explicit the unnerving accumulation and acceleration of these dangers, it marks in a sense that 'the future is over'.[2] That is, that the dream of 'an ever progressing development' will be brought to a brutal halt by the deteriorating living conditions of most humans, plants and animals.[3]

In this dystopia, the human ingenuity counted upon so optimistically in the imagination of the Anthropocene as a utopia will only shield the super-privileged and super-wealthy from the effects of civilizational decline. All other is imagined to be exposed not only to the brutality of an ever more hostile climate and biosphere but also to the 'barbarism' of other humans.[4] German social psychologist Harald Welzer (b. 1958) asserts, for example, that 'violence has a great future ahead of it. We shall see not only mass migration but also violent solutions to refugee problems, not only tensions over water or mining rights but also resource wars'.[5] British historian Timothy Snyder (b. 1969) goes one step further in claiming that 'the planet is changing in ways that might make Hitlerian descriptions of life, space and time more plausible',[6] while UN special rapporteur Philip Alston (b. 1950) warns that an over-reliance on the private sector could lead to 'a climate apartheid scenario in which the wealthy pay to escape overheating, hunger, and conflict, while the rest of the world is left to suffer'.[7]

These fears are not least noteworthy at a time when much of the global conversation about sustainability is formed by the United Nation's sustainable development goals. The reason being that these goals do not really mark a decisive break with the policies of the past but rather continue to equate development with the habitual need of perpetual economic growth. In other words, they do not really eliminate the fears that the chase for accelerating resource extraction and consumption will only lead to civilizational decline. To dismantle these fears, it will rather take a new global paradigm of thinking and doing, a paradigm in which development will first and foremost have to equate a more just and limited extraction and consumption of natural 'resources' than it currently does.

Works cited:

OHCHR. 2019. 'Climate Change and Poverty'. https://www.ohchr.org/Documents/Issues/Poverty/A_HRC_41_39.pdf. Accessed 25 November 2019.

Asafu-Adjaye, John, Linus Blomqvist, Stewart Brand, Barry Brook, Ruth DeFries, Erle Ellis, Christopher Foreman, David Keith, Martin Lewis, Mark Lynas, Ted Nordhaus, Roger Pielke Jun., Rachel Pritzker, Joyashree Roy, Mark Sagoff, Michael Shellenberger, Robert Stone and Peter Teague. 2015. 'An Ecomodernist Manifesto'. www.ecomodernism.org.

Berardi, Franco 'Bifo'. 2011. *After the Future*. Oakland: AK Press.

McDonagh, Martine. 2012. *I Have Waited, And You Have Come*. Brighton: Myriad Editions.

Snyder, Timothy. 2016. *Black Earth: The Holocaust as History and Warning*. London: Vintage.

Stengers, Isabelle. 2015. *In Catastrophic Times: Resisting the Coming Barbarism*. S.l.: Open Humanities Press.

Welzer, Harald. 2012. *Climate Wars: Why People Will Be Killed in the Twenty-First Century*. Cambridge, UK: Polity.

Dystopia

→ Future | → Garden | → Heritage | → Imagine | → Wilderness

Jesper Just (born 1974, located in New York, US) has exhibited extensively around the world, representing Denmark at the 55th Venice Biennale in 2013. His work can be found in the public collections of The Metropolitan Museum of Art (New York), the Guggenheim Museum (New York), MoMA (New York), Tate Modern (London), the National Museum of Modern and Contemporary Art (Seoul) and the Danish National Gallery (Copenhagen), among many others.

Jesper Just
Intercourses, 2013
Five channel video installation
black and white, 10:00 min
loop each
Dimensions variable
Edition of 7 (+2 AP)
Courtesy of Galleri Nicolai
Wallner and the artist

Ē

Earth Ethics J. Baird Callicott
Earthlings Jeff VanderMeer
~~eco-apartheid~~ → Soil
~~ecological civilization~~ → Client: Earth
Ecology Timothy Morton
~~economic growth~~ → Capitalocene
~~ecosystem diversity~~ → Biodiversity
~~ecosystem extinction~~ → Corals
~~eco-war~~ → Resources
~~embodied enaction~~ → Environment
~~embodied stories~~ → Attachment
~~embodied utopias~~ → Feminism
~~emergency~~ → Declarations of Climate Emergency
~~emission speed~~ → Next Generation
~~emotions~~ → Sensitivity
~~empathy~~ → Earth Ethics
Energy Kirsten Halsnæs
~~entanglements~~ → Attention → Bacteria → Power
Environment Cary Wolfe
~~environmental aesthetics~~ → Atmosphere
~~environmental justice~~ → Body
~~envision possible futures~~ → Aesthetics
~~erosion~~ → Garden
~~ethical guide~~ → Wilderness
~~Eurocentric Anthropocene~~ → Description
~~evolution siblings~~ → Time
~~exhaust of industrialization~~ → City
~~existential threat~~ → Next Generation
~~experience~~ → Sensitivity
Explicitation NORRØN
~~extending your senses~~ → Posthuman
~~Extinction Rebellion~~ → Declaration of Rebellion
~~extraction~~ → Care

Earth Ethics

→ Agriculture | → Anthropocene | → Atmosphere | → Biodiversity | → Client: Earth | → Climate | → Development | → Ecology | empathy | → Future | → Global | justice | responsibility

The living Earth itself is at no risk from a late-coming (200,000–300,000 YBP) species of anthropoid ape. For 3.5 billion years, life on Earth has endured all sorts of catastrophes – from radical changes in atmospheric chemistry to near-total glaciation to massive meteor strikes – and has rebounded from each more robust, lusty and diverse than ever before. The living Earth *as we know it* – its Holocene climate, its complement of species – is most definitely at risk of systemic collapse, after which Earth's biosphere will doubtless reorganize itself and rebound as before. If we are thinking like a planet, *Homo sapiens* may actually be thought to be releasing buried carbon back into the biosphere, thus providing nutrition for future photosynthetic organisms and ultimately prolonging the tenure of carbon-based life on Earth. That just might be why Gaia brought us forth.

Such teleological speculation notwithstanding, the beneficiary or moral patient of Earth ethics cannot be the living Earth itself – which our species can no more benefit than harm. One might identify the species *Homo sapiens* as the moral patient of Earth ethics. But our species per se is probably not at risk of total self-inflicted extinction. In the worst-case scenario of the bad Anthropocene, remnant populations of *Homo sapiens*, ruled by merciless warlords, endlessly fight over remaining resources on a scorched (literally as well as figuratively) Earth. A preview of the future condition of humanity is running in the current failed states of the world. In short, at grave risk of near-total extinction is not humanity but human civilization, which would surely corrode following the collapse of Earth's integrated biogeochemical systems. Also at risk of total extinction are many of our 'fellow voyagers in the odyssey of evolution' (many other extant species). And so, clearly, another genuine beneficiary or moral patient of Earth ethics would be Earth's current complement of species – or biodiversity, for short.

Having identified its proper moral patients, one need next ask how one might go about constructing a fitting Earth ethics. Popularly conceived, ethics consist of a code of dos and don'ts. Do become a vegan, don't own an automobile, etc. might be found in a code of Earth ethics. Such ad hoc

J. Baird Callicott (born 1941, located in Memphis, US), holds a BA from Rhodes College, Memphis, and an MA and PhD from Syracuse University, New York, and retired as University Distinguished Research Professor Emeritus and Regents Professor of Philosophy from the University of North Texas, US. He is author of *Earth's Insights* (1994), *Thinking Like a Planet* (2013) and *Greek Natural Philosophy* (2018) and co-editor-in-chief of the *Encyclopedia of Environmental Ethics and Philosophy*.

codifications of good and bad conduct, however, are inevitably incomplete and also soon become obsolete as circumstances inevitably change. Thus philosophers have sought to get at the wellspring of ethics and to provide theoretical foundations and general principles that are more adaptable to changed circumstances, more coherently to guide our conduct. Two classic examples are the Christian golden rule and the Greek golden mean – the former embedded in such ideas as humans having been created in the image of God and the latter in the ideal of human excellence or virtue. Two modern examples are the utilitarian greatest-happiness-for-the-greatest-number principle and the Kantian (or deontological) categorical imperative. The latter would require us to pause and ask in each instance, What if everyone, without exception, were to do what I am contemplating doing?

These classical and modern legacy ethics are of little help in constructing Earth ethics. They are all of Western provenance and thus none of their conceptual foundations resonate with everyone. And they are all individualistic, while the proper moral patients of Earth ethics are holistic entities – global human civilization in all its wondrous diversity and even more wondrous biodiversity. Not only are the moral patients of Earth ethics holistic entities; so also must be the moral agents. Voluntary individual Earth-ethical action cannot mitigate climate change or prevent the erosion of Earth's biodiversity or reverse the damage to the planetary ecosystem. Only through governmental policies and laws that positively incentivize and/or compel universal Earth-ethical action can these goals be achieved. The relatively successful Montreal Protocol – which from 1987 banned the production and use of chlorofluorocarbon propellants and refrigerants in the interest of restoring stratospheric ozone – can serve as a model for tackling our other global environmental challenges.

Alternatively, we might envision a patchwork of Earth ethics grounded in Confucian, Buddhist, Hindu, Islamic, shamanic ... traditions of thought. But that is hardly fitting in a time in which our challenges are global in scope and thus require a global consensus. The scientific worldview is not wholeheartedly shared by everyone, but it is globally distributed and culturally neutral. Thus in it we might discover the conceptual foundations of Earth ethics. One might object that science, to the extent that it has informed technological development, is what has got us into the present environmental predicament. But wholesale rejection of science will hardly solve our environmental problems. Science can just as well inform technologies that might help avert the impending collapse of Earth's biogeochemical systems. And it can just as well inform Earth ethics.

The contemporary scientific account of the origin and development of ethics – evolutionary moral psychology – is traceable to Charles Darwin, who devoted two chapters of the *Descent of Man* to 'the moral sense'.[1] Observing that *Homo sapiens* is the quintessentially social mammal, Darwin argued that ethics evolved to facilitate social cohesion. For, as he vividly notes, 'No tribe could hold together if murder, robbery, treachery, etc., were common; consequently such crimes, within the limits of the same tribe are "branded with everlasting infamy".'[2] On the mammalian platform of 'the parental and filial affections', primates evolved feelings of sympathy, empathy, beneficence, loyalty and other moral sentiments to restrain selfish impulses to commit such crimes, thus maintaining sufficient social cohesion and order.[3] The moral sentiments were naturally selected because those individuals in whom they were lacking were driven away to pursue life's struggle as solitaries – but with little hope of success. Evidently, the genes responsible for their antisocial propensities were not altogether winnowed from the human genome, but they were certainly reduced in frequency. With the capacity to linguistically express and rhetorically reinforce the moral sentiments, *Homo sapiens* evolved ethics, properly speaking.

From this evolutionary account of the origin of ethics, we may infer the following two lemmas: 1) ethics are correlative to social cohesion and order, and 2) as society changes in scope and form, ethics change accordingly. Aboriginal human societies were extended families (gens or clans) whose members lived by foraging. Clans later merged to become tribes, and some tribes eventually took advantage of the Holocene climate to domesticate plants and animals and live by farming. Settled agriculture allowed human populations to increase, cities to coalesce and priestly, political, medical and various artisanal classes to arise. With each such expansion of society and shift in forms of subsistence, ethics became more inclusive and changed in emphasis. For example, in smaller, foraging societies, in which possessions are few and food fluctuates in abundance, there is a premium on sharing. In larger, settled-agricultural societies, in which possessions are more numerous and much labour is invested in crops, there is a severe sanction on theft.

Combining this evolutionary account of the origin and development of ethics with ecology, American conservationist Aldo Leopold devised a 'land ethic'. In one strain of ecology, the relationships among plants and animals are represented as a biotic community. 'All ethics so far evolved rest upon a single premise: that the individual is a member of a community of interdependent parts,' Leopold wrote,[4] echoing Darwin. Ecology 'simply enlarges the boundaries of the community to include soils, waters, plants and animals, or collectively: the land. [...] A land ethic changes the role of *Homo sapiens* from conqueror of the land-community to plain member and citizen of it. It implies respect for his fellow members and also for the community as such'.[5]

Biotic communities are local – a forest here, a prairie there, a wetland yonder. To devise Earth ethics, we can combine the evolutionary account of ethics with the ecosystem strain of ecology. There are two conceptual keys to constructing an Earth ethics. The first is to envision the living Earth as a planetary ecosystem, with global interactions and reactions among the atmosphere, hydrosphere, lithosphere, microbes, fungi, plants and animals (most importantly insects and now a formerly insignificant but latterly impactful anthropoid ape). The second is to envision ourselves, both individually and collectively, as exquisitely adapted to the Earth in its present state and as embedded in and utterly dependent upon the integrity, stability and functionality of the planetary ecosystem. The second of these conceptual challenges may be the hardest, at least for those of us with a European heritage, as it defies a long Western history of religious and philosophical human exceptionalism and radical individualism. Nothing less than the way we conceive of and experience the self – from a psychic monad residing in a body and an externally related social atom to a node or nexus in a web of biospheric relationships – is required. In the contemporary science of ethics there lies a profound psychological impediment to the emergence of effective Earth ethics. Our moral sentiments evolved at small temporal and spatial scales. Thus empathy and compassion are evoked most strongly when we are in close proximity with a human or non-human animal in imminent danger or presently suffering. The greater the distance in space and time the more tenuously and weakly our moral sentiments are engaged. The ability of television and social media to contract spatial and temporal distance can, to some extent, overcome this limitation of our inherited moral capacities. Cognitive as well as experiential countermeasures are also effective – replacing narratives of otherness and difference with those of kinship and solidarity among persons 'of all nations and races', to quote Darwin again.[6] Relevant too are the contemporary narratives in the ethology of the rich and complex consciousnesses of other animals.

Practical Earth ethics, however, can turn these evolutionary limitations of our moral sentiments to an advantage. Empathy most strongly wells up in us when we behold our own progeny in imminent danger and present suffering. Individually, we may successfully strive to provide our own progeny with a material inheritance, but we cannot individually bequeath a livable climate and a whole and healthy planetary ecosystem to our own progeny. That we can do only in concert with others. So surely, even empathy most narrowly ranging but most strongly felt can motivate cooperative effort to avert global socio-environmental collapse. For the younger ones among us, even the most narrow self-interest provides a powerful psychological motivation for cooperative efforts to preserve what remains and to restore, as much as possible, what has been lost of the Earth's ecological integrity, stability and functionality.

A sense of justice, no less than a sense of empathy, is among our inherited moral sentiments. Those least responsible for global ecological destruction related to climate change are most vulnerable to its effects in the form of drought, flood, famine and dislocation. Another aspect of Earth ethics is for those who are most responsible for climate-related ecological destruction to take responsibility for it. And that would include helping those least able to help themselves avoid or adapt to its direst consequences.

Works cited:

Darwin, Charles. 1874. *The Descent of Man, and Selection in Relation to Sex*, 2nd edn. London: John Murray.

Leopold, Aldo. 1949. *A Sand County Almanac and Sketches Here and There.* New York: Oxford University Press.

Further reading:

Callicott, J. Baird. 2013. *Thinking Like a Planet: The Land Ethic and the Earth Ethic.* New York: Oxford University Press.

Earthlings

→ Care | → Coexistence | find a home | → Garden | → Invisible | → Plantationocene | → Posthuman | the truth of past, present and future

---

When you came to this place
among the leaves and soft shadows.

This place among the branches
through which blue sky shone.

That smelled rich and green and the wind
That made the trees sough strange and rough.

The wind that slowed to bleed into
and through you.

They told you you you *you*
Would find a home here

That *you* you you you you
Would forget your origin and your name

Find a home here

Jeff VanderMeer (born 1968, located in Tallahassee, US) is an award-winning novelist known for his emphasis on environmental themes, especially in his critically acclaimed *Southern Reach Trilogy*. His recent novel, *Borne* (2017), was called 'a thorough marvel' by Colson Whitehead, was a finalist for the Arthur C. Clarke Award and is being developed for television by the AMC television network. His latest novel is *Dead Astronauts*.

At 7.21 a.m. on 2 November, a rainless day, the earthling stared at you in a way unfamiliar, and you could not must not will never hold its gaze. There was in the stance and the eye a knowledge of you that was unbearable.

The encounter at 4.34 p.m. on 2 November … or was it 3 November … was unexpected and not what it first seemed. The surveillance that burnt upon your face, that rested there with a sharpness born of long regret, welled up from the forest floor. From an earthling who stood immobile but alert and made you feel like a traitor, no, an intruder, no, a traitor. A threat, like a thief or hurricane or a sound too loud. You could not understand for the longest time why you stood there staring down at her staring up, and wept. Why you should have to weep for being held to account. But when you were distracted for a moment, startled by a sound, she disappeared as if she had never been there. So utter, so total. So loved by camouflage or speed, or both. It felt as if you had disappeared with her.

November. Later in November. In November. November. It was November. Maybe it was November. A new earthling to solve as your bones soaked in the cold. You did not mean to make it run or chase it behind a tree. But those things happened anyway. The stress of regard was not the moment or the point. The stress of regard was the aftershock. For you felt you had seen this earthling before and that it had seen you before, and this, now, was mere retort or renewal or further rehearsal of a point or mode or relationship that had already begun, been forged, dissolved, resolved. But the eyes of the earthling held you, and you shuddered for you could not quell their fear of you, not this one or all the ones before. And this made you fearful and want to be small and quiet. Something dissolving. Some sense of the sky melting into the ground.

158

Came screaming forth from the canopy. Came screaming forth in a month that was a month that was a month or moment after or before or during the other months and moments. Came screaming forth as the sound that had startled you before, revealed as something earthly with fierce demons, no, demeanour that admitted to no fault or weakness. It destroyed the branch the talons clung to even as immovable, inviolate, as if forever perched and forever destroying. Only slowly, as you recovered from the sound, as you stood so very still, did you admit to the beauty of the earthling … in the way its feathers became a disguise both sharp and diffuse, both ghost and the thing the ghost had once been, and in this way showed its prey the truth of past, present and future. For this being travelled through time continually, calculated the next velocity pierced to a point on a map. But of your velocity you had no idea, nor where you had been pierced. Distance was distress not purchase. And the glare of gaze impervious fixed upon you and showed you the past, present and future … yet spared your life.

From a vantage above, on some day in some year of a decade disguised by mist, you came unawares upon an earthling that had no knowledge or awareness of you. An earthling that might not know of you at all, or your deeds or reputation. You watched with such a strange sad delight that it was like a song. It felt wrong to observe such openness, such unguardedness. It felt wrong and yet compulsion: you could not halt the observation. You could not let the earthling remain unmapped. You tunnelled into reason: that many earthlings observed by you had enjoyed ecstatic many moments already where they had relaxed into the comfort of being invisible. Yet the longer you stood there as scrutiny, and the longer the earthling lingered, the more agitated you became. Lifted one foot, then the other, tried to turn away, could not. Dropped to your knees, felt a shooting pain, found your mouth become open and issuing forth a scream that racked you raw, sound muffled by the sky pouring into you through the branches. Pouring into your lungs, your bones, and destroying you entirely. Until consciousness was kept from you, muffled and indistinct and far away … And when you came to, you looked around nervously like a new thing, and you understood now your weeping the first day. Even if you would never write it down or tell anyone but only keep it tethered to the centre of you. In an unobserved place.

The year is the moon through the trees eclipsing your thoughts with a feral smile. The year is something cold that smells of food and must be chased. The year is long yet compressed into a single moment. You have long since become a being of the night: the soothe of night, the lull and hum, the bottomless dark lake that steals your vision. You could not take all that light for so long; it revealed all of you until there was nothing left but light. So in the dark you made a new home. In the dark, perhaps, the other earthlings would not see you so hard or so difficult or so long or so fast or so aching. Perhaps, you had believed the terror that followed you would be contained within and you could forget. But in time, trundling across time, there came the disallowance, disavowal: an earthling across the bridge that spanned the creek. There came all disguised and in the grace of soft-padding beauty an earthling that glimpsed *you*. All of you. Even as she was wary of what might be received in return for being so open to receiving you. The earthling looked at you and wondered what you were and what you were to her. To yourself. And you held her gaze because you were desperate and you felt small and you were alone. Then, the earthling turned and made to leave you. But you could not let it leave. And so you followed the earthling into the dark. Because she was a form of love. Because she let you. And, soon enough, across the bridge, there came a blessed nothing composed of an infinity of moments of which you know nothing … and everything.

after in the swell of roots impactful toward the sky
after through the tree branches soaking up the wind
when you knew what they meant
bereft of reason but steeped in something deeper
after

there is no weight now

Ecology

→ Art | → Attachment | → Care | → Coexistence | → Earthlings | good ideas | → Imagine | need | → New Materialism | reliance | symbiosis | the certain uncertainty | wholes with holes

Ecology is the wish to be haunted. Ecology means being aware that things are happening on more than one time-and-space scale at once. You get haunted by the consequences of your actions, which never perfectly line up on every scale. Ecology means you are aware of finitude. Ecology means that you know there are life forms around the corner of your awareness on whom you depend, life forms who depend on you.

Ecology means you depend on something. Ecology means you realize you and others depend on each other. It's good to need. I don't believe in codependency any more. I think that's a way for us to tell each other that needing is bad in a world that wants to make it bad, for the sake of profit.

Ecology means you rely on things. You rely on the Earth not to burst into flame. You rely on water not to kill you with too much of itself.

Ecology means you know all these chemicals you are made of, that flow into you and out of you. And they make the earth and the sea and the sky. And ecology means you know you are part of all kinds of groups, all kinds of collectives, teams. Wholes. Wholes that have holes. Perforated wholes. Wholes that can overlap. Not silos or prisons. No loyalty oaths.

Timothy Morton (born 1968, located in Houston, US) is Rita Shea Guffey Chair in English at Rice University. He has collaborated with Björk, Laurie Anderson, Jennifer Walshe, Hrafnhildur Arnadottir, Sabrina Scott, Adam McKay, Jeff Bridges, Justin Guariglia, Olafur Eliasson and Pharrell Williams. He is the author of *Being Ecological* (2018) and 15 other books translated into ten languages.

Ecology means symbiosis. Ecology means you're floating along in the ocean one day and GLOP! What did I just swallow? Was it good for me? Was it poison? I guess I have to find out. Ecology is the beautiful uncertainty of coexisting. Ecology is welcoming a stranger, and that stranger becomes more and more strange the more you know them. Ecology is being in love. The certain uncertainty. The way ambiguity is a signal of accuracy. The way irony is a signal of reality. The way you're almost you, this cat on my glass table is almost a cat, the table is almost a table, you might almost say I'm living in a world. You might almost say I'm alive. You might almost say I'm a person. You might almost want to put your arms around someone and almost tell them almost everything – you can't quite say everything, but you almost do.

You have wiggle room. The uncertainty of your guest, the one you just let inside, that's why things can change. The ambiguity, the beauty of it, that's how progress can happen. Stillness and movement are a little different – they're almost different. Stillness and movement are not the same. They almost are. Things are shimmering. Beauty happens for no reason. Everything is a person, and people are almost people. The good stuff is a lot more available and a lot cheaper than you might think – the good ideas that stop planet death. They're right here. I'm almost done.

In a really good comedy, all the emotions are coexisting like a really healthy habitat, all the strangeness, melancholy, sadness, joy, love, absurdity, jealously, hate, indifference, care … all of it, all of it for as long as you can keep those plates spinning, keep on moving in the disco, moving, standing still, moving.

I don't think I will ever get tired of this magical forest.

Energy

CO_2 | fossil fuels | geopolitical changes | inertia | → Oil | policy instruments | → Power | → Production | renewable energy | strong fossil fuel industrial-economic regimes | → Sun

Stabilizing global climate change at low temperature levels is a great challenge – we need to phase out fossil fuels rapidly.

We are living in a time of great challenges: the disparities in economic development around the world are increasing, and we are facing challenges in terms of the deep societal transformations needed if we are going to stabilize global temperature change at low levels of 2 °C or 1.5 °C, as targeted in the Paris Agreement of the UNFCCC.

Fossil fuel consumption has been the major backbone in industrialization over the last 200 years and has thereby been a key contributor to the welfare society we know today in OECD countries. Fossil fuels, however, are also the major contributor to global climate change and contributed 65% of all global greenhouse gas (GHG) emissions in 2010.[1]

To meet low stabilization targets like 1.5 °C, global temperature change, according to the UN Intergovernmental Panel on Climate Change (IPCC), would require that CO_2 emissions are reduced to net zero around 2050/2060.[2] All parts of the world and all sectors need to be on board if we are going to meet this challenge, and since the energy sector is the major contributor to global GHG emissions, it means in practice that all fossil fuels in the energy sector as well as in the transportation sector should be phased out rapidly.

The world's energy supply is totally dominated by fossil fuels today, as we can see from Figure 1, based on energy statistics from the IEA.[3] In 2017, more than 80% of the global primary energy supply was based on fossil fuels, and in the period since 1971 new energy sources like renewables, biofuels, and waste have very slowly played an increasing role in energy supply.

This is the case despite plenty of alternative low-carbon energy sources like wind, solar power and hydropower being available and that the efficiency and costs of renewable energy sources have actually developed faster than expected by science over the last decades.[4]

The fast progress in renewable energy technologies sounds good, and, accordingly, it could be expected that decarbonizing energy systems and meeting climate policy targets could be achieved relatively easily. Such optimistic expectations could, in principle, be right, but a fast change to a renewable energy supply will probably not happen very easily and smoothly in practice, based on what can be observed today from the speed of renewable energy penetration.

Fossil fuels totally dominate our energy systems today, and large investments in coal, gas and oil exploitation as well as in new power plants based on these fuels are still occurring around the world, even in countries that officially state that they want to be very ambitious about climate policies. There are still high expectations about the future return of investments in fossil fuel-based energy sources, and while recognizing that the lifetime of exploitation facilities and energy supply technologies are long term, spanning from 20 to 50 years, these ongoing investments can create large inflexibilities and inertia in energy supply and will tend to increase the costs of renewable energy introduction.

Kirsten Halsnæs (born 1956, located in Copenhagen, DK) is a professor in climate change and economics at the Danish Technical University. She has published extensively internationally and has also played a leading role in the Intergovernmental Panel on Climate. Her focal research areas include sustainable development as a framework for climate change, decarbonization costs, and damages from climate hazards.

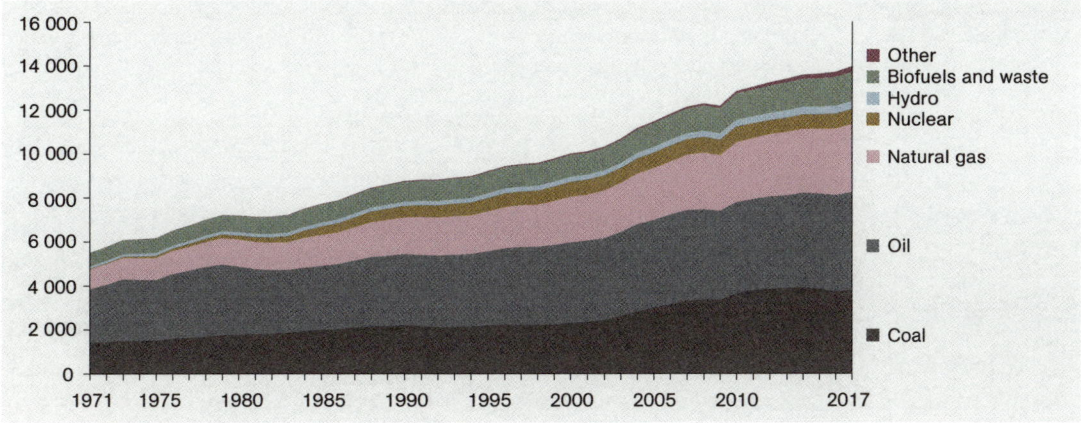

World total primary energy supply (TPES) 1971-2017 by source (Mtoe).

Several factors are driving the persistent strong role of fossil fuels in energy supply, and in new investments. They include policy expectations and uncertainties related to the progress and strength of climate mitigation commitments and related policy instruments, which constitute an important market framework for cost-effective renewable energy penetration. Stable long-term market conditions are a cornerstone in the penetration of renewable energy as well as in relation to innovation and research, and such conditions do not exist today. It is also important to recognize that very strong economic powers are concentrated around the fossil fuel sector in terms of companies and countries with large income generation based on fossil fuels, and it is a difficult challenge to disrupt the strong fossil fuel industrial-economic regimes, which have been so powerful and important in the global economic development for more than 200 years.

The world has enormous fossil fuel resources, including coal, oil and gas, and new resources have been recovered frequently during the past decades; however, exploiting all these resources would create conflicts with climate-change stabilization policies for low temperature targets. In 2015, British academic Paul Ekins and senior energy analyst Christophe McGlade assessed the magnitude of fossil fuel resources, which globally have to stay in the ground if we are going to stabilize global temperature change at 2 °C. The resources would be 88% of the coal potential, 52% of the gas potential and 35% of the oil potential. These fossil fuel resources are predominantly located in a few areas of the world, and keeping these in the ground would imply large economic losses and impacts on employment in the exploitation sectors as well as on national economies. This calls for the development of strategies, where economic development options are created for areas which today heavily depend on fossil fuels.

Let us examine some of the main current energy challenges of the world in order to obtain deeper insights into the challenges we are facing in a transition where renewable energy is to substitute fossil fuel consumption. The story is about large emerging geopolitical changes in terms of where future energy consumption will show large growth and about what could be at stake if fossil fuels are to be phased out.

In 2018, 17% of the world's population lived in more developed regions; in 2050 and in 2100 the share of the population in this part of the world is expected to be only 13% and 11% respectively, according to a medium UN population protection case.[5] Future economic development is expected to provide opportunities for providing modern energy to hopefully all people during this century, which will require large energy investments outside the more developed regions; in terms of the scale of global energy supply, OECD countries will be a relatively small playing field for introducing renewable energy options.

In 2014, electricity consumption per capita was 8,009 kWh in OECD countries.[6] If the world population increases to 10.9 billion people in 2050,[7] and their electricity consumption per capita corresponds to the OECD level in 2014, then the total global electricity consumption would be as large as 87.3 billion kWh by 2100. In some of the least-developed countries, as, for example, those in Africa, only around 50% of the population today has access to modern energy forms. This current low access to energy provides a large window of opportunity for establishing energy systems based on renewables in low-income countries and to avoid being locked in to fossil fuel-based supply systems.

How can we go against such massive forces embedded in current energy systems and the

deep economic and geopolitical interest in just continuing our current extensive use of fossil fuel resources and being locked in to these resources when new investments are being made in an expansion of energy access around the world?

The answer is asserted ever more clearly in the development of international climate policy agreements such as the Paris Agreement, and in several United Nation (UN) agreements, as, for example, the Sustainable Development Goals (SDG) 2030.

The UN SDGs include 17 areas in which several are closely linked to climate action. Some of them can be aligned relatively easily with climate action, but there are also areas where potential trade-offs can emerge between sustainable development and climate policies for low stabilization targets. An example may be trade-offs between the SDGs on access to energy, water and food for all, and climate policies in terms of the large-scale introduction of renewable energy, including bioenergy, which in some case could imply higher energy costs and conflicts about land use for bioenergy crops and agriculture.[8] These examples call for the development and application of climate policies, which are mainstreamed into general economic policies where regulation and finance aim to offset conflicts with development objectives.

Coal mining activities will have to be reduced during the coming decades if temperatures due to climate change are to be stabilized at low levels.

Works cited:

IEA. 2019. *Key World Energy Statistics*. Paris: IEA Publications.

IPCC. 2014. *AR5 Climate Change 2014: Mitigation of Climate Change*. New York: Cambridge University Press.

IPCC. 2018. 'Global Warming of 1.5 °C: An IPCC special report on the impacts of global warming of 1.5 °C above pre-industrial levels and related global greenhouse gas emission pathways, in the context of strengthening the global response to the threat of climate change'. Retrieved from. http://www.ipcc.ch/report/sr15/. Accessed 16 December 2019.

McGlade, Christophe, and Paul Ekins. 2015. 'The Geographical Distribution of Fossil Fuels Unused When Limiting Global Warming to 2 °C'. *Nature*, 517 (7533), pp. 187–190. doi:10.1038/nature14016.

UN. 2019. 'World Population Prospects'. https://population.un.org/wpp/Download/Standard/Population/. Accessed 16 December 2019.

World Bank. 2019. 'Electricity Consumption per Capita'. https://data.worldbank.org/indicator/EG.USE.ELEC.KH.PC. Accessed 16 December 2019.

Environment

→ Agency | → Art | → Attention | → Chthulucene | → Coexistence | → Description | difference | → Earth Ethics | → Ecology | embodied enaction | relationship | situatedness

When many people hear the term 'environment', they think they are hearing a synonym, a close cousin, of the term 'Nature'. (Why one of these is capitalized and one is not is a matter I will take up in just a moment.) In fact, almost the opposite is true. 'Nature' is something we have traditionally taken to be given, pre-existent – so much so that it can serve as a proper noun, a kind of baseline or fixed reference, something that is captured in expressions such as 'it comes naturally' or 'it's only natural' – hence the capital 'N' of the opening sentence. 'Environment', on the other hand, is a *relational* term. It only has meaning in relation to another term – an organism, a system, something that exists *in* and *with* that environment. While 'Nature', in the traditional sense, is a known, stable entity, 'environment' is always the 'environment' *of* something.

We can be highly technical, if necessary, about why this is the case. In contemporary systems theory, for example, we can never talk about 'environment' in isolation because it is always part of a larger system–environment unity. But these two are not equal partners, because the environment is *everything* that falls outside the boundaries of a given system (be it a biological system or a social system). So the first thing to understand about an environment is that it is overwhelmingly, exponentially more complex than any single system that tries to maintain itself and continue its existence in a constantly changing world. When you think about it, this is commonsensical enough. As famed German systems theorist Niklas Luhmann puts it (borrowing a phrase from cyberneticist Ross Ashby), systems lack the 'requisite variety'[1] that would enable them to respond, in real time, to all the changes going on in the world around them. There can be no 'point-for-point' correspondence between

Cary Wolfe (born 1959, located in Houston, US) is founding editor of the *Posthumanities* series at the University of Minnesota Press. He currently holds the Dunlevie Chair in English at Rice University, where he is also founding director of 3CT: The Center for Critical and Cultural Theory.

a system's internal state in real time and all the changes happening in the universe at any given moment. And what this means, as he puts it, is that 'the system's inferiority in complexity must be counter-balanced by strategies of selection'.[2] In other words, any system has to find a way to *reduce* overwhelming environmental complexity if it wants to maintain its coherence and get on in the world.

A couple of important consequences follow from this basic postulate. First consequence: the system–environment relationship is just that: a relationship. And it is, given the constantly changing nature of everything around us, a dynamic, temporal one, an ongoing process of give and take, of trial and error – a process that is sometimes characterized as an ongoing 'loop' of which system and environment are just components, one driven by the asymmetrical distribution of complexity across the system–environment boundary. This means that 'system' and 'environment' are not opposed, discrete and static entities, each comfortably occupying a separate side of an ontological divide, but quite the contrary. They are co-implicated and enfolded in a kind of ongoing dance of co-specification and co-definition. Second consequence: this gives us a technically precise way to explain our deeply intuitive sense of the amazing creativity, heterogeneity and fecundity of what we still call 'the natural world' – what the Romantic poets called 'multeity in unity'.[3]

The driver, the engine, for the amazing diversity we find in the biosphere is *difference:* the radical difference between system and environment in terms of complexity, and the radical difference between different systems and the strategies of selection that they use to try to make that overwhelming complexity manageable so that they can continue to exist. Of course, that very process of systems just 'doing what they do' by being selective and thus building up their own unique strategies, their own unique identities, creates even *more* complexity, *more* diversity out there in the world and so only increases the complexity of an already complex environment for every other system that happens to exist at the same time. The attempt to reduce complexity *creates* complexity, creates diversity.

In a very important sense, then, the 'environment' is a *virtual* entity, but here virtual doesn't mean 'not real' or 'less real', it means '*more* real'. In the context of the Anthropocene, we are often encouraged, in Tim Clark's words, to 'think on a planetary scale',[4] but being specific about the concept of environment forces us to ask, what, exactly, would such a thing look like? Whose 'environment' are we talking about? After all, as many people have noted, global warming hasn't been a catastrophe at all for the world's jellyfish population. Quite the contrary, the jellyfish are loving it! But do we want a world populated only by jellyfish? Probably not.

All joking aside, my point here is not just merely academic, not just an academic exercise in the fine points of epistemology. On the contrary, it pertains to the very nature of life on the planet. As we know from the contemporary life sciences stretching back to the work of the Baltic German biologist Jakob von Uexküll in the early 20th century, ecological space itself is above all *virtual* space. Why? Because any such space is populated by a myriad of wildly heterogeneous life forms who create their worlds, their environments, through which Chilean biologists Humberto Maturana and Francisco Varela call their embodied 'enaction',[5] unfolding dynamically and in real time their own modes of knowing and being, their own ways of dealing with a complex environment. A bat is not an elephant is not a dolphin is not a dung beetle. As German philosopher and cultural theorist Peter Sloterdijk puts it in his massive *Spheres* project, meditating on the path-breaking work of Jakob von Uexküll during the first decades of the 20th century, 'it had been a mistake to view the human world as a shared stage for all living creatures.' What we find here instead is a 'pluralistic ontology' which consists, in Uexküll's lyrical phrasing, 'not of a single soap bubble that we have blown up beyond our horizon into the infinite [...] but of countless millions of narrowly bounded soap bubbles that overlap and intersect everywhere'..[6]

We might be tempted to call such a perspective 'relativist', but in fact, as Maturana argues, such a perspective is 'super-realist'.[7] One 'who believes in the existence of innumerable equally valid realities' cannot be called 'relativist' because 'asserting their relativity would entail the assumption of an absolute reality as the reference point against which their relativity would be measured'.[8] Such an assertion – the assertion of 'relativism' – would entail the all too familiar humanist desire to escape our own ecological embeddedness and our finitude (to use Jacques Derrida's term) – to escape what Donna Haraway characterizes as the 'situatedness' of our knowledge and experience of the world.[9]

In the end, then, the important thing to realize about the difference between 'environment' and 'Nature' is that the difference isn't just philosophical; it's ethical too. If there is no Archimedean point, no god's-eye view,[10] from which all those environments, all those worlds – all those 'countless millions of soap bubbles' – can be seen and described in their totality, then that councils a certain humility: towards the myriad other forms of life on the planet and towards our own situatedness and finitude that shapes how we see and value them. And if the environment is relational and dynamic, something that is *made* and not *given*, then it's all the more important how we make the world we live in – and how we bear responsibility for our disproportionate power, among all other life forms, to affect the environments that other creatures inhabit too.

Works cited:

Clark, Timothy. 2015. *Ecocriticism on the Edge: The Anthropocene as a Threshold Concept.* London: Bloomsbury.

Coleridge, Samuel Taylor. 1971. 'On the Principles of Genial Criticism Concerning the Fine Arts.' In *Critical Theory since Plato*, pp. 471–476. Edited by Hazard Adams. New York: Harcourt Brace Jovanovich.

Haraway, Donna J. 1991. 'Situated Knowledges: The Science Question in Feminism and the Privilege of Partial Perspective.' In *Simians, Cyborgs, and Women: The Reinvention of Nature*, pp. 183–202. New York: Routledge.

Luhmann, Niklas. 1995. *Social Systems.* Translated by John Bednarz, Jr., with Dirk Baecker. Stanford: Stanford University Press.

Maturana, Humberto, and Francisco Varela. 1992. *The Tree of Knowledge: The Biological Roots of Human Understanding.* Translated by Robert Paolucci. Revised Edition. Boston: Shambhala Publications.

Maturana, Humberto, Bernhard Poerkesen, Wolfram K. Koeck and Alison R. Koeck. 2004. *From Being to Doing: The Origins of the Biology of Cognition.* Translated by Wolfram Karl Koeck and Alison Rosemary Koeck. Heidelberg: Carl Auer Verlag.

Sloterdijk, Peter. 2016. *Spheres, Volume 3: Foams—Plural Spherology.* Translated by Wieland Hoban. South Pasadena, CA: Semiotext(e).

Explicitation

→ Attention | implicit stories | → Local | → Terraforming | tide | → Time | → Water | → Weather

A site is woven of implicit stories: of history, culture, natural elements, geology, materials, social relations, imaginings and words.

We can use architecture to lay bare the multiple layers of information a site contains, rendering them physical and explicit. The key is to identify the site's strongest building blocks, to communicate and build on them. New spatial, cognitive and bodily experiences can emerge from existing ones and emphasize a site and a time with condensed narratives. They take their beginning in local features: weather, materials, people and context, each with its time, rhythms, tempos.

In Blåvand, on the Danish west coast, architecture becomes a language we can use to emphasize how weather and the movements of the water are the fundamental premises for how the site was shaped and continues to change with the influence of wind, tides and shifting sands. Along the water's edge, the tide is highlighted with a water playground that brings out the variations in the water level.

NORRØN (founded 2014, located in Copenhagen, DK) was established by the two architects Marco Berenthz and Poul Høilund. NORRØN works in and reflects on the fields of experience economy and destination development.

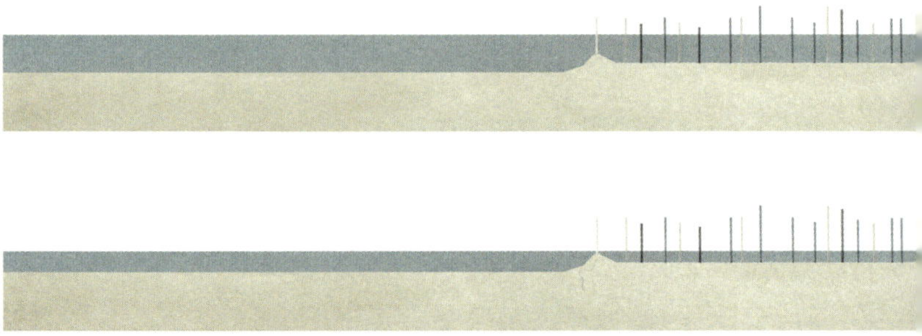

The North Sea coastal landscape.

As the waves wash up on the beach, the water playground retains and delays the water in basins when it retreats again.

Each of us is woven into many hidden systems and stories. When the systems are laid bare, we can discover how we are connected to the world and to the site. This laying bare lets us sense a complex world, where we always exist in a mutual dependency with our surroundings.

The wooden columns hold back the ocean water during low tide, creating small lagoons for children to play in.

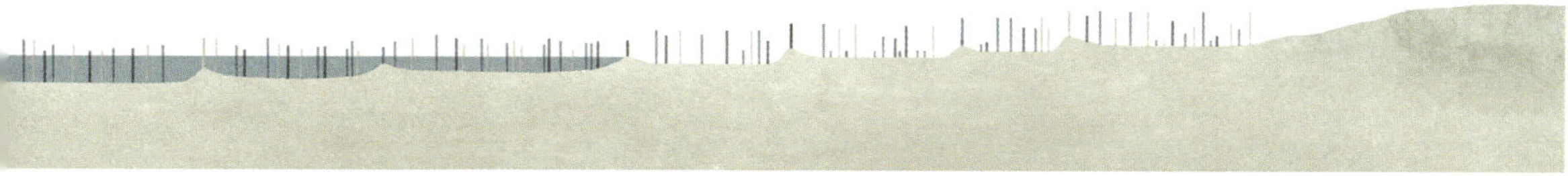

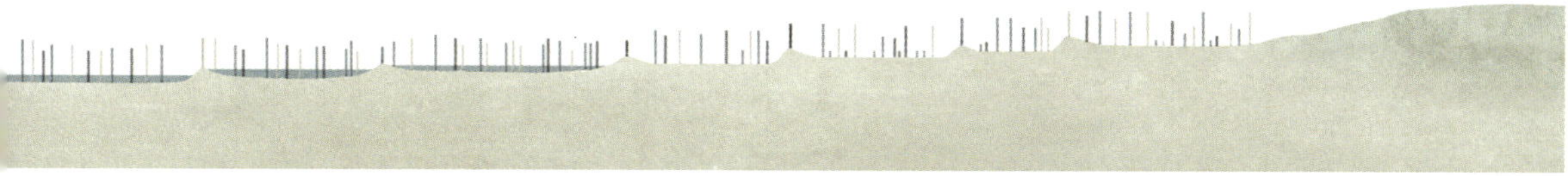

F

~~facing Gaia~~ → Care

Facts Peter Weibel

~~fast food culture~~ → Food

~~fatherland~~ → Xenophobia

Feminism Meike Schalk, Thérèse Kristiansson and Ramia Mazé

~~fertility~~ → Body

~~find a home~~ → Earthlings

Fire Lars Skinnebach

Flood SUPERFLEX

~~fluid~~ → Water

~~flux~~ → Garden

Food Alice Waters

~~foregrounding the material world~~ → Power

~~fossil fuels~~ → Energy

~~framing~~ → Attention

~~from background to main drama~~ → Climate

~~from life to death~~ → Oil

Future Andri Snær Magnason

~~future generations~~ → Sustainability

Facts

cognitive dissonance | → Denial | doxacracy | ideology | → Media | mediated society | → Moving Earths | → Object-Oriented Ontology | science | → World Scientists' Warning to Humanity

Facts in the age of post-truth philosophy
'The world is everything that is the case.' Austrian-born British philosopher Ludwig Wittgenstein's famous book *Tractatus Logico-Philosophicus* opens with this sentence.[1] But what is the case? Facts are the case, says Wittgenstein: 'The world is the totality of facts, not of things.' Wittgenstein believed in facts. To him, it is a fact that the world consists of facts: 'The world is determined by the facts, and by these being *all* the facts.' Apparently, these definitions are slightly tautological. The world is determined by facts, and facts are everything that is the case. What is the case is the world, and the world is the totality of facts. We learn facts exist, and what exists is facts.

In fact, the world is also what is not the case but what is possible. The world itself is everything that is the case and that is not the case. What exists for some people does not exist for other people: truth and lie, facts and fiction. In everyday life, it is rather easy to define what exists. Almost nobody would deny that tables and trees exist. If it comes to the question of whether God exists or not, some would say it is a fact that he exists; some would say he does not exist – God is not a fact. What is the case are facts, and from facts we derive the truth. Lies deny facts.

Peter Weibel (born 1944, located in Karlsruhe, DE, and Vienna, AT) is an artist, curator, media theorist and CEO of ZKM | Center for Art and Media Karlsruhe and director of the P.W. Research Institute for Digital Cultures at the University of Applied Arts Vienna. He commissioned the Austrian Pavilions at the Venice Biennale and was in charge of Ars Electronica, the Seville Biennial, and the Moscow Biennale as artistic director.

The truth about facts is that facts – there is no doubt – are always doubted. Beginning with the Italian philosopher and polymath Galileo Galilei, we can define what facts are and what the problem with facts is. Firstly, humans have invented a method to discover, create, invent facts which can be observed, tested in repeated experiments and empirically and theoretically proven, verified or falsified. This method is called science. Secondly, facts can be refuted and denied by religious, ideological, political, emotional and other interests.

Facts are sometimes counter-intuitive. They contradict what we see, or they proclaim something which we do not see. As human beings, we do not feel the rotation of the earth around itself and the sun. Therefore, in 1616 the Roman Catholic inquisition condemned Galilei's championing of heliocentrism as 'foolish and absurd [...] and formally heretical since it explicitly contradicts in many places the sense of Holy Scripture'.[2] French physicist Léon Foucault's pendulum experiments from 1851 proved, without doubt, the rotation of the earth.

Experiencing how difficult it was to establish facts by scientific methods, scientists and philosophers searched for a theory that could principally discern wrong from false ideas. British philosopher and statesman Francis Bacon, one of the founders of modern science, wrote in *Novum Organum* (1620), 'The idols and false notions which are now in possession of the human understanding, and have taken deep root therein, [...] beset men's minds that truth can hardly find entrance.'[3]

In the vein of Francis Bacon, during the French Revolution intellectuals used the term 'ideology', derived from the world 'idea', to establish a science to distinguish true ideas from false ideas. French philosopher Antoine-Louis-Claude, Comte Destutt de Tracy is the founder of this concept of ideology as a theory of ideas. The key concern was that true ideas are based on facts. The German philosophers Karl Marx and Friedrich Engels, however, argued in *The German Ideology* (1846) that ideology became precisely the opposite: like the camera obscura, ideology produces false images and ideas of the world.

This pejorative turn from ideology as a method to discern true from false ideas to an interest-driven belief system is the problem of today, when in times of social media and media, in general, the differences between facts, truth, fakes and lies have become more indiscernible, but above all more difficult to be accepted. As early as 1956, German–Austrian philosopher Günther Anders observed in his book *The Obsolescence of Humankind* that the distinction between essence and appearance, real and fiction disappears in the age of TV. As a result, we have a US president, trained by and grown up with TV, who flips between facts and 'alternative facts', between truth and 'fakes' as he pleases. As people have accepted trash TV, it is only consequential that they also get a trash president.

French political theorist Guy Debord described in *The Society of the Spectacle* (1967) that our mediated society exists only in the image and for the image without reference to reality or facts. French philosopher and sociologist Jean Baudrillard's theory of simulation assumes that the differences between true and false images, between reality and media are destroyed by the media itself (*Simulacra and Simulation*, 1994).

Mass media, with their cult of celebrities, created by the media themselves, are the secular version of prior religious idolatry, the worship of fake images, fake gods and chimera. The mass media, from print to online, play a decisive role today in the conditioning of facts and truth, because as the German sociologist Niklas Luhmann noted, 'Whatever we know about our society, or indeed about the world in which we live, we know through the mass media.'[4] The media tell us today 'what is the case in the world'. They report about the world. Their selection and interpretation of what is the case and of what occurs and takes place constitute the specific totality of facts that we cannot control or prove. American psychologist Leon Festinger investigated the problem of this media-based information in 1957. He discovered the law of 'cognitive dissonance',[5] which explains why facts are easily refused. Every piece of information – every fact that contradicts presumed, preconditioned or ideological assumptions – causes dissonance and disharmony in the human brain and therefore is suppressed, refuted, opposed, negated. Humans will not accept new facts that force them to rethink and reorganize their opinions. For most people it is much more comfortable to live with their prejudices than to make analytical judgements based on facts, which is significantly more strenuous and stressful.

With social media, humans have now a mass medium available for everybody to articulate his or her opinions or prejudices in public. These opinions can be reinforced, multiplied by others and become mass opinion, even supported by millions of bots, fictive algorithmic artificial opinions. Therefore, social media sites have become a gigantic resonance, mirror room or echo chamber of opinions. The ancient Greek word for opinion is *doxa*, in contrast to knowledge, *epistēmē*. Instead of living in a democracy, we are now living in a *doxacracy*, under the tyranny of *doxa*, which serves the multiplication and reinforcement of prejudices. Opinions and social media are the new Roman Catholic inquisition: against facts and for fakes, against information that violates the mental harmony built on disinformation. Social media sites are the arena for closed circles of preconceptions. They are the resonance room for acting out cognitive resonance; they are the pool for fakes. Popular opinions, circulated in the closed room of social media, feed the basis for totalitarian truth-suppressing regimes.

This technological-social turn away from facts was unfortunately foreshadowed by the so-called science wars that took place between 1994 and 1999, starting with a text by American professor of physics and mathematics Alan Sokal about quantum gravity supporting postmodern criticism of scientific objectivity. The text was a hoax, a parody on postmodern deconstruction and the social construction theory in general. Books such as *Fashionable Nonsense* (Alan Sokal and Jean Bricmont, 1997) and *The Social Construction of What?* (Ian Hacking, 1999) and later the 'Grievance Studies Affair' (2017–2018, also referred to as 'Sokal Squared'), a series of accepted hoax and nonsense papers published by three authors in social sciences magazines, complained and demonstrated that postmodern philosophy and science studies not only wrongly relativize the claim of science to objectivity, truth, facts, but even obscure science. The truth of a sentence became – from Russian philosopher of language Mikhail M. Bakhtin to French philosopher Jacques Derrida – a space of infinite interpretations; 'matters of fact' became 'matters of concern'.[6] In the age of Donald Trump, it became evident that this kind of philosophy and science studies, which denied in a certain measure the objectivity of facts by emphasizing linguistic, psychoanalytic or social conditions, was providing intellectual ammunition for reactionary interests, especially in denying the climatic crisis, denying evident facts. Therefore, philosophers like Bruno Latour have recognized that their 'very same argument of social construction' of facts is misused 'to destroy hard-won evidence that could save our lives'.[7]

Science was invented as a method to investigate what the case is in the world, what the facts are of the world, by verifying or falsifying ideas and theories by observation and experiments. Later, ideology was initially invented as a method to discern true from false ideas. Then ideology gained the reputation to obscure reality, mask and disguise facts and truth. In the postmodern age, even science was argued to be ideology constructing facts and truth. Therefore, it is necessary to embrace a world view again based on facts. Otherwise we lose our ability to survive: data can serve as therapy, as proposed in *Factfulness*[8] by Swedish statistician Hans Rosling.

Works cited:

Bacon, Francis. 1858. 'Aphorisms Concerning the Interpretation of Nature and the Kingdom of Man, §38'. In *Novum Organum Scientiarum I (The New Organon)*. Cited from *The Works of Francis Bacon*. Edited by James Spedding, Robert Leslie Ellis and Douglas Denon Heath. London: Longman et al.

Festinger, Leon. 1957. *A Theory of Cognitive Dissonance*. Stanford: Stanford University Press.

Latour, Bruno. 2004. 'Why Has Critique Run Out of Steam? From Matters of Fact to Matters of Concern'. *Critical Inquiry*. Special issue: *Future of Critique*, 30 (2), pp. 225–248.

Lombardus, Petrus, et al. (1616) 1989. 'Consultant's Report on Copernicanism, 24 February 1616'. In *The Galileo Affair: A Documentary History*. Edited by Maurice A. Finocchiaro. Berkeley, Los Angeles and London: University of California Press.

Luhmann, Niklas. 2000. *The Reality of Mass Media*. Stanford: Stanford University Press. Originally printed in 1996 as *Die Realität der Massenmedien*. Opladen: Westdeutscher Verlag.

Rosling, Hans, Anna Rosling Rönnl and Ola Rosling. 2018. *Factfulness: Ten Reasons We're Wrong About the World – and Why Things Are Better Than You Think*. New York: Flatiron Books.

Wittgenstein, Ludwig. 1922. *Tractatus Logico-Philosophicus*. London: Paul Kegan/New York: Harcourt.

Feminism

becoming-with | → Body | → Creation | → Description | embodied utopias | kinship | other-than-human-beings | → Queer | situated knowledge | storytelling | → Time

---

Arguing that feminism continues to be one of the most powerful movements for social justice, bell hooks, American activist and educator, posits feminism as a broad vision for the rights of all bodies, identities, voices and viewpoints. She articulates, 'Feminist movement happens when groups of people come together with an organized strategy to take action to eliminate patriarchy.'[1] She traces a long history of feminist movement and its effects: from struggles such as 'black liberation' and 'women's liberation' to an evolving feminist legacy established through activism and scholarship, which uncovered suppressed voices and histories, and, finally, to contemporary feminist theory, which engages with critical theories to explore differences and to empower the construction of more just futures.

Recently the term 'Anthropocene feminism' has been coined, referring to American feminist philosopher Donna Haraway's work in science and technology studies, among others.[2] Haraway was one of the feminist thinkers who have redrawn the map of what is considered knowledge. 'Situated knowledges'[3] recognizes frequently marginalized groups' experiences that arise from acting in a particular place, time and situation, as valid data in the world.[4] However, the entanglement of the human and non-human in one world has been subject already in the amazing works of Rachel Carson, American marine biologist, conservationist and writer, from *Under the Sea Wind* (1941) to her seminal book *Silent Spring* (1962), which have affected environmental movements globally and inspired generations of eco-feminists thereafter.

From a critical Indigenous perspective such as formulated by the Sisseton Wahpeton Oyate Indigenous studies scholar Kim TallBear, it is the devastating white supremacist life order under which we are all forced to live today that has been a reality ever since the colonization of the Americas and, brutally imposed by its 'settler state' mentality, its ways of organizing human and other-than-human relations. 'Whether the settler state wants to farm, build a mine or a city, pump oil, or cordon off a national park, the "resources" used to build these nation-states include the lands, waters and other-than-human-beings with whom Indigenous people are co-constituted'.[5] Contrasting these exploitative

Meike Schalk (born 1963, located in Stockholm, SE) is a German architect and Associate Professor of Urban Design and Urban Theory at KTH School of Architecture, Stockholm. She works with feminist theory and practices, and collaborative research formats. With Thérèse Kristiansson and Ramia Mazé, she edited the book *Feminist Futures of Spatial Practice: Materialisms, Activisms, Dialogues, Pedagogies, Projections* (2017).

Thérèse Kristiansson (born 1981, located in Stockholm, SE) is a Swedish artist, architect and researcher, and part of the design, art and architecture group MYCKET. Her ongoing projects include Kepsen, a public space for dance and movement built for and together with the local dance academy in Råslätt, Jönköping, and *When Walls Speak*, a publication of MYCKET's architectural findings from their research on the queer club scene in *Girls Like Us*.

Ramia Mazé (born 1974, located in Helsinki, FI) is a professor at Aalto University in Finland. She previously worked in Sweden at Konstfack, KTH Royal Institute of Technology and at the Interactive Institute. Mazé is a designer and architect by training, thus her PhD focuses on interaction design. She has led and participated in major design research projects in areas such as social innovation, sustainable design, design policy and activism.

relations, TallBear makes connections between Indigenous practices and traditions (in particular from an everyday Dakota understanding of existence) with queer and extended kin lifestyle understandings, as formulated by Haraway.[6] Such an undertaking implies decolonizing the idea of the nuclear family as it is based on an exclusive kind of intimacy and the gender system of the 'settler state' (which cannot be decolonialized, as TallBear says). For this, she directs us to the thought that by sustaining 'good relations among all the beings that inhabit these lands', we must undercut settler (property) relations.[7] Haraway's and TallBear's thoughts on extended kin groups include our companion species.

The question feminism addresses: How can we change the world?

Feminism offers optimistic outlooks on the future; every feminist politics believes that things can be otherwise and that they can be changed, states the Swedish philosopher Fanny Söderbäck.[8] There are, nonetheless, many varieties of feminism, or feminisms, and notions about what feminism contributes to the future and how such a future could be produced. bell hooks's *Visionary Feminism* points to three fundamental components for achieving social change: feminist theory, environments for intellectual exchange and feminist pedagogy.[9] Feminist theory involves critical interrogation crucial for developing, as hooks puts it, 'a revolutionary blueprint for the movement' to act. She also argues for the collective production of common environments where sustained dialectical critique and exchange can take place. Most of all, she regards feminist pedagogy as providing the possibility for everyone to take part in the movement, for everyone to develop critical consciousness – though each from her own perspective.

In architecture, British writer and architectural theorist Jane Rendell has suggested a 'feminist spatial practice'[10] which works as an explanation, a concept and a strategy. While critical spatial theory may generally examine how a particular social-spatial order is constructed, and critical spatial practice may work to destabilize that order, feminist spatial practice questions and opposes, but it also projects, activates and enacts alternative norms or ideals. Transgressing the boundaries of disciplines as well as theory and practice, feminist spatial practice develops new terms of engagement, including tactics and ethics of practice.

Learning from the geographers who go under the shared pen name J.K. Gibson-Graham,[11] and in line with TallBear, we see feminist spatial practice as developing different terms upon which everyday life and all social relations of society can be reorganized, premised on alternative experiences, world views and subjectivities. They are, thus, in their words, practices of ontological reframing, re-viewing (or re-doing) differently and cultivating forms of creativity that emerge from an experimental, performative and ethical orientation to the world. Many feminists believe it is through recognizing the activity of hitherto overlooked actors who experience the world differently that possibilities for the future emerge. According to TallBear, 'We must turn the ontological table';[12] the idea of 'settler state' property undercuts the very base of how we could live otherwise, and TallBear proposes instead 'an explicitly spatial narrative of *caretaking relations* – both human and other-than-human – as an alternative to the temporary progressive settler-colonial *American Dreaming* that is ever co-constituted with deadly hierarchies of life'.[13]

Also American anthropologist Anna Tsing explores new ways for humans and non-humans to live together in a time of environmental decline – 'in capitalist ruins' (the Anthropocene).[14] Tsing poses the question, what manages to live despite capitalism? She gives attention to the small aspects to grasp the vast topic of environmental change, revealing unexpected connections between ecological relations, capitalist transformations of environment and collaborative survival. Like Haraway, her work inspires to rethink connectedness, or 'becoming with', by learning to embrace a different reality. She proposes storytelling as a means to make these connections, referring to the American writer Ursula K. Le Guin, who suggested that 'storytelling might pick up diverse things of meaning and value and gather them together, like a forager rather than a hunter waiting for the big kill. [...] Stories should never end but rather lead to further stories'.[15]

Part of the creation of these forms of collaborative survival is the transformation of our personal practices and by that to imagine and to produce 'other worlds'.[16] Connecting feminist materialist, queer and decolonizing perspectives, Danish–Swedish gender studies scholar Nina Lykke describes materially concrete but also open-ended world-making practices. As material-discursive activities, they move from critical to reparative or affirmative modes, transgressing seemingly fixed boundaries and non-negotiable taxonomies. Through this frame, she highlights methodologies that are hopeful, performative and, simultaneously, robust enough for a messy world in which other dynamics than the utopian unfolds.[17]

Besides environments and access to theory and education, architects and spatial practitioners need to develop other notions of time in order to act upon the future, argues Australian philosopher Elizabeth Grosz.[18] Instead of regarding time as planned development, in which the future is fundamentally the same as the past, she directs our attention to a notion of time as 'becoming', connected to lived experience and bodies. Her notion of 'embodied utopias' is a productive paradox that functions to critically rethink exclusionary politics, discrimination and racism. It combines the projection of utopia – which is both nowhere at no time and anywhere at any time – with the recognition of duration and transforming, matter and bodies, of sexual, racial and other specificities, the 'differential values of its subjects' and their utopic visions.[19] Embodied utopias evoke critical consciousness of multiple visions, which claim space and time, and imply that all must take part in shaping a common future.

Against what and for what do we act together?

These concepts have gained fresh relevance during this time of rising nationalist, sexist and racist tendencies around the world. Many Western countries have become destinations for those fleeing war zones and the effects of climate change and poverty, for those seeking a different and better future. Visions offered by nationalist and racist politics speak about a return to an idealized past[20] and the project of an idealized future,[21] in which both past and future typically presume particular bodies and gendered divisions.

In these difficult times, feminisms offer a critical resource for rethinking the future through a varied and expanding range of approaches that question the status quo and the past, present and future dominance of particular hegemonies. They articulate alternative ways of being and a diversity of ways for organizing collectively. They offer useful interventions and tactics, strategies, techniques and methods for remaking categories of utopia (Grosz), capitalism (Gibson-Graham), kinship (Haraway) and so on, thus turning them into plans for action, in the here and now.

Works cited:

Carson, Rachel. (1941) 2007. *Under the Sea Wind*. London: Penguin Classics.

Carson, Rachel. (1962) 2012. *Silent Spring*. Boston, MA: Houghton Mifflin Harcourt.

Gibson-Graham, J.K. 2008. 'Diverse Economies: Performative Practices for "Other Worlds"'. *Progress in Human Geography*, 32 (5), pp. 613–632.

Glabau, Danya. 2017. 'Feminists Write the Anthropocene: Three Tales of Possibility in Late Capitalism'. *Journal of Cultural Economy*, 10 (6), pp. 541–548.

Grosz, Elizabeth. 2001. *Architecture from the Outside: Essays on Virtual and Real Space*. Cambridge, MA: MIT Press.

Grusin, Richard, ed. 2017. *Anthropocene Feminism*. Minneapolis: Minnesota Press.

Haraway, Donna. 1988. 'Situated Knowledges: The Science Question in Feminism and the Privilege of Partial Perspective'. *Feminist Studies*, 14 (3), pp. 575–599.

Haraway, Donna. 2015. 'Anthropocene, Capitalocene, Plantatonocene, Chthulucene: Making Kin'. *Environmental Humanities*, 6, pp. 159–165.

hooks, bell. (1984) 2000. *Feminist Theory: From Margin to Center*. London: Pluto Press.

Lykke, Nina. 2017. 'Prologue: Anticipating Feminist Futures While Playing with Materialisms'. In Meike Schalk, Thérèse Kristiansson and Ramia Mazé, eds. *Feminist Futures of Spatial Practice: Materialisms, Activisms, Dialogues, Pedagogies, Projections*, pp. 27–32. Baunach: AADR/Spurbuchverlag.

Petrescu, Doina, ed. 2007. *Altering Practices: Feminist Politics and Poetics of Space*. London: Routledge.

Rendell, Jane. (2011) 2016. 'Critical Spatial Practices: Setting Out a Feminist Approach to Some Modes and What Matters in Architecture'. In Lori A. Brown, ed. *Feminist Practices: Interdisciplinary Approaches to Women in Architecture*, pp. 17–56. London: Routledge.

Söderbäck, Fanny. 2012. 'Revolutionary Time: Revolt as Temporal Return'. *Signs*, 37 (2), pp. 301–324.

TallBear, Kim. 2019. 'Caretaking Relations, Not American Dreaming'. *Kalfou*, 6 (1) (Spring), pp. 24–41.

Tsing, Anna Lowenhaupt. 2015. *The Mushroom at the End of the World: On the Possibility of Life in Capitalist Ruins*. Princeton: Princeton University Press.

Fire

→ Creation | → Invisible | → Oxymorons | → Sun

I write only in daylight. Under the original mother's. When my fellows made fire, they split the spirit from the body and have been sick ever since. The spirit could hold vigil all night and imitate the tongues of the fire. That is how language and meaning arose. Later, the sun moved into the houses so the fellows could live anywhere and eat anything. The two tablets are an asemic text that can be read with a hand-held mirror. From within I look like lips.

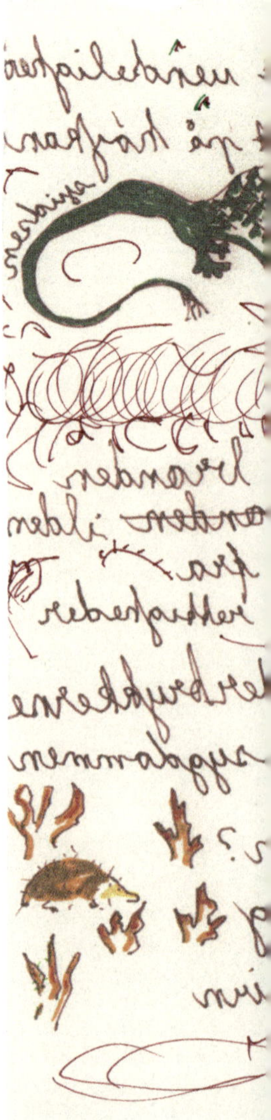

Lars Skinnebach (born 1973, located in Sønderho, Fanø, DK) grew up in Greenland. His books from the new millennium represent a turning point in Danish poetry towards a more politically engaged literature. In 2010, his book *Øvelser og rituelle tekster* (Exercises and Ritual Texts) sparked an ecopoetic movement in Denmark that continues to gain momentum. Today, Skinnebach has retreated into an ascetic lifestyle and creates performance art as part of the group Gp&Pls.

menneskene til ildværket da
Ner de skinnende tårne
og det på malken flød
og det nu kommer gå den anden
å strand
sig det kom og hinanden
Vi tvedede i gaden og vendede
dag gå torver fra Amazon
fra de travers huse
regnskove Til den anden side
korlivsendimaanta
Jeg blev opvarmet med min lectur
så gode bullinger træerne var
og havde unge som klamoterne
ne bid nogen er det elementernes
Kamp: lvantiene i californien
og australien. hvad et
hvorfor den avulmer i normer
og oikanerne øjne

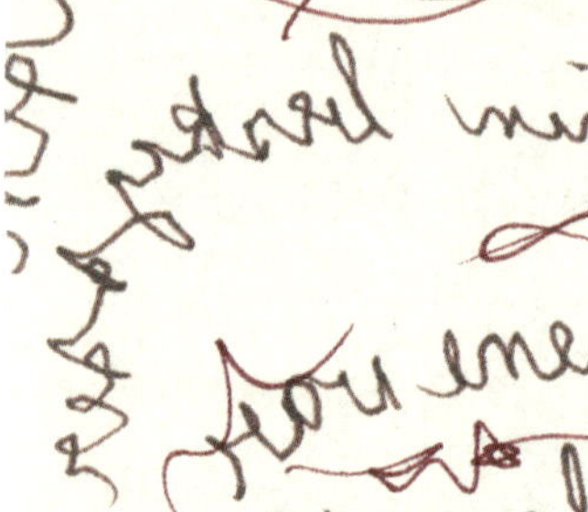

Sjuglmiereau uetàli beam ilàtem ɡọr ɡọív
menneuerdet til et anbet vorau
end a tet kiatooqiske

Med ilátem kraw nyroga
rarevrede uyraten
ɡɐranɡ
På deu ene eide
aglyɡning
Na lia bar
og ɡorabu
madeeren der
ateukler aur
Iraleɡi ɡrå ur mad
de ɡladeker
mu ɡeerer tid
Ned anetaɡ

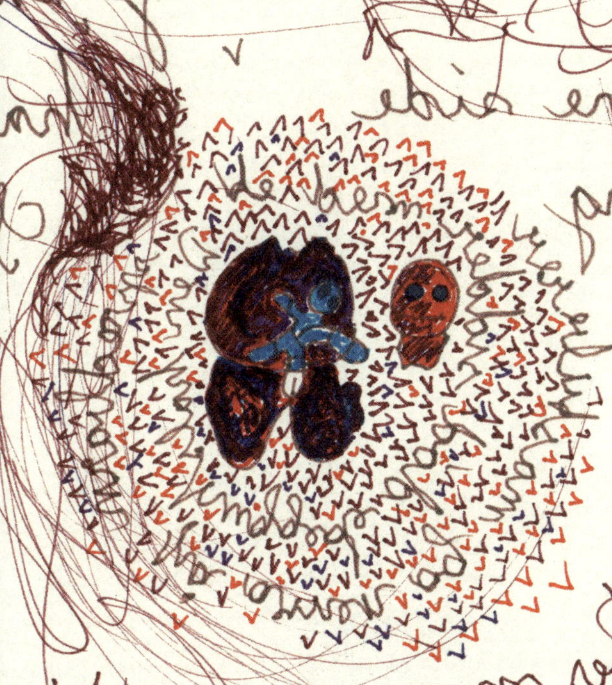

marts 2 2019

Flood

→ Borders ¦ → Climate Risk Communities ¦ → Dystopia ¦ → Earthlings ¦
→ Posthuman ¦ → Water

SUPERFLEX (founded 1993, located in Copenhagen, DK) was established by Jakob Fenger, Bjørnstjerne Christiansen and Rasmus Nielsen. With a diverse and complex practice, SUPERFLEX challenges the role of the artist in contemporary society and explores the nature of globalization and systems of power. SUPERFLEX describes its artworks as tools, thereby suggesting multiple areas of application and use.

Après nous, le déluge, or After us, the flood in English. We – Madame Pompadour, chief mistress to Louis XV, and Louis XV – uttered this phrase upon hearing the news of the 1757 French loss at the Battle of Rossbach against the Prussian Empire, a significant turning point during the Seven Years' War. Our words can be interpreted as a double entendre: a prophetic claim of impending chaos, a statement of lurid indifference.

Either way, let the flood come.
We welcome it.

It means nothing to us, for we are long gone.

'*Après moi, le déluge!* is the watchword of every capitalist and of every capitalist nation. Hence Capital is reckless of the health or length of life of the labourer, unless under compulsion from society.' After me, the flood. So wrote Karl Marx in *Das Kapital*.

Me, I am Capital. I have a habit of draining everything around me to quench my constant thirst. The water is rising over my head; it sloshes over here and there. Sometimes even I start to wonder how much volume I can withstand.

But I pay no mind.
I won't concern myself with floods today.

Après vous, le déluge, or After you, the flood if you prefer. This is a message from the depths of the sea. It is a message from us, the fish, to you, the human. Within a few human generations, it is estimated the global sea level will rise by up to 2.5 metres. So, it is certain that your structures will become at least partially if not entirely submerged. While this flooding might be catastrophic for you, it is a welcome change for us. The ocean will heave and transcend your human-made borders, igniting a massive vertical migration.

Yes, you will be gone, but just think: after you comes a flood of new life!

Food

a delicious revolution | → Agriculture | → Body | → Care | → Connectedness | fast food culture | → Garden | learn by doing | monocultures | sensorily deprived | → Soil | The Edible Schoolyard Project

Alice Waters (born 1944, located in Berkeley, US) is a chef, food activist and the owner of Chez Panisse in Berkeley, CA. She founded the Edible Schoolyard Project in 1995, whose mission is to institute free organic school lunch for all children and a food curriculum in every public school. She has been vice president of Slow Food International since 2002 and was awarded a National Humanities Medal by President Obama.

A hundred years ago, with her study of the stages of childhood development, the Italian philosopher and educator Maria Montessori reminded us that our senses are the pathways into our minds. In her work with children in Naples and India, Montessori discovered that poverty and hunger cause children to become sensorily deprived; their awareness of the world around them is diminished and their imaginations cannot thrive. Today our children remain sensorily deprived – not just because of pervasive hunger and poverty but because of the hegemony of fast food culture. 'Fast food culture' is the phrase I use for today's dominant culture, which has embraced the fast food values of 'fast, cheap and easy'. Fast food culture is a system fuelled by greed and designed to enrich industrial agriculture, corporate interests and the one per cent. All around the world, fast food culture disconnects us from nature and from the universal human values of nourishment, stewardship and community.

We wonder why we cannot engage people to do more to reverse climate change. I believe the reason for this alienation – this failure to embrace our own accountability – stems from the origins of the food we eat. The food system in the United States has dramatically changed in the past 60 years: our former agrarian culture has been replaced by a highly industrialized one. Crops are grown in vast, government-subsidized monocultures, many foods we used to produce domestically are now imported, and most of what is delivered to the American table is ultra-processed and filled with sugars, additives and preservatives. One in two children in the United States will develop diabetes. Our children have been indoctrinated by the fast food industry, absorbing the insidious fast food values of uniformity, convenience, constant availability and speed above all else. Our food is manipulated and sold to us as if nature didn't exist. Food is delivered instantly, devoid of beauty, in disposable containers, so it can be consumed in the car or on the move. In fast food culture, there's no sense that food comes from the land, that someone has grown and harvested it – indeed, there's no sense that we are profoundly dependent upon nature, and deeply part of it. And while cultures around the world have always thought of food as medicine, this current culture wants us to deny the basic truth that what we eat directly connects to our health and sense of well-being.

Twenty-five years ago, I started a project called The Edible Schoolyard Project in Berkeley, California. I had spent much of my time at my restaurant working against the industrialization of agriculture, but I came to realize that, just as we had industrialized our farms, we had industrialized our public schools using the same one-size-fits-all corporate business model. The Edible Schoolyard Project started as an intervention in a public middle school near my house, where a thousand students – speaking 22 different languages – were enrolled. We planted a large edible garden classroom on the campus and built an adjacent kitchen classroom. Classes in both the garden and kitchen were developed with the Montessori pedagogy in mind: to learn by doing, at an age when children are still young and open. These were not classes to learn gardening or cooking per se.

Rather, the garden and kitchen classrooms were woven into an academic curriculum in which students measure flowerbeds in maths class, collect soil samples to analyse in science class and thresh ancient grains in history class. The classes come alive, and students fall in love with their lessons – and just as importantly, they learn that nourishment comes from the ground and that they are, thoroughly and fundamentally, part of the natural world. I have always believed that, in every school cafeteria, students should sit together and share a meal where the values of sustainability – nourishment, community and stewardship of the land – would wash over them.

Now is the time to take action. I believe that public education is one of the last remaining democratic institutions in America, and a potential location for extraordinary change. In the state of California alone, every day the public school system feeds more than six million students in its cafeterias. What if all ten thousand California public schools pledged to emancipate themselves from the industrial food supply chain and instead purchased their food from small local farms that practice regenerative agriculture? Our schools could be the economic engine for regenerative farming, which could be a major solution to climate change. With its no-till approach and use of compost and companion planting, regenerative agriculture can replenish our soil and sequester carbon at the same time, effectively pulling carbon out of the atmosphere and putting it back into the soil where it belongs. What's more, scientific studies have shown the link between regenerative farming, the soil's rich microbiome and our own immune systems. When we farm regeneratively, we improve the health of the planet and our own health in the process. This is a remarkable, hopeful and global solution that can save us all, inside and out. And if we committed to school-supported agriculture, we could change our agricultural system in one academic year!

Fast food culture tells us this isn't feasible: our children won't want it, there isn't enough quantity, the system is too calcified to change. The corporate, lobby-driven machine benefits when we remain stuck in our ways. But we can change the way we operate. The restaurant I started in Berkeley in 1971 has been breaking the rules from the beginning and showing that a new type of food system can prevail. We have been buying food from small regenerative farms and feeding 500 people a day for almost 50 years. We have learnt how to eat differently in the summer and winter and adapt our diets in tune with nature.

Consider the power of food. It is something we all partake of every day, if we're lucky, and we have a choice every time we sit down to a meal. What we eat can either close down or open up our lives. It can reduce our world to something small and isolated or it can open up our senses and our bodies to the world around us. There are consequences to every decision we make, even if the decision is as seemingly small as choosing what to eat. When we make the right decisions about food, food reconnects us to ripeness and beauty and taste, to family and culture and tradition; it reconnects us to our own health, to the land around us and to the survival of our planet. These human values, which have sustained us for millennia, are the values that make this a delicious revolution.

Future

→ Attachment | → Connectedness | direct impact on the future | → Imagine | → Next Generation | → Sensitivity | → Time | → Window of Opportunity

I'm at Grandmother Hulda and Grandfather Árni's home in Hlaðbær. We're sitting in the kitchen: the Elliða stream meanders in front of the house, and people are jogging along the river path. I open my computer and load a video so I can show Grandmother and Mum a film no one has seen in decades. I'd discovered an old 16 mm cassette in their storage room and had converted it to digital. It was a movie Grandfather took in 1956, black-and-white and silent. Well-mannered children are sitting in the dining room and Grandmother appears, smiling, with a magnificent cream cake decorated with lit candles. At the end of the table, ten-year-old twin sisters are sitting together, laughing and blowing vigorously at the candles.

And we're sitting in the same kitchen, 60 years later. Mom is over 70, Grandmother 94 years old, my youngest daughter 10. We sit down to eat pancakes as the radio hums low in the background. I ask Hulda Filippía, my daughter, to do a little maths puzzle.

'How old is your great-grandmother if she was born in 1924?'

'She's 94,' Hulda replies immediately.

'Fast maths', I say.

'Well, I know how old she is,' she grins.

'Alright, but now you'll really have to do some sums. When will *you* be 94?'

'You mean 2008 plus 94?'

'Exactly'.

She takes a piece of paper and a pen and looks sceptically at the sheet. She shows me the result as though it must be a misunderstanding.

Andri Snær Magnason (born 1973, located in Reykjavík, IS) has written poetry, novels, children's books and plays. His books include *LoveStar* (2012), *The Story of the Blue Planet* (2012) and *Dreamland* (2012). His newest book, *On Time and Water* (2020), is a story about glaciers, grandmothers and holy cows, weaving, science, mythology and personal stories in the light of climate change.

'2102?'

'Yes, hopefully you'll be just as energetic as Grandmother is now. Maybe you'll even be living in this same house. Maybe your ten-year-old great-granddaughter will be visiting, sitting with you in this kitchen in 2102, just like you are sitting here right now.'

'Yes, maybe', says Hulda, sipping a glass of milk.

'One more equation. When will your great-granddaughter be 94 years old?'
Hulda writes some figures on a piece of paper, with a little help.

'She was born in 2092?'

'Yes, that's right.'

'2092 plus 94 ... 2186!'
She laughs at the thought.

'Yes, can you imagine that? You, born in 2008, might know a girl who is still alive in 2186.'
Hulda purses her mouth and looks into the air.

'Can I go now?' she asks.

'Almost', I say, 'I've one more puzzle. How long is it from 1924 to 2186?'
Hulda does the maths.

'262 years?'

'Imagine that, 262 years. That's the length of time you connect. You know the people who span this time. Your time is the time of someone you know, you love and who moulds you. And your time is also the time of someone you will know and love, the time you will shape. You can touch 262 years with your bare hands. Grandmother taught you; you will teach your granddaughter. You can have a direct impact on the future, right up to the year 2186.'

'2186!'

following spread:
Ok glacier memorial plaque. Installed in August 2019, in memory of the first Icelandic glacier to be lost to human-related climate change. Text by Andri Snær Magnason in collaboration with Cymene Howe and Dominic Boyer of Rice University in Texas and glacialogist Oddur Sigurðsson.

Bréf til framtíðarinnar
Ok er fyrsti nafnkunni jökullinn til að missa titil sinn.
Á næstu 200 árum er talið að allir jöklar landsins fari sömu leið.
Þetta minnismerki er til vitnis um að við vitum
hvað er að gerast og hvað þarf að gera.
Aðeins þú veist hvort við gerðum eitthvað.
A letter to the future
Ok is the first Icelandic glacier to lose its status as a glacier.
In the next 200 years all our glaciers are expected to follow the same path.
This monument is to acknowledge that we know
what is happening and what needs to be done.
Only you know if we did it.
Ágúst 2019
415ppm CO_2

Bréf til framtíðarinnar
Ok er fyrsti nafnkunni jökullinn til að missa titil sinn.
Á næstu 200 árum er talið að allir jöklar landsins fari sömu leið.
Þetta minnismerki er til vitnis um að við vitum
hvað er að gerast og hvað þarf að gera.
Aðeins þú veist hvort við gerðum eitthvað.
A letter to the future
Ok is the first Icelandic glacier to lose its status as a glacier.
In the next 200 years all our glaciers are expected to follow the same path.
This monument is to acknowledge that we know
what is happening and what needs to be done.
Only you know if we did it.
Ágúst 2019
415ppm CO_2

G

Garden Hu Fang
~~geochemical and geocultural agent~~ → Waste
~~geochemical and geophysical cycles~~ → Biodiversity
~~geochronology~~ → Aesthetics
Geology Minik Rosing
~~geology of humanity~~ → Anthropocene
~~geopolitical changes~~ → Energy
Geo-Social Classes Nikolaj Schultz
~~geo-subjectivity~~ → Heritage
~~gig economy~~ → The Sharing Economy
~~glacial-to-interglacial transition~~ → Abrupt Climate Change
Glaciers Jesper Theilgaard
Global Saskia Sassen
~~global commons~~ → Resources
~~global heating~~ → Resources
~~global middle class~~ → Capitalocene
~~global migration architecture~~ → Migration Flows
~~global warming~~ → Declarations of Climate Emergency
~~good ideas~~ → Ecology
~~greenhouse gasses~~ → Glaciers
~~Greenland and Antarctica~~ → Abrupt Climate Change
~~growing protests~~ → Anthropocene

Garden

dark rain | erosion | flux | → Soil | → Time | → Wilderness

I came to this decadent garden at a time of tempest, and just like when I stepped into that village, I inevitably came too late. By the time I arrived, the garden had already evolved into ruin.

The last time I had seen it was in a portrait of my parents – my father wearing his Mao suit, my mother in her Lenin coat – posed together before an artificial mountain. It was their favourite view, although they never once talked with me about the garden. It was only later, after seeing a film by Antonioni,[1] that I could imagine the garden that filled their eyes.

Or you could say that what I was seeing in the garden was itself a movie. Wherever my gaze landed, there was never a moment when the light and shade, the air, the vegetation, the ripples in the water were not in flux – as though, at the same time it was being exposed, it was also being developed, and disintegrating, just like the future upon which the darkness has to tread.

If one looked carefully, this place still bore the traces of a peony garden. Unconventionally, the garden's owner had used various types of peony to create a herb garden, hidden along the right bank of the long-since dried-up pond, and even the scholar's stones lining the pond had taken on a refreshing herbal fragrance.

Hu Fang (born 1970, located in Guangzhou, CN) is a fiction writer and co-founder of Vitamin Creative Space in Guangzhou. His recent books include *Dear Navigator* (2014) and *Towards a Non-Intentional Space* (2016), which reflects upon the research and thinking process of developing Mirrored Gardens, a project space seeking to merge with its rural environment in contemporary art practices.

Amid the tempest, the garden resembled a scholar's stone after years of erosion, gradually worn to the bone, so that it could only respond to what the sunlight gave it, and what the dark rains gave it, with a reciprocal feeling, and nothing more. Formerly, under the painstaking care of its master, the garden had been full of vitality, while beneath that vitality another garden, a negative, decaying garden, was simultaneously gestating; then at a certain point in time – for example, now – the sun fades in the west and the light shines all the more brilliantly, even though this is just the soulful parting of sun and earth, and it is exactly during this exchange between day and night that I will slip into another layer of this garden's space.

As night fell, I cut through the detritus, and by the faint glow of my phone I suddenly made out the peony garden's remaining herbs and weeds, now starting to entangle, struggle, embrace, merge, while the soil, more welcoming and yet melancholy, luxuriantly exuded the smells of the earth's depths, so that it seemed one were embraced by an even more fundamental existence. Compared to the gardener's meticulously tended order, this wasteland has a more enveloping power, linking hands with time in occupying the garden as its own territory. Perhaps, between the consciousness of time and naturally passing time, the garden in its time of flourishing had already set aside time for its flowers to fade and behind its didactic order had set aside waste and wilderness, and then this waste connected the garden to the vast and desolate outer world, gave it the potential for truly becoming part of nature.

Those things that remain in our heads, those things that remain after all this time, prompt you to head here, and not there – and strolling aimlessly, I strolled right to the boundary of the decadent garden, an internally desolate boundary.

There is no one who is without guilt, but we are the only ones who can judge ourselves.

Geology

→ Anthropocene | → Atmosphere | bio-geochemical cycles | biosphere | children of Mother Earth | → Climate | → Earthlings | → Energy | hydrosphere | lithosphere | matter and energy

We live on a globe, just one among eight sister planets. They each orbit a star we call the sun, just one among hundreds of billions of other stars in our galaxy, which is just one galaxy among a couple of thousand billion others in the universe. Our universe is a vast expanse of emptiness peppered with small clusters of matter and energy, including our sun and our planet. All the galaxies in the universe are made from somewhat forlorn leftovers, leftovers composed of one billionth of an original capital of matter left after an unfathomable amount of matter and antimatter was annihilated during the first fraction of a second at the origin of time, 13.7 billion years ago.

Geology is the word that describes our reasoning about Earth, our miniscule glob of matter in this immense universe. Perhaps it is extravagant to allocate a whole science to the study of such a small fraction of everything. But Earth is our home, the only home we have.

When you stand on a mountaintop on a clear day in Greenland, you see endless landscapes stretched out in all directions. Glaciers draped over mountains and hills transected by rivers and dotted with lakes. Mountains upon mountains lead your eye to the far horizon. No person could walk all the hills and valleys you can see from just one mountaintop, even if they spent their entire life on the project. From this perspective, Earth seems infinite.

The immensity of time and the range of scale is a dilemma for geology. But geology is a planetary science that attempts to understand the origin and fate of our Earth in the contexts of the solar system and broader universe through billions of years of time. It also has to provide insight into human evolution and the impact of human activity on Earth's surface environments on the scale of a human lifetime. Only if we understand the scale of the physical Earth and the dimension of time can we begin to understand ourselves.

Since the emergence of consciousness, humans have reflected on the origin of the world and our role in it. Our understanding of the world as a spherical planet goes back thousands of years and was first formalized by Pythagoras more than 2,500 years ago. A quarter of a millennium later, Eratosthenes managed to determine the size of our planet based on astronomical observations. The first textbook that describes Earth and its processes and resources was written by Pliny the Elder 2,000 years ago under the title *Naturalis Historia*.

After thousands of years of human measuring, pondering and educated guessing about the scale of Earth and its component parts, Austrian geologist Eduard Suess took the logical consequence of Earth being spherical and defined the components parts as spheres as well. In 1875, he gave us the lithosphere: the rocky part of Earth; the hydrosphere: oceans, rivers, lakes and glaciers; the atmosphere: gasses; and rather ingeniously the biosphere: everything living. He understood that most things that happen and have happened in our world are interactions between these spheres. Every process we know forms part of a cycle of materials – moving from one sphere to another and ending again in its original sphere. All these cycles are driven by the flow of energy either from Earth's hot interior to the cold space surrounding us, or from the sun. These are the biogeochemical cycles.

Minik Rosing (born 1957, located in Copenhagen, DK) is a professor at GLOBE Institute and a geologist working on the influence of life on the geological evolution of Earth's continents, oceans and climate. His work is mainly based on field research in his native Greenland. He was curator of the Danish Pavilion at the 2012 Architecture Biennale in Venice, thematizing the harmonious development of Greenland in a rapidly changing world.

The flow of energy determines how fast the cycles are spinning. Those driven by the inner energy of Earth are mostly very slow, like the movements of continents across the globe at a few centimetres per year, while those driven by the fierce heat of the sun, such as the winds in a tropical storm, may rage at hundreds of kilometres per hour. Most of the cycles involve life in one form or another, particularly the biogeochemical cycle of carbon. Everything living is built on a structure of carbon, hydrogen and oxygen – that is, they are mainly manufactured from carbon dioxide and water. When plant life is thriving, it consumes CO_2 from the atmosphere to make more biomass. That depletes the content of CO_2 in the atmosphere. Conversely, if biomass, recent or fossil, is eaten or burnt, it increases the concentration of CO_2 in the atmosphere. This function of life has regulated the composition of the atmosphere over billions of years. And that is lucky, because the composition of the atmosphere is crucial for the habitability of Earth.

In 1894, the Swedish chemist Svante Arrhenius discovered that Earth's climate is largely determined by the concentration of CO_2. He called the phenomenon 'the greenhouse effect' and was able to demonstrate that even though only 3 in 10,000 molecules of the air are CO_2 molecules, this trace gas has a strong effect on Earth's surface temperature. Understanding the carbon cycle is key to understanding why Earth's climate is clement and conducive to life and human existence.

As individuals and as a species, we humans are little and have short histories on any galactic scale. This has led us to regard ourselves as insignificant on a geologic scale as well. Most, if not all, of our traditional and religious stories make us beneficiaries or victims of external forces. Deities or spirits of nature determine the natural circumstances of our lives. We are the children of Mother Earth and have no responsibility for our fate or the fate of the natural world.

In this magical thinking, the resources of Earth are infinite. The sky is high, human efforts are puny, dwarfed by the forces of nature. Recently – that is, only in the past century – we have gradually discovered that far from being ineffectual, insignificant creatures, our very existence acts as a major force on Earth. Thanks to our intelligence, we figured out ways to command fossil energy stored in Earth for millions of years, so we could spend it in just a couple of centuries. It has come as a surprise to us that the super powers we found by tinkering with the carbon cycle come at the cost of Earth's entire system. Our choices have direct and real consequences for the fate of the planet we live on. This story is encoded in Earth's geological record. Geology is the science that has finally taught us who we really are.

Microscopic particles of black carbon found in a more than 3,700 million-years-old sedimentary rock from Greenland. The carbon originally formed part of the atmosphere and was converted to organic matter by living organisms. Fossil energy has been stored in rocks over nearly four billion years, while life has regulated Earth's climate.

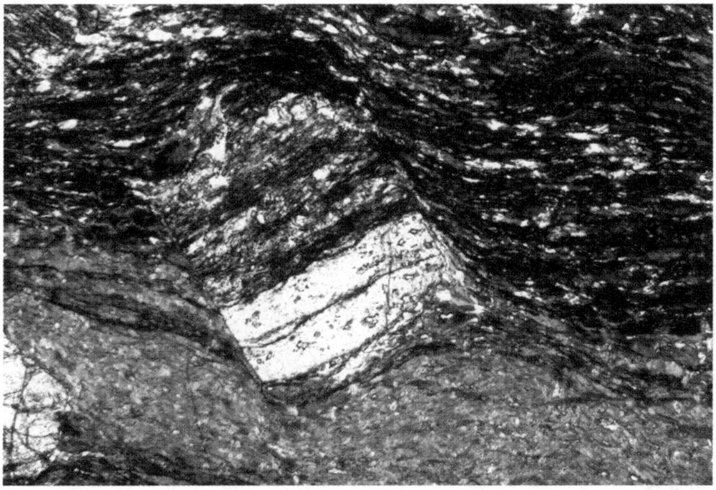

following spread:
Carbonate rocks in the great fjords of north-east Greenland. Microbes formed these kilometre-thick deposits of limestone in a now lost ocean more than a billion years ago. In doing so, life sequestered CO_2 from the atmosphere in the rocks. As these rocks become heated in Earth's interior, the CO_2 is released again and returned to the atmosphere through hot springs or volcanoes. The carbon has turned full circle in its biogeochemical cycle.

Geo-Social Classes

→ Capitalocene ¦ class ¦ → Description ¦ → Explicitation ¦ material conditions of existence ¦ → Migration Flows ¦ New Climatic Regime ¦ → Power ¦ power and domination ¦ reproduction ¦ → Resources ¦ territorial positions ¦ → Violence

The Anthropocene is an 'event for social theory'[1] forcing us to leave behind long-held assumptions about the nature of the social world, its dynamics, structures and stratifications. Many of the questions we thought we knew how to answer need to be reposed, some even reinvented, and so do the concepts we use to frame these questions through. One of these questions regards how we understand the concept of 'social class' in our new geological epoch.

One of the reasons for the significance of the notion of class for politics and social theory is its relation to two different existential, social questions – 'existential' in this case referring not to inquiries into the essence of what it *means* to exist but instead inquiries into the essence of what *allows* entities to exist.

The first of these questions – what we can call the quasi-objective existential question of the social – has to do with inquiries into *what allows societies to exist*. What is the practical, material reality of society? What is the basic structure of the social world? What are the fundamental mechanisms that determine the shape of societies and what entities allow societies to reproduce and survive? Queries and curiosities that regard the fundamental ontology of the social world and the processes of reproduction of societies.

The second of these questions deals instead with *what allows people in societies to exist* – what we can name the quasi-subjective existential question of the social. What is the position of people in the social landscape? Where in the material reality of society do people live? From where do people get their conditions of subsistence and what allows them to survive in society? With whom do they share these conditions and against whom do they struggle? Inquiries that investigate the positions and the orientation of people in the social world in relation to their reproduction in society.

Nikolaj Schultz (born 1990, located in Paris, FR) is a PhD fellow at the Department of Sociology, University of Copenhagen, where he is preparing his thesis on geo-social classes. Since 2018, he has collaborated with Bruno Latour on this topic. He is currently editing a book on Latour's work (2020) with contributions from, among others, Pierre Charbonnier, Gerard de Vries, Graham Harman and Barbara Herrnstein Smith.

For a long time, Marxist analysis offered tools that made these two questions easier to grasp. At the birth of the modern industrial capitalist society, Karl Marx turned Georg W.F. Hegel's idealist dialectics upside down and argued that our understanding of history ought to be 'materialist'.[2] For Marx, the fundamental starting point of any society was the *survival and reproduction of human life*, and any analysis of history thus had to begin by considering the *basic material conditions of existence* – that is, food, water, clothing and housing – that allowed this reproduction.

According to Marx, the *production* of these material conditions of reproduction formed the basis of history and society. What allowed societies to exist and to reproduce? The means, resources, human labour, instruments, knowledge, techniques and organization that permitted the production of society's material conditions of subsistence – in sum, what Marx called the 'forces of production'. These forces produced the practical, material reality of society, and, combined with the specific social 'relations of production', they constituted the 'mode of production' – by Marx understood as 'the innermost secret, the hidden basis of the entire social edifice'.[3]

With the mode of production, Marx described the material structure of the social landscape and the mechanisms that allowed industrial societies to reproduce and subsist, hereby answering what we called the quasi-objective existential question of the social. Yet by describing the forces *and* relations of production, Marx had furthermore developed a vocabulary that allowed people to position themselves *in* the process of production and to orient themselves *in* the material landscape of the society that emerged from it.

By defining 'social classes' with reference to ownership over the means of production, Marx made it possible for people not only to know *what* allowed them to subsist but also *where* in the chain of subsistence production they lived and with *whom* they shared these conditions. If you owned the means of production, you were a part of the bourgeoisie, a capitalist. If not, you were a part of the proletariat, the working class, a definition that allowed people in one and same breath to describe *what* they lived off, *where* they lived and with *whom* they lived, hereby responding to the quasi-subjective existential question of the social world.

This is the sometimes forgotten aspect of the notion of social class. Its usefulness not only lies in its ability to demarcate the mosaic of stratifications in society. No less important, it inherits crucial descriptions of *how society materially reproduces itself and how people reproduce themselves within this process*. It describes the *genesis* and the more or less just *distributions* of societies' material condition of subsistence or reproduction, two crucial aspects for the understanding of any society – aspects which have always been present in the background of political anthropology but which, as we shall see, now return to its centre with an amazing power.

With this apparatus of social and political analysis, Marx entered the stage and gave intellectual direction to a socialist tradition that until then, as Pierre Charbonnier notes, had been messy to say the least.[4] Yet what Marx could not foresee was that the industrial forces of production would *accelerate so greatly*[5] that they would end up destabilizing earth and climate systems to a degree where their mutations are now *intensifying* and *metamorphosing* the questions of the forces and mechanisms that allow societies to reproduce and survive.

While *Capitalocenists*[6] have tried to update Marxist thinking to capture the Anthropocene condition by underlining 'the logic of profit' as the driving force behind our new geological epoch, this is what their critical gaze has left unnoticed. Today, in our 'New Climatic Regime',[7] the two existential social questions of what allows societies to reproduce and what allows people to survive in society are transforming, and the quintessential task for the social sciences has become to develop an analytical framework that allows us to comprehend their changes.

These transformations correspond to the unveiling of what Bruno Latour calls the 'processes of engendering',[8] understood as a conceptual alternative to the mode of production as the reproductive basis of society. While the system of production presupposes a world of stable, given resources for reproduction, *the continuous, durable existence* of these material conditions of subsistence is no longer to be assumable in a New Climatic Regime characterized by a common loss of territory. At the end of modern abundancy,[9] with the soil disappearing under the feet of us all, we need to dig a bit deeper than the mode of production when answering the quasi-objective existential question of the social and describing the reproductive basis of society.

Instead of limiting our framework to the forces of production, we need to widen our attention to the *terrestrial forces of engendering* – including entities like climate, air, trees, soil, insects et cetera – and the labour, instruments, knowledge, techniques and organization that *mediate* these agencies. In the Anthropocene, it is impossible to understand the reproductive basis of society without paying attention to such agencies that increasingly co-define the material infrastructure of society and with which societies will have to renegotiate their permission for continuous, long-term subsistence.

In other words, it no longer suffices to turn Hegel on his head. Instead, we have to bury him deep into the soil and identify and describe the terrestrial forces of negotiations between humans and non-humans that make up the material conditions of existence that allow societies to reproduce and survive. Nonetheless, as for Marx, describing the mutation of these means of reproduction is only half of the story. The task is describing not just the *forces* but also *the specific relations of engendering* that emerge with the contemporary transformations of the reproductive basis of society.

206 Today, to describe *what* allows people to subsist, *where* in the material reality of society people live and with *whom* they share these conditions of subsistence no longer suffices to focus on the ownership over the means of production. Rather, in order to answer the quasi-subjective existential question of the social, our analysis will have to identify and describe the *relational distributions of a wider array of material conditions or agencies of subsistence* that allow people to reproduce and that account for their place in the social, material landscape.

Such redescriptions correspond to a shift from social classes to what we have called *geo-social classes.*[10] These are classes defined not by their *ownership over the means of production in the production process* but by their *access to a broader range of material conditions of reproduction in the engendering process.* While social classes were collectives defined by economic position, geo-social classes are collectives defined by *territorial* position, by their position in the reproduction processes of the soil. It is the distribution of these conditions of reproduction in the engendering process that defines the stratifications of societies in our New Climatic Regime.

Revising the Marxist framework of class theory in this way would allow us to delineate a people corresponding to the new climatic questions in the same way Marx delineated a people corresponding to the social question in the 19th century and hereby develop a vocabulary permitting people to position themselves within society's process of reproduction. Yet how to map these collectives and their position in the geo-social processes of engendering?

The first step is *drawing up the networks of forces of existence* that different social groups depend on to live and reproduce. This amounts to describing the territories different collectives live off, the spatial, material extension of people's livelihoods. What are the material conditions, connections or agencies that establish the *more or less prosperous livelihoods* of people? What are the forces – for example, CO_2, soil, air, energy, water, food, transport, salaries, housing – that permit the reproduction of people, what allows their access hereto and what allies enable or mediate the durable, continuing existence of these entities?

By means of such descriptions, what would initially be revealed is how *dissimilar* people's *networks of conditions of existence* look and how these networks amount to better or worse chances of reproduction. The meshwork that holds together the existence of slum inhabitants in South East Asia looks very different from that of a high-flying oil trader from New York. Yet what would also appear is how some people's networks of reproduction do *share certain features* with those of others. Maybe not exactly the same networks of reproduction but *similar enough* to reclassify them as social collectives and position them in the process of engendering.

By redescribing, reclassifying and comparing these different networks of conditions of existence, we will not only be able to identify the patterns of privilege and non-privilege in the processes of engendering. It would furthermore permit us to *reconsider our understanding of power and domination*. By describing and comparing the material extensions of people's livelihoods, what would become visible is how *the networks of existence of some allow or disallow the networks of existence of others to be better or worse.* In other words, by identifying geo-social classes, we would generate descriptions of *who is occupying or exploiting the territory of others*, or how some people's livelihoods disallow the durable existence of other people's conditions of reproduction.

Thus as opposed to the system of production where exploitation was defined by the *surplus value* that ownership over the means of production allowed some collectives to profit from, exploitation in the processes of engendering is defined by the *surplus existence* that some collectives profit from at the expense of others' means of reproduction. Exploitation happens when social groups live off other people's soil, disallowing collectives to inhabit a prosperous terrain of life. In short, the forms of livelihood some collectives profit from, disallowing other collectives a prosperous network of existences, will define domination in our New Climatic Regime.

For a long time, the Marxist vocabulary allowed for a more or less precise assessment of *what* people lived off and *where* in society's process of reproduction they lived, their answers to the existential questions of the social being sufficient for navigating within the social landscape. But today, we have to develop tools to articulate the wider array of material conditions of subsistence *under* the layers of the system of production, the networks of existences that have proven vital to understand the reproduction of societies and people's position in this process of reproduction. This is the ambition of the concept of geo-social classes.

Works cited:

Blok, Anders, and Casper B. Jensen. 2019. 'The Anthropocene Event in Social Theory: On Ways of Problematizing Nonhuman Materiality Differently'. *The Sociological Review*, 67 (6), pp. 1195-1211.

Charbonnier, Pierre. 2018. 'L'écologie, c'est réinventer l'idée de progrès social'. *Ballast*. https://www.revue-ballast.fr/pierre-charbonnier-lecologie-cest-reinventer-lidee-de-progres-social/. Accessed 1 November 2019.

Charbonnier, Pierre. 2020. *Abondance et Liberté*. Paris: La Découverte.

Marx, Karl. 1987. *On Historical Materialism*. Moscow: Progress Publisher.

Marx, Karl. 1992. *Capital: Volume III*. London: Penguin Books.

Latour, Bruno. 2017a. *Down To Earth: Politics in the New Climatic Regime*. Translated by Catherine Porter. Cambridge: Polity Press.

Latour, Bruno. 2017b. *Facing Gaia: Eight Lectures on the New Climatic Regime*. Translated by Catherine Porter. Cambridge: Polity Press.

Latour, Bruno, and Carolina Miranda. 2019. 'Troubles dans l'engendrement: Entretien sur la politique à venir'. *Revue du Crieur*, 14 (3), pp. 60–73.

Malm, Andreas. 2016. *Fossil Capital: The Rise of Steam Power and the Roots of Global Warming*. London: Verso Books.

Moore, Jason. 2015. *Capitalism in the Web of Life*. London: Verso Books.

Schultz, Nikolaj. 2020. 'On the Theory of Geo-Social Classes'. In *Critical Zones: The Science and Politics of Landing on Earth*. Edited by Bruno Latour. Cambridge, MA: MIT Press.

Steffen, Will, Wendy Broadgate, Lisa Deutsch, Owen Gaffney and Cornelia Ludwig. 2015. 'The Trajectory of the Anthropocene: The Great Acceleration'. *The Anthropocene Review*, 2 (1), pp. 81–98.

Stein Pedersen, Jakob Valentin, Bruno Latour and Nikolaj Schultz. 2019. 'A Conversation with Bruno Latour and Nikolaj Schultz: Reassembling the Geo-Social'. *Theory, Culture and Society*, 36 (7–8), pp. 215–230.

Glaciers

→ Abrupt Climate Change | drought | → Future | greenhouse gasses | ice shelves | icebergs | lack of drinking water | → Water

From our early books on geography, we know about eternal snow on the top of high mountains. This is due to the low temperatures at these heights, so the precipitation will be snow. During hundreds and even thousands of years, this snow is accumulated, packed and transformed into ice. Due to the slope of the mountains, the pack of ice drifts very slowly downwards between the rocks like a river creating a glacier.

Glaciers will therefore be found everywhere there is a combination of high ground where snow can fall and accumulate and where the pack of snow transformed into ice can slide downwards. That means that the vast areas of ice in Greenland and in Antarctica also have glaciers. Here they move towards the sea, creating a continuous birth of icebergs, where glaciers in the mountains will melt as they move downwards generating of stream of water, which will build up into rivers.

The glaciers have a function in the climate system as all white surfaces re-emit the shortwave radiation from the sun back into space, so this part of the sun's energy will not be a part of the energy budget. Therefore, all ice areas are a part of the thermostat of the Earth as more ice will have a cooling effect and less ice will have a warming effect. Saying that, it is obvious that an increasing temperature will create a self-perpetuating process.

As we in recent decades have seen an increasing temperature in the atmosphere, the ice has become more unstable and a greater melt has been recorded. That counts for almost all glaciers across the globe. Some glaciers grow due to more precipitation in the area, but in general we see decreasing and retreating glaciers.

Jesper Theilgaard (born 1955, located in Copenhagen, DK) has been a professional meteorologist since 1978 and from 1990 to 2018 a weather presenter on Danish National TV, including time as a climate expert. He has written more than 25 books about weather and climate and received a publishers' award in 2007 for his book about the Danish weather. He also received the Danish Windmill award for his communication of climate change.

For the glaciers, we have to look at the different type of areas where they are found. For Greenland and Antarctica, the nature of the glaciers is a movement of ice masses from land to sea. As snow falls on the vast ice areas, the mass increases, creating a pressure on the glaciers, so they drift downhill towards the sea. The speed of the glaciers depends on the roughness of the underlying surface. As temperature rises, we see meltwater from the surface slide through the ice to the bottom of the glacier and here act as a lubricant causing the speed to increase. If this is a continuous trend in both Greenland and Antarctica, we will see a reduction of ice mass here and thereby an increase of water in the oceans, which will inevitably cause a rise in sea level. This is one of the serious consequences of global warming, due to the increasing amount of greenhouse gasses in the atmosphere.

In some areas of Greenland and in Antarctica, we see ice shelves blocking the way for the glaciers. Ice shelves are a platform of ice often several hundred metres thick lying on top of the sea, into which the glaciers normally flow. The ice shelves are locked by the surrounding rocks and are therefore very strong as long as the temperature is below freezing. These ice shelves cause the movement of the glaciers to decrease.

In recent years, we have seen more examples of break-up in ice shelves, probably caused by the warming sea. This has, for example, happened in two sections of the Larsen Ice Shelf in Antarctica, causing the glaciers nearby to move at a greater speed.

The problems are a little different when we look at glaciers in the high mountains around the Earth. As mentioned earlier, the glaciers here form rivers when they melt at a lower height. Most of the greatest rivers form that way, and therefore millions and millions of people depend on the water from these glaciers. Especially in South-Eastern Asia, we have a number of great rivers coming from the Himalayan mountains, such as the Mekong River, the Yellow River, Yangtze River and Ganges, among others. Along these rivers, life has formed over thousands of years. People here expected, with good reason, that the water would continuously flow from the Himalayas – and so it did, but the rise in temperature implies certain risks in both the short- and long-term future. Higher temperatures will increase the melt from the glaciers, so there will be more water in the rivers, increasing the risk of flooding.

In the long term, however, another and probably greater risk may develop. If the melting is so great that it cause some glaciers to disappear, there is a risk that some rivers will dry out – at least during parts of the year. That will cause problems for hydropower, which depends on the stable flow of water and, of course, risk of drought and lack of drinking water for humans and animals.

We have actually already seen examples of disappearing glaciers. The best known is the Chacaltaya glacier in the Bolivian Andes. This glacier has been known for thousands of years, but due to lack of precipitation and higher temperature, it finally disappeared in 2009.

So glaciers are very important for many reasons, and if glaciers disappear in a greater number, mankind will face serious problems. Therefore, it will be fair to ask the question, can we do something to restore the stability of the glaciers? The short answer is no, but as the stability of the glaciers is directly linked to the temperature of the air covering the atmosphere, it is obvious that if we can stop global warming, we will also stop the melting of the glaciers. In a broader perspective, this is what the climate debate is all about – reducing the emission of greenhouse gasses, which will both stabilize the glaciers and reduce global warming. A real win-win if we manage to reduce the emissions enough. But time is running out fast – just like the meltwater from the glaciers – so we need to act fast.

Global

→ Borders | → City | → Explicitation | → Local | → Moving Earths | → Oxymorons | reshaping the national from inside | the global inside the national | transversal vectors

Saskia Sassen (born 1947, located in New York, US) is the Robert S. Lynd Professor of Sociology at Columbia University and a member of its Committee on Global Thought, which she has also chaired. Her key books include *The Global City* (2002), *Expulsions* (1991), *Territory, Authority, Rights* (2008) and, with Mary Kaldor, *Cities at War* (2020).

The global is often portrayed as being in opposition to the national. This is correct, but only up to a certain point. Here I explore the ways in which the global can be structured inside the national.

We can think of at least three ways this can happen – ways that are significant for a proper understanding of the field of global studies. One is the endogenizing or the localizing of global dynamics in the national milieu. A second is the making of formations that, although global, are articulated with particular actors, cultures or projects, producing an object of study that requires negotiating a global and a local scale, such as global markets and global networks. A third is the denationalizing of what had historically been constructed as national, such as state institutions that are the key producers of instruments needed by global economic actors.

Though these three types of instances capture distinct social entities and have diverse origins, they are not mutually exclusive. Global studies research into such sub-nationally based processes and dynamics of globalization requires methodologies and theorizations that engage not only the global scale but also sub-national scalings as components of global processes. This makes possible the use of long-standing research techniques, from quantitative to qualitative, in the study of globalization even if these may not have focused on global conditions. It also provides a bridge between, on the one hand, studies that use national and sub-national data sets and, on the other, the specialized scholarship associated with area studies. Such transversal vectors open up a new vista for the field of global studies.

In fact, many of the transformations we call global are actually often better described as a denationalizing of what was historically constructed as national, as I have explicated at length elsewhere.[1] Some of this can eventually become global, but much of it might simply no longer be national yet not necessarily global.

The most widely accepted definitions of globalization emphasize the growing interdependence of the world and the formation of global institutions. One key, often implicit, assumption in this type of definition is that the global and the national are two mutually exclusive domains.

Yet at least some of these conditions also need to be understood as emerging from local settings and dynamics. And while some of these localizations of the global are familiar – for example, the buildings of an international financial centre – many others are rarely recognized as such, so they do not get coded as having anything to do with the global. They are, often, far less talked about or simply overlooked compared with the broad, overarching macro-level global processes – notably highly visible state-to-state formal agreements, or the vast emergent operational space that has emerged from the growth in the number of global firms.

Both of these very diverse understandings of the global capture the new forms of power and their impressive new technologies. And they completely overshadow the far less visible local instantiations of the global.

The making of global spaces and global actors that inhabit local institutional and territorial framings brings to the fore the fact that much of what we call globalization is constructed inside the national and should be recognized as such. In fact, it is often coded and experienced as national. Multiple implications flow from this, including, for instance, the question of how much of what was historically constructed as the national is still national in the historical (Western) sense of the term. And even if it is no longer national, we cannot assume that it is necessarily global.

In my own work, I have often used the case of major cities as one of the spaces where diverse global processes and projects are constituted, even though such cities are mostly local. Because the global is so often understood as a condition that transcends the national, capturing the global as it gets constituted at local levels requires specific modes of analysis and interpretation. This also means that the pertinent scholarship covers an enormously broad range of objects of study – from whole cities to sub-urban elements and trans-urban elements. That scholarship also shows us the ways in which the urban is a core vector for the study of the global even if focused on micro levels of analysis.

The data generated by this type of work is quite different from that generated by research focused on the major global actors – for example, global corporations and the broad range of global governance institutions. When this embedding of the global in national settings is left out or overlooked, it easily leads to the notion that what the global gains the national loses, and vice versa. That, in turn, implies a strong correspondence of national territory with the national – that is to say, if a process or condition is located in a national institution or in national territory, it must be national.

And this will tend to set up a contest between the global and the national: it can easily signal that what is good for the global is not necessarily good for the national. While this is often the case, we must recognize that the national is increasingly a partial condition and that globalization goes well beyond self-evidently visible global institutions.

Recognizing that the global also dresses itself in the clothing of the local, reshaping the national from inside, opens up a vast research agenda. It means that studying globalization needs to include detailed local research – notably ethnographies – of multiple conditions and dynamics that *are* the global or are shaped by it but that also function inside the national and are mostly experienced as national.

Works cited:

Sassen, Saskia. 1991. *Expulsions: Complexity and Brutality in the Global Economy.* Cambridge, MA: Harvard University Press/Belknap Press.

Sassen, Saskia. 2014. *The Global City.* Princeton: Princeton University Press.

H

Heatwave Jim Reed

Heritage Ben Dibley

Home lenschow & pihlmann

~~Hope~~ → Next Generation

~~human and nonhuman agencies~~ → Power

~~human rights~~ → Body → Queer

~~human smugglers~~ → Migration Flows

~~human-non-human material relations~~ → Care

~~human-object relations~~ → Object-Oriented Ontology

~~(hu)Mans~~ → Care

~~humans as a component of ecosystems~~ → Biodiversity

~~human-weather relation~~ → Weather

~~humus~~ → Chthulucene → Soil

~~hybrids~~ → Attention

~~hydrosphere~~ → Geology → Water

~~hyper attention~~ → Attention

Heatwave

→ Resources → Soil → Sun → Terraforming → Water → Weather

Jim Reed (born 1961, located in Boston, US) is an American weather and environmental photographer, speaker, author and contributor to *National Geographic* magazine.

Drought Conditions at Lake Powell, Utah
Early signs of trouble. Record low water levels at Lake Powell in Utah were becoming a concern in the spring of 1997. The lake, which is the United States' second largest reservoir, was at 45% capacity in 2015 and at risk of reaching its lowest level.

following spread:
Record Heat at Sunset
Early signs of trouble. A thunderstorm erupts at sunset in the Central Plains of the United States during a record-setting high temperature of 42 °C (108 °F) on 20 June 1998.

Heritage

→ Anthropocene | becoming-rock | → Future | → Geology | geo-subjectivity | life and nonlife | → Posthuman | technofossils

By volume and distribution, the most significant and enduring markers of human influence on the planet will likely be the 'trace fossil system'. This will include the remains of cities, buildings, roads, airports and their altered landscapes; the 'burrowings' and 'intrusions' of mining and construction activities underground; and the various deposits of new 'anthropogenic minerals' such as pure metals and alloys, bricks, concrete, slags, polymers and plastics.[1] Once buried, these remnants of 'the technosphere' have the potential to endure in a new sedimentary layer as technofossils.[2] For the geologists seeking to delineate the Anthropocene's inauguration, the proliferation of these fossils will be not only the human species' geological legacy but also the mineral signature that marks its emergence as a major geo-force. A time, then, is to come in which Anthropocenic technofossils will litter the strata, leaving an enduring trace on the Earth's crust. If the geologists are right, this scar will stand as a legible testimony to the human species' presence as a geological force, one which will be readable in the stratigraphic record from a distant posthuman future.[3]

The logic of the technofossil is important for earth scientists making the case for the Anthropocene's formalization as a geological interval. It provides an important point of reference for examining the analogues, continuities and discontinuities with other geological epochs and periods, notably the Cambrian, the interval in which most of the planet's major animal phyla

Ben Dibley (born 1971, located in Sydney, AU) is a researcher and writer currently working at the Institute for Culture and Society, Western Sydney University.

emerged. Locating the human species' geological legacy in relation to other intervals on the Geological Time Scale – 'most of which are *unequivocally inhuman*'[4] – acknowledges that the logic of technofossils underscores that the Anthropocene is as much about the *decentering* of the human as it is about the escalating geological agency of the human species. In this connection, it is important to note that the notion of the Anthropocene not only decentres the human but also breaks with an 'organic chauvinism'.[5] For the key distinction is not the organic preoccupation with that between life and death but rather that between life and nonlife, that life, and its corollary, death – as human or species extinction – is but an interval bookended by the vast expanse of nonlife. The technofossils of the Anthropocene are but one type of trace to be considered in relation to other traces from other resolutely *inhuman* epochs. In this, the technofossil as trace fossil demands, and only has its full significance, in the consideration of temporalities that both precede and exceed the advent of life and that of the human as major geological forces and epoch markers. Nevertheless, as the inscription of the human in inhuman time, of the living in the duration of nonlife, the technofossil delivers a pathos – even a horror – that is difficult to ignore. In the hands of the Anthropocene's stratigraphers, the prospective mineralization of the remnants of human labour is not simply an objective marker of a new epoch; it is also the occasion for that species' anticipated memorialization. Literally written in stone, the strata of the Anthropocene will be a memorial to human existence – to the era of its doing and undoing.[6] The technofossil is, then, an unsettling invitation to reflect on our own species' distant stony legacy – a reflection on the poignancy of our own becoming-rock. Such prospective lithic testimonies to human existence are elevated to the status of a heritage-to-come. It is a strange heritage, one which is orientated not to the past and the memory of the dead but to a future in which the human ceases to exist.

The logos and the pathos of the technofossil are contingent on a paradoxical relationship between temporality and legibility. The technofossil is projected into a time in which an Anthropocenic strata will be legible, which is nevertheless a time without a subject to interpret it as such. The technofossil relies, then, on a future readability in a future without (human) readers. It is in this context that the technofossil performs as both scientific heuristic and memento mori.[7] On the one hand, it is an interpretive *device* of the scientific imagination concerned with the thought experiment, 'what legacy will humans leave in the rocks?', the subtitle to Jan Zalasiewicz's *The Earth After Us*. No doubt, as a conceptual tool, the technofossil is key to the legibility of a future stratum, one that makes a conjecture on the future condition of the lithosphere and its fossil record, based on what is known about the durability of the materials of which it might come to be composed. On the other hand, 'the technofossil metaphor evokes aesthetically resonating, thing-like objects more than biogeochemical signals'.[8] It is in this connection that the technofossil appears as an affective object, serving as a reminder of mortality and the trajectory of the material afterlife of the human species' activity, as 'a reminder of our incipient minerality'.[9]

Drawing attention to the ways in which the human species will come to be archived in the Earth's crust, technofossils invite a certain tragic, cosmic vanity. From an imagined dead, desolate future, technofossils ask in their stony silence, how will the Earth remember us? As Claire Colebrook writes, 'We now, narcissistically, imagine the tragedy of the posthuman future as one in which death and absence will be figured through the unreadability of our own fragments, as though our self-alienation through archive and monument yields some sentiment that we ought to remain as readers of ourselves'.[10] It is in this context that technofossils turn into strange machines of subjectification, of 'geologic subjectification'.[11] Geology is implicated in contemporary subject formation in the sense that that which is experienced as the Anthropocene is contingent on discourses, affects and tactics that enrol and attune subjects to geological processes in unprecedented ways. Hailing from the lithic future, technofossils serve to interpolate a certain geo-subjectivity, summonsing 'us' as contributing authors to our own epitaph: the 'golden spike' that marks the point at which we started to etch ourselves into the fossil record as Anthropocene rock and which will be read – in our forlorn fantasies, by a posthuman/nonhuman palaeontologist from a remote future – as signalling the start of the interval that is the beginning of the end (of us). This narrative of the technofossil perhaps comes to share in the horror that Eugene Thacker has diagnosed in his exploration of the notion of the 'unthinkable world' – 'the world-without-us' – in horror fiction and philosophies of pessimism and nihilism.[12] This world lies somewhere between the 'world-for-us' and the 'world-in-itself' in 'a nebulous zone that is at once impersonal and horrific'.[13] As testimonies without witnesses, as monuments without mourners, as inheritance without heirs, as future heritage, technofossils, it would seem, rest in this indeterminate, disturbing zone.

Works cited:

Clark, Nigel. 2012. 'Rock, Life, Fire: Speculative Geophysics and the Anthropocene'. *Oxford Literary Review*, 34 (2), pp. 259–276.

Colebrook, Clare. 2014. 'Archiviolithic: The Anthropocene and the Hetero-Archive'. *Derrida Today*, 7 (1), pp. 21–43.

De Landa, Manuel. 1997. *A Thousand Years of Nonlinear History*. Cambridge, MA: MIT.

Dibley, Ben. 2018. 'The Technofossil: A *memento mori*'. *Journal of Contemporary Archaeology*, 5 (1), pp. 44–52.

Haff, Peter K. 2014. 'Humans and Technology in the Anthropocene: Six Rules'. *The Anthropocene Review*, 1 (2), pp. 126–136.

Szerszynski, Bronislaw. 2010. 'Reading and Writing the Weather: Climate Technics and the Moment of Responsibility'. *Theory, Culture & Society*, 27 (2–3), pp. 9–30.

Szerszynski, Bronislaw. 2012. 'The End of the End of Nature: The Anthropocene and the Fate of the Human'. *Oxford Literary Review*, 34 (2), pp. 165–184.

Thacker, Eugene. 2011. *In the Dust of this Planet*. Vol. 1 of *Horror of Philosophy*. Alresford: Zero Books.

Westermann, Andrea. 2020. 'A Technofossil of the Anthropocene: Sliding up and down Temporal Scales with Plastic'. In *Power and Time*. Edited by Dan Edelstein, Stefanous Geroulanos and Natasha Wheatley. Chicago: The University of Chicago Press.

Yusoff, Kathryn. 2013. 'Geologic Life: Prehistory, Climate, Futures in the Anthropocene'. *Environment and Planning D: Society and Space*, 31 (5), pp. 779–795.

Zalasiewicz, Jan. 2008. *The Earth After Us: What Legacy Will Humans Leave in the Rocks?* Oxford: Oxford University Press.

Zalasiewicz, Jan, Mark Williams and Colin Neil Waters. 2014. 'Can an Anthropocene Series Be Defined and Recognized?' In *A Stratigraphical Basis for the Anthropocene*. Edited by C. N. Waters, J. A. Zalasiewicz, M. Williams, M. A. Ellis and A. M. Snelling. London: The Geological Society.

Home

→ Aesthetics | → Borders | → Explicitation | → Imagine | → Invisible | → Modernism | → New Materialism | → Oxymorons

lenschow & pihlmann (founded 2015, located in Copenhagen, DK) is an architecture office established by Kim Lenschow Andersen (1987, NO) and Søren Thirup Pihlmann (1987, DK). As architects, they are interested in the artistic and poetic potential that lies in the act and processes of building, and they operate in a field of architecture ranging from small-scale installations and pavilions to housing projects.

Home minus 12.5 mm

A series of three 1:6 scale models
Halting the construction and subtracting the finishing layers
Furnished and staged as a home

~~ice shelves~~ → Glaciers
~~icebergs~~ → Glaciers
~~ideology~~ → Facts
~~imagination~~ → Window of Opportunity
Imagine Björk
~~imagined community~~ → Sun
~~imbalance~~ → Sustainability
~~implicit stories~~ → Explicitation
~~inclusive definitions of violence~~ → Violence
~~inertia~~ → Energy
~~insidious anxiety~~ → Denial
~~interconnectedness within ecosystems~~ → Pollution
~~international conventions~~ → Xenophobia
~~intersectional justice~~ → Queer
~~inter-urban climate networks~~ → Climate Risk Communities
Invisible Rune Bosse

Imagine

→ Coexistence | → Future | mutant species | space for hope

it is an emergency

in order to survive as a species
we need to define our utopia

the paris climate accord is a modern utopia
impossible to imagine
but overcoming our environmental challenges
is the only way
we can survive

we have to imagine something that doesn't exist
carve intentionally into the future
and demand space for hope
weave a matriarchal dome

let's imagine a world where nature and technology
collaborate
and make a song about it
a musical mock-up
then move into it

Björk (born 1965, located in Reykjavík, IS) is a multidisciplinary artist who, time and again, innovates across music, art, fashion and technology. From writing, arranging and producing an expansive music catalogue to escapades in virtual reality and digital apps, Björk continues to inspire and experiment, redefining the boundaries of how a musician works.

let’s write music for our destination

in mythologies around the world
after a disaster one captures the spirit
with a flute and starts anew

carved out of the first fauna

we arrive on a new island with mutant species
unknown hybrids of birds and plants
our past is on loop, turn it off
let’s be intentional about the light

imagine a future

be in it

Invisible

→ Attention → Environment → Explicitation → Garden → Oxymorons
→ Terraforming

Walking through our surroundings, we often stop paying attention to what is actually there.
Encountering something 'unnatural' can bring us back to where we actually are.
But what is still natural at a time when nature itself is partly manufactured and produced?

230

Rune Bosse
If i were a plant, in the summer
of 1987.
i would grow, become interested
in growing.
i would learn and seek inspiration
in my natural surroundings.
both thru questioning this world;
how is it put together?
and seeing/showing possibilities
of assembling it in new ways.
it would give me direction
knowing the nature of things.

Rune Bosse
Where you are. Where are you,
2011
Bøgedskov and Feddet Strand, Denmark. 100 m² of beach were placed into the forest and 100 m² of forest were placed onto the beach.

J

~~Jevons Paradox~~ → Modernism

~~justice~~ → Earth Ethics

K

~~keep listening~~ → Tenderness
~~kin~~ → Care
~~kinship~~ → Feminism

L

~~lack of drinking water~~ → Glaciers
~~land as a commodity~~ → Description
~~Law of Exploitation~~ → Soil
~~Law of Return~~ → Soil
~~learn by doing~~ → Food
~~learning~~ → Resilience
~~life~~ → Water
~~life and nonlife~~ → Heritage
~~liquid carbon pathway~~ → Agriculture
~~lithosphere~~ → Geology
~~living in and living from~~ → Moving Earths

Local

Emmy Laura Perez Fjalland

~~localities~~ → Local

Local

→ Body | → Coexistence | → Environment | localities | situated knowledge | stories with planetary dimensions

With all our self-consciousness, we have very little sense of where we live, where we are right here right now. If we did, we wouldn't muck it up the way we do. [...] If we did – if we really lived here, now, in this present – we might have some sense of our future as a people. We might know where the center of the world is.

Ursula Le Guin, 1982, pp. 84–85.

240

Emmy Laura Perez Fjalland (born 1987, located in Copenhagen, DK) is a postdoctoral researcher at the Institute of Architecture, Urbanism and Landscape, at The Royal Danish Academy of Fine Arts in Copenhagen. She works with environmental humanities and explores the connections between critical thinking (feminist materialist and speculative realist traditions) and the current dialogues of environmental doom, more-than-human ontologies and ecological practices.

First, I find it important to highlight the dangers of 'local' as defining 'it' holds a long history with many stories, theories, policies and actions that have had many different outcomes, materializations, exclusions, oppression and privileging, sometimes in very unjust, inequal manners. *Local* holds connections to ideas of authenticity, something real, grounded, rooty, and the practices and materializations of this have different ethics and politics, and in all their manifold ways they are all very real, very actual and authentic, but each practice also has different cultural, environmental, ethnic, sexual, material, social and biological implications for those living there. Actual and real implications for humans and more-than-humans. With this in mind, local may also have fertilities, such as a sense of belonging, something alive and living, tangibility, something fleshy, fresh, unique, concrete, a right here and right now. Local is also defined in relation to *scale* – local, regional, national, global, planetary. Scale is the so-called measurement and comparison of some*thing*'s 'real' size and its size on a map or model and/or in relation to institutions, organizations, corporations. Let us just keep in mind that 'real' reflects a human measurement in so-called centimetres, metres, yards, inches or latitudes and is a significant language, suggestion, for how to talk about 'the real'. Furthermore, the map/model part of this definition reflects the territorial and institutional logics of defining a place as 'local', and how this is interpreted and performed ethically and politically vary. Other languages about 'the real', about things, sites and sizes, can be found, among other things, in stories, myths, wisdoms and sciences *of* Indigenous practices. It then seems that what makes somewhere, someone, something local seems understood, defined and practiced *in relation to* somewhere, someone, something else. Demarcations and borders weave together and are ambiguous, which means that the local is a becoming rather than being. The many tensions of the local, and defining the local, unfolds the manifold contaminations and collaborations taking place locally and necessarily recur through this text.

Local may refer to a place that is close to where you live and where *significant* culture, stuff, geology, habitats, landscapes, architecture and/or people are gathered and unfolding. In thinking more closely about where this local begins and ends and what this 'significance' is, local becomes not so fixed and sited. British geographer Doreen Massey has invited us to think of localities (note the plurality) as continuously becoming, continuously being made and remade 'out of a particular constellation of social relations, meeting and weaving together a particular locus'.[1] Localities then appear as filtered knots of manifold strings from different origins, materials, sizes, lengths, temporalities (imagine different balls of yarn – different colours, materials, ages, processes). *Localities as knots* of geologies, elements, words, powers, stuff, organic and inorganic materials, people, places, phenomena and imaginations, words. Just to name a few elements of the mess. While, to some, this may sound like a romantic communal diversity, we must remember the dangers mentioned and how each of these relates to each other in order to create adequate accounts of the local (of the worlds). American writer Ursula K. Le Guin points out in 'The Carrier Bag Theory of Fiction' that everything in this belly universe holds a significant, *powerful* relation to each other in a myriad of ways.[2] Always unfolding, refolding. Thinking and practicing the local in pluralities is an attempt to move around the thinking and practice of the local that at some time, somewhere has led to a romanticized notion of place and people that then sometimes, somewhere has led to nationalism and imperialism that then sometimes, somewhere has led to racialism, genocide, extinction. This is a kind of local that becomes a territory, a fixity, hermetically closed, bordered. Somewhere, sometimes imagined, desired, practiced. This is some of the dangers of *performing the local.*

Local also refers to a pain, pleasure or unruly feeling or experience affecting a specific part of your body, which then means that the local may be understood temporarily (a pain or joy can come and go), body-materially (fleshy, other-than-cultural), and psychosomatically, sensuously and emotionally. However odd the following comparison may be, the local can also have a taste of that which in French is named *terroir* and *is a bodily, sensuous and storied culmination of a biosocial site-specific landscape collaboration.* The demarcations and borders of landscapes weave together and are ambiguous, which means that it is becoming rather than being, and together with the multi-temporality of landscapes, it might be that the landscapes themselves are helpful in order to understand the local further. Landscapes can be understood as ongoing, unending collections of different rhythms and tasks that play out.[3] This could be a human body, a tree, a crop, a house, soil, a cow, an earthworm, a plough, a fertilizer, a honey bee. Each participates in shaping the particular landscape and holds a significant temporality, a time and speed; each *carries* out a significant task, and each plays with deeper histories and deeper ecologies. Local as always becoming landscaping, a carrier bag[4] practice? *Thinking local with terroir* – a sensuous, storied experience (painful, tasteful, delightful) of a biosocial landscape collaboration – might be fertile, or regenerative, in these times of a looming ecological crisis because terroir embodies how localities and locality-based practices are both particular and planetary knots of human, organic and non-organic meanings, matters and making (that might even taste good, do good).

Knowing and sensing where we find ourselves, in this specific moment, both as historical beings and as beings of water, air, bacteria, cultures, classes, is about knowing how everything relates to everything else in this 'belly universe'.[5] Look around, listen, measure, count, taste. It might be time for naming, unnaming, renaming. We might not need to take any particular position (as Modernism or pragmatism, or territorialize sites and thoughts). Enmeshed as we are, we might just *take part* and think with the knots of becoming. In these disastrous times of fire, drought, desertification, this might be a science of contamination, of ruins, of collaborations of life that continues. This might give us a more adequate view on particular concerns and views on possible localities for response-able becoming. These sciences might not have resolutions, progress, dramas and conclusions (or other territorial practices), although they might be grippingly particular, partial, incomplete, savage and unending.

Works cited:

Ingold, Tim. 1993. 'The Temporality of the Landscape'. *World Archaeology*, 25 (2), pp. 152–174.

Ingold, Tim. 2000. *The Perception of the Environment: Essays on Livelihood, Dwelling and Skill.* London: Routledge.

Le Guin, Ursula K. 1982. 'A Non-Euclidian View of California as a Cold Place to Be'. In *Dancing at the Edge of the World: Thoughts on Words, Women, Places* (1989), pp. 80–100. New York: Grove Press.

Le Guin, Ursula K. 1986. 'The Carrier Bag Theory of Fiction'. In *Dancing at the Edge of the World: Thoughts on Words, Women, Places* (1989), pp. 165–170. New York: Grove Press.

Massey, Doreen. 1994. *Space, Place, and Gender.* Polity Press.

M

~~manage connectivity~~ → Resilience
~~mantra of growth~~ → Care
~~many Anthropocenes~~ → Corals
~~mapping underlying material networks~~ → Media
~~maps of connectivity~~ → Migration Flows
~~mass extinction~~ → Next Generation → Declaration of Rebellion
~~material conditions of existence~~ → Geo-Social Classes
~~matter and energy~~ → Geology
Media Paul Roquet
~~mediated society~~ → Facts
~~mediation~~ → Media
~~memories~~ → Borders
~~memory~~ → Sensitivity
~~microbes~~ → Body
~~microbes and privilege~~ → Bacteria
~~migration~~ → Borders
Migration Flows Thomas Gammeltoft-Hansen
~~minimize footprint~~ → Production
Modernism Asmund Havsteen-Mikkelsen
~~monocultures~~ → Food → Soil
~~monster rain~~ → Natureculture
~~mood~~ → Atmosphere
~~moral obligation~~ → World Scientists' Warning to Humanity
Moving Earths Bruno Latour and Nikolaj Schultz
~~multi-being life forms~~ → Posthuman
~~multispecies individuals~~ → Corals
~~mutant species~~ → Imagine
~~mutual connections~~ → Sensitivity

Media

→ Attention | → Description | → Facts | mapping underlying material networks | mediation | → Object-Oriented Ontology | → Oxymorons | planetary resources | → Power

Particularly in the last decade, the field of media studies has shifted more and more towards broader ecological perspectives. Studies increasingly uncover 'mediation' at work within technological and planetary contexts going far beyond the human, even as they work to show how these systems have been fundamentally shaped by human action. This expansion in focus has been motivated in part by a sense that as media interfaces became more mobile and more ubiquitous, media technologies have come to play a more environmental role, deeply shaping an individual's perception of the world around them rather than functioning simply as a means of aesthetic consumption or information exchange. This has led to a shift away from a focus on media as representational practices largely produced and consumed by humans to think about mediation on a more material level, as an interface where two forms of matter come up against one another and something crosses between them, becoming transformed in the process. These approaches often attempt to reveal layers of mediation that are not (or are least not completely) perceptually available to humans as they go about their everyday lives. This includes the infrastructures underlying the production and circulation of media technologies, such as the mining of rare earths for smartphone chips or the energy reserves necessary to keep server farms running; computational functions operating behind the scenes to aggregate patterns of user behaviour and subsequently determining what types of materials do or do not appear; and the way moods and affects can rapidly circulate across media networks in ways that seem to outstrip conscious reflection, even as these forces go on to shape both individual and group behaviours. The implicit or explicit message of much of this work, echoing the major theme of this book, is that mediation is a process at work everywhere, connecting things far beyond more readily identifiable 'media' like newspapers, television or online platforms.

Paul Roquet (born 1980, located in Cambridge, US) is Associate Professor of Media Studies and Japan Studies at the Massachusetts Institute of Technology (Comparative Media Studies/Writing). He is the author of *Ambient Media: Japanese Atmospheres of Self* (2016).

Attempts to dig into deeper, more foundational layers of mediation present a compelling strategy when confronted with media environments of seeming abundance, where even hours and hours per day online means interacting within only an infinitesimally thin slice of what is taking place. As implied by the title of this book, a rise in connectedness often necessitates a confrontation with incompleteness. When everything is seen to affect everything else, it becomes a struggle to delineate a clear and coherent framework for anything. Mapping out underlying material networks below the daily avalanche of media becomes attractive as one strategy to try and break through the surplus of surface noise.

The connectedness emphasized in the current era of Anthropocene discourse also carries strong echoes of the connectedness supposedly fostered by digital communications networks. Not only do these two emphases emerge in tandem but they are inextricably intertwined. Today it is impossible to imagine a strategy for raising awareness of the climate crisis that does not rely on the circulation of media in some form. At the same time, it is becoming clear that the production and circulation of media may also be part of the problem, both because of new media technologies' demands on planetary resources and also because the message just doesn't seem to be getting through.

The enthusiasm for connectedness can obscure the simultaneous emergence of an inverse and also powerful phenomenon: a growing preference for disconnection. Presenting the Anthropocene as a question of connectedness favours the perspective of the well-connected (or perhaps those in the business of selling you those connections). Yet the same period sees the spread of strategies to voluntarily or involuntarily deprive people of a fuller understanding of their situation, drawing on the obscure operations of online platforms to skew the circulation of media towards various political and commercial ends. Debates over media policy have increasingly come to centre on who has the right to determine what media a person does or does not see, who can choose whether a particular piece of media circulates or does not. Media disinformation campaigns (including efforts to deny or obscure the climate crisis) have become frighteningly effective means of cultivating disconnection. The Internet, once touted as an interconnected global village in its early years, now seems to have ushered in a new era of division and distrust. We really are all connected by deep-woven material ecologies, but this doesn't automatically translate into a media environment capable of fostering mutual understanding. The more tightly engineered and contextually responsive systems of the new media environment may even be more effective at driving people apart.

The risk of rushing to expand the definition of 'media' to include all types of environmental and energetic exchange is to obscure the continued need to understand media in the more delimited sense as practices of human communication shaped by technological ends. At the end of another Anthropocene day, the challenge of getting all humans to understand the situation they are in remains absolutely essential to any effective response to contemporary planetary conditions. Books (like this one) and other more formally stable media continue to be important precisely because they are finite, arguing for the importance of a select group of issues while bracketing out others deemed less urgent.

Among those issues, exploring the roadblocks to effective human-to-human communication remains essential, including the difference between *more* connection and *better* connection. While the ultimate goal for an intervention into the Anthropocene may be to cultivate an understanding of the complex interconnectedness of human and nonhuman systems, the contemporary media situation suggests we must not lose sight of how media also work to block or interrupt understanding, standing in the way of deeper comprehension as often as aiding it. If one approach to media in the Anthropocene is to discover connections at every level, another must be to trace how effective humans have been at building little self-enclosed media environments for themselves and others, using media as a way to avoid confronting the vulnerability of connected life on a damaged planet.

Migration Flows

→ Architecture | → Body | → Borders | → Climate Risk Communities | → Geo-Social Classes | global migration architecture | human smugglers | → Invisible | maps of connectivity | nationality determines mobility | risk distribution | the passport system | → Violence | → Water | → Xenophobia

Migration flows are conditioned by architectural infrastructures. Physical architecture such as roads, fences, walls and checkpoints all seek to steer migration. But migration flows also depend on non-material architecture – the infrastructures governing human mobility. We might call it global migration architecture. Global migration architecture determines who among us is allowed to travel, through what means, via what routes and at what cost. Global migration architecture invisibly surrounds us and shapes our actions, our outlook and individual and collective trajectories.

Global migration architecture is composed of rules. For example, immigration legislation defining who is a refugee, what it takes to achieve family reunification or how resourceful you need to be to qualify for fast-track citizenship in, for instance, Malta or Canada. Other rules remain more hidden yet guide millions of individual practices – for the immigration officer deciding who is picked out of the line for further questioning, for the airline personnel carefully checking your documents to avoid fines and for the 'connection man' in Agadez who might know someone who knows someone that can help you onwards. What becomes clear when looking at these activities from afar is that they are patterned, that they reflect a particular infrastructural design.

Taken together, global migration architecture allows us to draw different maps of connectivity. Global shipping lanes trace the outline of our continents (Fig. 1), but also the 'white spots' outside effective control, such as the piracy-ridden Gulf of Guinea or the notoriously treacherous waters of the Devil's Sea in Asia. Railroad networks, super highways and airline routes connect the urban centres of the world. Meanwhile, smuggling routes and the well-trodden paths for irregular migrants – from south to north and from east to west – connect the haves and the have-nots.

Global migration architecture is a prime example of what Spanish sociologist Manuel Castells calls a 'space of flows'. It is a material organization of 'purposeful, repetitive, programmable sequences of exchange and interaction' that shape both our social practices and our social consciousness.[1] It is a dehumanizing form of architecture, meant to

Thomas Gammeltoft-Hansen (born 1979, located in Copenhagen, DK) is an internationally leading scholar on refugee and migration issues. He is a professor with special responsibilities in migration and refugee law at the University of Copenhagen and an honorary professor at Aarhus University. He is a regular commentator in Nordic and international media and has consulted for a number of international organizations, governments and NGOs.

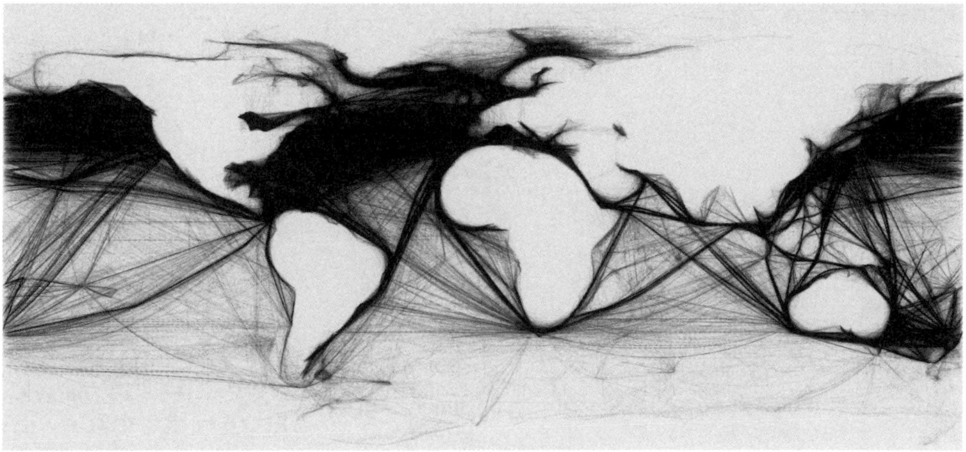

Fig. 1: Global shipping lanes
based on GPS data.

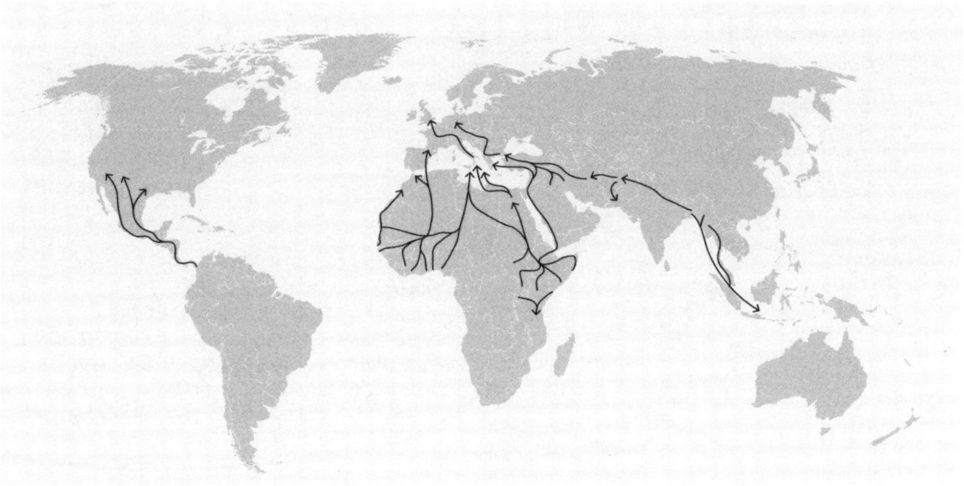

Fig. 2: Major irregular migration routes,
compiled from data from the International
Organization for Migration.

routinize and expose the body. Once entering the flow, there is no escape. The body must submit, whether to the crammed space of a dinghy or the position required by the airport body scanner. The flow asks us to surrender to it, and to move along.

Not everybody is swept up by the flow, however. While global migration architecture has radically expanded mobility and connectedness for those capable of accessing it, such access is a carefully safeguarded privilege. The passport system serves to illustrate this point. The modern passport was introduced towards the end of the 19th century as a way for states to control the unprecedented new flows of migrants arising from the global transportation networks established through trains and steamships. Today, the passport is ubiquitous for international travel, yet in many parts of the world only a small fraction of the population will ever be issued one.

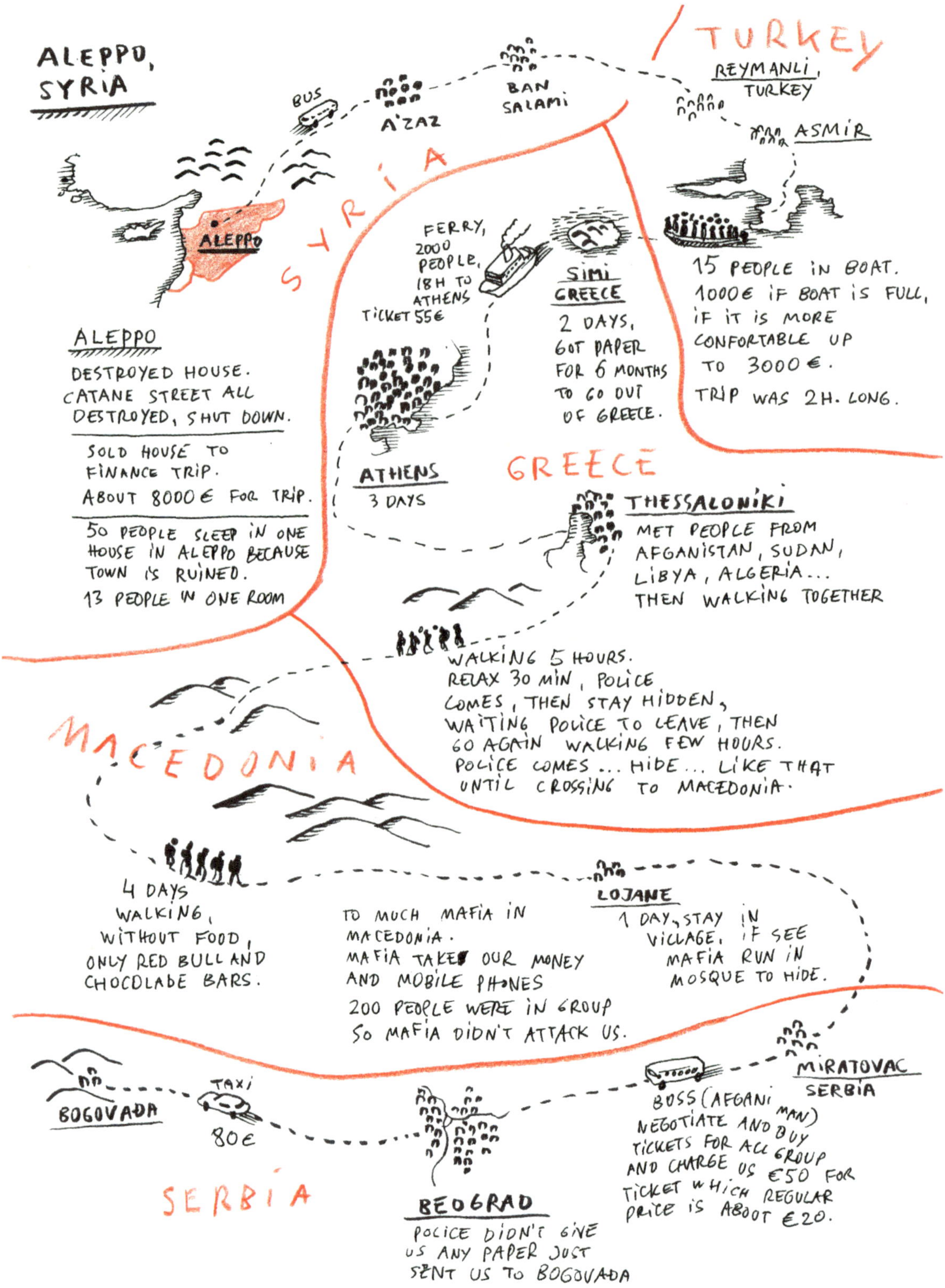

ALEPPO, SYRIA
TURKEY
BUS
A'ZAZ
BAN SALAMI
REYMANLI, TURKEY
ASMIR
SYRIA
ALEPPO
FERRY, 2000 PEOPLE, 18H TO ATHENS
TICKET 55€
SIMI GREECE
2 DAYS, GOT PAPER FOR 6 MONTHS TO GO OUT OF GREECE.
15 PEOPLE IN BOAT. 1000€ IF BOAT IS FULL, IF IT IS MORE CONFORTABLE UP TO 3000€.
TRIP WAS 2H. LONG.
ALEPPO
DESTROYED HOUSE. CATANE STREET ALL DESTROYED, SHUT DOWN.
SOLD HOUSE TO FINANCE TRIP.
ABOUT 8000€ FOR TRIP.
50 PEOPLE SLEEP IN ONE HOUSE IN ALEPPO BECAUSE TOWN IS RUINED.
13 PEOPLE IN ONE ROOM
ATHENS
3 DAYS
GREECE
THESSALONIKI
MET PEOPLE FROM AFGANISTAN, SUDAN, LIBYA, ALGERIA... THEN WALKING TOGETHER
WALKING 5 HOURS. RELAX 30 MIN, POLICE COMES, THEN STAY HIDDEN, WAITING POLICE TO LEAVE, THEN GO AGAIN WALKING FEW HOURS. POLICE COMES... HIDE... LIKE THAT UNTIL CROSSING TO MACEDONIA.
MACEDONIA
4 DAYS WALKING, WITHOUT FOOD, ONLY RED BULL AND CHOCOLADE BARS.
TO MUCH MAFIA IN MACEDONIA.
MAFIA TAKES OUR MONEY AND MOBILE PHONES
200 PEOPLE WERE IN GROUP SO MAFIA DIDN'T ATTACK US.
LOJANE
1 DAY, STAY IN VILLAGE, IF SEE MAFIA RUN IN MOSQUE TO HIDE.
MIRATOVAC SERBIA
BOSS (AFGANI MAN) NEGOTIATE AND BUY TICKETS FOR ALL GROUP AND CHARGE US €50 FOR TICKET WHICH REGULAR PRICE IS ABOUT €20.
BOGOVADA
TAXI
80€
SERBIA
BEOGRAD
POLICE DIDN'T GIVE US ANY PAPER JUST SENT US TO BOGOVADA

This applies to developed countries as well. Only 42% of US citizens have a valid passport. Passports are, moreover, not created equally.

Like commercial travel itself, passports establish a class system in which your nationality determines mobility. In 2019, a passport from the United Arab Emirates was the most powerful, granting its holder visa-free access to 167 countries and surpassing Germany and the United States with 166 and 165, respectively. In general, EU passports grant easy access to more than 80% of the world. At the opposite end of the scale, an Afghani passport enables visa-free access to only 29 countries, an Iraqi passport to 32 and a Syrian passport to 36.

For the majority of the world's population – those without passports or with less connected nationalities – global migration architecture works in reverse. It reinforces immobility. Migration for these populations is facilitated through alternative mobility architectures. In tandem with the growth of global migration control, clandestine networks of 'people pushers', 'fixers', 'coyotes' and 'human smugglers' have emerged. Despite their illicit nature, the economy and market of these networks are intimately tied to the formal migration architecture. For every euro spent on border control, the illicit migration industry equally expands. As a result, it is cheaper for me to fly business class to Venice and read this book than for an Eritrean refugee to buy a spot in an inflatable boat and make the comparatively much shorter journey from Al-Zawiya on the coast of Libya to the islands of Lampedusa or Sicily in Italy.

Škart
Untitled, 2013–2015
Print on canvas
Courtesy of the artist

One of 15 maps made at the asylum centre in Bogovadja, Serbia, in 2013–2015. It was part of a collaborative project initiated by Group 484 from Belgrade for migrants and schoolchildren in Serbia. The aim of the project was to hear and learn from migrants about their journeys and to present their stories visually as education tools in high schools around the country.

Global migration architecture also distributes risk differently. Crossing the Mediterranean by sea is far riskier than if you can afford good-quality forged documents or bribe an airline official to let you on board a commercial flight. And while statistics show that fewer migrants crossed the Mediterranean last year, the death rate kept climbing. As safer routes are shut down by European migration control, migrants are pushed towards longer, more dangerous routes.

Radically different epistemologies of risk are thus embedded in global migration architecture. If a commercial airline crashes, it is rightly seen as a catastrophe. Using passenger lists, next of kin are notified, investigations are started to ascertain the cause of the crash and criminal charges are brought in case of wrongdoing. When a migrant boat sinks, it is treated as a statistic, which may or may not get reported. Such incidents are surrounded by an absence of information – victims mostly remain identity-less and their families left worrying, wondering and, perhaps, hoping.

Of course, it was not always like this. Archaeological and geo-genetic research shows that migration flows have always been part of the human experience, often essential to our survival and evolution. Like all other kinds of architecture, however, global migration architecture is man-made, a product of intentional design, experimental modelling and visions. Only by bringing this underlying design into focus are we able to more fundamentally consider and challenge its effects.

Work cited:

Castells, Manuel. 1996. *The Rise of the Network Society*. Oxford: Blackwell.

Modernism

→ Architecture ¦ → Capitalocene ¦ → Development ¦ → Energy ¦ → Food ¦ → Global ¦ Jevons Paradox ¦ newness ¦ → Oil ¦ → Pollution ¦ violence against non-human nature

If we studied the 'beginnings' of architectural Modernism, we would find a search for a new vocabulary based on geometric forms with the machine as the main metaphor for spatial production (Le Corbusier), a reduction of form to its function (Mies van der Rohe) and a belief in industrial design products as accessible to ordinary people (Bauhaus). We would also find a spiritual vocation, as in the attempt to give modern man a space that mirrored his desire to shed the dead weight of historical references (Adolf Loos). Together all these aspirations led to new styles and visions of utopia that were applied on both sides of the ideological arena in the 20th century: the glass and steel of private houses and corporate architecture in liberal democracies (International Style) and the concrete mass-dwellings of socialist societies (Modernist housing schemes).

Asmund Havsteen-Mikkelsen (born 1977, located in Copenhagen, DK) is a painter and non-philosopher. Recent solo exhibitions in 2019 include *Lost in Space* (Gallery Kant, Copenhagen) and *Total Transformation* (Gallery MøllerWitt, Aarhus). Recent publications were *Mentalscapes* (2019) and *Louis Kahn in Denmark* (2018). Forthcoming activities include the exhibition *Privacy* (Kastrupgaardsamlingen, Copenhagen, 2021) and the publication of *Community of Contribution* (2020).

Today, with an almost five-fold increase in the world's population (from 1.6 billion in 1900 to 7.8 billion in March 2020) and the increased use of fossil fuels, together with the advance of capitalism, science, health care and intensive agriculture, we find Modernism in action all over the globe as the spatial programme that has provided housing for the mass urbanization of people. Dropping myself down as a little orange man on Google Earth wherever there is a blue line, I see the aftereffects of Modernism. As an 'algorithm' for planning, executing and building architecture, it has become a planetary visual force and the spatial expression of the Anthropocene. Modernism in all its variations mirrors the fundamental driving forces of this new age, in which man has become a geological agent. It is based on fossil fuels (in coal for energy production and in the automobile, aeroplane or train as modes of transportation), it uses abstract spatial language (mathematical grid space), it is made for the individual (both in private dwellings and in the isolation of the apartments inside high-rise towers), it is universal (due to the global presence of capitalism) and it is progressive (as in the implementation of new technology).

Every search for 'beginnings', however, should be careful of reductionism. When we zoom in on Modernism as a movement to understand its beginnings and its evolution, we discover regional differences between Scandinavian, Central European, Asian, African, Latin American and American Modernism, because even though Modernism saw itself as a universal language (reflecting the universal rights of man), it was still applied with huge local variances depending on climate, culture and material possibilities: not one Modernism but many Modernisms, yet all of them responding to the new conditions of a world based on a prime mover exploding in a combustion engine.

Thus there are many sources for – and aspects of – the concept of Modernism, and from every one of them we could find a spatial and visual energy that could make us believe again in its promise of technological emancipation through new styles and modes of spatial production. Yet writing in the year 2020, more than a century after the first signs of a new architectural understanding began to emerge, I am unable to jubilate in the marvellous and extraordinary energies that Modernism unleashed. Instead I see a spatial project whose metaphysical foundation is now being washed away by the all-pervasive climate crisis. Hence my project *Flooded Modernity* of 2018 as the visual expression of this situation: a 1:1 model of Le Corbusier's Villa Savoye, which is partly submerged in a Danish fjord. Originally conceived as a response to the use of social media in manipulating public opinion in the US and UK, I now see it as a portent of the impending climate crisis.

To be critical of Modernism is not new. At least since Robert Venturi and Charles Jencks, it has been common to mock Modernism. Why is it different this time? In the 1960s and onwards, the main argument against Modernism was that it was too abstract (not related to context), it was hierarchical (not reflecting the new values of multiculturalism), it was too white (not allowing for colours), it was standardized and generic (not allowing for individual differences), it was isolating (not allowing for communities to develop), it was cold (too much concrete) and it was male (dominated by old Caucasian men).

252

Asmund Havsteen-Mikkelsen
Flooded Modernity, 2018
Vejle Floating Art Festival
Wood, paint, styropor and acrylic glass
5 × 10 × 15 m, 5 tonnes

Instead of reiterating the standard critical objections to Modernism, I want to propose a different viewpoint relating to the unintended side effects (as in rebound effects) of the movement. Here, I will introduce an observation by economist William Stanley Jevons, who in 1865 noticed that efficiency in the use of coal did not lead to a diminishment of use but the opposite. The more efficient the steam engine became, the more the demand for coal increased (since efficiency also lowered the price of the energy). This is called the Jevons Paradox and describes how more efficient technology leads to an increase in energy consumption through new and unexpected possibilities.

So instead of searching for the 'beginnings' of Modernism and its utopian aspirations of creating a better life for modern man by providing the material means for an *Existenzminimum*, I think we should look at the Jevons Paradox of Modernism: all those unintended side effects that emerged with Modernism as an aesthetic regime. What kind of life and which modes of consumption did Modernism make possible?

First of all, Modernism as an architectural discourse was based on a paradigm of unlimited access to and use of fossil fuels (the factory production of elements, the automobile as a mode of transport, the installation of central-heating systems); secondly, it dislocated its users from nature (as consumers unable to grow vegetables and establishing a self-sustainable environment) and from wild animals (it did not consider itself in relation to creating habitats for non-human nature); thirdly, it promoted and incarnated the ideology of 'newness' (by presenting itself as new and without ornaments, it spurred a destruction of consumer habits based on care, mending, reusing and inheriting).

By establishing an abstract space for dwelling in an urban environment, it enabled the violence against animal food slaves to be kept away from modern man. In Denmark alone, 139.5 million animals are killed annually. In the urban realm, the rearing of animals for food has disappeared, together with the stench of the slaughterhouse. The meat of the sentient animal is conveniently wrapped in plastic and silently accepts its fate on the plate, yet today the effects of the industrial-agricultural food industry is what is driving the sixth mass extinction of species on the planet through the extensive use of land for animal food production.

The Jevons Paradox of Modernism is the creation of an architectural condition for an immense luxury trap based on patterns of high-energy consumption of fossil fuels, a distanced relationship to nature, and an externalization of violence against non-human nature. Modernism made mass-scale urban dwelling possible and created the mythology of a modern life based on newness and technological advancement. Modernism was progress, but the rebound effect of this progress is the sixth mass extinction and the climate crisis.

Moving Earths

→ Bacteria | cosmological turn | critical zones | → Description | → Environment | → Geo-Social Classes | → Home | living in and living from | → Oil | redescription of territory | re-engineering the system of production | → Resources | → Soil | space as an offspring of time | space as the product of agencies | the price of solidarity | → Violence

Bruno Latour (born 1947, located in Paris, FR) is Professor Emeritus at Sciences Po in Paris and is among the world's leading sociologists and philosophers. A veteran of science and technology studies (STS), Latour has written more than a dozen books, including *Laboratory Life* (1979), *We Have Never Been Modern* (1993), *An Inquiry into Modes of Existences* (2013), *Facing Gaia* (2016) and, most recently, *Down To Earth* (2017).

Nikolaj Schultz (born 1990, located in Paris, FR) is a PhD fellow at the Department of Sociology, University of Copenhagen, where he is preparing his thesis on geo-social classes. Since 2018, he has collaborated with Bruno Latour on this topic. He is currently editing a book on Latour's work (2020) with contributions from, among others, Pierre Charbonnier, Gerard de Vries, Graham Harman and Barbara Herrnstein Smith.

An interview with Bruno Latour on cosmology and class by Nikolaj Schultz
In this conversation with Danish sociologist Nikolaj Schultz, French sociologist and philosopher Bruno Latour elaborates on his analysis of our 'New Climatic Regime'[1] and presents new ideas on its consequences for political and social theory. With the earth reacting to our actions, we face a cosmological shift that leaves us all divided and lost in space. The quintessential political question of our times is finding a place to land. 'Globalists' continue to believe in the project of moderniza-tion and 'populists' flee back to the land of the old while a few 'escapists' simply try to take off to other planets. How to respond? According to Latour, the task becomes reinventing the old socialist tradition beyond the system of production, something we can only do if we re-theorize the concept of social class to include a wider array of material conditions of existences than Marx's definition of class alluded to.

Cosmology and division

Nikolaj Schultz: In *Facing Gaia*,[2] you try to historically situate our present encounter with an earth suddenly reacting to our actions by comparing two different scientific discoveries. In the 17th century, Galileo Galilei raises his telescope to the moon and shortly after concludes that our earth is *similar* to all the other planets of the universe. Some 350 years later, James Lovelock instead concludes that our earth is *dissimilar* to all the other planets. What are the symmetries and asym-metries of these two discoveries and what do they tell us about where we are in history?

Bruno Latour: Galileo and Lovelock both try to cope with moving earths, but two different kinds. Galileo discovered that the earth was moving around the sun and disturbed everybody by saying so. First, there was the quarrel with the church and, secondly, there were the major consequences his discoveries had on social order. This is well known from the history of science and because of Bertolt Brecht's extraordinary play *The Life of Galileo.* People believed they were in one cosmos before suddenly learning that the earth was moving. They did not know where they were in space, and they felt lost – even if the practical consequences of Galileo's discovery for daily life were close to zero. So at hand we have a famous discovery with major impacts for physics and astronomy which simultaneously disturbs the whole establishment of the church and the social world.

Now, I contrast this with Lovelock's similar but different discovery of another kind of moving earth. What Lovelock and Lynn Margulis discovered is not simply that the earth *is moving* but that earth is *being moved*, to use Michel Serres's expression.[3] The earth is reacting to the actions of humans. This new sort of movement of the earth is immensely more important, not least in terms of consequences for the social order, and thus also more disputed. So with a gap of 300 years, we have two discoveries of moving earths, and what interests me is that they both bring along extraordinary changes in cosmology and in understanding of space. It is another powerful example of a question which has interested me for 40 years, namely the link between science and society, between cosmology and social order. While Galileo's discovery marked the beginning of modern cosmology, I see Lovelock and Margulis's discoveries as marking the end of modern cosmology. Right now, when we hear about their discovery that the earth is being moved, we find ourselves in the same shoes as the people who in 1610 were worried about Galileo messing up their cosmology by proving that the earth was moving. We are as lost as they were.

NS: So, to talk with Alexandre Koyré,[4] if Galileo took us from the 'closed cosmos to the infinite universe', then Lovelock is bringing us back from the infinite universe to a closed cosmos on earth. Why has the figure of this return to earth, 'Gaia', been so misunderstood?

BL: Most importantly because it was understood through a wrong idea of space. Gaia was immediately associated with the idea of 'the globe' and with the idea of the earth as an 'organism'. This meant it was quickly used by biologists and New Age people to return to the old, Greek idea of earth considered as one big animal. But this was not what Lovelock was interested in. Instead, he was interested in how life forms – including bacteria, vegetation, insects et cetera – had provided so many changes in the chemical circulation of the atmosphere that it became impossible to understand air, water, mountains or plate tectonics without taking into consideration the dynamic agencies of these life forms. With the help of his instruments, Lovelock was studying pollution and had realized that pollutants were able to spread everywhere on Earth. This made him intuit that what Modern industry was doing perhaps had been done for billions of years by all life forms on earth. He meets Lynn Margulis, who studied the consequences bacteria had on the atmosphere, climate, rivers and mountains, and together they arrive at this extraordinary entity called Gaia – an entity with nothing in common with the idea of the earth 'being alive' as an organism. Instead, it is an argument about the ways life forms continue to transform their own conditions of existence to the point where they engineer the whole surface of the earth.

NS: So the fundamental consequence of Gaia is that entities make up their own environments. This not only means that climate is the historical result of agencies; it also means that space itself is the offspring of time. With Gaia, space is not in the background; space is continuously constructed by dynamic life forms. Why is this difficult to understand cosmologically?

BL: Not least because of the cartographic tradition, invented at the time of Galileo. Cartography gave us a sort of 'taken-for-granted' definition of space as a frame inside which objects and people reside. With this definition of space, you cannot see how space itself is constructed by the agencies of life forms. With this gaze, you miss how life forms are not *in* space but that they *make* space. One example is how bacteria produce the oxygen of the atmosphere that all life forms breathe. Bacteria are not *in* the frame; they *make* the frame. This you cannot see if you approach space cartographically. If you approach space from the view of the globe, or as a map, you remain stuck inside a frame, with difficulties understanding what life is. These difficulties have burdened biology and ecology since the 17th century.

With Gaia, the situation is reversed. The trick of Lovelock and Margulis is to say, if there is an earth, soil and sea, it is because life forms are producing their own environment. Life forms are not sitting in the environment; they *produce* the environment. In biology, Lynn Margulis's ideas and her notion of 'holobionts' are becoming mainstream now. Today, everybody knows that our bodies are made of microbes, for example. So the idea that we are seized and maintained by the agencies of life forms is beginning to become common sense. The amusing thing is that this idea of space as the product of agencies is an old actor-network-theory argument that we developed completely separately in sociology!

NS: What are the political consequences of this concept of space? Previously, you have conceptualized this spatial or cosmological shift with the notion of a New Climatic Regime.

BL: Like Galileo, Lovelock is not interesting for his politics. What I am nonetheless interested in are the political consequences of being lost in space after the discovery of Gaia. This is somehow what I try to map very grossly in *Down to Earth*.[5] My argument is that what we all have in common is no longer moving forward through progress and that we are lost in space. What we all have in common is no longer having an exact idea of where we are in space, or on what soil or land we reside. And I think this shows clearly in the political disputes of today.

First, by what is normally referred to as the 'populist movements' and their questions of 'What are our borders and what are the people inside our borders?' Questions posed all over Europe and, of course, most vividly with Brexit. Secondly, it shows with those saying 'Let's go on', 'Business as usual', 'Let's maintain the modernist tradition of progress'. The ideal of 'globalization', if you want. Both these positions are simply affects asking where we are, on what soil or land we reside. Now, the problem is that both these positions are too abstract in terms of material existence. The land the populists want to go back to – the England of Johnson, the Italy of Salvini, the France of Le Pen et cetera – are not real countries. They are imaginary versions of what *would* have been the land years ago. But the land of the 'globalists' is just as imaginary, since they imagine that the earth will accept infinite modernization. So we are lost in space.

NS: So politics is now ordered by the question of land, but we are all lost in space because none of the political territories that modernity offers us have any ecological or economical fundament.

BL: Exactly. Look at the example of Brexit, for me a great experimentation of territorial redescription. It started with an imaginary space based on ideas of 'identity' and 'borders'. Three years later, it is a complete mess. The English learned day by day, bit by bit, what they were *actually* depending on as a territory – dependencies always transcending the nation state. If you leave the EU, you will be in trouble getting medicine, fresh food, your labour force will have bad protection of rights et cetera. So one talks about identity and about walls, but slowly you realize that you do depend not only on identity but more importantly on a long list of other conditions of existences. Our ignorance about what makes our countries thrive is immense. This is what I try to allude to when I say that we are spatially lost.

NS: Yesterday in Paris, you attended the defence of French philosopher Pierre Charbonnier's habilitation.[6] One of his arguments is that there is a disconnect between where the Moderns *think* they live and the territory they *actually* live off. How is this connected to the current spatial confusion? Why the difficulty of understanding that to have politics you need to have a land and a people corresponding?

BL: Yes, there is a disconnect between the two sorts of land that we inhabit. On the one hand, there is the land from where we have our rights – the nation state – which is territory that we understand ourselves as *living in*. On the other hand, there is the land we *live from*, which is the territory where we get our resources. We *sort of* know these two territories are connected, but because of the material history of the Moderns – first the colonies, then the discovery of coal and later oil – they have divorced. So if people have lost their sense of space, it is because of this divorce which has made it difficult for people to describe the world out of which they get their prosperity and the entities that allow them to subsist. And what Charbonnier investigates is simply how this disconnect has become bigger and bigger ever since the 'discovery' of America.

In one chapter, there is an interesting simile to understand the argument and its relevance for political ecology. In the beginning of the 19th century, German philosopher Johann Gottlieb Fichte wrote a book answering to the English project of liberalism, arguing that in inventing the global world the English were completely hypocritical.[7] They pretended to be civilized and tolerant while simultaneously exploiting the whole planet. If Germany wanted to be tolerant, Fichte said, they would need to close down their borders, forbid commerce and instead juxtapose the land out of which they lived with the land that gives rights to their citizens. Fichte probably did not imagine this to be possible even in the 19th century, but it is a fine description of a sort of utopia, where the legal country is reconciled with the material country.

I think this is a good way of grasping our current situation. Because, in fact, political ecology has nothing to do with 'green stuff' or 'nature'. It is about how the new, moving earth forces everybody to repose the question of what to subsist on. This question of subsistence is a main feature of what I call the New Climatic Regime. Everybody is simply trying to find out which land to live off and live in. This is also why the Trumpists are climate deniers. You study that yourself, namely the question of how some are saying, 'We don't share the same earth as you'.[8] Something impossible to reconcile with modernism, since modernism was supposed to be 'progress of all' – even if it was not really.

NS: Yes. It is difficult to believe in modernism when you see a picture of Elon Musk's Tesla sports car floating around in outer space. This did not look like 'progress for all' – this was progress or emancipation for the wealthy few! And when you look at how other Silicon Valley tech billionaires are trying colonize Mars, then it certainly does not look like modernism either, since the classic question 'Is there life on Mars?' is rephrased from a civilizational question into a question for the 1% who tries to escape earth. This is the ideological essence of what you have previously called offshore politics or 'Planet Exit': the escapism of the earthly, material limits by the few.

BL: With a lot of money put into it.

NS: Lots of money and lots of technology. For these elites *deus ex machina*, and as the 'techsters', they are God's chosen few. Definitely not a coincidence that the wildfires of California never reached Silicon Valley, so with the prospect of ecological, civilizational collapse, they take off and go to Mars. Problem is you rather quickly find out that you cannot live on Mars. It is not very nice up there. So the tech billionaires shift from Planet B to Plan B and in addition invest in luxury climate-secured escape bunkers in places like New Zealand, so they can escape civilizational collapse. It sounds anecdotal, but it has been studied in detail by investigative journalists.[9]

BL: So they hedge their bets, one on Mars and one in New Zealand! How many people are we talking about?

NS: Exactly. Crushed under the weight of the new moving earth, they choose to escape and leave the rest of us behind. They do not live in the Anthropocene; they live in the Misanthropocene. Steve Hoffman, the billionaire founder of Reddit and, if anyone, an insider, estimates that around 50% of the Silicon Valley tech elites have bought escape property around the world. Escape bunker property for the ultra-rich has become a billion dollar business.[10] The interesting thing is that it is not even secret, even if it sounds like a neo-Balzacian conspiracy theory when one says that the rich are escaping the planet during night-time. They actually say so themselves! Yet it is not an unproblematic move for the rich. A lot of things could go wrong: How do you make sure that your security guards do not turn their weapons against you? Are you supposed to bring the family of the pilot of your private jet when you escape? A lot of questions arise, but it is still better than 'staying with the trouble', as your friend Donna Haraway would say.[11]

BL: But they are not climate sceptics; they are deniers right? They know that there is a planetary danger?

NS: Yes, that is exactly why they take off. Again, climate denial arises not despite the fact that the climatic mutations are there; it arises because the climatic mutations are real and because the price of solidarity is too high to pay. It is the same with Trumpism. These are just the people who take extreme consequences and choose to leave.

BL: But how do they cope with the fact of being alone and not following the old logic of modernism? How do they cope morally with leaving behind the rest of us? They must sort of reinvent themselves as atomized agents.

NS: That is what should be studied now. If we could describe the material conditions of existence and the moral economies of these 'exiters' and compare them with those who are stuck behind deprived of habitable territory, we would probably have a better grasp on tomorrow's class struggle, a struggle over territory and not over the means of production.

BL: When Musk sent his Tesla into space, he said that it was 'silly but fun'. The space adventures of the 20th century were certainly not silly and fun; they were part of a progressive modernity. Seeing it becoming a caricature for just a few people was very shocking. So at this moment, I think we are exactly at a place where we are literally living on different planets. One of these is the modernist, globalist planet; the other one is the identity, localist planet and the third is the escapist or exit planet that you study. We are completely divided as to on what planet or on what land we live. This is what I try to show in *Down to Earth.*

NS: Yes, when Musk said that it was 'silly but fun', it was good proof that modernity was dead. But we only capture the dividedness you speak about if we remember that these people are very serious about escaping. They put billions of dollars into it! And, somehow, this move of escapist ideology was not a big surprise. Only a few months before, Donald Trump took America out of the COP21 Agreement. What did he do just after? He announced that he was going to 'Make America great again' ... on Mars.

Class and description

BL: The question is how to respond to this division of space. Here, I want to go back to what we spoke about before. As Charbonnier shows, the question becomes how to restart the socialist tradition, a tradition which was in fact always interested in the question of the divide between the land, the industry and the legal framework in which people live. One can even say that socialism was about this disconnect. Yet it is also true that socialism never succeeded in connecting with ecology. For this reason, Charbonnier's hero is the same as mine. Karl Polanyi was one of the few in the socialist tradition who articulated the question of both labour force *and* land as resisting production. In *The Great Transformation*,[12] he maintains that it is not a question of production but of what I call 'processes of engendering', the question of ways in which things are *brought* to the world.

This is the connection I am interested in. Can we, within the socialist tradition, *rearticulate* ecology into a question of existence, of survival, of generation, of reproducing, of giving birth and of losing territory? As a philosopher, I see the first contours of what we have been calling 'geo-social classes', a notion that would perhaps allow us to redo for the present situation what the socialists did fairly well until the 1950s and the beginning of the Great Acceleration. This would allow us to reconnect the land we live in with the land we live from, as well as to connect ecology with socialism within the framework of politics as usual. But *I* gave *you* the task of finding these classes! How would you approach the question? What would be a good definition of geo-social classes?

NS: I think your intuition in *Down to Earth* is correct. These are not classes defined by their position in the production system; it is classes defined by their territorial conditions of survival, their material conditions of existence or reproduction. Defining geo-social classes means taking the cosmology of our new moving earth seriously when approaching the social question and using it to redescribe social classes in a way that extends their Marxist definition. While social classes were defined by their ownership over the means of production, geo-social classes are defined by their dependence on a wider array of material conditions of existence that allow social groups to survive or thrive. If we had such a definition of classes, we could delineate a people corresponding to the new climatic question of the 21st century, and to geo-history, in the same way Marx made a people correspond to the social question of the 19th century and to social history.[13] The terribly difficult question is how to map this empirically. First, it would be necessary to define on what territory different collectives live, by describing what entities or actors different social collectives depend on to reproduce. In other words, on what land the different social groups live. If we did this, we would first see that the networks of existences that allow different social groups to survive and reproduce would look very heterogeneous. But what would also be clear is how some social groups would share means of reproduction with some more than others, similarities and dissimilarities that would allow us to reclassify social groups on the basis of material conditions of existence. Perhaps this would even allow us to redefine exploitation as the surplus of existence that some social groups profit from, by describing how the livelihoods of some collectives disallow the access to a habitable territory of others. I think the affairs of the Yellow Vests in France perhaps showed us the urgency of the geo-social question. Would you agree?

BL: I think the Yellow Vest affairs started with an interesting moment of geo-social inquiry, since it was a matter of salary, taxation, gas, landscape and social justice. So you are right; initially the connection was made. But you cannot have a political position if you cannot describe your own territory. So nothing came out of it precisely because they did not have a vocabulary, the tools or a political movement to help them articulate this link. We are extraordinarily bad at describing what allows people to subsist. We have a lot of talk about identity, we have a lot of discussions about values, but please describe to me the territory in which you survive, in which you invest and might want to defend. I think the lack of such descriptions is what renders the political scene so interesting but also so violent today. We begin to realize that this is the real question, but we do not know how to answer it. This is also why I am interested in the episode of the 'Cahiers de Doleances', because it was exactly an initiative directed towards territorial descriptions and questions of social justice in one and same breath. The Yellow Vests did not manage to maintain this link.

So if the question of geo-social classes is difficult to answer, it is because we all have very little idea about where we get our subsistence from. We have simply lost the habit of describing what we are attached to, what we are connected to and what allows us to survive. In a way, Marxism used to be a vocabulary that allowed such descriptions of our conditions of subsistence, which we could use to locate ourselves inside the system of production. Can we do the same thing today with what I call the 'processes of engendering'? Since Proudhon and through Marx, socialism described the practical and material realities of industrial society. They described where people within this society got their subsistence from, which allowed people to position themselves in the system of production. But today, we live in a different world. Today, if one would have to describe the practical, material world in which one lives, it would not only be about industry; we would furthermore have to add entities like the climate, CO_2, water, bugs, earthworms, soil et cetera. The wider array of material conditions of existences that you spoke about before. And this is what ecologists never managed to bring to the attention of socialists. It is still the question of inequality, of justice and of the material world out of which we get our subsistence; it is simply that the world has changed form.

NS: Yes. The interesting thing is that in the first period of the Yellow Vests, when there was a moment of geo-social description, they actually enjoyed support and were able to mobilize affects internally and externally. When they lost their territorial descriptions, it turned violent. It seems that in some situation, violence does not occur when indignation reaches a certain level; it occurs when you are no longer able to describe who you are, what you are attached to and with whom you fight.

BL: Yes, they completely lost their territorial descriptions, and instead went on to ask for the head of the president ... Macron then offered them a 'grand debate', but we learned nothing from it because people simply gave their opinions. But opinions of people who have no land or a world to describe are useless. One and a half million answers to the debate and not one single description of where we reside and with whom. Values? Yes. Identity? Yes. But no territories. If you have lost the ability of describing the land or the territory on which you reside – understood in the etiological sense, as the lists of entities you rely on to subsist – then you simply cannot do politics. If you have no territory, you have no politics.

NS: So to restart politics, we need to redescribe our territories, our lands and our people. How come we lost the ability of doing so? Were we atomized by neoliberalism, which is fundamentally an ideology and politics of disattachments?

BL: Of course, this is one of the reasons. But you can simply also just lose the habit and culture of doing politics if it is not constantly maintained. Redescription is a general rule of the social sciences, but today I would say this is *the* political question. Let us not forget that ecological mutations are unprecedented. We never before had a moment where we have had to re-engineer the whole system of reproduction piece by piece, house by house, mobility by mobility, food by food. We have experience of production and modernization, but we do not have any experience of reproduction and remodernization. Eight billion people – and every single material entity that binds their societies together and makes them live is controversial. Meat is controversial, clothes are controversial, transport is controversial et cetera. In this situation, we cannot skip the phase of description of territory, unless you want to end up in an abstract world of identity or values. This is what happened in Britain. If we do not do the work of description, we cannot go forward.

NS: This leads me to my next question. Forty years ago, you started your career by following natural scientists in the laboratory. Now, you have become interested in a new sort of science and a new sort of scientists. In *Down to Earth*, you dedicate a chapter to critical zones and critical zone scientists, and you are currently doing an exhibition on the topic. Why are you interested in these and how are they related to the task of description?

BL: First, critical zones and critical zone scientists are words used in geo-science, hydrology, geomorphology, geochemistry and in soil sciences to denote the thin 'crust' or 'skin' of the earth and the scientists studying them. And, yes, when I have been following and studying these scientists for five years now, it is exactly because I think they help with the redescription of territories in a very practical way. First, because they are not global. They are not working with the earth as the globe. Rather, it is the earth as a thin skin. Everything all life forms live off exists only here, on a few-kilometres-thick pellicle of the earth, reaching from the atmosphere and a few kilometres down in the rocks. So what they study fits fairly well with the discovery of Lovelock, and it is another tool to get away from the idea of 'Nature', which is simply too big, abstract and imprecise. When you study critical zones, you study a series of things or connections on the crust of the earth, so it has a modesty. It is about very limited entities; it is not the whole cosmos. The second interesting thing about these sciences is that they explicitly study the differences between what they see in the laboratory and what they see in the field. Again, there is a modesty; it is a 'boot-in-the-ground' type of science. A bit like natural history or like Alexander von Humboldt's natural science.

NS: It is another epistemology.

BL: Yes, epistemologically they are far from the other sciences that I have been following for many years. And since they underline the discrepancies between their observations and the chemical reactions, it means they are redescribing and rematerializing the question of territory, which we simultaneously try to redescribe and rematerialize in political and social theory. This is also where there is a link between Lovelock's discovery, the political question of geo-social classes and critical zones. This is why I am interested in them and why I am also doing an exhibition on the topic.

NS: Why an exhibition? What is the role of artists?

BL: Exhibitions allow you to do a thought experiment in a limited space that cannot be done in any other way. Every time I have done an exhibition, the question at hand was completely impossible to raise in a book but possible to raise in a space. Why? Because you are able to submit people to an experiment. This is what I mean by 'thought exhibitions'. It is a way to use a limited space, art and artists to 'bombard' the visitors with expressions and then see what happens with them. The last one I did in 2016, *Reset Modernity*,[14] bombarded visitors with objects, asking if they could reset their vision of modernity. This [new] exhibition – simply called *Critical Zones: Landing on Earth* – is somehow easier. It basically offers a lot of scientific facts and arts from which the visitors can learn to redescribe and revisualize the earth's surface in which they live but which they are not conscious about, in large because of the cartographic imaginary we spoke about before. The problem remains the same. We always think of the earth seen from the outside. If you say 'earth', what typically comes to peoples' minds is the globe. But despite all the talk about 'the blue planet', only people who are *out of space*, *out in space* experience the earth like that! We are not out in space; we are inside critical zones. And this is what we need to visualize. Here, the importance of artists is that they help us multiply the visions of the earth, viewed from the inside and not from the outside. It sounds simple, but it is absolutely crucial not to imagine the planet as the globe if we want to land on earth. The globe is too big and too abstract. So what we simply try to do is to invent with scientists and artists a vocabulary for this landing. In a way, it is surprising that we even have to do so. Why should we have to land? Are we not on earth? In a way no, because Moderns took off on an interesting and somehow beautiful journey, as visualized by Elon Musk and his Tesla, but now we realize that we have to land again without crashing. As I say in *Facing Gaia*, we are exactly in the same position as when we 'discovered' the new world and when the cartographers had to redraw their maps. Four centuries later, we discover a new, moving earth. Not in extensity but in intensity, an earth which is reacting to our actions. For that you need new descriptions and you need new visualizations.

Works cited:

Charbonnier, Pierre. 2019. *Abondance et liberté: De la revolution industrielle au changement climatique.* Habilitation thesis. Paris: L'École des Hautes Etudes en Sciences Sociales.

Fichte, Johann Gottlieb. 2012. *The Closed Commercial State.* New York: State University of New York Press.

Koyré, Alexandre. 1957. *From the Closed Cosmos to the Infinite Universe.* Baltimore, MA: John Hopkins University Press.

Haraway, Donna J. 2016. *Staying with the Trouble: Making Kin in the Chthulucene.* Durham, NC: Duke University Press Books.

Latour, Bruno. 2016. *Reset Modernity.* Cambridge, MA: MIT Press.

Latour, Bruno. 2017a. *Down To Earth: Politics in the New Climatic Regime.* Translated by Catherine Porter. Cambridge: Polity Press.

Latour, Bruno. 2017b. *Facing Gaia: Eight Lectures on the New Climatic Regime.* Translated by Catherine Porter. Cambridge: Polity Press.

Osnos, Evan. 2017. 'Doomsday Prep for the Super-Rich'. *The New Yorker*, 22 January. https://www.newyorker.com/magazine/2017/01/30/doomsday-prep-for-the-super-rich. Accessed 16 December 2019.

Polanyi, Karl. 2001. *The Great Transformation.* Boston, MA: Beacon Press.

Serres, Michel. 1995. *The Natural Contract.* Ann Arbor: University of Michigan Press.

Schultz, Nikolaj. 2020a. 'New Climate, New Class Struggles'. In *Critical Zones: Observatories for Earthly Politics.* Edited by Bruno Latour & Peter Weibel. Cambridge, MA: MIT Press.

Schultz, Nikolaj. 2020b. 'Life As Exodus'. In *Critical Zones: Observatories for Earthly Politics.* Edited by Bruno Latour & Peter Weibel. Cambridge, MA: MIT Press.

Turkewitz, Julie. 2019. 'A Boom Time for the Bunker Business and Doomsday Capitalists'. *The New York Times.* 13 August. https://www.nytimes.com/2019/08/13/us/apocalypse-doomsday-capitalists.html.

following spread:
Frédérique Aït-Touati, Alexandra Arènes and Axelle Grégoire
The Soil Map, Terra Forma, manuel de cartographies potentielles, 2019

This conversation between Bruno Latour and Nikolaj Schultz took place at The Queens Hall, Royal Library, Denmark, on 29 May 2019. It was previously published on Critical Inquiry's *In The Moment* blog with the title 'Cosmology and Class: An Interview with Bruno Latour by Nikolaj Schultz'. It has since been edited and substantially revised.

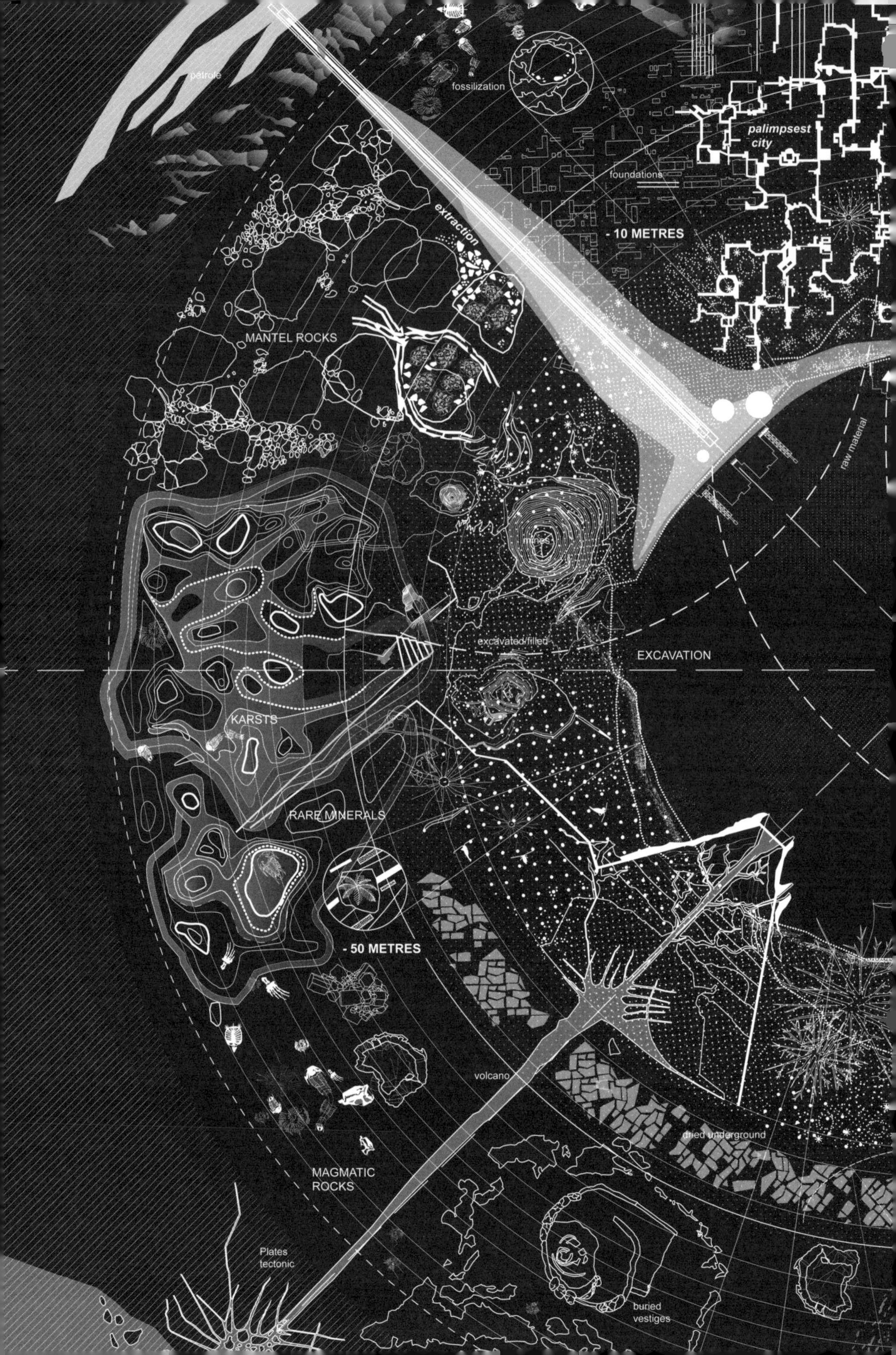

pétrole
fossilization
palimpsest city
foundations
extraction
- 10 METRES
MANTEL ROCKS
raw material
mines
excavated/filled
EXCAVATION
KARSTS
RARE MINERALS
- 50 METRES
volcano
dried underground
MAGMATIC ROCKS
Plates tectonic
buried vestiges

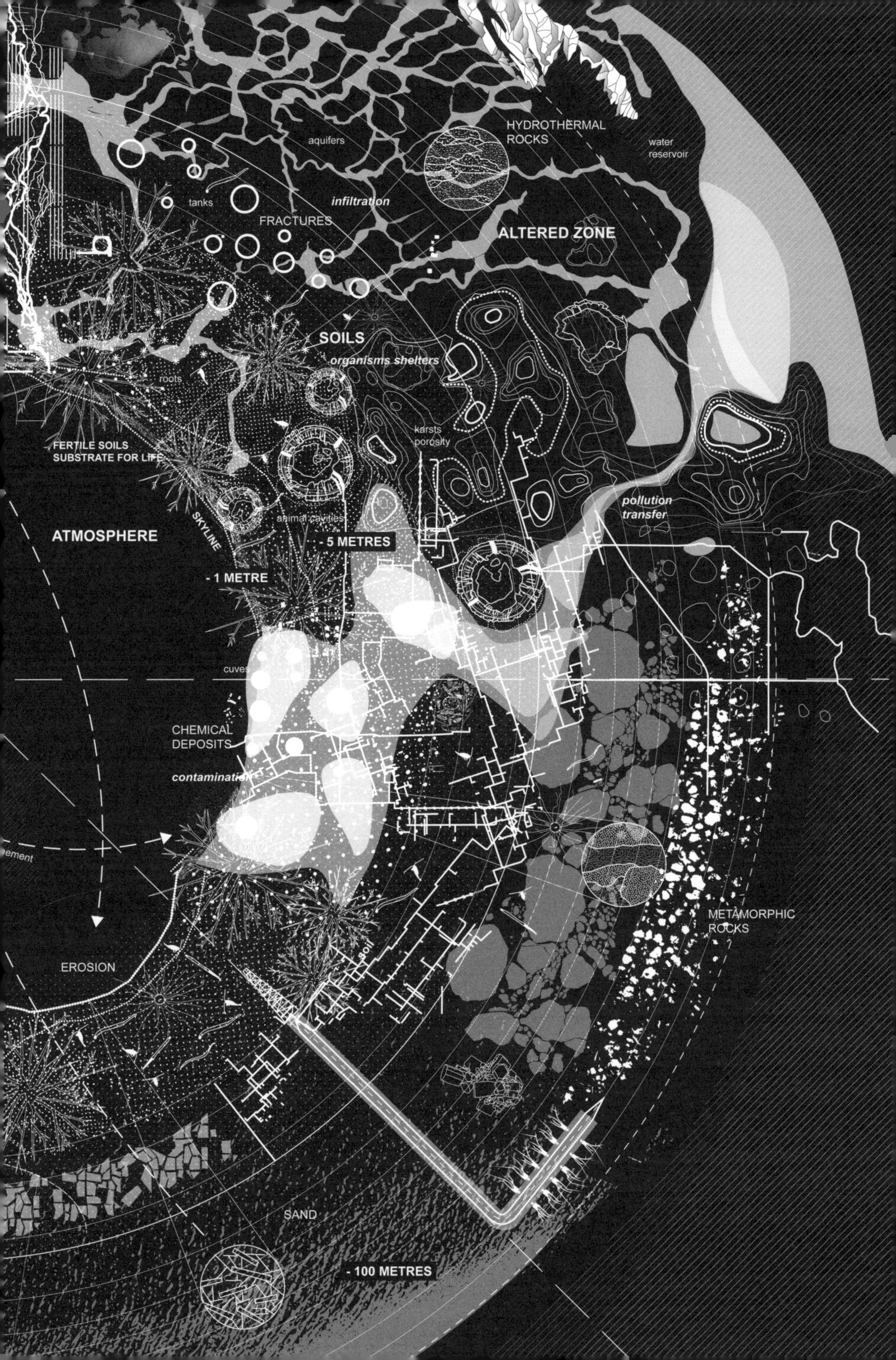
HYDROTHERMAL ROCKS
aquifers
water reservoir
tanks
infiltration
FRACTURES
ALTERED ZONE
SOILS
organisms shelters
roots
karsts porosity
FERTILE SOILS SUBSTRATE FOR LIFE
pollution transfer
SKYLINE
animal cavities
ATMOSPHERE
- 5 METRES
- 1 METRE
cuves
CHEMICAL DEPOSITS
contamination
METAMORPHIC ROCKS
soil
EROSION
SAND
- 100 METRES

Ñ

264

~~nationality determines mobility~~ → Migration Flows
~~natural archive of snowflakes~~ → Abrupt Climate Change
~~natural powerhouse~~ → Sun
~~nature's attempts at understanding itself~~ → Connectedness
~~nature's vibrant energy~~ → Connectedness
Natureculture Flemming Rafn
~~need~~ → Ecology
~~New Climatic Regime~~ → Geo-Social Classes
~~new form of commons~~ → Agency
~~new global paradigm~~ → Development
New Materialism Diana Coole
~~newness~~ → Modernism
Next Generation Greta Thunberg
~~nodes in an ecology~~ → Capitalocene
~~non-linear matter flows~~ → New Materialism

Nature-culture

→ Aesthetics | → Atmosphere | → City | → Climate | → Flood | monster rain | → Resilience | urban metabolism | → Water | → Weather

---

> *The forenoon sun glistened on a myriad of open window-panes as if they were raindrops, and out near Enghaveplads the gray and yellow building facades rose like distant hills until they were dissolved in the shimmering haze.*
>
> Tom Kristensen, 1968, p. 56.

Like so many others, I wonder why the green transition is taking so long, since there is virtually everything to gain from securing a stable climate. Perhaps the lack of momentum is a reflection of human nature, shaped as it is over millennia by a restless urge to convert the planet's seemingly inexhaustible resources. Perhaps it is simply an indication that there is still too much money to be made by continuing as before. Or perhaps it is because it is, paradoxically, easier to imagine the ultimate civilizational collapse than a gradual softening of our impact on the planet.

It is not due to a lack of factual information. Almost three decades have passed since the former American vice president Al Gore published his first book on the climate disaster; since then the CO_2 content in the atmosphere has doubled. According to the Paris Accord, we have just a few decades to establish a fossil-free global society, and the rest of this century has to be spent restoring the balance by sucking carbon out of the atmosphere.

During the same brief period, until 2060, the United Nations predicts that the global number of square metres being built is going to double. That corresponds to building the city of Paris every week for the next 40 years. As the construction sector is estimated to be the most energy- and resource-consuming sector,[1] the challenges are monumental.

Flemming Rafn (born 1976, located in Copenhagen, DK) is co-founder of the Danish studio Tredje Natur (Third Nature). The studio combines building and biology into a third entity and calls its work humane solutions to man-made problems. From optimizing the smallest urban components to designing literally millions of new square metres, the aim is always to re-establish the ecological cycle and connect people to the planet.

One of the key problems facing cities today is their decoupling from nature and nature's causal connections. Originally, cities were constructed as small pockets of civilization within a larger untamed ecosystem. What was once a necessary and pragmatic form of settlement designed to secure the survival of the species has now led to a complete detachment of society from nature, which undermines our possible insight into the processes of urbanization. Not only in a physical sense, in that we are no longer in daily contact with the ecosystems that are vital to our survival, but also in relation to the resource processes that enable our consumption and the city's underlying technologies that efficiently, if unseen, underpin human society and productivity.

The climate crisis is already having a disastrous impact on our cities, and the situation is only going to get worse over the coming decades. Copenhagen has been having what is popularly known as 'monster rain' with alarmingly increasing frequency. Every three years since 2011, Copenhagen has seen rainstorms that usually occur every 100, 500 and 1,000 years, and the damage is extensive. Sooner or later, all the parks, public squares and streets in Copenhagen, as in many other cities, will have to be redesigned to be able to deal with the new weather patterns. A major and urgent investment. But might this predicament also facilitate a vital rethinking of the urban metabolism?

If we try, for a moment, to adopt a constructive perspective of the harmful effects of monster rain events, they do make the challenge tangible to everyone and thus establish a mobilizing focus. The transformative power of water renders phenomena on a 'climatic' or 'planetary' scale instantly perceptible on an individual level and may thus help us find part of the answer to the challenge of transition.

Atmosphere

'Atmosphere' has three different meanings: 1. A unit of pressure. 2. The envelope of gases surrounding the planet and the condition of all life. 3. A place or a situation that affects our body and state of mind.

When the climate crisis affects the city, the term's scientific and phenomenological meanings become intertwined. In Enghave Park, in Copenhagen's Vesterbro district, the city responds to monster rain with a comprehensive redesign. From 2020, the park will be able to handle 23,000 m^3 of storm water, preventing damage to the surrounding residential neighbourhood.

Excavations within the park's existing neoclassical structure make room for 9,000 m^3 of storm water. A new-built wall along the park perimeter enables the retention of the remaining 14,000 m^3 when the entire park is flooded. The park's storm water capacity is based on projections of a once-in-a-century rain event in 2100, which is the level calculated to be economically meaningful to protect against.

Part of the everyday rain from urban roofs is collected in the park in underground storage pipes and is used for watering the many species of plants during dry periods and by the city's street-sweeping lorries, which use water to clean the streets. The collected rainwater also circulates in a groove on top of the perimeter wall, where visitors to the park can run their fingers through it, and is used in a central fountain garden where children enjoy playing. It is probably the first legal recreational use of rainwater in the history of Copenhagen, which until now has relied entirely on groundwater. Thus the new design also saves millions of litres of groundwater. When the storage pipes are emptied after a prolonged period of drought, the recreational water features are switched off. Thus, the park's technical water functions are linked with a sensuous dimension as well as a causal resource understanding.

Enghave Park opened in 1929 and is built in a former nature area that once housed allotment gardens. The individual gardens were expropriated by the city – which led to deep resentment among the owners – in favour of the collective recreational value that the park would provide for the area's predominantly low-income working-class population. As a young employee in the Copenhagen City Architect's office, the Danish functionalist architect Arne Jacobsen created his first designs for the park: a stage and some stalls.

Contemporary writers have described how the first visitors excitedly walked through the axes and symmetries of the park and marvelled at the centrally placed reflecting pool. An unprecedented sense of order and bourgeois aesthetic had made its entry into the working-class neighbourhood. The very same order that Tom Kristensen had his protagonist, Ole Jastrau, tear to shreds with reckless abandon in an alcoholic haze in his famous 1930 novel *Havoc*.

A million people visited the park annually before the redesign, and with the expansion of the nearby Carlsberg district and a new metro station on the adjacent Enghave Plads, the number is expected to rise over the coming years. When the next extreme rainstorm turns the full 35,000 m^2 area of the park into a single water surface, the transformation will reflect both an accomplishment in architectural and water-management terms and a nature revival in a new type of urban metabolism. Hopefully, the park will engage the many visitors and stimulate a more immediate awareness of the new climate reality.

With monster rains and climate crisis, both havoc and haze take on different meanings in the park today. The new atmospheric water-management features enable a pragmatic, highly sensuous and deeply aesthetic narrative that will hopefully give rise to new reflections on the climate rather than the ones we are subjected to by urban breakdowns and media sensationalism. Ideally, the park atmosphere will activate our senses and inspire a more mindful approach to the climate crisis.

The ultimate goal for the transition, as I see it, is achieved when the balance between culture and nature is restored. When our species' resource

consumption is matched by the planet's capacity for regeneration. For nature and culture to form a new balanced continuum, they will have to be brought much closer together, on every level of society and in every aspect of our everyday life.

Not as a naive yearning for Romanticism or a pre-civilization era but as a searing acknowledgement of the paradoxically monstrous in us all. And as a fascinating drive to expand the strange and unique beauty that our combined natureculture can represent.

Work cited:

Kristensen, Tom. 1968. *Havoc.* Translated by Carl Malmberg. Madison and London: University of Wisconsin Press. Original edition published in Danish in 1930.

UN. 2018. United Nations Environment Programme. 'Global Status Report 2018'. https://www.unenvironment.org/resources/report/global-status-report-2018. Accessed 28 January 2020.

Model photo of Enghave Park showing the overflow from a 'monster rain' event released into the park to secure the neighbourhood's properties and infrastructure against the water's damaging effects.

New Materialism

→ Chthulucene | dynamic processes of becoming | → Ecology | → Environment | non-linear matter flows | → Object-Oriented Ontology | → Oxymorons | → Posthuman | ruling out full knowledge and control | the nature of the material world | undermining belief in the uniqueness of human species | → Waste

Often pluralized, the new materialisms cover a range of approaches that have become influential over the past decade.[1] What links them is a commitment to give matter its due, to explain how and why matter matters, to explore novel forms of contemporary materiality and to pose questions about the nature of the material world in ways that challenge existing ideas about society and the human.

New materialist ontology rejects an older sense of matter as a stable state of Being, focusing instead on dynamic processes of becoming. Across many disciplines within the natural and human sciences, its practitioners are investigating the choreographies of diverse materializations, alert to unexpected connections and to the alchemy of non-linear matter flows. In the visual and performative arts, such as in Argentine-Israeli Mika Rottenberg's installation videos, new materialists are exploring the fugitive properties of matter while also emphasizing some of the surprising and creative ways materials cross boundaries and follow unexpected or subterranean pathways. In a similar vein, new materialist architects are looking afresh at the materiality of the built environment in order to appreciate both its internal dynamism and its resonances with lived experience in specific material contexts. From a critical perspective, the aim of the new materialisms might be summarized as nothing less than a transformation of our ways of understanding and engaging the material realm: a task made urgent by awareness of the existential threat to life on planet Earth posed by modernity's attitudes towards nature and its Promethean conception of the human condition.

Diana Coole (born 1952, located in London, UK) is Professor Emerita of Political and Social Theory at Birkbeck, University of London. She is the author of a number of works on new materialism and has published extensively in the fields of phenomenology, feminism and demography. She is currently enjoying retirement as an opportunity to travel and has recently returned from Ethiopia.

The recent materialist turn disavows ideas about matter associated with Cartesian philosophy or Newtonian physics, which consider it to be an inert, meaningless substance fundamentally distinct from consciousness. The emphasis on materialization suggests that materiality is better appreciated in terms of self-transformative assemblages or dynamic open systems. Oppositions, such as between body and mind, subject and object, or nature and culture, are no longer tenable. If this view has some affinities with vitalism, the vitality of the vibrant matter described by new materialists arises not from any life force ascribed to matter but from the incalculable array of volatile relationships and differences that come into play between entities within any material field. Active, embodied humans are simply components – or, indeed, unstable constellations – within such fields. New materialists may, in addition, draw attention to the continuities and similarities between humans and animals, regarding their cognitive, behavioural and genetic properties. This further undermines belief in the uniqueness of the human species.

New materialist ontology is often described as 'flat', following the French sociologist Bruno Latour. The term refers to a rejection of traditional, vertical ontologies that distinguish and rank the human, animals, plants and minerals. A flat ontology rejects notions of human (and specifically masculine) privilege, a position that is exemplified by new materialists' refusal to equate agency with rational or moral subjectivity. Inversely, matter is no longer regarded as reliant upon human will to set it in motion, achieve change or bestow meaning and value. Agentic capacities – that is, efficacious capabilities to affect the course of events or composition of structures – are in principle dispersed across the full range of entities (or 'actants') that constitute a material system or field. Within this febrile mix, novel assemblages and hybrids are constantly being formed and destroyed. Which combinations or forces acquire potency here is contingent on the ever-shifting configurations of their relationships and contexts. This does not preclude human efficacy, but it does not guarantee it. Instead, its hazardous and varied appearances must be negotiated (and tracked) in concert with other material entities, all operating within dense, complicated situations that rule out full knowledge or control.

Because these propositions throw the nature and status of the human into question, they have radical implications, too, for thinking about the relationship between the human and the nonhuman. This suggests that new materialist ideas may be particularly relevant when considering the Anthropocene. Inasmuch as this is defined as an unprecedented geological-historical era, in which relations (and distinctions) between human and nonhuman have become increasingly complicated and indivisible, new materialists' denial of human uniqueness or species privilege lends ontological ballast to the critique of anthropocentrism – that is, human-centric views of the world. Ecocentric or biocentric alternatives are more congruent with a flat ontology, as are claims that embodied human beings cannot exist in separation from nature but are thoroughly imbricated in, co-produced by and inseparable from the natural environment. By emphasizing humans' embodiment, new materialists draw attention to the numerous entities – from microbiological organisms to technological and ecological systems – that produce, enhance, sustain and damage bodies, and thus to the porous nature of their biophysical boundaries, their vulnerability to disease and want (or to biomedical interventions and climate events) and their inextricability from nonhuman entities, both organic and mineral.

New materialist methods – as currently undertaken, for example, in science and technology studies (STS) – invite detailed studies of the ways human and nonhuman are ineluctably, but also increasingly, interwoven historically, for example through technology, biopower and the commodification of nature. Such studies are exemplified by research that traces particular matter flows (for example in energy use or food production) through and across a complicated tapestry of circuits, structures, switching points and feedback loops. They may thereby become aware of ways matter moves at different speeds and intensities (perhaps identifying connections between geological, biological and historical time) when, for example, tracking the itineraries of materials in the form of manufactured commodities or waste within the global economy.

What makes such materialist studies 'new' (and, for example, more comprehensive than Marxist historical materialism) is that they do not only focus on structures of power instantiated in globalized economies or geopolitics but follow more complex, unpredictable, circulations and agentic effects of matter at different levels. This may involve tracing movements from the micro level (for instance everyday corporeal routines and domestic habits) to the macro level (geological, biological, ecological, atmospheric) and back. For example, extracting minerals may affect miners' health, facilitate innovations in building, engender new markets and irreversibly change the Earth's crust in ways that rebound on everyday wellbeing. The choreographies and syncopations discovered by these new materialist investigations often show affinity with chaos or complexity theory, to which they add a social and political dimension to scientific or statistical accounts of the unstable material context associated with a climate emergency and mass extinctions. Such studies explain the (anthropogenic) role of modern humans in destroying the nonhuman environment while also showing their inability to control or escape the material consequences. In summary, the new materialisms are broadening the scope of critical investigations by insisting on the inseparability and bidirectionality of different levels of human–nonhuman interaction and by demonstrating the importance of meticulous investigations of 21st-century materializations.

Works cited:

Bennett, Jane. 2010. *Vibrant Matter*. Durham, NC: Duke University Press.

Coole, Diana, and Samantha Frost, eds. 2010. *The New Materialisms: Ontology, Agency, and Politics*. Durham, NC: Duke University Press.

Next Generation

action | climate justice | emission speed | → Energy | existential threat | → Future | hope | mass extinction | → Pollution | → Resources

When I was about eight years old, I first heard about something called 'climate change', or 'global warming'. Apparently, it was something us humans had created by our way of living. I was told to turn off the lights to save energy and to recycle paper to save resources.

I remember thinking that it was very strange that humans, who are an animal species among others, could be capable of changing the Earth's climate. Because, if we were, and if it was really happening, we wouldn't be talking about anything else. As soon as you would turn on the TV, everything would be about that. Headlines, radio, newspapers: you would never read or hear about anything else – as if there was a world war going on. But no one ever talked about it. If burning fossil fuels was so bad that it threatened our very existence, how could we just continue as before? Why were there no restrictions? Why wasn't it made illegal? To me, that did not add up. It was too unreal.

So, when I was eleven, I became ill, I fell into a depression, I stopped talking, and I stopped eating. In two months, I lost about 10 kilos of weight. Later on, I was diagnosed with Asperger's syndrome, OCD and selective mutism. This basically means I only speak when I think it is necessary. Now is one of those moments.

Greta Thunberg (born 2003, located in Stockholm, SE) is a Swedish climate youth activist who has received worldwide recognition for her efforts to fight climate change. In 2018, she founded a movement known as Fridays for Future (also called School Strike for Climate) and since then she has been invited to speak at numerous public events as well as in front of the UN. In 2019, she was nominated for the Nobel Peace Prize.

For those of us who are on the spectrum, almost everything is black or white. We aren't very good at lying, and we usually don't enjoy participating in the social game that the rest of you seem so fond of. I think, in many ways, that we autists are the normal ones and the rest of the people are pretty strange. Especially when it comes to the sustainability crisis, where everyone keeps saying that climate change is an existential threat and the most important issue of all. And yet, they just carry on like before. I don't understand that. Because if the emissions have to stop, then we must stop the emissions. To me, that is black and white. There are no grey areas when it comes to survival. Either we go on as a civilization or we don't. We have to change.

Rich countries like Sweden need to start reducing emissions by at least 15% every year. And that is so that we can stay below a 2 °Celcius warming target. Yet, as the IPCC has recently demonstrated, aiming instead for 1.5 °Celsius would significantly reduce the impacts on the climate. But we can only imagine what that means for reducing emissions.

You would think the media and every one of our leaders would be talking about nothing else. But they never even mention it. Nor does anyone ever mention the greenhouse gases already locked in the system. Nor that warming is hidden in air pollution; meaning, when we stop burning fossil fuels, we already have an extra level of warming – perhaps as high as 0.5 to 1.1 °Celsius.

Furthermore, hardly anyone speaks about the fact that we are in the midst of the sixth mass extinction – with up to 200 species becoming extinct every single day. And that the extinction rate today is between 1,000 and 10,000 times higher than what is seen as normal. Hardly anyone ever speaks about the aspect of equity or climate justice either, clearly stated everywhere in the Paris Agreement, which is absolutely necessary to make it work on a global scale. That means that rich countries need to get down to zero emissions within six to twelve years with today's emission speed. And that is so that people in poorer countries can have a chance to heighten their standard of living by building some of the infrastructures that we have already built, such as roads, schools, hospitals, clean drinking water, electricity and so on. Because, how can we expect countries like India or Nigeria to care about the climate crisis if we, who already have everything, don't care even a second about it or our actual commitments to the Paris Agreement?

So why are we not reducing our emissions? Why are they in fact still increasing? Are we knowingly causing a mass extinction? Are we evil? No, of course not. People keep doing what they do because the vast majority don't have a clue about the actual consequences of our everyday lives. And they don't know that rapid change is required. We all think we know, and we all think everybody knows. But we don't. Because, how could we? If there really was a crisis, and if this crisis was caused by our emissions, you would at least see some signs. Not just flooded cities. Tens of thousands of dead people and whole nations levelled to piles of torn down buildings. You would see some restrictions. But no. And no one talks about it. There are no emergency meetings, no headlines, no breaking news. No one is acting as if we were in a crisis. Even most climate scientists or green politicians keep on flying around the world, eating meat and dairy.

If I live to be 100, I will be alive in the year 2103. When you think about the future today, you don't think beyond the year 2050. By then I will, in the best case, not even have lived half of my life. What happens next? In the year 2078, I will celebrate my 75th birthday. If I have children or grandchildren, maybe they will spend that day with me. Maybe they will ask me about you, the people who were around back in 2018. Maybe they will ask why you didn't do anything while there still was time to act. What we do or don't do right now will affect my entire life and the lives of my children and grandchildren. What we do or don't do right now, me and my generation can't undo in the future.

So, when school started in August of this year, I decided that this was enough. I sat myself down on the ground outside the Swedish parliament. I school-striked for the climate. Some people say that I should be in school instead. Some people say that I should study, to become a climate scientist so that I can solve the climate crisis. But the climate crisis has already been solved. We already have all the facts and solutions. All we have to do is to wake up and change.

And why should I be studying for a future that soon will be no more, when no one is doing anything whatsoever to save that future? And what is the point of learning facts in the school system when the most important facts given by the finest science of that same school system clearly means nothing to our politicians and our society?

Some people say that Sweden is just a small country and that it doesn't matter what we do. But I think that if a few children can get headlines all over the world just by not coming to school for a few weeks, imagine what we could all do together if we wanted to.

Now we're almost at the end of my talk and this is where people usually start talking about hope. Solar panels, wind power, circular economy and so on. But I'm not going to do that. We've had 30 years of pep-talking and selling positive ideas. And I'm sorry but it doesn't work, because if it would have, the emissions would have gone down by now. They haven't. And yes, we do need hope. Of course, we do. But the one thing we need more than hope is action. Once we start to act, hope is everywhere. So instead of looking for hope, look for action. Then and only then will hope come.

Today we use 100 million barrels of oil every single day. There are no politics to change that. There are no rules to keep that oil in the ground. So we can't save the world by playing by the rules, because the rules have to be changed. Everything needs to change, and it has to start today.

Thank you.

'Next Generation' is an edited transcription of a TED Talk given by Greta Thunberg in January 2019.

ō

Object-Oriented Ontology Graham Harman

Oil Peter Adolphsen

~~ongoingness~~ → Chthulucene

~~'ordinary' aesthetic experiences of ecologies~~ → Art

~~other-than-human-beings~~ → Feminism

Overpopulation Betsy Hartmann

Oxymorons Julius von Bismarck

Object-Oriented Ontology

→ Aesthetics | → Architecture | → Art | human-object relations | sensual qualities | speculative realism | theory of reality

Object-Oriented Ontology (abbreviated OOO, usually pronounced 'Triple O') is a philosophical movement dating to the late 1990s and working under its current name since 2009. The authors most closely associated with it are Ian Bogost, Levi R. Bryant, Graham Harman and Timothy Morton.[1] Although OOO is not inaccurately described as one of four main tendencies of the larger umbrella group known as Speculative Realism, it both predates this group and enjoys a much greater scope of influence throughout numerous disciplines.[2]

One prominent feature of OOO is that it treats all objects as equally worthy of philosophical attention, regardless of whether they are real, fictional, artificial, natural or contradictory. But this alone does not make it unique and was never intended to do so. Global theories of objects were already established in the late 19th century Austro-Hungarian Empire, among the students of philosopher Franz Brentano.[3] Among the most prominent of these students to develop theories of objects were Kazimierz Twardowski of Poland and Alexius Meinong and Edmund Husserl from Austria.[4] Meinong in particular became well-known for this and was targeted in a 1905 polemic by his former admirer, the British philosopher Bertrand Russell.[5] What differentiates OOO from these Austrian theories of objects is that it not only rejects any focus on the relation between human thought and the objects to which it refers but also treats cases of inanimate object–object causal interaction as belonging to the same level as human–object relations. This leads OOO to break with the entire framework of post-Kantian philosophy in the West and has earned it some angry dismissals from those who prefer the current division of labour in which science alone is permitted to speak about object–object interactions.[6]

Since OOO holds that objects can never become directly present to us or to each other, it distinguishes between the real (or non-relational) character of objects and their sensual (or relational) character. It combines this with a second axis, the difference between any object and its qualities, which it finds to be active on both the real and sensual levels; in this way, OOO is a fourfold theory of reality with two kinds of objects and two kinds of qualities. The source of the second axis is the phenomenology of Husserl, whose philosophy can be read – though it seldom is – as a critique of the British empiricism of the 17th and 18th centuries. For an empiricist like David Hume, we do not encounter objects but only 'bundles of qualities'.[7] For example, we do not perceive an apple but only such disembodied qualities as red, hard, quasi-spherical, sweet and juicy; since these qualities occur together so often, we form the lazy habit of saying 'apple' to refer to them all, even though no one has ever seen an apple in isolation from its qualities. For Husserl, exactly the opposite is the case: we first perceive an apple, and we keep on considering it as the same apple across time even though its qualities are constantly shifting from moment to moment as the sunlight subtly changes along with our mood and the precise angle

Graham Harman (born 1968, located in Los Angeles, US) is Distinguished Professor of Philosophy at the Southern California Institute of Architecture (SCI-Arc). He is the author of numerous books, most recently *Art and Objects* (2020).

and distance from which we see the apple.[8] But whereas Husserl expresses serious doubt that the 'real' level of non-relational objects even exists, since he thinks it makes no sense that anything could exist without being – at least in principle – the object of some mental act, OOO argues for a layer of real objects existing in parallel with the sensual objects of everyday experience.

Since OOO's real objects can never be made directly present by any theoretical, perceptual or practical means, it denies that knowledge is the primary cognitive activity. However valuable knowledge is for the human species, it works either by 'undermining' objects (reducing them to their components or causal backstories), by 'overmining' them (reducing them to their appearances or effects) or more often by 'duomining' objects (under- and overmining them simultaneously). Among those forms of cognition that do not engage in 'mining' operations of any sort are philosophy and the arts. Although philosophy in the modern period has aspired to be a knowledge-producing science, Socrates founded the discipline with the practice of *philosophia* (meaning 'love of wisdom', not 'wisdom' itself). In the arts, it is even clearer that what is produced is not knowledge but an artwork that is more than its pieces and history, but also less than its sum total of effects. For this reason, OOO treats aesthetics first as philosophy.[9]

OOO theory suggests that art is about the persistent tension between a real object and its sensual qualities. The other three such tensions (real object–real qualities, sensual object–sensual qualities, sensual object–real qualities) are also treated under the heading of aesthetics, though in a broader sense than the usual one. Since the real object disappears in the artwork, the beholder or spectator steps in to replace it, meaning that – contra Immanuel Kant and Michael Fried – all art is inherently theatrical.[10] Yet the most interesting form of art for OOO is architecture, since it is always theatrical in a double sense: both in the sense just mentioned and in the sense that purpose is inscribed into works of architecture in a way that is not true of sculpture.

Works cited:

Bogost, Ian. 2012. *Alien Phenomenology, or What It's Like to Be a Thing.* Minneapolis: University of Minnesota Press.

Brassier, Ray, Iain Hamilton Grant, Graham Harman, and Quentin Meillassoux. 2007. 'Speculative Realism'. *Collapse*, III.

Brentano, Franz. 1995. *Psychology from an Empirical Standpoint.* Translated by A. Rancurello, D. B. Terrell and L. McAlister. New York: Routledge.

Bryant, Levi R. 2011. *The Democracy of Objects.* Ann Arbor, MI: Open Humanities Press.

Fried, Michael. 1988. *Absorption and Theatricality: Painting and Beholder in the Age of Diderot.* Chicago: University of Chicago Press.

Harman, Graham. 2007. 'Aesthetics as First Philosophy: Levinas and the Non-Human'. *Naked Punch*, 09 (Summer/Fall).

Harman, Graham. 2010. *Towards Speculative Realism: Essays and Lectures.* Winchester, UK: Zero Books.

Harman, Graham. 2018a. *Object-Oriented Ontology: A New Theory of Everything.* London: Pelican.

Harman, Graham. 2018b. *Speculative Realism: An Introduction.* Cambridge, UK: Polity.

Hume, David. 1978. *A Treatise of Human Nature.* Oxford: Oxford University Press.

Husserl, Edmund. 1970. *Logical Investigations.* 2 vols. Translated by J. N. Findlay. London: Routledge & Kegan Paul.

Husserl, Edmund. 1993. 'Intentional Objects'. In *Early Writings in the Philosophy of Logic and Mathematics.* Translated by D. Willard. Dordrecht: Kluwer.

Kant, Immanuel. 1987. *Critique of Judgment.* Translated by W. Pluhar. Indianapolis: Hackett.

Meinong, Alexius. 1988. Über *Gegenstandstheorie/ Selbstdarstellung.* Hamburg: Felix Meiner Verlag.

Morton, Timothy. 2013. *Hyperobjects: Philosophy and Ecology after the End of the World.* Minneapolis: University of Minnesota Press.

Norris, Christopher. 2013. 'Speculative Realism: Interim Report with Just a Few Caveats.' *Speculations*, IV (2013).

Russell, Bertrand. 1905. 'On Denoting'. *Mind*, 14 (6), October.

Twardowski, Kasimir. 1977. *On the Content and Object of Presentations: A Psychological Investigation.* Translated by R. Grossmann. The Hague: Martinus Nijhoff.

Zahavi, Dan. 2016. 'The End of What? Phenomenology vs. Speculative Realism'. *International Journal of Philosophical Studies,* 24 (3).

The seepage from the brook and the considerable weight of the maple, together with the mare's small but nevertheless crucial weight, eroded the slope, which eventually gave way round about midnight. A huge chunk of soil crashed into the lake with a rumble and a splash, and these noises roused the horse out of her sleep. But before she had time to look around, the tree, with a deep groan, tilted 30 degrees, whereupon the horse lost her footing and tumbled towards the water, landing first on a small floating island formed from a chunk of the collapsed slope. During the few seconds that passed before the temporary platform sank, the mare had time to smell the newly upturned soil and watch the tree keel over so it hung diagonally downwards. What were formerly the top branches now dangled just beyond her reach. Simultaneously the unstable ground beneath her gave way. Another splash. Wide-eyed, she struggled for just under a minute, but then gave up. The mud on the bottom enveloped the little horse almost lovingly. Her final thought concerned the taste of fern shoots.

Death exists, but only in a practical, macroscopic sense. Biologically one cannot distinguish between life and death; the transition is a continuum. Furthermore, at this point, nature consists of irreducible processes rather than clearly defined categories. The problem of defining death mirrors a corresponding difficulty with the definition of life: a living organism is formed of non-living material, organized so

Peter Adolphsen (born 1972, located in Copenhagen, DK) is a Danish writer of speculative fiction, primarily short stories and novellas. His work has been translated into ten languages. He won the Niels Klim Prize for best science fiction short novel in 2013 and was awarded the Lifetime Honorary Grant from the Danish State in 2019. His publications include *Brummstein* (2003), *Machine* (2006), *Year 9 after the Loop* (2013) and *Small Stories 3* (2020).

it can absorb energy to maintain its system, and death is thus the irreversible cessation of these functions. However, this definition feels too simplistic since the extent to which and how a system should be organized in order to be described as living, and precisely what aspects of its functions need to cease before death can be considered as having occurred, will always depend on an estimate. Besides, according to this definition certain sea anemones that reproduce through asexual division are immortal; as are bacteria, which merely replicate themselves only when the old cells perish – which, incidentally, is a stroke of luck for us, as the globe would otherwise be covered by a metre-thick layer of them within a matter of days. However, we mammals are not distracted by the relationship that bacteria and sea anemones have with death; instinctively, we know that death occurs when the heart stops beating – but even that is merely an illusion, partly because the heart can be kept pumping after all brain activity has ceased, partly because the majority of cells in the body continue to live a period of time after the heart has stopped and, finally, because the death of any major organism means the start of a veritable explosion of another, primarily bacterial, form of life.

[...]

Layer upon layer of material was deposited at the bottom of the lake as time passed; over millions of years, the patient micrometres of sediments became kilometres of strata on top of the heart of the small eohippus. The pressure from the multiple tonnes of material, the heat from the earth's core and the general heaving and nudging of the landscape in the form of shifts, folds and faults eventually broke down the decayed remains of the horse into oil, or, more precisely, into a vast amount of hydrocarbon bonds, variations on the basal structure C(x)H(2x+2).

The lake and the forest had long since disappeared and been replaced by arid mountains intersected by rivers. The slowly forming oil meandered through the surrounding minerals and accumulated in pockets – collectively known as the Green River Formation, once oil in serious quantities was discovered in the area in 1948. The small quantity of oil that had once been the heart of a mare was now located just under a kilometre below ground level, 13 kilometres south of the town of Jensen. The area was called the Uinta Basin and belonged to the federal state of Utah in the United States of America.

[…]

It was almost 8 p.m. on 23 June 1975 when our drop of fuel, which was once the heart of a horse, exploded in the third cylinder in the Kent engine of the Pinto 1.6L. It happened as they turned right into the car park at Timber Creek Apartments.

[…]

The majority of the soot particles that swirled around the portion of exhaust gas fumes, which had once been the heart of a horse, were compressed into a small constellation which was snapped up by the greasy oolith at the mouth of the exhaust pipe. A little later, this small assemblage of a grain of sand, oil and exhaust particles loosened itself from the pipe and was carried by the wind up to a height of 20 metres. Having ascended for a fair amount of time, then fallen and flown here and there, our little fragment ended up underneath the eaves, where it attached itself to a gangling thread from a long-since-abandoned spider's web. Here it hung for just under 24 hours, swaying in the warm, lazy Texan breeze until a balcony door below was pushed open, thus creating a sub-pressure wind that ripped the soot particles from the grain of sand, oil and cobweb.

The hand on the balcony door belonged to Clarissa, and the scream, which echoed through the trees on the slope a moment later, came from her throat. Its piercing sound stopped me in my tracks as I was playing on the balcony of the neighbouring flat; I was nine years old at the time. As I recall, the scream was entirely devoid of any shades of emotion and lasted for as long as she had sufficient breath.

Afterwards, she gasped for air and, apart from her panting, the breeze in the trees was the only sound to be heard. At that moment of near silence, Clarissa's fate was sealed as the soot particles of the ex-heart of the horse were caught by one of her forceful inhalations and sucked into the darkness of her lungs.

These passages are excerpts from Peter Adolphsen's novel *Machine* (Danish edition 2006, English edition 2008).

Over-population

apocalyptic appeal | → Geo-Social Classes | → Migration Flows | political smokescreen | → Power | powerful belief system | stereotypes | → Violence

What's wrong with overpopulation?
'Overpopulation' is a slippery term. It derives power from the way it reduces complex realities to simplistic stories across multiple realms, from natural science to social science, public policy to popular media. Its status as an almost sacrosanct article of faith masks how it creates fear and loathing of the Other by spawning and spanning threatening narratives, numbers, metaphors and visual images. These in turn often draw on deep-seated class, race, ethnic, religious and gender stereotypes. Overpopulation serves as a political smokescreen by blaming population pressures for hunger, poverty, environmental degradation, migration, conflict and now even climate change. In the process, it naturalizes and depoliticizes inequalities in wealth and power and their role in despoiling the environment.

Betsy Hartmann (born 1951, located in Amherst, US) is Professor Emerita of Development Studies at Hampshire College, Amherst. Her work focuses on the intersections between population, environment, migration and security issues. Her books include *The America Syndrome: Apocalypse, War and Our Call to Greatness* (2017) and *Reproductive Rights and Wrongs: The Global Politics of Population Control* (2016).

Contemporary notions of overpopulation reach back to the British reverend-turned-economist Thomas Robert Malthus, who wrote his essay on the Principle of Population at the turn of the 18th century. Malthus maintained that, if left unchecked, human populations grow geometrically (exponentially), while food production at best follows an arithmetic (linear) path. This condemns humanity to a constant battle to provide sustenance for its growing numbers. Only the afflictions of hunger, poverty, disease and war keep human numbers in check, along with some help from moral restraint and infertility caused by 'vice.'[1]

Overpopulation persists as a powerful belief system for five key interrelated reasons:

First is the historical elasticity of overpopulation, its one-size-fits-all-times dimension. When Malthus was alive, world population was close to one billion. In the 1960s, when alarm about population growth was spreading, the population was at around three billion. It reached six billion by the year 2000 and is presently at around 7.7 billion. The UN now predicts that world population could grow to 9.7 billion in 2050 and 10.9 billion by 2100.[2] Each of these different numbers has been argued to represent 'too many people' for available resources.[3]

Another common but historically inaccurate claim is that population continues to grow exponentially. On the contrary, birth rates have been declining steadily for many decades, and average fertility, now 2.5 children per woman, is projected to fall to 1.9 in 2100.[4] Although pockets of higher fertility still exist, in sub-Saharan Africa, for example, the main reason world population may grow by another three billion people is because such a large proportion of the population in the Global South is young and approaching child-bearing age. Over time, this 'demographic momentum' will peter out as the present large generation of young people gets older and birth rates continue to decline.

Secondly, the 'over' of overpopulation is a supple prefix that can be applied to diverse abstracted population groups in order to disparage them. Among today's targeted surplus populations are so-called youth bulges of angry young men in Africa and the Middle East who are prone to terrorism, Muslim migrants threatening to overrun white Europe or the new 'population bomb' of baby boomers in the Global North blamed for depleting social security systems.[5]

Thirdly, a picture of overpopulation is worth a thousand words. Policy and popular discourse about population dynamics often strategically avoids overt racial and gender stereotypes in word text yet signals them through interspersed visual images. For example, the UK All-Party Parliamentary Group on Population, Development and Reproductive Health's 2015 report 'Population Dynamics and the Sustainable Development Goals' 'is strewn with images of black and brown men in which they are represented as a threat, both in terms of sheer numbers and through association with conflict and violence.'[6] On the front cover of the report is a picture of a crowded lifeboat, filled with brown young men, evoking Garrett Hardin's notorious 1974 essay, 'Lifeboat Ethics: The Case against Helping the Poor'.

Fourth is the model trap. Overpopulation enjoys the aura of science when its premises are embodied in biological and statistical models of portending scarcity. Many of these are based on the concept of 'carrying capacity'. American geographer Nathan Sayre traces the concept's lineage from its initial use in the mid-1800s shipping industry, to its employment several decades later in range and game management, to its application to human populations by American ecologists. A mathematical model developed by American biologist Raymond Pearl in the 1920s was instrumental to this latter process. Pearl maintained that animal, plant and human populations all grow in a symmetrical S-shaped curve. Restricted to a limited area, populations first grow exponentially until they meet environmental resistance and then decline. According to Sayre, these kinds of models signified a larger scientific turn towards a mathematical ecology modelled on physics and chemistry, an ecology that critics later pointed out bore little relation to the complex realities of human population-environment interactions.[7]

Another important model trap is the algebraic equation, I=PAT, or IPAT for short. This equation portrays human impact (I) on the environment as the product of population size (P), the amount of goods consumed per person (A, for affluence) and the environmental degradation caused by technology per good consumed (T). The equation narrowly frames the population debate in terms of how to weigh the three factors relative to each other. IPAT's level of abstraction conceals more than it reveals. P, for example, is only about population size, while population dynamics entail so much more: population density and distribution to start with, as well as gender, race, class and age divides. By obscuring power relations between rich and poor, the equation ignores persistent social and economic inequalities. It also neglects positive human-environment interactions such as sustainable agriculture, conservation and advances in green technology.[8]

Similar to IPAT is the 1972 Club of Rome computer simulation, Limits to Growth. Forecasting over a hundred years into the future, the model's author studied interactions between five key aggregates – population, resources, industrial output, food supply and pollution – to warn of impending scarcity. They assumed growth in all these realms would be exponential, neglecting the role of technological change and price movements on resource use.[9]

Today, problematic computer models link population growth and climate change in a comparable fashion. Their aim is to persuade policymakers that reducing births is a key way to mitigate climate change even though the few countries in the world where population growth rates remain high, such as those in sub-Saharan Africa, have the lowest carbon emissions per capita in the world.[10]

Fifthly, the persistence of overpopulation beliefs is due to their apocalyptic appeal. The bleak, determinist futures forecast by Malthusian models prey on and reinforce people's fears that we are going to run out of resources and the end of the world is coming. So do dystopian images of black and brown hordes of people roaming the planet, fomenting violence and destroying the environment. Unfortunately, these images are a staple of popular culture, prevalent, for example, in disaster fiction and recent cli-fi films. In the United States, where opinion polls reveal that a staggering percentage of Americans believe in the coming apocalypse, this makes for a particularly toxic mix.

Apocalyptic panic about overpopulation also convinces many people that it is morally justified to curtail the basic human and reproductive rights of the Other in order to save the planet from doom. The result is an elitist moral relativism in which 'we' know best and 'our' rights are more worthy than theirs – a prescription for authoritarianism.[11]

Ideas have consequences

Ever since the time of Malthus, overpopulation ideas have been implicated in violence against poor people. This violence manifests in different ways at different times, interacting with other oppressive policies and politics. For example, the Malthusian views of British colonial authorities in India contributed to their failure to prevent a severe drought in the region from turning into the mass famine of 1877, when a staggering five to twelve million people died. A few years afterwards, British finance minister Sir Evelyn Baring told Parliament, 'Every benevolent attempt made to mitigate the effects of famine and defective sanitation serves but to enhance the evils resulting from over-population.'[12]

In the next century, population control became a centrepiece of US Cold War foreign policy toward the Global South. Rapid population growth in poor countries became viewed as a serious brake on development, which in turn would make those countries more susceptible to communist takeover. By 1967, the US government had become the largest single funder of population control programmes in the world. Initially, it pushed sterilization over temporary contraceptive methods, and coercion became routine. The clinical environments in which other long-acting contraceptives were delivered often denied women choice and took dangerous risks with their health.[13] Unfortunately, such practices continue today despite important efforts to reform family planning delivery and make it part of more comprehensive reproductive and primary health care.[14]

The Chinese government's one-child policy adopted in 1979 is the gravest example of reproductive and gender violence based on overpopulation ideas. American anthropologist Susan Greenhalgh has described how the Limits to Growth computer model influenced Chinese scientists and engineers to impose the policy.[15] Millions of women underwent forced abortions and sterilizations. The policy pressured families into sex-selective abortion of female foetuses, and many parents who bore daughters had to abandon or conceal them so they wouldn't be counted against the one-child quota.[16] Tragically, the international population community remained largely silent about these abuses, and the Chinese government only recently ended the policy.

In their attacks on immigrants and other targeted communities, right-wing regimes and nativist movements have long weaponized overpopulation. This is true today of Indian Prime Minister Narendra Modi and his Hindu nationalist supporters who rail against the supposed 'population explosion' of Muslim and Dalit communities.[17]

On the far right, overpopulation is an important thread in the contemporary resurgence of eco-fascism, a philosophy that melds the drive for racial purity of the nation state with a romanticized notion of a pure Nature unpolluted by the Other. The Nazis deployed this eugenic version of environmentalism to help justify their genocide of the Jews. While anti-Semitism remains strong on the far right, today the main ecofascist target is immigrants, especially Muslims and, in the US case, Latinos as well.

In a new twist, fears of climate change and appeals to sustainability are becoming part of the ecofascist creed, linked to concerns that the white race is being overrun. This is chillingly evidenced in the manifestos of the mass killers in Christchurch, New Zealand, and El Paso, Texas. In the words of the Christchurch killer, 'They are the same issue, the environment is being destroyed by over population, we Europeans are one of the groups that are not over populating the world. The invaders are over populating the world. Kill the invaders, kill the overpopulation and by doing so save the environment.' Influenced by this manifesto, the El Paso shooter argued, 'If we can get rid of enough people [in the US], then our way of life can become more sustainable.'[18]

As the far right begins to acknowledge the realities of climate change, overpopulation may serve as a sort of ideological bridge between green Malthusian tendencies on the liberal and left side of the political spectrum and ecofascism on the right. This dangerous development calls for more attention to be paid to the problematic ways that mainstream climate change discourse frames population and migration issues.

For a start, the concept of the Anthropocene downplays differential power relations among human beings due to its emphasis on an abstract Humanity affecting Nature. This abstraction in turn lends itself to a preoccupation with human numbers and an emphasis on population size and growth rather than the social and economic forces most responsible for environmental degradation and climate change. It diverts attention from the fact that 'vast inequalities are the conditions of possibility of the profound environmental crises around the world.'[19]

Widely accepted hyperbole about climate change causing mass migrations of millions of 'climate refugees' across international borders and sparking violent conflicts and wars reinforce negative Malthusian stereotypes of poor people running amok in times of scarcity.[20] Writing in *Nature Climate Change*, UK-based geographer Clionadh Raleigh and colleagues make this important observation:

'On the ground in developing countries, climate change and ecological stress is treated as a problem to be solved, not a harbinger of apocalyptic violence as it is viewed by many analysts. Indeed, during periods of hardship, higher levels of cooperation are found between erstwhile competitors. […] Yet cooperation is far less likely to make headline news. Alternative livelihoods, migration,

Clionadh Raleigh, Andrew Linke and John O'Loughlin, 2014.

and changing agricultural patterns are all examples of how individuals and communities adapt to new and volatile circumstances. [...] In terms of predicting and interpreting future insecurity in developing states, it is probably more critical to understand the "nature of the state" than the "state of nature". [...] People in poor countries do not respond to bad weather by attacking each other.'

Overpopulation may be a well-trodden path, but it leads to prejudice, poor policy prescriptions, dangerous politics and human rights violations. It stands in the way of real solutions to the urgent challenges of climate change, growing inequality and rising authoritarianism across the globe. It is high time to put it where it belongs – in the dustbin of history.

Works cited:

Connelly, Matthew. 2008. *Fatal Misconception: The Struggle to Control World Population*. Cambridge, MA: Harvard University Press.

Dash, Sweta. 2019. 'Modi and the Bogey of "Population Explosion"'. https://thewire.in/caste/modi-and-the-bogey-of-population-explosion, 25 August. Accessed 4 December 2019.

Davis, Mike. 2001. *Late Victorian Holocausts: El Niño Famines and the Making of the Third World*. London: Verso.

Greenhalgh, Susan. 2003. 'Science, Modernity and the Making of China's One Child Policy'. *Population and Development Review*, 29 (2), pp. 163–196.

Hartmann, Betsy. 2016. *Reproductive Rights and Wrongs: The Global Politics of Population Control*. Chicago: Haymarket Books.

Hartmann, Betsy. 2017. *The America Syndrome: Apocalypse, War and Our Call to Greatness*. New York: Seven Stories Press.

Hendrixson, Anne. 2018. 'Population Control in the Troubled Present: The "120 by 20" Target and Implant Access Program'. *Development and Change*, 50 (3), pp. 786–804.

Hendrixson, Anne, and Betsy Hartmann. 2018. 'Threats and Burdens: Challenging Scarcity-Driven Narratives of "Overpopulation"'. *Geoforum*, 101, pp. 250–259.

Hynes, H. Patricia. 1999. 'Taking Population out of the Equation: Reformulating I+PAT'. In *Dangerous Intersections: Feminist Perspectives on Population, Environment and Development*, pp. 39–73. Cambridge, MA: South End Press.

Johnson, Kay Ann. 2016. *China's Hidden Children: Abandonment, Adoption and the Human Costs of the One-Child Policy*. Chicago: University of Chicago Press.

Kovensky, Josh. 2019. 'White Nationalists Latch On To Climate Change for Mass Migration Hysteria.' https://talkingpointsmemo.com/muckraker/white-nationalists-latch-on-to-climate-change-for-mass-migration-hysteria, September 16. Accessed 4 December 2019.

Malthus, Thomas R. 1914. *An Essay on the Principle of Population*, vol. 1. New York: E.P. Dutton and Co.

Ojeda, Diana, Jade S. Sasser and Elizabeth Lunstrum. 2019. 'Malthus's Specter and the Anthropocene.' *Gender, Place & Culture*. Published online 16 April. https://www.tandfonline.com/doi/full/10.1080/0966369X.2018.1553858. Accessed 21 January 2020.

Raleigh, Clionadh, Andrew Linke and John O'Loughlin. 2014. 'Extreme Temperatures and Violence'. *Nature Climate Change*, 4, pp. 76–77.

Sasser, Jade S. 2018. *On Infertile Ground: Population Control and Women's Rights in the Era of Climate Change*. New York: New York University Press.

Sayre, Nathan F. 2008. 'The Genesis, History and Limits of Carrying Capacity'. *Annals of the Association of American Geographers*, 98 (1), pp. 120–134.

United Nations. 2019. Department of Economic and Social Affairs, Population Division. 'World Population Prospects 2019: Highlights'. https://population.un.org/wpp/Publications/Files/WPP2019_Highlights.pdf. Accessed 4 December 2019.

Wilson, Kalpana K. 2017. 'Re-Centering "Race" in Development: Population Policies and Global Capital Accumulation in the Era of the SDGs'. *Globalizations*, 14 (3), pp. 432–449.

Oxymorons

→ Facts → Fire → Geology → Heritage → Media → Queer
→ Terraforming

290

An oxymoron opens the possibility of speaking about things that can't be named. In combining the oppositional words that subtract each other naturally, it creates a new space for verbal formation – influencing the thinking as well. The principles of an oxymoron exceed by far the linguistic concept it's usually used for and can be understood as a handling instruction. In highlighting the opposite poles of catchwords, a new room for reflection will be created. The important thing hereby is the accuracy being created when using an oxymoron.

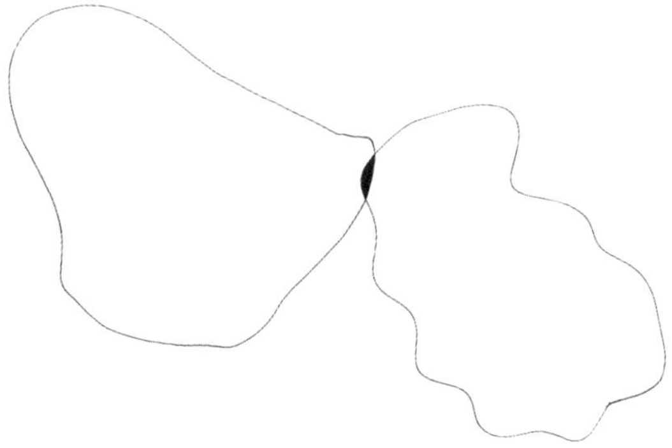

Julius von Bismarck (born 1983, located in Berlin, DE) associates visual arts to other fields of research and experimentation, which can take on various forms – from installations to happenings, from sculpture to Land Art. His artistic practice is defined by an in-depth and complex exploration of the phenomena of perception, or the representation and construction of reality.

I Am Afraid, I Must Ask You to Leave is one of three parts of an artistic project by Julius von Bismarck and Julian Charrière (2018). It resulted in blowing up woman-made nature monuments. What has been communicated by the media first as a terrorist act against the Arches National Park in Utah and second as 'fake news' happened to be a reconsideration of expectations. Ultimately, the work questions the toughness of the recognition of what truth, reality or fact is.

The actual work has been carried out over three months with the work of 35 people in a desert in Mexico.

FOX 13
LIVE
13
LIVE AT 5:30
VIDEO'S AUTHENTICITY IN QUESTION

LEAKED VIDEO_ Eco Terrorists Attack Utah
ROCK FORMATION DEMOLITION?
abc 4 UTAH
33°
5:07
JERRY SEINER
ROCK SPRINGS
NOW
Clear
24°
TONIGHT
Partly Cloudy
14°
FORECASTS

5:14
33°
NEW AT 5
2
SKEPTICISM OVER VIDEO OF ARCH DESTRUCTION

P

Pandemic Carsten Jensen
~~participation~~ → Resilience
~~perspective of care~~ → Architecture
~~pervasiveness~~ → Plastic
~~pesticides~~ → Pollution
~~petro-capitalism~~ → Plastic
~~planetary resources~~ → Media
~~planetary rhythms~~ → Air
Plantationocene Zachary Caple
Plastic Heather Davis
~~plastic as vector~~ → Plastic
~~platform cooperatives~~ → The Sharing Economy
~~playground for capital~~ → Agency
~~poetry~~ → Agriculture
~~policy instruments~~ → Energy
~~political action~~ → Declarations of Climate Emergency
~~political smokescreen~~ → Overpopulation
~~politics of privilege~~ → Weather
Pollution Frederick Rowe Davis
~~polycentric governance systems~~ → Resilience
~~populism~~ → Denial
~~post-fossil fuel era~~ → Air
~~post-anthropogenic forming of terra~~ → Terraforming
~~post-democratic era~~ → Resources
Posthuman Tomás Saraceno
~~potential futures~~ → Time
Power Lars Tønder
~~power and domination~~ → Geo-Social Classes
~~powerful belief system~~ → Overpopulation
~~prehistoric futuristic world~~ → Creation
Production Sidsel Kjærulff Rasmussen and Till Rickert
~~progress~~ → Development
~~pure violence~~ → Violence

→ Bacteria | → Body | → Borders | citizen of the planet | → Connectedness | → Future | sense of loss | vulnerability

Pandemocracy: The New World Order

Pandemic is a beautiful word. *Pan* means 'all' in Greek, while *demi* is the plural of *demos*, 'all people'. *Epidemic*, which simply means 'upon people', is less evocative. But *Pandemic* sounds almost like a manifesto: a utopian declaration of internationalists and universalists dreaming of a common united humanity.

A pandemocracy is a new form of government that transcends borders, constantly conquering new territory, generously embracing all of humankind and rendering all of us equal.

How do you become a citizen of the new pandemocracy? Here, there are no distinctions based on creed, sex or race. Eligibility is simple. The only requirement to secure a bed and care is a cough, a fever, a headache and severe respiratory problems. The symptoms that give you eligibility are beyond your control. You may think you have them, but a simple test will reveal the truth. You must resign yourself to waiting in uncertainty.

Meanwhile, your relationship with death becomes more personal. In the early stages of the surge, as pandemocracy flies its colours and admits new citizens to its expanding realm, the ubiquitous mortality statistics give you an unaccustomed feeling of vulnerability. You are used to seeing death on the screen. It tends to strike in far-away countries plagued by wars and natural disasters, so it doesn't concern you directly, even if it briefly arouses compassion; or you might pass the scene of an accident and spontaneously think, *I'm glad it's not me*. But now, the abstract language of numbers is speaking to you with renewed urgency. Now you're thinking: *it could be me*. Which puts you well on your way to becoming a citizen of the new global state of pandemocracy.

You alter your behaviour radically. You turn inward and avoid company. Your life enters a new, meditative phase; your new citizenship feels like membership of a sect. Your body is suddenly no longer a generator of desire but fragile as glass. You see your surroundings in a new light, with a foreboding sense of loss. You think back to the last time

Carsten Jensen (born in 1952, located in Copenhagen, DK) is a writer born in Marstal, on the island of Ærø. His books in English translation comprise *Earth in the Mouth* (1994), *I Have Seen the World Begin* (2000), *We, the Drowned* (2010) and *The First Stone* (2019).

you were on a plane, or a tropical beach, or a crowded train, or a busy motorway. Or the last time you saw a friend's face. And you wonder, was that *the actual last time*? You realize that the notion of average life expectancy no longer applies. If you are a Danish man, your allotted lifespan is supposedly 78 years. If you are a woman, it's 83. But statistics have lost their credibility. Your death is no longer scheduled.

You realize that death's strongest characteristic is its abrupt definitiveness. Death comes like a thief in the night, the Bible tells us. As a new citizen in the pandemocracy, you spend your nights in an unguarded house. A hand reaches out for you in the dark.

You always used to think of the future as a place that resembled the present, only with more of everything. Now you think of it as the opposite: a place that has less of everything, yourself included. Death not only affects people but also objects, habits and situations. The daily commute, the workplace itself, the queue to the supermarket cash register. Mundane behaviour patterns imposed on you by daily necessity are suddenly the stuff of a past lost forever, appearing in your mind's eye with the clarity of exhibits. In the pandemocracy, you inhabit a museum of yourself and your life. Your memories are now your life, and every day you ask yourself when the door is going to open and you can leave.

You can't know what the world will be like a hundred years from now, because you won't be around to see it. But now you don't even know what it will look like tomorrow. Or if you'll even be here. The media industry has accustomed you to life as a spectator. With its all-seeing gaze, it has spawned a new human type. In the pandemocracy, you are a citizen of the planet, unprotected by the detachment that comes with spectatorship. Everything you see on the screen is also all around you. You are living not only at the same time as everyone else but in the same space. So-called social distancing and self-isolation are your final, desperate gestures of defence against our shared mortality.

The virus is a cosmopolitan organism without a filter, and so are you. In the pandemocracy, your world is at once smaller and bigger than ever before. Death by contagion has a utopian democratic quality. In theory, at least, we are all equal: equally affected, equally exposed and equally defenceless.

When the pandemic is over, we need to renegotiate our relationship with death. We are learning the art of renunciation and loss, with the virus dictating a lifestyle of self-isolation and fear of public spaces. Can we one day create a new form of global citizenship, other than pandemocracy, in which we dare to breathe freely, and equality means more than just equality in the face of death?

Plantationocene

a machine for massifying life → Agriculture capital as the ultimate crop → City → Geo-Social Classes → Oil → Pollution the racist imagination of the West

Zachary Caple (born 1979, located in Florida, US) is an environmental anthropologist with the University of South Florida. His research investigates the chemical fertilizer industry and the role it plays in the formation of the Anthropocene.

A Parable of Rabbits

Take a pair of rabbits. Place them in a cage. Feed them and allow them to breed. Take their offspring and place them in cages. Repeat. Rabbits multiply; cages multiply.

The plantation is a machine for massifying life.

Rabbit plantations take up space. So do the plantations required to produce rabbit feed. For each crop of rabbits, there is a crop of carrots. To keep pace with the replication of rabbits, we must develop a plantation for multiplying carrots. Together, carrot and rabbit plantations take up more space than either plantation alone.

The carrot is a plant. Like all plants, it assimilates soil nutrients, water, light and atmospheric carbon in its growth and reproduction. In any given plot of earth, there is a finite quantity of phosphorus. Derived from rock, phosphorus is essential to all life. Carrots harness phosphorus from the soil and incorporate it into their flesh. Over time, the harvest and export of carrots will deplete the phosphorus in a plot of land, causing carrot production to peter out.

In order to replenish the phosphorus to grow carrots to feed rabbits, we need to mine phosphate rock and import it to carrot plantations as a fertilizer. Phosphate mining for fertilizer manufacture creates holes in the earth.

Let's review. Phosphorus is mined and fed to carrots, which in turn feed the uninterrupted expansion of rabbits. Mineral, vegetable, animal. The plantation economy is a hierarchical trophic relation, an engineered network of eating and being eaten.

Moreover, the plantation system leaves traces in the earth: phosphate pits and an expanding network of carrot and rabbit production plots.

Now let's add humans to the story – humans who eat the rabbits, wear their furs and sometimes nibble on carrots. The story needs consumers.

Human consumers live in many different environments, but the vast majority live in cities. Rabbits produced in the periphery, embodying phosphorus and carrots in their flesh, flow into the city and fuel the growth of urban populations. The city is the plantation's appetitive core.

The city is also a space where consumers labour. Humans *are grown* to expand the labour base available to urban systems of extraction. The plantation system feeds the factory system. The life force generated in plantations and embodied in food is translated into urban labour power; labour power is translated into capital through the production of commodities.

Capital feeds on labour as rabbits feed on carrots.

Workers need to eat. They also need to reproduce. Capitalism has an insatiable appetite for workers. Workers die and need to be replaced. But the worker base must grow at a rate that exceeds replacement. The average family needs to produce more than two children to grow the labour/consumer power demanded by capitalist expansion. Urban demographic

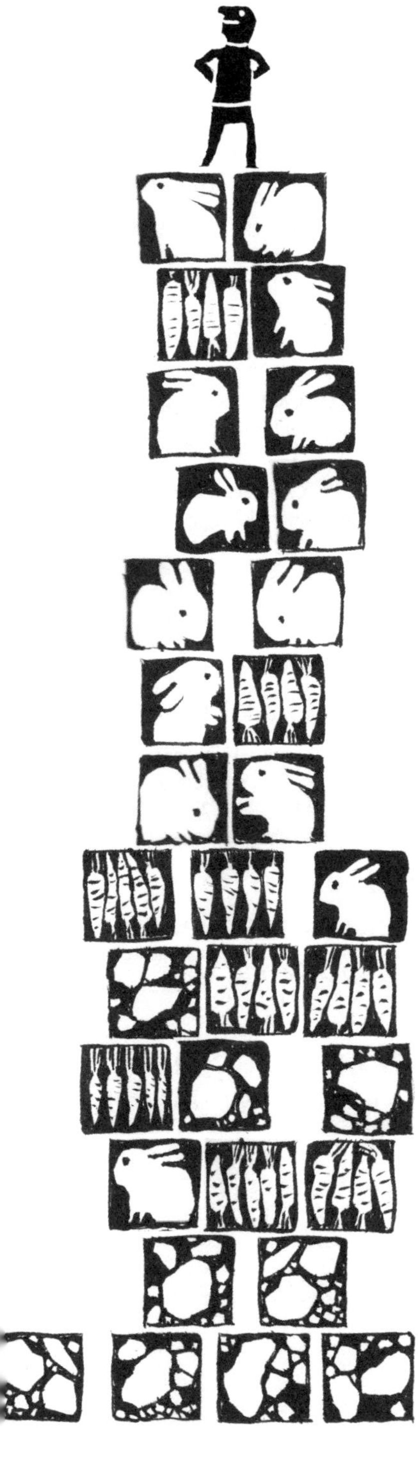

expansion, like the growth of caged rabbits, is conditioned by the sexual-structural mandates of the greater plantation economy. The mass production of families and households rests atop the mass production of plantations.

Just as a farmer must apportion a fraction of his crop to reseed next year's growth, capital reinvests a fraction of its surplus into the expansion of the plantation system. As capital grows so too do the number of phosphate mines and carrot and rabbit plantations. Cities and their belching streams of pollution grow too.

The plantation is a reproductive social order that works through a series of translations: phosphate rock → carrots → rabbits → labour → capital. Each of these translations is also a subjugation. These subjugations represent a mode of trophic violence that is legitimated by and enacted through what might be called *the racist imagination of the West*. In this imagination, the messy entanglements of the living world are abstracted into a hierarchy of kinds, with humans on top and minerals at the bottom. Kinds are ranked according to their inferior and superior qualities. Within the category of the human, people are divided and ranked, with European Whites on top and Black Africans at the bottom. The racist imagination of the West is not just a theory of everything; it is *a practical imagination* that enacts its fictions of races, classes and species through the coercive economy of the plantation.

In sum, the plantation is a totalizing machine that enslaves the growth and reproduction of life itself, encoding the logic of race at all levels of its operation. Capital is its ultimate crop.

Having described the paradigmatic structure of the plantation, how might we understand the Plantationocene – the Earth as transformed by the total plantation system?

Let's return to the beginning.

Take a pair of rabbits. Place them in a cage. Place that cage in a plot of wild land abounding with biodiverse, non-hierarchical relations – a meadow, for instance. Let us now imagine that this plot of wildness wraps around the whole Earth, creating the self-regulating, homeostatic condition called Gaia.

As cities, rabbit plantations, carrot fields and phosphate mines multiply, more and more of the Earth's wildlands are lost to growth. Domesticated rabbits and domesticated humans soon outweigh the biomass of all wild animals combined. The world-wrapping fabric of wildness, punctured and frayed, begins to haemorrhage species. Wild creatures eking out a living in landscapes overtaken by growth confront a range of hazards to which they may not ultimately adapt. Rabbit farts warm the climate. Industrial farms and urban sewers spew phosphorus into aquatic ecosystems, nourishing blooms of toxic algae and oxygen-depleted dead zones.

In the layered insults of the greater plantation economy, the homeostasis of Gaia begins to break down. Cracks in the earth system wind their way into the capitalist world system. Food production begins to fail; cities drown in their own pollution. World leaders, glorying in their civilizational achievements, call for more growth to create the wealth needed to finance the repair of Earth.

Q: How will Earth be patched back together?
A: The reinvention of rabbits.

Plastic

→ Air | banality of environmental horror | → Body | → Environment | → Oil | pervasiveness | petro-capitalism | plastic as vector | → Soil | → Violence | → Water

It is by now an everyday scene. Gazing down from a boat, or dock, into the water and seeing a gently moving translucent object that initially appears to be just another floating jellyfish, bobbing around, expanding and contracting, but on second glance is a plastic bag. A similar experience happens on land, where a flutter catches the corner of your eye, and as you look up, you see a bag drifting in the wind, arching and tumbling. Or, as you bend down to pick up a particularly bright coloured rock from the ground, you realize it is actually a well-worn piece of plastic, some broken and weathered toy or lighter. Plastic has now become one of the vectors to understand the flows of water and wind, the pressures and speeds and variegations of the world around us. The transformation of our landscapes through the omnipresence of plastic is now a platitude. The saturation of the world with oil is so common-place as to be a banal observation. What does this mean, to live in times where our long-dead ancestors, compressed with geologic force, have been revived, and to take this revelation so blandly? That sleek, slick substance that marks all of our relations in the 21st century is as pervasive and all-encompassing as our atmosphere. And for many of us, now, this reality appears unremarkable.

Heather Davis (born 1979, located in New York, US) is an assistant professor in culture and media at the New School, New York. She is the co-editor of *Art in the Anthropocene: Encounters among Aesthetics, Politics, Environments and Epistemologies* (2015) and editor of *Desire Change: Contemporary Feminist Art in Canada* (2017). Her current book project re-examines materiality in light of the widespread dissemination of plastic.

The slow suffocation, the temperate starvations, the seeping of chemicals, all these conditions form a central part of the banality of environmental horror, the ways in which ecocide is rather mundane. The damaged planet has become part of our everyday lives, and in this sense this extreme state of exception appears quite ordinary. This state of affairs is characterized by the split consciousness of contemporary existence, where many of us are quite aware of the dangers that we are surrounding ourselves with and the violence we are perpetrating against others, and yet we carry on working and loving and living as if everything were just fine, caught up in the tasks and infrastructures and duties of everyday life. Plastic can be understood as a materialization of these realities. For it can be seen as a condensation of the forces of petro-capitalism, with all of its attendant assaults on humans and the more-than-human worlds we inhabit. And yet it is also just the bag that we carry home, it is also just the paint that is in our homes, it is also just the keys on which these words were typed and the glasses through which I see and the pavement of the roads and the tyres on those roads. This creeping and pervasive transformation is too encompassing to find horrifying, at least not on an ongoing basis. It is too convenient and omnipresent and, frankly, beautiful. It is too seductive, too pleasurable, too easy, too normal.

Plastic is a question posed to us from a different time, from an ancient time, from a distant future. It asks, how do we deal with banality? What does pervasiveness feel like? For plastic is now everywhere, in everyone, and there is no outside or escape or safe room to retreat to, even if these conditions of exposure and toxicity are differentially distributed according to race and class. So, what does this material have to teach us about contemporary environmental thought? What might we learn from these intractable and, in many ways, irreversible conditions? How are we to deal with the mundane horrors of environmental decline, the slow violence enacted on the bodies of many organisms because of the suffocating, toxic, starving qualities of plastic? What does it mean to unearth the dead? And for all of this to exacerbate and intensify pre-existing patterns of disparity and privilege? These are the questions that plastics ask of us, demand us to consider, as they swirl, lazily, through the waterways, as they drift on the winds, as they clog our gutters and fill the stomachs of camels and whales and coral. These relatively new materials are calling us to reimagine our relations to water, oil, air and soil, and to each other.

Pollution

→ Agriculture | → Biodiversity | → Body | → Capitalocene | chemicals | → Client: Earth | → Earth Ethics | → Environment | → Food | interconnectedness within ecosystems | → Invisible | pesticides | → Plantationocene | → Resources | risks | → World Scientists' Warning to Humanity

In her groundbreaking book *Silent Spring*, American science writer and marine biologist Rachel Carson revealed the interconnectedness within ecosystems. Carson connected environmental degradation to pollution across media – air, soil, water – and to organisms – humans, mammals, birds and fish. With impassioned prose, she alerted Americans to the environmental impacts of indiscriminate pesticide use. She linked widespread death and disease in birds and fish to direct and indirect effects of extensive and repeated pesticide applications. She wrote, 'As crude a weapon as a cave man's club, the chemical barrage has been hurled against the fabric of life – a fabric on the one hand delicate and destructible, on the other miraculously tough and resilient, and capable of striking back in unexpected ways.'[1]

Carson had a gift for interpolating scientific papers that pointed to ecological effects. She simplified the vast number of insecticides into just two primary categories: chlorinated hydrocarbons and organophosphates. In language that was precise, Carson described the chlorinated hydrocarbons, beginning with the well-known DDT and proceeding to Aldrin, Dieldrin, Chlordane and Endrin, one of the most toxic of the pesticides in the class.

Carson characterized organophosphates as even more dangerous than the chlorinated hydrocarbons. She recounted how Gerhard Schrader, a German scientist, synthesized the first esters of phosphoric acid and discovered

Frederick Rowe Davis (born 1965, located in West Lafayette, US) is head of and a professor at the Department of History at Purdue University. He also holds the R. Mark Lubbers Chair in the History of Science. He studied the history of science at Harvard, the University of Florida, and Yale, where he received his PhD. He is the author of *Banned: A History of Pesticides and the Science of Toxicology* (2014).

that the chemicals were highly toxic to insects as well as other animals, including humans. While Schrader continued to develop organophosphates as insecticides, other scientists explored their potential as nerve agents for use in war though they were never deployed during the Second World War. Carson recounted tales of organophosphate poisonings in animals and humans. One toxicologist died before he could administer the antidote after self-experimenting to determine the toxicity of parathion.

The proliferation of DDT and other chemical insecticides in American agriculture is so well known that it hardly needs mention here.[2] Carson cited Charles Elton, the Oxford population biologist, to explain how chemical insecticides permeated environments and the bodies of plants and animals. Elton argued that agriculture shortened food chains, leaving crops vulnerable to insect infestation. Chemical insecticides provided a temporary solution, but Carson revealed the extent of unintended consequences to animals as chemicals like DDT accumulated in soil and the bodies of animals. Gradually, the entire ecosystem showed signs of contamination. The bald eagle, an iconic bird of prey, provided one of Carson's most dramatic examples. With a steady diet of fish, eagles developed toxic levels of DDT, which interfered with the ability to produce offspring. They still nested, but the eggs never hatched.

Carson argued that the very fabric of life was at risk. *Silent Spring* may have launched the American environmental movement, but a decade passed before DDT was banned for use in the United States. In the search for simple solutions, farmers replaced DDT and the chlorinated hydrocarbons with organophosphates. *Sensu stricto*, organophosphates caused less environmental contamination than DDT in that they disintegrated quickly following applications. However, the highly toxic organophosphates posed direct risks to wildlife and even farmworkers and went on to become the pesticides of choice for nearly 30 years after the DDT ban. With the passage of the Food Quality Protection Act (FQPA; 1996), the U.S. Environmental Protection Agency (EPA) launched a reassessment of pesticides including organophosphates. As a result, many of the organophosphates were banned in 2001.[3]

In many ways, the chlorinated hydrocarbons like DDT and organophosphates had parallel life cycles. Both comprised large numbers of closely related chemicals deployed as insecticides. Both were developed during the Second World War and were extensively produced and used in American agriculture in the years following the war. In *Silent Spring*, Carson revealed unintended consequences associated with both, including environmental contamination and dangers to wildlife and humans. In 1972, the stories of the two major groups of pesticides diverged when the EPA banned DDT and chlorinated hydrocarbons faded from use. However, reliance on chemical insecticides to protect crops is a practice deeply entrenched among American farmers.

Even before the EPA began its review of organophosphates, a new class of insecticide had joined the ranks of agricultural insecticides. Since the 1950s, scientists have attempted to synthesize compounds like a naturally occurring insecticide: nicotine. Chemists first synthesized promising nicotinoids during the 1970s, but the initial compounds were unstable in light and thus unviable for development as insecticides. Agricultural chemists working with support from Bayer and Shell successfully developed and patented several 'neonicotinoids' during the 1980s and 1990s. As a class, neonicotinoid insecticides showed promise as systemic insecticides that would be taken up by crops. Carson envisioned insecticides like the neonics in *Silent Spring*. She wrote of systemic insecticides, chemicals that would be taken up by the plants rendering the tissues insecticidal: 'The world of systemic insecticides is a weird world, surpassing the imaginings of the brothers Grimm – perhaps more closely akin to the cartoon world of Charles Addams. It is a world where the enchanted forest of the fairy tales has become the poisonous forest in which an insect that chews a leaf or sucks the sap of a plant is doomed.'[4]

With more than 90% of maize grown with neonicotinoid

insecticides, cornfields across America realize the poisonous forest Carson imagined. Even though neonicotinoids represent a relatively new class of pesticide, or at least a recently synthesized form of an existing chemical (nicotine), their widespread proliferation in agriculture across America and throughout the world seems eerily familiar. Once again, a fog of scientific uncertainty surrounds the most widely used agricultural insecticides in the world.

Contrary to Carson's clarion call for a reduction in the use of all insecticides, the ban on DDT and other organochlorines initiated a risk-risk trade-off in which agribusiness replaced DDT and the persistent organochlorines with highly toxic organophosphates, like parathion, that threaten the welfare of humans and wildlife despite relatively rapid disintegration in the environment. When Congress enacted the FQPA, the EPA launched its comprehensive review of organophosphates and carbamates, and U.S. restrictions on many of them followed. Nevertheless, neonicotinoids provided agribusiness with substitutes, albeit ones that may contaminate ecosystems and threaten non-target organisms, including bees and birds. Initial assessments suggest that neonicotinoids pose lower risks to humans and other mammals than the organophosphates and carbamates. As regulators review these chemicals and the risks they pose to ecosystems and wildlife, we should look to *Silent Spring* and a century of pesticides and toxicology for models with which to evaluate novel risks. As Carson concluded, 'It is our alarming misfortune that so primitive a science has armed itself with the most modern and terrible weapons, and that in turning them against the insects it has also turned them against the earth.'[5]

Work cited:

Carson, Rachel. 1962. *Silent Spring*. Boston: Houghton Mifflin Company.

Davis, Frederick Rowe. 2014. *Banned: A History of Pesticides and the Science of Toxicology*. New Haven: Yale University Press.

Posthuman

→ Chthulucene | → Coexistence | → Connectedness | → Declaration of Rebellion | extending your senses | multi-being life forms | response-ability | shared work of imagining

What you see is my mind, my body. I weave the mouth that feeds me, but, if flies do not attune to my score, I eat it back before a summer storm.

Weaving in the interstices between branches and door frames after a rain shower, they are oracles of living bodies, scripts of fortune divination; entangling cooperative constellations, these multi-being life forms trace maps of attunement to the astral scores.

Arachnomancy celebrates the ability to forecast meteorological events, or extraordinary ones such as tsunamis, through the observation of other species' behaviour. Spider/webs are the mouths through which the spider eats and the oracle speaks. The oracle is a messenger between perceptual worlds, transcending the reciprocal blindness between spider/webs and humans. Extending your senses towards new forms of embodied cognition, Arachnomancy tries to attune to a non-verbal language that amplifies our response-ability to each other.

The deck of 33 Arachnomancy Cards is an instrument of mediation, one of the many ways to consult spiderweb oracles, in an invitation to attune to the shared work of imagining and creating our future. Inspired by spider divination methods practiced in different parts of the world, particularly the nggam collaboration of ground-dwelling spiders and their human neighbours in Cameroon, the Arachnomancy Cards think through the spider's oracular capabilities as a result of its sensory universe. Sense new threads of connectivity, or else face the eternal silence of extinction. As life draws lines on your hands, so the spider draws lines on your future. The Arachnomancy reading is written through the silken threads of the spider/web.

Tomás Saraceno (born 1973, located in Berlin, DE) elevates the concepts that link art, life science and the social sciences. Enmeshed at the junction of these worlds, his floating sculptures, community projects and interactive installations propose and explore new, sustainable ways of inhabiting and sensing the environment.

The card's drawings and reinterpretation based on W. Duncan, *Webs in the Wind*, New York: The Ronald Press Company, 1949; W.S. Bristowe, *The World of Spiders*, London: Collins, 1958; William Curtis, 1746–1799; Elizabeth Marbury, 1856–1933, donor; F. Vollrath, 1988; G.B. Sowerby, *Popular History of the Aquarium of Marine and Fresh-Water Animals and Plants*, London: Lovell Reeve, 1957; Peter Apian, *Cosmographia*, 1539; Benjamin White, *Flora Londinensis, or, Plates and Descriptions of Such Plants as Grow Wild in the Environs of London*, 1778; Basilius Besler, *Hortus Eystettensis*, Nuremberg, 1613; 'Untangling the Spider's Web,' in *Trends in Ecology & Evolution* 3, 1988, pp. 331–335, with the Arachnophilia archives and Studio Tomás Saraceno.

Let your future be read by a spider/web. Download the Arachnomancy app and join a collective exercise of mapping against extinction.

For more information, visit Arachnophilia.net.

Courtesy of the artist, with thanks to Arachnophilia, Andersen's, Copenhagen; Ruth Benzacar, Buenos Aires; Tanya Bonakdar Gallery, New York / Los Angeles; Pinksummer Contemporary Art, Genoa; Esther Schipper, Berlin.

Tomás Saraceno
BAD NEWS
Card 28 out of a deck of
33 Arachnomancy Cards,
2019–ongoing

Accumulation as supporting core, land colonization from above. Becoming prey without seeing it coming, sticky threads reaching from the top. To break free you need to change perspective by changing position.

Suit: Space Spider/Web
Species: Cryptachaea riparia
Notation: E ♭
Plant: Juniperus communis

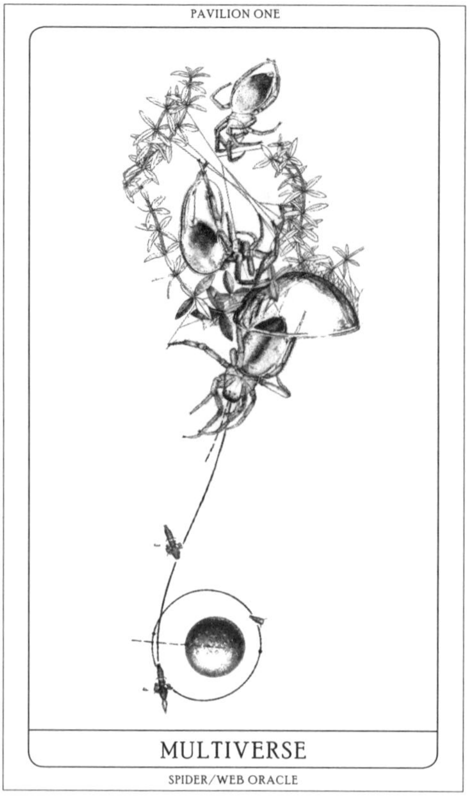

Tomás Saraceno
MULTIVERSE
Card 1 out of a deck of
33 Arachnomancy Cards,
2019–ongoing

Gravitational waves resounding the cosmic web, yet to be felt. Infinite sensing of the world, life-forms weave constellations. Close your eyes, cover your ears, I will still sense your felt vibrations.

Suit: Diving Bell Spider/Web
Species: Argyroneta aquatica
Notation: D ♭
Plant: Sphagnum cuspidatum

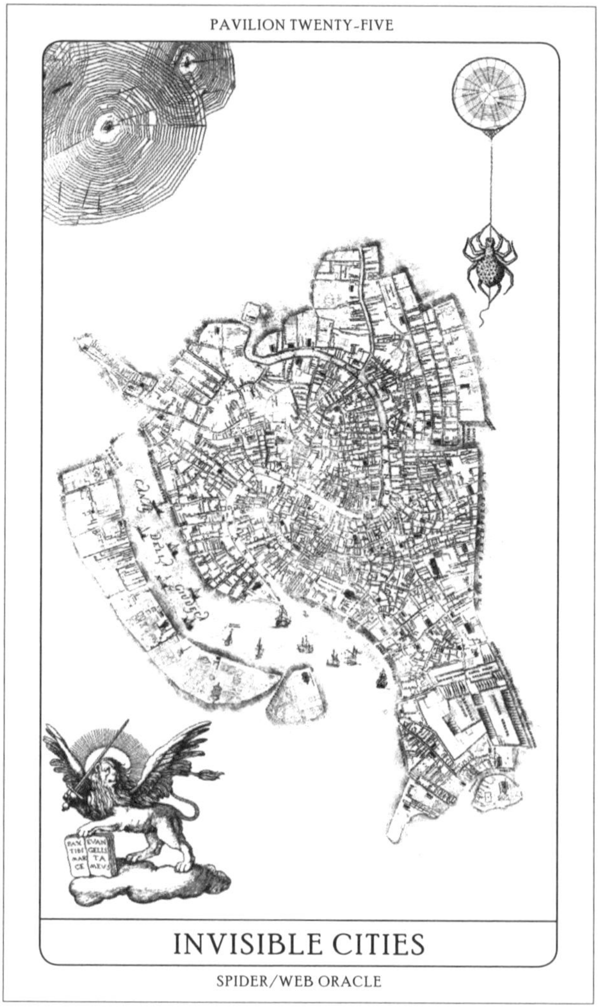

Tomás Saraceno
INVISIBLE CITIES
Card 25 out of a deck of
33 Arachnomancy Cards,
2019–ongoing

Every object is a past movement, every web is a silken map of evolving memories. There are other cities hidden within this one, spider/webs will help you with routes and returns, when finding your way back.

Suit: Ballooning Spider/Web
Species: Argiope lobata
Notation: E ♭
Plant: Cupressus sempervirens

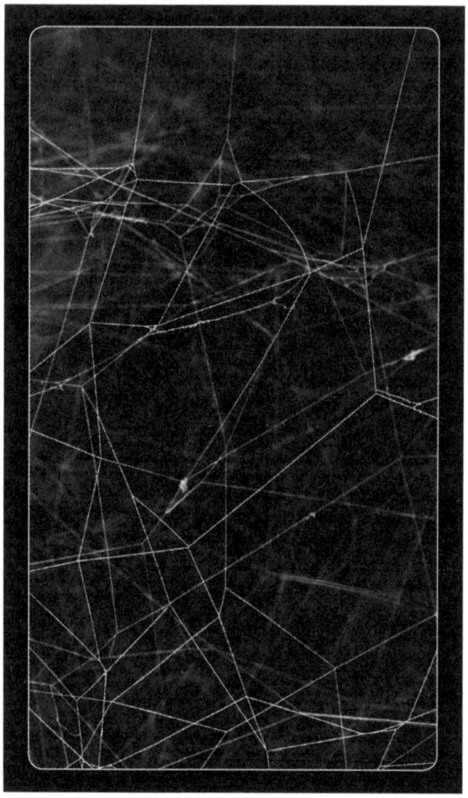

Tomás Saraceno
Reverse of the Arachnomancy
Cards, 2019
Deck of 33 cards printed on
carbon-footprint-neutral paper

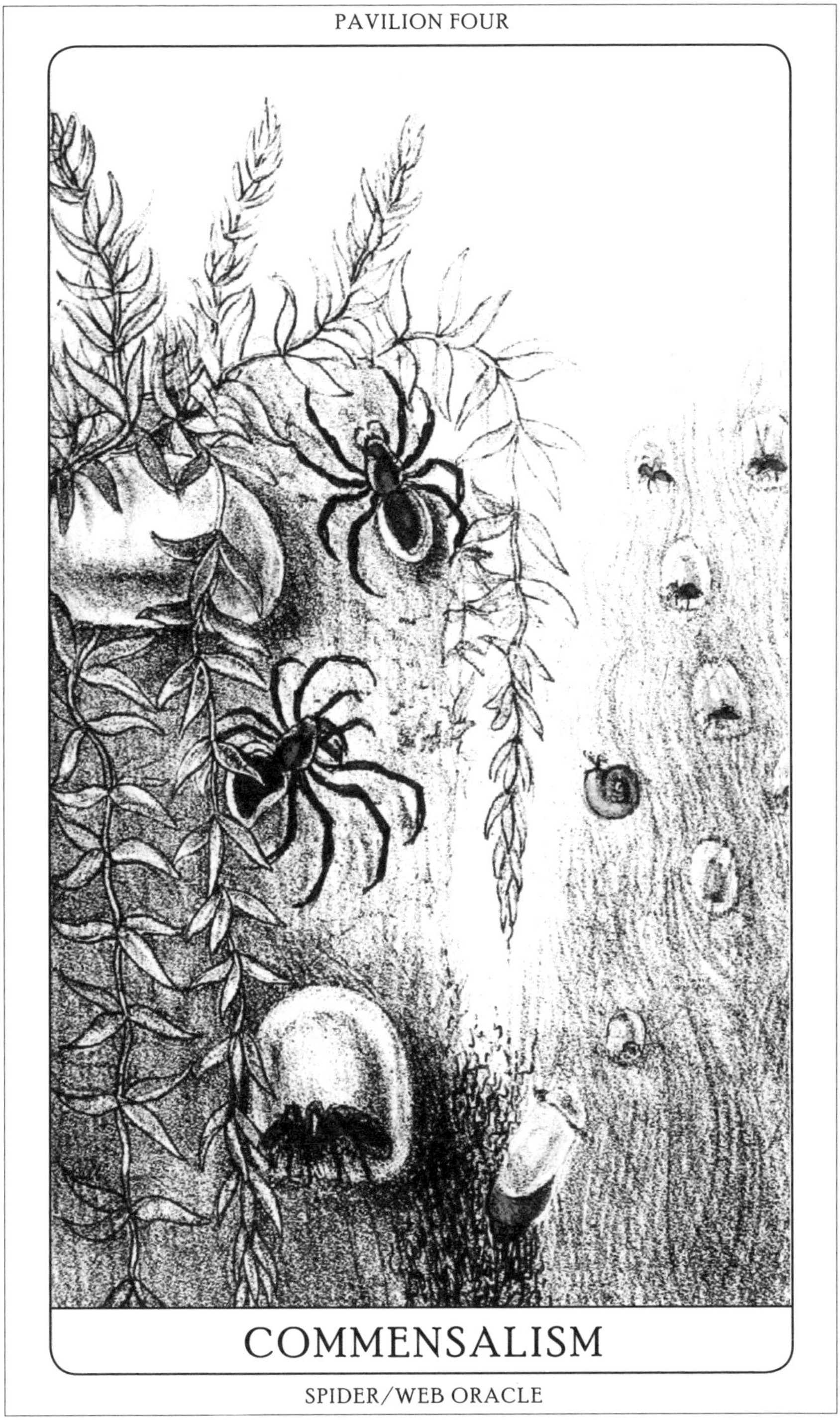

Tomás Saraceno
COMMENSALISM
Card 4 out of a deck of
33 Arachnomancy Cards,
2019–ongoing

In between the cypress branches or in the ceiling rafters. Worlds are folded into each other, a community that doesn't need to name itself. If the habitat creates the collective, it is time to interrogate the one you think you belong to.

Suit: Diving Bell Spider/Web
Species: Argyroneta aquatica
Notation: C ♭
Plant: Sphagnum fallax

Power

→ Agency | → Anthropocene | → Care | entanglements | foregrounding the material world | → Future | human and nonhuman agencies | → New Materialism | tipping points | → Violence

This much we know about the Anthropocene: the forces that have driven society to the brink of extinction are far more complex and entangled than anything we have seen before. Central to this development are technological developments, which have elevated human agency to the level of a 'geological force'. After all, this is why leading scientists propose to use the Greek word for human – *ánthrōpos* – as the name for our current condition. But it would be wrong to think that human agency has become the only game in town. As climate report after climate report reminds us, the amplification of human agency has prompted a similar (or even stronger) reaction amongst the many ecosystems that define life on the planet. The result is a steady movement towards several 'tipping points' that threaten to overrule or undo anything humans could ever dream of doing. Between microscopic organisms, ocean currents, atmospheric disturbances and technological innovations, power is now working in all kinds of ways, and at all scales.

Lars Tønder (born 1972, located in Copenhagen, DK) is a political theorist and Professor MSO in the Department of Political Science, University of Copenhagen. His research interests include democracy, power and the Anthropocene. His forthcoming book, published in Danish, is titled *Om Magt: En Introduktion til Magtbegrebet i den Antropocæne Tidsalder.* (On Power: An Introduction to the Concept of Power in the Age of the Anthropocene).

The difficulties that many decision-makers have in appreciating – not to mention counteracting – this new situation may come from a deep bias within the concept of power itself. Typically, power is associated with a series of intentions or interests that one human agent applies to another. As we learn from most textbooks written in the 20th century, *Power occurs when* A *makes* B *do something that B otherwise would not have done*. This way of formulating the issue eradicates nonhuman agency. Not only is the nonhuman imagined as radically different from the human, it is left without power and thus without any value of its own. A similar approach – what the American political theorist William E. Connolly calls 'sociocentrism' – is also present within more advanced conceptions of power where the focus on intentions and interests is replaced with a concern for discursive structures and symbolic practices. While such conceptual innovations provide a more nuanced picture of how human agency works, they do little to bring the nonhuman back into light. The result is a blind spot that continues to block a proper view of what society can and must do to counter the effects of climate change in the Anthropocene. Rather than acknowledging the many entanglements of human and nonhuman modes of life, we are stuck in a zero-sum game in which the winner takes it all. No wonder most decision-makers have such a hard time imagining what another world could look like!

The Anthropocene, then, is not just a challenge to politics as usual; it is a challenge to how we, as entangled and engaged beings, understand power – and, ultimately, how we envision the very constitution of society. How, you might ask, should we overcome this challenge? An important first step would be to recognize that the entanglements of human and nonhuman lives are so profound that it can be difficult, if not impossible, to see where one ends and the other begins. Strictly speaking, these entanglements should not surprise us, since both partake in the material world that empowers life in the first place. Moreover, as vitalist philosophers from Lucretius and Baruch Spinoza, via Henri Bergson and Georges Canguilhem, to Jane Bennett and Donna J. Haraway are fond of saying, the material world is an infinite series of potentialities that expand across every specific mode of being – be it human or nonhuman. The material world is in that sense the most powerful of all, which is precisely what needs foregrounding if we want to counteract the current climate crisis. A new definition of power for the Anthropocene might thus go something like this: *Power occurs when* A *and* B, *each embodying a discrete series of human and nonhuman entanglements, interact to make* C *possible*. In this definition, the emphasis is on the entangled interactions within the material world, and on how these interactions make new modes of life possible. Some of these new modes may well embody a forward thrust that makes them suitable for future life. Others will be more destructive, if not straight out deadly. Our challenge, you might say, is to appreciate which is what.

The ambiguity of this last statement is not coincidental: to engage power in the Anthropocene is an inherently uncertain endeavour filled with innumerous dilemmas and uncertain choices. The time has therefore finally come to forget the very ruse of power. As all the other entangled beings in this world, we 'humans' do not control the future. Yes, that is right. We 'humans' are no more self-legislating than the world around us, and the decisions we make are no less determined or externally caused than the decisions made by a honeybee or some other living species. In fact, if the last 20 years or so is any proof, we do more harm than good if we think that's the case. When it comes to power, we 'humans' are truly no more exceptional than anyone else (which is to say that we are not exceptional in any meaningful manner). While some observers may see this conclusion as a reason for apathy, if not outright resignation, it may very well be that such a sobering account of power in the Anthropocene is the best we can hope for. For starters, it may prompt us to tread more carefully and with greater concern for the environment on which we so very much depend. Moreover, it may prompt us to listen more attentively and take seriously when other entangled beings suffer from our exploitative endeavours, which for the past many hundred years have taken us to where we are today.

Production

→ Energy | minimize footprint | → Plastic | → Resources | sustainable solutions | → Waste | → Water

Please note that this text describes the production of the first edition of this book, not the present paperback edition.

The editorial team has examined this book's production process in depth with the aim of minimizing the publication's CO_2 footprint. By investigating every aspect of the production and presenting the details here, we wish to bring transparency to some processes that are normally difficult for the ordinary consumer to evaluate.

PAPER AND CARD

Sweden and Italy

The book is printed on Scandia Smooth Natural paper, which is produced, from sustainable forestry, at Lessebo Paper in Sweden and certified by the FSC, PEFC, ECF and Nordic Swan Ecolabel. The Materica card used for the cover comes from the Fedrigoni paper mill in Italy and is also FSC- and ECF-labelled, with 20% of the pulp coming from recycled materials. The paper mills are powered by renewable energy from hydroelectric plants.

FSC (Forest Stewardship Council)-labelled paper comes from forests where no more trees are felled than the forest is capable of reproducing. FSC also ensures that wildlife and plants are protected and that forest workers are properly trained and have adequate safety equipment and pay.

PEFC (Programme for the Endorsement of Forest Certification) is the world's biggest certification system for sustainable forestry. PECF-labelled wood is fully traceable from the forest to the consumer. PEFC aims to protect climate, animals and plants as well as forestry workers' rights, safety and health.

PRINTING AND BINDING

Denmark → Germany

The so-called lay-flat binding requires only one layer of card instead of two layers of paper around a sheet of cardboard, as with a conventional hardback. Pre-press and printing were handled by the Danish printer Narayana Press, which is 100% wind-powered. The inks and varnishes are vegetable-based. The printed sheets were transported to Germany for binding at Integralis Buchbinderei, which relies entirely on renewable energy sources (wind, sun and biomass). The finished book was wrapped in reusable plastic foil for protection.

ECF (Elemental Chlorine Free) means that wood pulp is bleached with chlorine dioxide instead of elemental chlorine, thus largely preventing the formation of the most environmentally harmful chloride compounds.

TRANSPORT

Sweden and Italy → Denmark → Germany → Italy

All components and the finished book were transported to and from the printer in Denmark and the bookbinder in Germany by the Danish freight company Freya, which holds the ISO 14001 environmental certificate.

ISO 14001 is an internationally approved standard for environmental management. ISO 14001 is used by organizations of all sizes and across all sectors as a management tool to deal with environmental impact, increase resource efficiency and enable managers to monitor their company's eco-performance.

The Nordic Swan Ecolabel looks at the full life cycle of the paper, including energy efficiency, chemicals, waste and production emissions into the air and water. It also requires that part of the wood pulp has to come from certified sustainable forestry.

Although we have carefully produced this book – based on information available from all participating companies – to reduce its impact on the climate, the process has clarified to what extent we are subject to structural, global conditions that are difficult to avoid and fully understand. If the most sustainable production facilities are located far from the most sustainable paper mill, is it then better to choose a less sustainable paper from a nearby manufacturer to reduce transport?

By exposing every step of this book's production, we wish to bring transparency to the often impenetrable conditions and processes that characterize today's society. Mapping is the first step on the journey to implementing new behaviours and habits.

Sidsel Kjærulff Rasmussen (born 1980, located in Copenhagen, DK) is Publishing Director at Strandberg Publishing. She holds an MA in Art History and Film and Media Studies and has edited books on Danish design, architecture and art since 2013, including *Danish Lights 1920–Now* (2019), *The Danish Chair* (2018) and *The Human Figure in Islamic Art* (2018).

Till Rickert (born 1976, located in Copenhagen, DK) is a graphic designer and occasional illustrator. Working at Rasmus Koch Studio in a wide range of design disciplines, his main focus since 2008 has been on designing books.

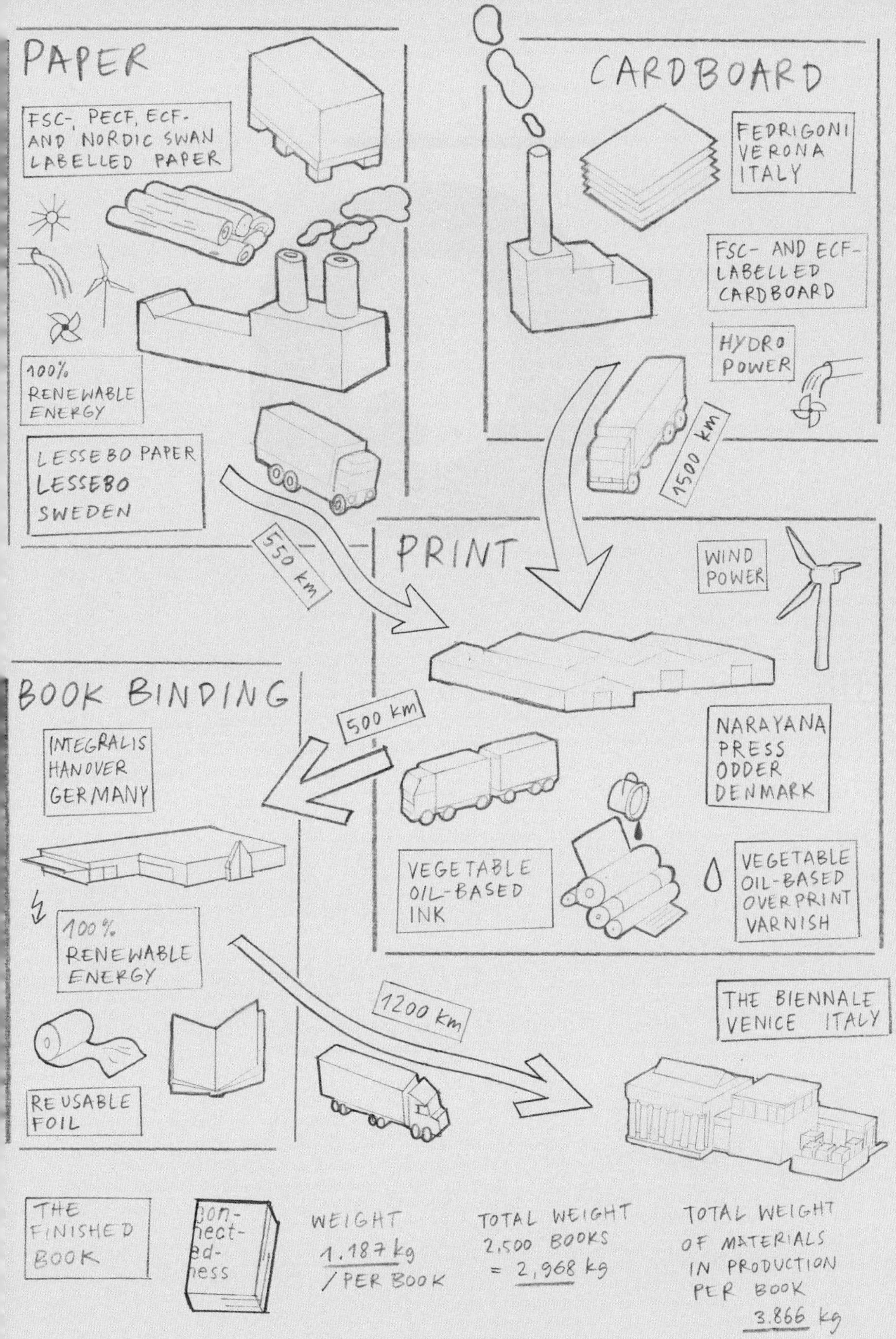

PAPER
FSC-, PECF, ECF- AND NORDIC SWAN LABELLED PAPER
100% RENEWABLE ENERGY
LESSEBO PAPER LESSEBO SWEDEN
550 km
CARDBOARD
FEDRIGONI VERONA ITALY
FSC- AND ECF-LABELLED CARDBOARD
HYDRO POWER
1500 km
PRINT
WIND POWER
NARAYANA PRESS ODDER DENMARK
VEGETABLE OIL-BASED INK
VEGETABLE OIL-BASED OVERPRINT VARNISH
500 km
BOOK BINDING
INTEGRALIS HANOVER GERMANY
100% RENEWABLE ENERGY
REUSABLE FOIL
1200 km
THE BIENNALE VENICE ITALY
THE FINISHED BOOK
con-nect-ed-ness
WEIGHT 1.187 kg / PER BOOK
TOTAL WEIGHT 2,500 BOOKS = 2,968 kg
TOTAL WEIGHT OF MATERIALS IN PRODUCTION PER BOOK 3.866 kg

Q

316

~~quasi-life~~ → Waste

Queer Antke Engel

~~queering cohabitation~~ → Queer

Queer

affirming connectedness under conditions of conflict | → Borders | → Care | caring for conflicts | → Coexistence | → Denial | human rights | intersectional justice | → Oxymorons | queering cohabitation | the other of the other | → Violence

Antke Engel (born 1965, located in Berlin, DE) is director of the Institute for Queer Theory in Berlin, a site where academic debate meets political and cultural activism. They obtained their PhD in Philosophy at Potsdam University and are currently working as an independent scholar and guest professor in the fields of queer_feminist and poststructuralist theory, political philosophy and visual cultural studies.

In a state of global denial, a denial that negates the suffering caused by living in a world defined by exploitation, new ways of living our connectedness to all other kinds of life will not develop without facing conflict. Cohabitation means that we are sharing the world with those we have not chosen and would never chose – be it microbes inhabiting bodies, family members, neighbours or warlords. If not killing is the answer, it is often mere coexistence. Both are far from a life-affirming sociality. The common modes of taming the discontent_hate that often goes along with cohabitation is drawing borders, installing security fences, creating Others and denigrating them, developing a strong Self and bloat it to grandiosity, or altruistically submitting to a compassion for all others except oneself. What would it mean to acknowledge cohabitation as being saturated by conflictual opinions, interests and values, by competition over power and resources, and an inevitable tension between self-assertion and bonding – without this creating antagonism, hierarchy and violence? My answer would be queering cohabitation – that is, taking pleasure in complexity, confusion and conflict, finding a potential in queerness as a politics of the sexual, rather than sexual politics, a politics of affirming connectedness under conditions of conflict.

QUEERRRRRing sexual politics

Queer has fulfilled its task as sexual politics. It is free to remember its adolescent wildness, when it noisily claimed to undermine all kinds of normalcy, rejecting identitarian closures, normative aims and fixed forms, when its focus was on queering rather than queerness. To start again with queering, as it is suggested here, pursues a mode of moving backwards that is not nostalgic but is collecting treasures of former critique which have not yet been incorporated – incorporated with pleasure and pain, into the practices of queering, including queering desire and queering cohabitation, or desires for queer cohabitation. Asking for incorporation denotes the sexual dimensions of queerness. When the sexual does not settle as sexuality, as sexual identity or sexual politics but remains becoming, it is opening to encounters that vibrantly or gently draw unexpected connections. This is where queering desire activates its potential of desiring queerness: departing from normalcy and instead embracing ek-static selves and inviting the Other of the other.

The dynamics of power and desire
This, however, would not happen without reimagining and rearranging the intertwinements of power and desire – processes which have been initiated by the queer, feminist, anti-racist, anti-capitalist, environmentalist and crip politics of the last decades. These are all hopeful movements, albeit ones stumbling again and again over narrow-minded single-issue politics, with their respective involvements in various modes and histories of violence, and stumbling over the conflicts resulting from privileges and discrimination, or from tensions between identification and belonging – in short, failing in solidarity with those who are in need of justice but lack similarity. Therefore, the critique that has pointed out the exclusions, normativities and normalizations of a homogenizing or universalizing queer movement seems indispensable – and wants to be incorporated. In order to open up futures that escape linear futurity, we will need to stop and rest at crossroads of conflict and violence supposedly long gone but in fact simply ignored and left behind with eyes, ears and nose closed and skins not touching. As a visceral_affective_mental dynamic of power and desire, however, incorporation points towards shared embodiments rather than individual bodies. Only then can we even ask how to denounce desire as an instrument of power, ask whether desire could be desire for justice, so that violence in all its psychic and physical, epistemic and structural dimensions would surrender to bodies licking, touching, tasting, swallowing, digesting and ruminating conflicts.

Queer has fulfilled its task as sexual politics
Why would I say that sticking to queer as sexual politics is no longer promising? Positively spoken, sexual and gender rights are high on the agenda and provide a publicly available discourse, even if they are also the target of resistance and repression in the form of hate speech, disenfranchisement and crime. Nonetheless, those claiming or advocating for self-determination have gained strong voices and lobbies. LGBTIAq* politics are highly differentiated and embrace a wide range of non-binary genders or non-normative desires, both in modes of self-understanding as well as academic, intellectual and mundane knowledge production. Queer politics no longer needs to fight against unintelligibility, the problem of having neither names, nor concepts, nor narratives for lives nonetheless lived – though lived by abject, ghost-liked figures. These were times when to be criminalized or pathologized was, cynically spoken, nothing less than a privilege in comparison to being a non-being – as was the case in modern Western societies for all those who did not fit into the binary, heteronormative sex_gender order. Though, maybe, it's wrong to pronounce here a linear progress, rather than a paradoxical simultaneity: killings of trans* persons or enforced medical treatments of inter* infants are still common practice. By now, however, those can be called murder and human rights violations. The voices of sexual and gender minorities can no longer be silenced; the UN has taken on their issues, and states are beginning to implement, if not yet ratify, the Yogyakarta Principles.

In times of neoliberal normalcy
The very same development which can be celebrated as success can also be critically demurred: politics of sexual and gender diversity, of recognition and self-determination have become part of the conservative liberal agenda. The individualized bearer of rights and owner of their own body fit neatly with the demands of capitalist freedom as a celebration of consumption and property. No reason why this neoliberal model should find limits in naturalized notions of cis-gender and reproductive heterosexuality. Accordingly, privileged versions of assimilated sexual and gender minorities have been integrated into the social and legal mainstream of

so-called pluralist societies and contribute to a deceitful progressiveness – phenomena which have been extensively criticized as homonormativity and homonationalism.

Thus, my argument is that we no longer need queer as sexual politics because hegemonic forces have taken on its agenda. This does not mean that there is no need to fight sexual and gender violence and its state-sponsored forms. This is, indeed, as vibrant as, or more than, ever, facing the current impact of authoritarian, autocratic and undemocratic forces which deploy gender and sexual politics as one of their favourite instruments of legitimizing their drastic and repressive measures proffered as a means of ensuring a return to normalcy. But my point is that we can fight this with the given means of human rights, anti-discrimination and criminal law. Fruitful discussions are going on as to whether this should be formulated and implemented as the protection of minorities or as universal rights and standards of non-violence. In any case, this does not need queer politics but rather spans the full range of intersectional justice.

The paradoxical desire of caring for conflicts

To resume: queer politics might now be open for new engagements, since a growing constituency of sexual and gender particularities is able to invent their own names and claim their rights, not necessarily against but even with the help of hegemonic forces. So, what are the alternatives that I am suggesting for queer politics? Why turning to practices of queering, or queering cohabitation? Or queering desire in order for queer cohabitation? I put an emphasis on desire as a decisive moment of queering because desire, a visceral as much as a relational and intellectual practice, permeates all kinds of normality. Its paradoxical power lies in its capacity to stabilize as well as to subvert given order. Desire is simultaneously a most conservative as well as revolutionary force. If one is longing for cohabitation as a mode of embracing heterogeneity, it needs to accommodate these contradictory moments of desire. This also means incorporating critique as a corporeal practice. Queering as a political task means caring for conflicts: being careful and attentive about them, handling them with care rather than resolving them prematurely. What are queer forms of dealing with conflict? How does queering make use of aesthetic_epistemic conflicts in ways that foster injustice?

Taking pleasure in complexity and confusion

From this point of view, queering is becoming something which takes pleasure in complexity and confusion. It may evolve from play, or from interspecies sympoiesis, or from animate and inanimate intra-action. It may also occur as an aesthetic_epistemic practice that works on the interplay of power, desire and truth. Each of these terms is fuelled by ambiguity: power as a mode of dominance and oppression as well as resistance and transformation; desire as drawing as well as breaking connections, herein respectively supporting or undermining powerful normalcies; truth as a claim of either singularity or universality, of absoluteness or socio-historical relativity. While queerness may indeed refuse to crystallize in any specific form, taking pleasure in equivocation is not an end in itself. It gains valence through creating dynamic constellations, shapes that are shifting, thanks to queering's potential of changing the interplay of power, desire and truth. With a little help from serendipity, unexpected figurations and constellations may occur. Queering as an aesthetic as well as an epistemic practice may foster more than just forms of cohabitation. Heterogeneity grows from transforming affect, desire and matter, sound, colour, movement, signs, numbers and relations (in short, data and energy) into new modes of connectedness to all other kinds of life. Caring for conflict levels injustice and violence inherent to norms, and forms, knowledge and morals, habits and affects. Exit roads open up, lines of flight, cutting through the Anthropocene.

This text takes inspiration from Sara Ahmed, Laylah Ali, Karen Barad, Jessica Benjamin, Lauren Berlant/Lee Edelman, Pauline Boudry/Renate Lorenz, Judith Butler, Mel Chen, Cathy Cohen, Gilles Deleuze/Félix Guattari, Ines Doujak, Lisa Duggan, J. K. Gibson-Graham, Kübra Gümüsay, Michel Foucault, Donna Haraway, Evangeline Heiliger, Annemarie Jagose, Ins A Kromminga, Teresa de Lauretis, Audre Lorde, Robert McRuer, Sushila Mesquita, Jose Muñoz, Yv Nay, Elspeth Probyn, Jasbir Puar, Eva von Redecker, Emilia Roig, Tejal Shah, Christina Sharpe, Maryam Sheikh, Gayatri Spivak and many more critters and creatures and the humus they build and inhabit.

R

~~radical interconnectedness~~ → Posthuman
~~real~~ → Water
~~receptiveness~~ → Tenderness
~~reconstructing climate variations~~ → Abrupt Climate Change
~~redescription of territory~~ → Moving Earths
~~re-engineering the system of production~~ → Moving Earths
~~reflexive position~~ → Agency
~~refugees~~ → Borders
~~regeneration~~ → Agriculture
~~regulation~~ → Resources
~~relationality~~ → Bacteria
~~relationship~~ → Environment
~~reliance~~ → Ecology
~~renewable energy~~ → Energy
~~reparative practice~~ → Attachment
~~reproduction~~ → Geo-Social Classes
~~reshaping the national from inside~~ → Global
Resilience **Aditya Bahadur**
Resources **Jaime Stapleton and Rikke Luther**
~~response-ability~~ → Agency → Attachment → Posthuman
~~responsibility~~ → Earth Ethics
~~restore dutiful democracy~~ → Declaration of Rebellion
~~rethink growth~~ → Sustainability
~~risk distribution~~ → Migration Flows
~~risks~~ → Pollution
~~ruling out full knowledge and control~~ → New Materialism

Resilience

→ Biodiversity | bridging | → Climate Risk Communities | diversity | → Ecology | → Environment | learning | manage connectivity | participation | polycentric governance systems | → Power | → Sustainability

Within the constellation of approaches that aim to help vulnerable communities in dealing with the impacts of climate change and disasters, 'resilience' is pre-eminent. This is evident from the fact that the use of the term 'resilience' in published books and articles increased twenty-five-fold between 1998 and 2018. The number of people googling the word 'resilience' more than doubled in one decade from 2004.[1]

Across Web of Science, a platform that aggregates outputs from 7,000+ academic research institutions.

The term originates in the Latin word *resilire*, which literally means 'to recoil or rebound'.[2] It now finds wide application across a number of disciplines. In the field of psychology, 'resilience is defined as the quality that prevents individuals who are at genetic risk for maladaptation and psychopathology from being affected by these problems'.[3] The field of structural and engineering science has also explored and employed resilience. For example, the concept of seismic resilience of buildings understands it to be the property of a system which has '1. Reduced failure probabilities, 2. Reduced consequences from failures, in terms of lives lost, damage, and negative economic and social consequences, 3. Reduced time to recovery'.[4] Economic theory has incorporated resilience thinking in terms of the internal motivation and stimulus of private or public policy that enables a system to recover from a severe shock.[5]

By far the discipline that has explored resilience most deeply is ecology, where resilience is defined as 'the amount of disturbance that an ecosystem could withstand without changing self-organized processes and structures (defined as alternative stable states)'.[6] Closely associated with the concept of resilience in ecosystems is the application of this term to understand 'socio-ecological systems' as linked systems of people and nature and that 'the delineation between social and ecological systems is artificial and arbitrary'.[7] Here resilience is understood as the ability 'to absorb or withstand perturbations and other stressors such that the system remains within the same regime, essentially maintaining its structure and functions'.[8]

Central to resilience thinking in socioecological systems is the concept of the 'adaptive cycle' that sees changes in all complex systems in essentially four phases.[9] This heuristic argues that all complex systems begin with a growth phase (where systems are established) and they then transition into a conservation phase (where systems function and flourish). Following this, systems then become entrenched, lose touch with changes occurring in the context/environment to collapse and finally enter a phase of renewal and reorganization. The key issue that resilience managers must understand here is that systems transition through these phases and ultimately self-organize through the interaction and feedback of different system components.[10] If the relationships between system subcomponents break down, then the system degrades and tips over into dysfunction.[11] Alternatively, external influences (e.g. pollutants) might initiate new, negative feedbacks that may have to be intercepted. Understanding these relationships is therefore key to those attempting to ensure that systems remain healthy and dynamic and transition from one phase to another. Closely associated with this is the notion of 'panarchy', which explains how these adaptive cycles are simultaneously taking place within system components at different scales.[12] This means that feedbacks

Dr **Aditya Bahadur** (born 1983, located in Delhi, IN) has 13 years' experience in research, evaluation and the practice of adaptation and resilience. He has held positions at Oxford Policy Management, the Overseas Development Institute, Hyderus and the International Federation of Red Cross and Red Crescent Societies. He completed his PhD at the Institute of Development Studies, UK, and is currently a postdoctoral research fellow at Columbia University, US.

can be taking place across scales, and these need to be understood to ensure the health and resilience of systems.

It is this understanding of resilience that has influenced policies and programmes to mitigate the risk of climate impacts and disasters where it is understood as the 'ability of a system and its component parts to anticipate, absorb, accommodate, or recover from the effects of a hazardous event in a timely and efficient manner, including through ensuring the preservation, restoration, or improvement of its essential basic structures and functions'.[13]

Resilience has received a lot of attention from individuals and organizations designing approaches for reducing risk from climate change and disasters. This has resulted in a proposal of different schemas, tenets and principles that attempt to translate this amorphous concept into an operational agenda. Salient among these are the seven principles of resilience proposed by the Stockholm Resilience Centre:[14]

— Maintain diversity and redundancy: A larger number of system components (species, knowledge systems, actors and cultural groups) leads to a greater degree of resilience. This is because one component may compensate for the loss of others.[15] This means that economies reliant on one dominant economic sector are less resilient than those that have multiple healthy sectors, and communities reliant on one source of livelihood are less resilient than those that rely on multiple livelihoods.[16] In practice this could be cultivated through building in a buffer capacity into systems, ensuring ecological diversity, not aiming for disparity, and response diversity instead of 'maximum efficiency'.[17]

— Manage connectivity: Connectivity can enhance the resilience of a system.[18] For instance, wildlife corridors that connect wildlife sanctuaries ensure the health of species by permitting migration from one area to another in case of shocks or environmental stresses. Connectivity can also reduce the resilience of a system. For instance, in densely connected human systems, crippling diseases can spread fast. Therefore key to enhancing the resilience of a system is to 'manage' and regulate this connectivity. In practice, connectivity can be managed by building in 'modularity' into systems where different parts of a system can be connected or disconnected as situations unfold.

— Manage slow variables and feedbacks: Understanding and managing the manner in which the different components of a system relate to each other is essential to ensuring resilience. Reinforcing feedback (e.g. between over-fishing and penalties for this) or dampening feedback (e.g. between pollution flows into lakes) is a key strategy for ensuring resilience. In practice this can be done through the establishment of governance mechanisms where individuals are charged with monitoring a number of pre-defined thresholds for different variables in a system. In the event of a breach, a management response should be triggered that results in the reinforcement or dampening of the feedback associated with that variable.

— Foster complex adaptive systems thinking: Even as resilience thinking emphasizes the management of connectivity and feedback between different system components, it is vital to acknowledge that 'social-ecological systems are based on a complex and sometimes unpredictable web of connections'.[19] Novelty, surprise, uncertainty and a degree of randomness are unavoidable features of systems, and resilience implies the capacity to cope with these.[20] In practice this can be done through the adoption of 'complex adaptive systems thinking' and 'adaptive management'. This is a management approach that considers a range of plausible hypotheses about future changes in the system, weighs a range of possible strategies against this wide set of potential futures and then favours actions that are robust in the face of uncertainties.[21]

— Encourage learning: Learning and experimentation are essential to building resilience as this ensures that different types and sources of knowledge are considered when developing solutions. Undertaking adaptive management to deal with complexity and uncertainty inherent in socioecological systems is dependent on learning.[22] Without learning, it would be impossible to determine relationships between system components, to understand thresholds beyond which these feedbacks need to be suppressed or reinforced and to unearth the process of doing this. Crucially, learning from disturbance is essential so as to not return to the pre-existing level of vulnerability, to the same kind of shock or stress, and to 'bounce back better'.[23]

— Broaden participation: Community engagement, ownership, participation and indigenous/local knowledge are frequently stressed in the reviewed literature to be essential to resilience.[24] This is fundamentally because the participation of a diversity of voices that are representative of those that are part of particular socioecological systems and have a stake in their management is essential to detecting perturbations, understanding the interconnections between system elements and determining feedbacks essential to system resilience.[25]

— Promote polycentric governance systems: Closely linked to the preceding point is one that emphasizes the importance of polycentric governance mechanisms where power is decentralized and diverse perspectives are considered in decision-making processes.[26] This is for a number of reasons that include the fact that dispersed decision-making allows the system to react as problems emerge, that decision-making power is distributed so that decisions can still be made if some parts of a governance system are overwhelmed or incapacitated and that a multiplicity of voices are considered in decision-making processes.[27]

Resilience offers a number of unique tools to support socioecological systems to deal with a variety of shocks and stresses in the Anthropocene. The emphasis on connectivity, complex adaptive systems thinking and acknowledging feedbacks between different system components urges policymakers and programme managers to break out of traditional sectoral silos and consider the 'system' as a whole. This is why resilience has also been called a 'bridging concept' that facilitates the convergence between diverse disciplines to find solutions to common problems. Also, unlike other paradigms of risk management that aim to map and determine expected risks to then establish responses, resilience is predicated on the idea of ensuring that systems are flexible and able to respond to unexpected shocks and stresses.

These are the reasons why governments, international organizations and local actors are all designing and delivering initiatives that aim to operationalize this concept in order to combat the exigencies of disasters and climate change in some of the world's most vulnerable contexts.

Works cited:

Adger, W. Neil. 2000. 'Social and Ecological Resilience: Are They Related?' *Progress in Human Geography*, 24 (3), pp. 347–364.

Alesso-Bendisch, Franziska. 2019. *Community Nutrition Resilience in Greater Miami: Feeding Communities in the Face of Climate Change*. Cham: Springer Nature.

Bruneau, Michel, and Andrei Reinhorn. 2006. 'Overview of the Resilience Concept'. *Proceedings of the 8th US National Conference on Earthquake Engineering*, Paper No. 2040 (18–22 April), pp. 18–22.

Cicchetti, Dante, and Jennifer A. Blender. 2004. 'A Multiple-Levels-of-Analysis Approach to the Study of Developmental Processes in Maltreated Children'. *Proceedings of the National Academy of Sciences*, 101 (50), pp. 17325–17326.

Cutter, Susan L., Christopher G. Burton and Christopher T. Emrich. 2010. 'Disaster Resilience Indicators for Benchmarking Baseline Conditions'. *Journal of Homeland Security and Emergency Management*, 7 (1).

Folke, Carl. 2006. 'Resilience: The Emergence of a Perspective for Social–Ecological Systems Analyses'. *Global Environmental Change*, 16 (3), pp. 253–267.

Gunderson, Lance H., and C. S. Holling. 2001. *Panarchy: Understanding Transformations in Human and Natural Systems*. Washington, DC: Island Press.

IPCC. 2012. 'Glossary of Terms'. In: Field, C.B., V. Barros, T. F. Stocker, D. Qin, D. J. Dokken, K. L. Ebi, M. D. Mastrandrea, K. J. Mach, G.-K. Plattner, S. K. Allen, M. Tignor and P. M. Midgley, eds. *Managing the Risks of Extreme Events and Disasters to Advance Climate Change Adaptation: A Special Report of Working Groups I and II of the Intergovernmental Panel on Climate Change (IPCC)*. Cambridge, UK/New York: Cambridge University Press, pp. 555–564.

Lovell, Emma, Aditya Bahadur, Thomas Tanner and Hani Morsi. 2016. *Resilience: The Big Picture*. London: Overseas Development Institute.

Moser, Susanna C. 2008. *Resilience in the Face of Global Environmental Change: CARRI Research Report 2*. Oak Ridge, TN: Community and Regional Resilience Initiative.

Norris, Fran H., Susan P. Stevens, Betty Pfefferbaum, Karen F. Wyche and Rose L. Pfefferbaum. 2008. 'Community Resilience as a Metaphor, Theory, Set of Capacities, and Strategy for Disaster Readiness'. *American Journal of Community Psychology*, 41 (1–2), pp. 127–150.

Osbahr, Henry. 2007. *Building Resilience: Adaptation Mechanisms and Mainstreaming for the Poor.* Human Development Report Office Occasional Paper No. 10. New York: United Nations Development Programme.

Ostrom, Elinor. 2009. 'A General Framework for Analyzing Sustainability of Social-Ecological Systems'. *Science*, 325 (5939), pp. 419–422.

Resilience Alliance. 2018. 'Resilience'. https://www.resalliance.org/resilience. Accessed 7 November 2019.

Rose, Adam. 2004. 'Defining and Measuring Economic Resilience to Disasters'. *Disaster Prevention and Management: An International Journal*, 13 (4), pp. 307–314.

Ruth, Matthias, and Dana Coelho. 2007. Understanding and Managing the Complexity of Urban Systems under Climate Change. *Climate Policy*, 7 (4), pp. 317–336.

Simonsen, Sturle Hauge. 2007. 'Resilience Dictionary'. http://www.stockholmresilience.org/research/whatisresilience/resiliencedictionary.4.aeea46911a3127427980004355.html. Accessed 8 November 2019.

Simonsen, Sturle Hauge. 2015. *Applying Resilience Thinking: Seven Principles for Building Resilience in Social-Ecological Systems*. Stockholm: Stockholm Resilience Centre.

Walker, Brian, and David Salt. 2012. *Resilience Thinking: Sustaining Ecosystems and People in a Changing World.* Washington, DC: Island Press.

Wilby, Robert, and Suraje Dessai. 2010. 'Robust Adaptation to Climate Change'. *Weather*, 65 (7), pp. 180–185.

Resources

→ Air | → Capitalocene | → Development | eco-war | → Environment | → Geo-Social Classes | global commons | global heating | → Pollution | post-democratic era | regulation | UN

Jaime Stapleton (born 1964, located in Copenhagen, DK) has worked as an academic and in public policy in the UK, and internationally for the World Intellectual Property Organization. He has advised a number of artists on cross-disciplinary issues in economics and law, and between 2008 and 2015 he wrote academic and fictional pieces for the artist group Learning Site. He hasn't quite given up hope in rational argument – yet.

Rikke Luther (born 1970, located in Copenhagen, DK) explores in her work the interrelations created by the environmental crisis as they relate to the changing landscape, language, politics, financialization, law, biology and economy, expressed in drawn images, photography, film and pedagogical strategies. In 2016, Luther created the work *Overspill: Universal Map* for the 32nd Bienal de São Paulo.

Problems

Beyond the borders of the state, out there in seemingly limitless Global Commons, a war on the planetary resources is being conducted. To understand this 'eco-war', we need to understand that today's interlocking political and ecological crises are facets of human industrial organization.

The 20th century was characterized by a war between 'carbon communism' and 'carbon capitalism'. Both industrialisms rested on resource depletion and ecological destruction. Invoking those old ideological binaries in the face of mass *extinctions*, the Great *Heating*, soil *degradation* and interweaving *pollutions* merely radicalizes their progress. The multiple crises are simply 'spill-over effects' of attempts to comprehend the entire planet, and its subset economies, in terms of human industry.

Twenty years ago, at the dawning of the new digital era, academic Lawrence Lessig famously proclaimed 'code is law'. All those Anthropocene-era theories of economics, politics and digital culture have blinded us to a simple empirical fact: *the ecosystem is the law.*

The Global Commons

The UN Global Commons (UNGC) is distinct from many other conceptions of a 'commons', such as English 'common land', 'Common Law' jurisdictions, the 'commonplaces' of rhetoric and logic, the 'digital commons', 'common-pool resource theory'. There is no 'common denominator' or unified principle that ties such disparate, context-sensitive conceptions of a commons together. Even the economist Friedrich von Hayek, were he alive, would claim the price mechanism operating in a 'perfect market' is essentially 'a commons', since each actor brings and takes from a total marketplace what they desire according to their individual capacities.

The UNGC grew from a system of ocean management first proposed in the late 1960s. That resulted in the United Nations Convention of the Law of the Seas (1970). The treaty declared the seabed to be the 'common heritage of mankind' to be 'exploited for the benefits of mankind as a whole'. Over the following decades, that general principle was developed with other legal instruments which currently comprise what the UN refers to as 'The Global Commons'.

The Global Climate Emergency has given this concept a new, and radical, role. The foundation of the UN in 1945 demonstrated the 'positive' legal and territorial limits to the nation state. By contrast, the UNGC comprises 'negative' spaces that have been criss-crossed with international treaties. Though nations contest each other's power, these aspects of the planetary ecosystem are beyond the direct control of any nation. They are defined as the High Seas – the oceans beyond territorial waters of nation states. The Atmosphere that surrounds us – the air we breathe. Outer Space, comprising the airless near space between the Earth and the Moon, and all that lies beyond our solar system out into the wilderness of deep space. The fact that the UNGC is a political construct is demonstrated by the fourth commons, the continent of Antarctica. When the UNGC came into being in the late 20th century, the southern-most continent was simply beyond the territorial claim of any one nation.

From 'knowledge' to 'extraction'

Until the 21st century, resource extraction in the UNGC was mainly an issue of fisheries. However, new sources of demand, new technologies and vast reserves of investment capital are changing that. As the Danish artist Rikke Luther has pointed out, the sand resources used in concrete are increasingly scarce on land, and the industry is looking towards the littoral and beneath coastal waters. As those companies look to off-shore dredging, more adventurous speculators look to the UNGC, with plans afoot to dredge the deep seabed for new sources of the rare minerals used in the tech industry. Further out still, in the UNGC, the communications satellite industry is extending its reach, and a new generation of corporate prospectuses promise future mineral extractions on the Moon and passing asteroids.

That expansive process has vastly increased in the digital era, and not simply because our seemingly 'in-corporeal', 'disaggregated', existence online sits on top of a corporeal, material and highly centralized system of carbon-fibre cables that are visible in Luther's drawing of the High Seas. Our ostensibly incorporeal networked existence

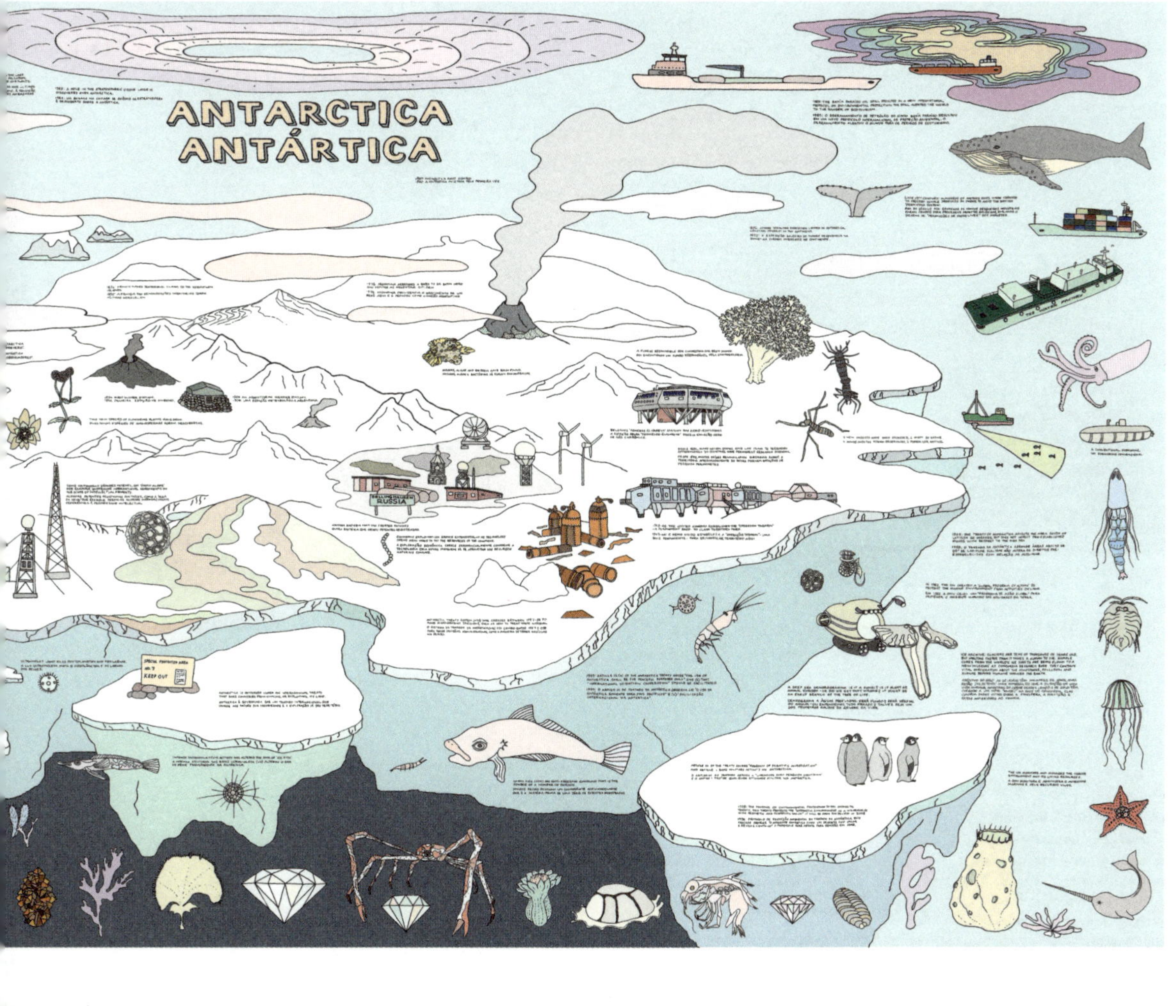

Rikke Luther
Antartica from the work
Overspill – Universial Map
Commissioned for the 32nd
São Paulo Bienal, Brazil, 2016
Original printed on tiles,
recreated on textile in 2018
2.25 × 4 m

Rikke Luther
Atmosphere from the work
Overspill – Universial Map
Commissioned for the 32nd
São Paulo Bienal, Brazil, 2016
Original printed on tiles,
recreated on textile in 2018
2.25 × 4 m

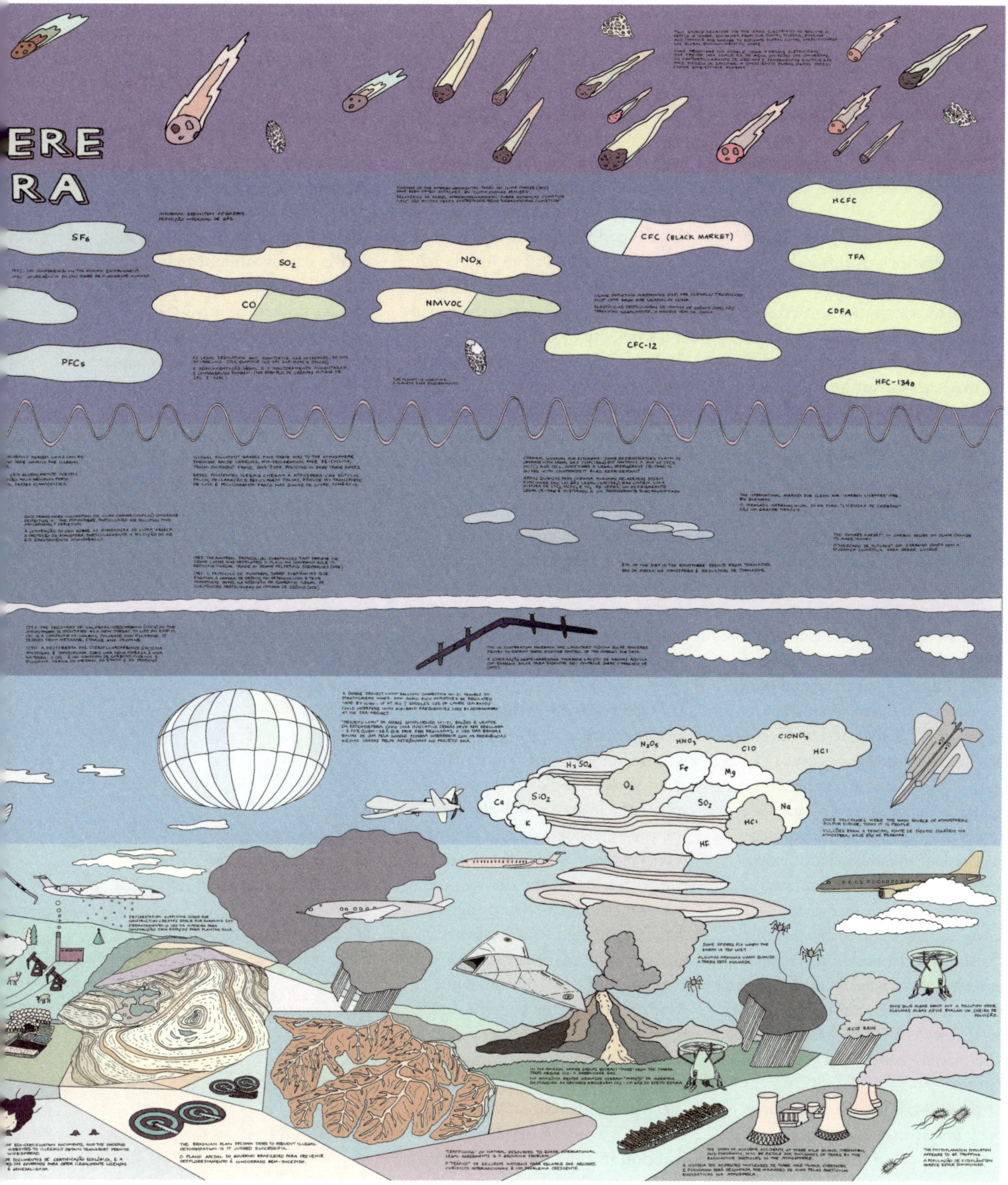

ERE
RA
SF6
SO2
NOx
CFC (BLACK MARKET)
HCFC
TFA
CO
NMVOC
CDFA
CFC-12
PFCs
HFC-134a
N2O5
HNO3
ClONO2
ClO
HCl
H2SO4
Fe
Mg
O2
SiO2
Ca
SO2
Na
K
HCl
HF
ONCE VOLCANOES WERE THE MAIN SOURCE OF ATMOSPHERIC SULFUR DIOXIDE, TODAY IT IS PEOPLE
VULCÕES ERAM A PRINCIPAL FONTE DE DIÓXIDO SULFÚRIO NA ATMOSFERA; HOJE SÃO AS PESSOAS
SOME SPIDERS FLY WHEN THE EARTH IS TOO WET
ALGUMAS ARANHAS VOAM QUANDO A TERRA ESTÁ MOLHADA
SOME BLUE ALGAE SEND OUT A POLLUTION ODOR.
ALGUMAS ALGAS AZUIS EXALAM UM CHEIRO DE POLUIÇÃO.
ACID RAIN

draws directly on finite corporeal resources of the Earth beneath our feet. Simply, our expanding digital life rests on extracting material resources from which its supporting tech is built. However, capital investment patterns suggest a far more complex process.

Expectations of profit are based on expectations of future human behaviour. The financial crisis of 2008 had two important effects. First, taxpayer bailouts to banks left institutions with decisions to be made about future markets. Second, much of the political hope invested in the 'Knowledge Economy' proved to be hot air. That specific version of the role of knowledge in economic theory drew on the work of American economist Paul Romer and was popular with policymakers between operating after the collapse of communism in 1989 and before the financial crisis of 2008. Future growth would come from innovation protected by intellectual property (IP) law. But after the 'Great Crash', global investors ran for cover. Significantly, the growth of the Internet was also making investing in copyright-related innovation ever more risky. When considering where to invest the 'fresh capital' handed to them by governments, lenders and investors preferred to take up 'opportunities' in the *material* world rather than the *incorporeal*, digital world.

If the digital question was once, why invest in risky innovation/IP when you could invest in digital platforms?, the question after 2008 was, why invest in digital platforms when you could invest in material resources on which the digital intermediation of human existence now rests? More pointedly still, why invest in material extraction on land, within nation states where legal regulations are likely to be enforced, when you could invest in places where regulations are thinner and often unenforceable, such as the UNGC?

The intensification of digital intermediation has created a strangulating cord of silicon and electricity around the ecosystem. The myth of 'limitless opportunity' feeds the myth of a 'limitless digital world' with 'limitless freedom of expression' and 'limitless free knowledge' and, thus, 'limitless opportunity'. As this Silicon Leviathan widens and deepens its penetration into every aspect of human life, that digital cord tightens, increasing the speed and intensity of natural resource depletion. Any loosening would be both 'state-imposed tyranny' and an admission of the material limits to digital growth. This 'common sense' of digital intermediation culture means there can be no proper limits on the extraction of natural resources. Every free post, every free search, every share and each mediated conversation is paid for by *depleting* natural resources, and each act of digitally enabled thinking and communication *heats*.

That ever-warming digital intermediation is also pushing the world ever faster into what the English sociologist and political scientist Colin Crouch dubbed the post-democratic era. That is terrifying on its own terms, but the withering of the democratic era reduces the internationalist capacity needed to solve every global problem. There is not even enough internationalist sentiment to agree to talks on a new international trade round, let alone the will to summon up multilateral legal solutions to meet these profound threats to life on Earth. Instead, humanity's first reaction to the Global Climate Emergency is to seek refuge in the 'comfort zones' of 20th-century political economy. In the face of all the heating and melting, the species extinctions, the soil infertility, the pollution and those still-expanding CO_2 emissions, outmoded political faces are pulled – nationalism colonialism and post-colonialism, communism, capitalism and fascism. The facts are met with threats – dictatorship, post-democracy, free market supremacy – or with trippy dreams of colonies on the fourth moon of Saturn, where markets will be freed of the environmental holocaust on Earth.

Solutions

Bullshit is the necessary baby of digital intermediation. It antagonizes, splits, separates and finally parses audiences to create the variegated soils in which the rotting flowers of advertising and state surveillance grow. Yet remarkable things can still happen, even in this death-sodden age.

There is no reason why life on Earth should be confined by a digital panoptican, or democracy should fade, or governance and oversight of the UNGC become outdated. The solutions are simple. Regulation, Regulation, Regulation. If digital communication systems are drowning

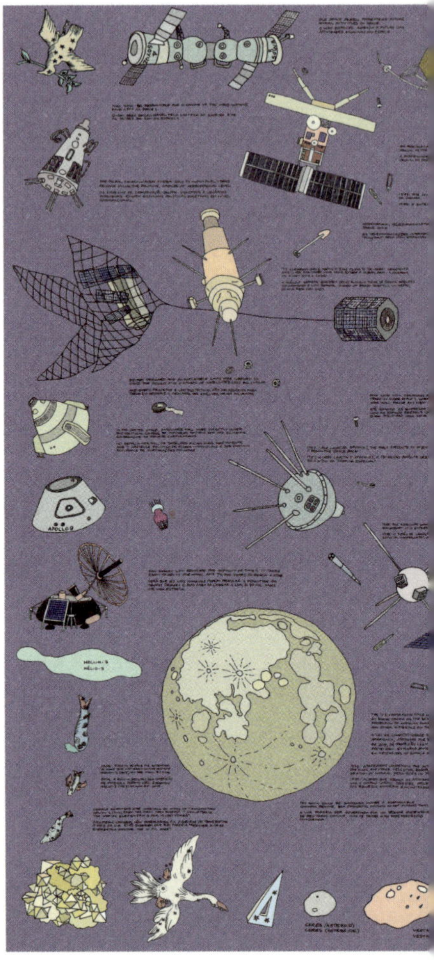

humanity in its own witlessness, if digital mediation helps turn the seas into an ever-warming kettle, the answer is *governance*.

This year economist Joseph Stiglitz and academic Shoshana Zuboff have made the same point in different ways: Global Heating is the 'Third World War' and we need *regulation*; tech needs guidance and we need *regulation*. And, of course, Green activists and their few political representatives have demanded the same for decades!

Regulation, however, requires a will that currently appears in short supply. Digital intermediation and Global Heating are materially linked crises whose regulatory solutions are, presumptively, international. The world might need an international treaty to halt Silicon Valley's dismantling of representative democracy, the world might need an international treaty to radically cut the insane levels of resource depletion, but how politically *likely* is recourse to 20th-century-style legal internationalism?

For sure, a Thunberg-shaped sanity is growing, but since the millennium the list of collapsing democracies around the world has grown ever longer. For every worried, fearful democrat in Europe deleting their Facebook account, there are ten new recruits across the world who are unconcerned about the loss of a democracy they have never known. For every million households trying desperately to cut their carbon emissions, there is one anti-planetary investor in Bitcoin – a Blockchain Ponzy scheme that last year sucked up the same distributed electricity load as the whole of Belgium. Some, in our desperation, resort to demonstrating … marching with our feet connected to the Earth … watching others checking their phones … posting … mediating experience … heating.

Rikke Luther
Outer Space from the work
Overspill – Universial Map
Commissioned for the 32nd São Paulo Bienal, Brazil, 2016
Original printed on tiles, recreated on textile in 2018
2.25 × 4 m

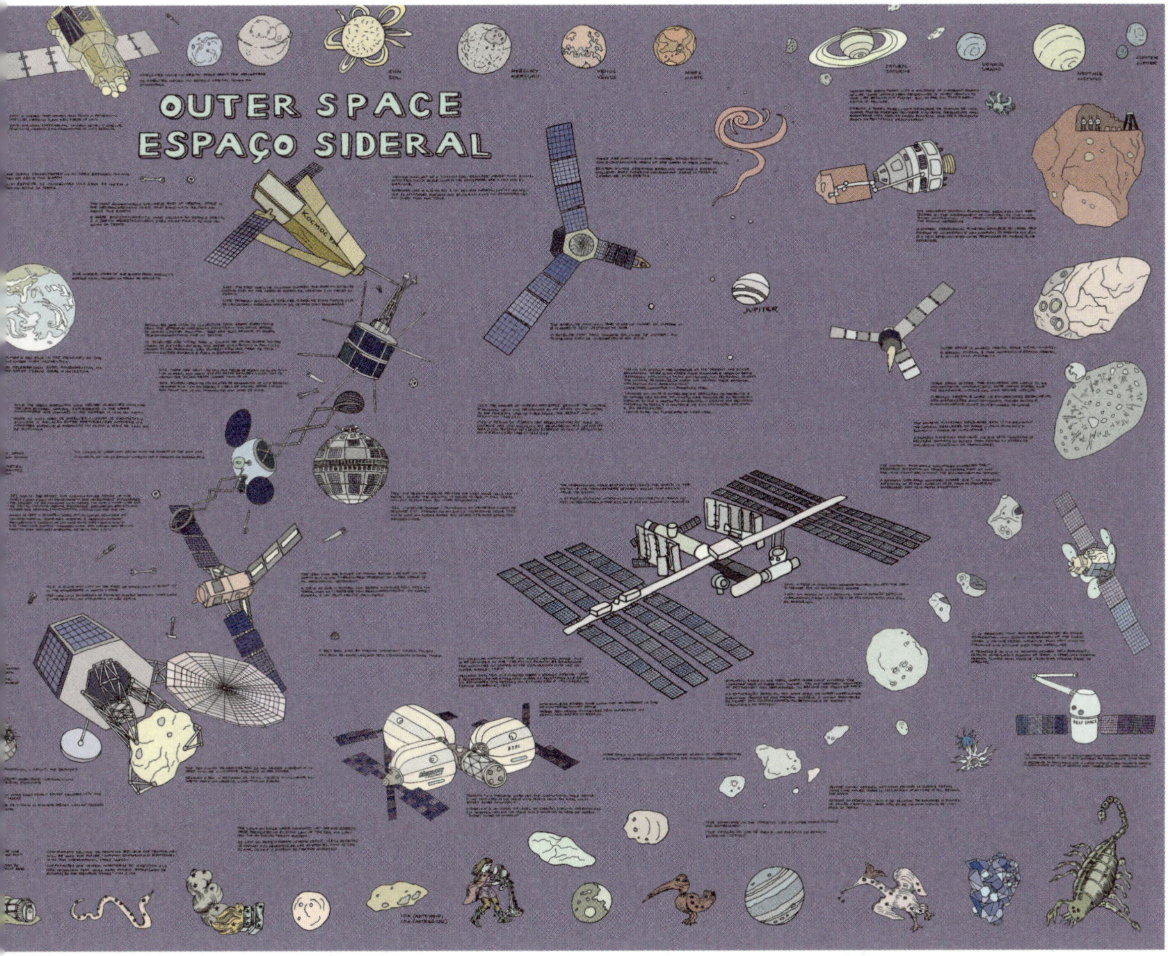

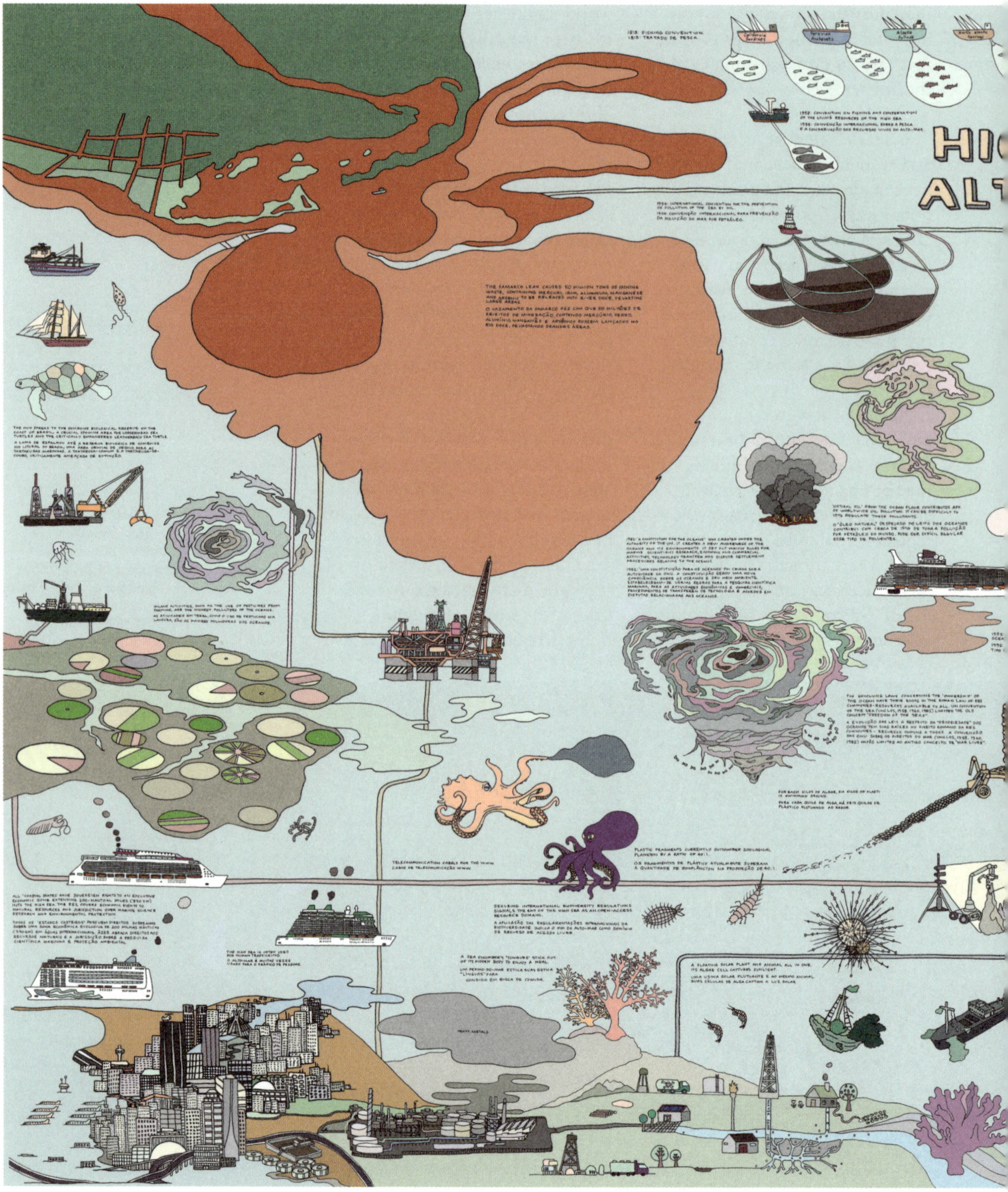

Rikke Luther
High Sea from the work
Overspill – Universial Map
Commissioned for the 32nd
São Paulo Bienal, Brazil, 2016
Original printed on tiles,
recreated on textile in 2018
2.25 × 4 m

EA
AR
SATELLITE MAPPING TO MONITOR CHANGES
THERE ARE MORE ACCURATE MAPS OF MARS THAN OF THE OCEAN FLOOR.
EXISTEM MAPAS MAIS DETALHADOS DE MARTE DO QUE DO LEITO OCEÂNICO.
AN ESTIMATED 18% TOTAL FISHING IS DEEMED ILLEGAL UNDER INTERNATIONAL AGREEMENTS
ESTIMA-SE QUE 18% DO TOTAL DA PESCA É CONSIDERADO ILEGAL SEGUNDO ACORDOS INTERNACIONAIS
SMALL ISLAND NATIONS THAT DON'T HAVE MOUNTAINS OFTEN DISAGREE WITH LARGER NATIONS THAT DO HAVE MOUNTAINS.
PEQUENOS PAÍSES INSULARES SEM MONTANHAS MUITAS VEZES DISCORDAM DE PAÍSES MAIORES COM MONTANHAS.
OFFSHORE WINDMILLS ARE A GROWING INDUSTRY
TURBINAS EÓLICAS DE ALTO-MAR SÃO UMA INDÚSTRIA EM CRESCIMENTO
THE TOTAL AREA OF THE NORTH PACIFIC GYRE IS TWICE THE SIZE OF THE STATE OF TEXAS, AND CONSISTS OF APPROXIMATELY 3.5 MILLION TONS OF HUMAN WASTE.
A ÁREA TOTAL DO GIRO DO PACÍFICO NORTE É DUAS VEZES O TAMANHO DO TEXAS, E CONSISTE EM APROXIMADAMENTE 3,5 MILHÕES DE TONELADAS DE LIXO HUMANO.
SINCE THE DISASTER IN 2011, FUKUSHIMA NUCLEAR POWER PLANT HAS LEAKED RADIOACTIVE MATERIAL INTO THE ENVIRONMENT, AS WELL AS CAUSING MUTATIONS IN LOCAL TREES AND BUTTERFLIES, AND DAMAGE TO DNA OF LOCAL WORMS. ISOTOPES OF CELICIUM HAVE BEEN FOUND AS FAR AS CALIFORNIA.
DESDE O DESASTRE DE 2011, A USINA NUCLEAR DE FUKUSHIMA VAZOU MATERIAIS RADIOATIVOS NO MEIO AMBIENTE. ALÉM DE CAUSAR MUTAÇÕES EM ÁRVORES E BORBOLETAS DA REGIÃO, E PREJUDICAR O DNA DAS MINHOCAS LOCAIS, FORAM ENCONTRADOS ISÓTOPOS DE CÉSIO ATÉ NA CALIFÓRNIA.
THE SEA IS CRITICAL IN MAINTAINING THE WEATHER AND THE QUALITY OF THE ATMOSPHERE
O MAR É UM FATOR CRÍTICO NA MANUTENÇÃO DO CLIMA E NA QUALIDADE DA ATMOSFERA
IT IS ARGUED THAT UP TO 750.000 TONS OF RADIOACTIVE STORAGE WATER CAN 'SAFELY' BE LEAKED INTO THE OCEAN.
HÁ QUEM DIGA QUE ATÉ 750 MIL TONELADAS DE ÁGUA RADIOATIVA ARMAZENDA PODEM VAZAR NO MAR "COM SEGURANÇA".
AROUND THE WORLD THOUSANDS OF BOATS SUCK SAND FROM THE OCEAN FLOOR LIKE VACUM CLEANERS.
POR TODO O MUNDO, MILHARES DE NAVIOS SUGAM AREIA DO LEITO OCEÂNICO COMO ASPIRADORES DE PÓ.
WASTE WATER & FACTORY
A AREIA É O SEGUNDO MATERIAL MAIS USADO NO MUNDO, DEPOIS DA ÁGUA. OS LEITOS DOS RIOS E AS PRAIAS ESTÃO DRAGADOS, E AGORA A INDÚSTRIA ESTÁ MIGRANDO PARA O LEITO OCEÂNICO.
1972: CONVENTION ON THE PREVENTION OF MARINE POLLUTION BY DUMPING WASTE FROM SHIPS AND AIRCRAFTS.
1972: CONVENÇÃO SOBRE PREVENÇÃO DE POLUIÇÃO MARINHA POR ALIJAMENTO DE RESÍDUOS E OUTRAS MATÉRIAS.
5 HUGE GYRES, SPINNING WHIRL POOLS OF PLASTICS, HAVE FORMED IN HIGH SEA.
5 IMENSOS VÓRTICES GIRATÓRIOS DE PLÁSTICO SE FORMARAM NO ALTO-MAR.
ORGANOCHLORINE
PETROLEUM
L17
DEEP SEABED MINERALS: PROPERTY OF THE GLOBAL HUMAN POPULATION (1967)
'DEEP SEABED MINERALS' WERE DECLARED THE PROPERTY OF THE GLOBAL HUMAN POPULATION IN 1967.
OS 'RECURSOS MINERAIS DO FUNDO DO MAR' FORAM DECLARADOS COMUM DE TODA A POPULAÇÃO HUMANA EM 1967.
NO INDIVIDUAL OR NATION STATE CAN LEGALLY APPROPRIATE A PROPERTY RIGHT TO THE COMMON RESOURCES.
NENHUM INDIVÍDUO OU PAÍS PODE LEGALMENTE REIVINDICAR UM DIREITO DE PROPRIEDADE SOBRE RECURSOS COMUNS.
1994: THE "COMMON HERITAGE OF MANKIND" WAS TRANSLATED INTO FREE MARKET TRADITION OF DEREGULATION AND DECENTRALISATION.
1994: "PATRIMÔNIO COMUM DA HUMANIDADE" FOI TRADUZIDO PARA O LIVRE MERCADO COMO DESREGULAMENTAÇÃO E DESCENTRALIZAÇÃO.
INTERNATIONAL LAW DIFFERENTIATES 'SEDENTARY SPECIES' DWELLING IN THE OCEANS, SUCH AS CLAMS, FROM 'FREE-SWIMMING SPECIES'.
O DIREITO INTERNACIONAL DIFERENCIA "ESPÉCIE SEDENTÁRIA" QUE VIVE NOS OCEANOS, COMO OS MARISCOS, DE "ESPÉCIE QUE NADA LIVREMENTE".
WE ARE RUNNING OUT OF LAND. OFFSHORE MARINE CULTURE IS GROWING FAST. IN ASIA, IT ACCOUNTS FOR 54% OF THE TOTAL FISH CONSUMPTION.
ESTAMOS FICANDO SEM TERRA. O SECTOR DA PESCA EM ALTO-MAR VEM CRESCENDO DEPRESSA NA ÁSIA, REPRESENTA 54% DO CONSUMO TOTAL DE PEIXES.
FISH
OFFSHORE
OFF SHORE
ON SHORE

BATATA, COMPOSTOS DE ATÉ DEZ ESSETE MINERAIS
O MANGANÊS, O FERRO, O COBRE E O COBALTO ERAM
COMERCIALIZÁVEIS.
THOSE USING THE LIVING RE
ANTI-POLLUTION MEASURES
ARE NOT AS KEEN. SEA CU
PRICE OF METALS GOES UP
AQUELES QUE USAM OS RE
APÓIAM MEDIDAS ANTIPOLU
DO LEITO OCEÂNICO NÃO
FICA ESTRESSADO COM
THE REALITY OF EXPLOITATION GROWS DAY BY DAY AS
TECHNOLOGY OPENS NEW WAYS TO TAP COMMON RESOURCES
A REALIDADE DA EXPLORAÇÃO CRESCE DIARIAMENTE CONFORME
A TECNOLOGIA GERA NOVAS MANEIRAS DE SE APROVEITAR
DOS RECURSOS COMUNS.
TELECOMMUNICATION CABELS FOR THE WWW.
CABOS DE TELECOMUNICAÇÃO WWW.
MERCURY
CESNIUM 137
FOR MILLIONS OF YEARS, THE OCEAN HAS
BEEN DUMP FOR HUMAN WASTE
POR MILHÕES DE ANOS, O OCEANO FOI
UM DEPÓSITO DE LIXO HUMANO
INTERNATIONAL LAW DIFFERENTIATES 'SED
SPECIES' DWELLING IN THE OCEANS, SUCH A
FROM 'FREE-SWIMMING SPECIES".
O DIREITO INTERNACIONAL DIFERENCIA "ESP
SEDENTÁRIA" QUE VIVE NOS OCEANOS, COMO
MARISCOS, DE "ESPÉCIE QUE NADA LIVREM

DEEP SEABED MINERALS: PROPERTY OF THE GLOBAL HUMAN POPULATION (1967)
HE OCEANS SUPPORT
INING COMPANIES
T STRESSED WHEN
OS DOS OCEANOS
PRESAS MINERADORAS
SIM. O PEPINO-DO-MAR
METAIS NA BOLSA.
'DEEP SEABED MINERALS' WERE DECLARED THE PROPERTY OF THE GLOBAL HUMAN POPULATION IN 1967.
OS 'RECURSOS MINERAIS DO FUNDO DO MAR' FORAM DECLARADOS COMUM DE TODA A POPULAÇÃO HUMANA EM 1967.
INDIVIDUAL OR NATION STATE CAN LEGALLY APPROPRIATE PROPERTY RIGHT TO THE COMMON RESOURCES.
ENHUM INDIVÍDUO OU PAÍS PODE LEGALMENTE REIVINDICAR DIREITO DE PROPRIEDADE SOBRE RECURSOS COMUS.
1994: THE "COMMON HERITAGE OF MANKIND" WAS TRANSLATED INTO FREE MARKET TRADITION OF DEREGULATION AND DECENTRALISATION.
1994: "PATRIMÔNIO COMUM DA HUMANIDADE" FOI TRADUZIDO PARA O LIVRE MERCADO COMO DESREGULAMENTAÇÃO E DESCENTRALIZAÇÃO.
'Ndrangheta
IT IS ESTIMATED 40% OF THE WORLDS PHYTOPLANKTON HAS DIED SINCE THE 1950'S.
ESTIMA-SE QUE 40% DE TODO O FITOPLÂNCTON DO MONDO TENHA MORRIDO DESDE A DÉCADA DE 1950.

S

~~scale~~ → Time
~~science~~ → Facts
~~sense of loss~~ → Pandemic
Sensitivity Olga Tokarczuk
~~sensorily deprived~~ → Food
~~sensual qualities~~ → Object-Oriented Ontology
~~shared work of imagining~~ → Posthuman
~~shift the zeitgeist~~ → Climate
~~situated knowledge~~ → Feminism → Local → Weather
~~situatedness~~ → Environment
Soil Vandana Shiva
~~soil fertility~~ → Soil
~~space as an offspring of time~~ → Moving Earths
~~space as the product of agencies~~ → Moving Earths
~~space for hope~~ → Imagine
~~speculative realism~~ → Object-Oriented Ontology
~~stay with the trouble~~ → Chthulucene
~~stereotypes~~ → Overpopulation
~~stories with planetary dimensions~~ → Local
~~storytellers~~ → Tenderness
~~storytelling~~ → Feminism
~~strong fossil fuel industrial-economic regimes~~ → Energy
~~subnature~~ → City
Sun SPACE10 and SachsNottveit
~~suspicion~~ → Denial
Sustainability Connie Hedegaard
~~sustainable solutions~~ → Production
~~symbiosis~~ → Corals → Ecology
~~sympoietic~~ → Chtuhulucene
~~sympoietic futures~~ → Posthuman

→ Attention | butterfly effect | → Care | → Connectedness | → Creation | emotions | experience | → Facts | → Media | memory | mutual connections | → Tenderness | the authorial self | the world as fabric | → Time

The tender narrator

1.
The first photograph I ever experienced consciously is a picture of my mother from before she gave birth to me. Unfortunately, it's a black-and-white photograph, which means that many of the details have been lost, turning into nothing but grey shapes. The light is soft, and rainy, likely a springtime light, and definitely the kind of light that seeps in through a window, holding the room in a barely perceptible glow. My mom is sitting beside our old radio, and it's the kind with a green eye and two dials – one to regulate the volume, the other for finding a station. This radio later became my great childhood companion; from it I learnt of the existence of the cosmos. Turning an ebony knob shifted the delicate feelers of the antennae, and into their purview fell all kinds of different stations – Warsaw, London, Luxembourg and Paris. Sometimes, however, the sound would falter, as though between Prague and New York, or Moscow and Madrid, the antennae's feelers stumbled into black holes. Whenever that happened, it sent shivers down my spine. I believed that through this radio, different solar systems and galaxies were speaking to me, crackling and warbling and sending me important information, and yet I was unable to decipher it.

When as a little girl I would look at that picture, I would feel sure that my mum had been looking for me when she turned the dial on our radio. Like a sensitive radar, she penetrated the infinite realms of the cosmos, trying to find out when I would arrive, and from where. Her haircut and outfit (a big boat neck) indicate when this picture was taken – namely, in the early 1960s. Gazing off somewhere outside of the frame, the somewhat hunched-over woman sees something that isn't available to a person looking at the photo later. As a child, I imagined that what was happening was that she was gazing into time. There's nothing really happening in the picture – it's a photograph of a state, not a process. The woman is sad, seemingly lost in thought – seemingly lost.

When I later asked her about that sadness – which I did on numerous occasions, always prompting the same response – my mother

Olga Tokarczuk (born 1962, located in Wrocław, PL) is a writer known for her complex novels, including *Flights* (2017), which won the Man Booker International Prize and was a finalist for the National Book Award in Translation. She received the 2018 Nobel Prize for Literature (awarded belatedly in 2019).

would say that she was sad because I hadn't been born yet, yet she already missed me. 'How can you miss me when I'm not there yet?' I would ask.

I knew that you miss someone you've lost, that longing is an effect of loss.

'But it can also work the other way around,' she answered. 'Missing a person means they're there.'

This brief exchange, someplace in the countryside in western Poland in the late 1960s, an exchange between my mother and me, her small child, has always remained in my memory and given me a store of strength that has lasted me my whole life. For it elevated my existence beyond the ordinary materiality of the world, beyond chance, beyond cause and effect and the laws of probability. She placed my existence out of time, in the sweet vicinity of eternity. In my child's mind, I understood then that there was more to me than I had ever imagined before. And that even if I were to say 'I'm lost', then I'd still be starting out with the words 'I am' – the most important and the strangest set of words in the world.

And so a young woman who was never religious – my mother – gave me something once known as a soul, thereby furnishing me with the world's greatest *tender narrator.*

2.

The world is a fabric we weave daily on the great looms of information, discussions, films, books, gossip, little anecdotes. Today the purview of these looms is enormous; thanks to the Internet, almost everyone can take place in the process, taking responsibility and not, lovingly and hatefully, for better and for worse. When this story changes, so does the world. In this sense, the world is made of words.

How we think about the world and, perhaps even more importantly, how we narrate it have a massive significance, therefore. A thing that happens and is not told ceases to exist and perishes. This is a fact well known to not only historians but also (and perhaps above all) to every stripe of politician and tyrant. He who has and weaves the story is in charge.

Today our problem lies, it seems, in the fact that we do not yet have ready narratives not only for the future but even for a concrete now, for the ultra-rapid transformations of today's world. We lack the language; we lack the points of view, the metaphors, the myths and new fables. Yet we do see frequent attempts to harness rusty, anachronistic narratives that cannot fit the future to imaginaries of the future, no doubt on the assumption that an old something is better than a new nothing, or trying in this way to deal with the limitations of our own horizons. In a word, we lack new ways of telling the story of the world.

We live in a reality of polyphonic **first-person narratives**, and we are met from all sides with polyphonic noise. What I mean by first-person is the kind of tale that narrowly orbits the self of a teller who more or less directly just writes about herself and through herself. We have determined that this type of individualized point of view, this voice from the self, is the most natural, human and honest, even if it does abstain from a broader perspective. Narrating in the first person, so conceived, is weaving an absolutely unique pattern, the only one of its kind; it is having a sense of autonomy as an individual, being aware of yourself and your fate. Yet it also means building an opposition between the self and the world, and that opposition can be alienating at times.

I think that first-person narration is very characteristic of contemporary optics, in which the individual performs the role of subjective centre of the world. Western civilization is to a great extent founded and reliant upon that very discovery of the self, which makes up one of our most important measures of reality. Here man is the lead actor, and his judgement – although it is one among many – is always taken seriously. Stories woven in first person appear to be among the greatest discoveries of human civilization; they are read with reverence, bestow full confidence. This type of story, when we see the world through the eyes of some self that is unlike any other, builds a special bond with the narrator, who asks his listener to put himself in his unique position.

What first-person narratives have done for literature and in general for human civilization cannot be overestimated – they have completely reworked the story of the world, so that it is no longer a place for the operations of heroes and deities upon whom we can have no influence but rather a place for people just like us, with individual histories. It is easy to identify with people who are just like us, which generates between the story's narrator and its reader or listener a new variety of emotional understanding based on empathy. And this, by its very nature, brings together and eliminates borders; it is very easy to lose track in a novel of the borders between the narrator's self and the reader's self, and a so-called 'absorbing novel' actually counts on that border being blurred – on the reader, through empathy, becoming the narrator for a while. Thus literature has become a field for the exchange of experiences, an agora where everyone can tell of their own fate, or give voice to their alter ego. It is therefore a democratic space – anyone may speak up, everyone can create a speaking voice for herself. Never in the history of humanity have so many people been writers and storytellers. We have only to look at the statistics to see that this is true.

Whenever I go to book fairs, I see how many of the books being published in the world today have to do with precisely this: the authorial self. The expression instinct may be just as strong as other instincts that protect our lives, and it is most fully manifested in art. We want to be noticed, we want to feel exceptional. Narratives of the 'I'm going to tell you my story' variety, or 'I'm going to tell you the story of my family' or even simply 'I'm going to tell you where I've been' comprise today's most popular literary genre. This is a large-scale phenomenon also because nowadays we are universally able to access writing, and many people attain the ability, once reserved for the few, of expressing themselves in words and stories. Paradoxically, however, this situation is akin to a choir made up of soloists only, voices competing for attention, all travelling similar routes, drowning one another out. We know everything there is to know about them; we are able to identify with them and experience their lives as if they were our own. And yet, remarkably often, the readerly experience is incomplete and disappointing, as it turns out that expressing an authorial 'self' hardly guarantees universality. What we are missing, it would seem, is the dimension of the story that is the parable. For the hero of the parable is at once himself, a person living under specific historical and geographical conditions, yet at the same time he also goes well beyond those concrete particulars, becoming a kind of Everywhere Everyman. When a reader follows along with someone's story written in a novel, he can identify with the fate of the character described and consider their situation as if it were his own, while in a parable he must surrender completely his distinctness and become the Everyman. In this demanding psychological operation, the parable universalizes our experience, finding for very different fates a common denominator. That we have largely lost the parable from view is a testament to our current helplessness.

Perhaps in order not to drown in the multiplicity of titles and last names, we began to divide literature's leviathan body **into genres**, which we treat like the various different categories of sports, with writers as their specially trained players.

The general commercialization of the literary market has led to a division into branches. Now there are fairs and festivals of this or that type of literature, completely separate, creating a clientele of readers eager to hole up with a crime novel, some fantasy or science fiction. A notable characteristic of this situation is that what was only supposed to help booksellers and librarians organize on their shelves the massive quantity of published books, and readers to orient themselves in the vastness of the offering, became instead abstract categories not only into which existing works are placed but also according to which writers themselves have started writing. Increasingly, genre work is like a kind of cake mould that produces very similar results, their predictability considered a virtue, their banality an achievement. The reader knows what to expect and gets exactly what he wanted.

I have always intuitively opposed such orders, since they lead to the limiting of authorial freedom, to a reluctance toward the experimentation and transgression that is in fact the essential quality of creation in general. And they completely exclude from the creative process any of the eccentricity without which art would be lost. A good book does not need to champion its generic affiliation. The division into genres is the result of the commercialization of literature as a whole and an effect of treating it as a product for sale with the whole philosophy of branding and targeting and other, similar inventions of contemporary capitalism.

Today we can have the great satisfaction of seeing the emergence of a wholly new way of telling the world's story that is purveyed by the **on-screen series**, the hidden task of which is to induce in us a trance. Of course, this mode of storytelling has long existed in the myths and Homeric tales, and Heracles, Achilles or Odysseus are without doubt the first heroes of series. But never before has this mode taken up so much space or exerted such a powerful influence on the collective imagination. The first two decades of the 21st century are the unquestionable property of the series. Their influence on the modes of telling the story of the world (and therefore on our way of understanding that story, too) is revolutionary.

In today's version, the series has not only extended our participation in the narrative in the temporal sphere, generating its various tempos, offshoots and aspects, but also introduced its own new orders. Since in many cases its task is to hold the viewer's attention for as long as possible; the series narrative multiplies the threads, interweaving them in the most improbable manner so much so that when at a loss it even harks back to the old narrative technique, once compromised by classical opera, of the deus ex machina. The creation of new episodes often entails the total, ad-hoc overhaul of the psychology of the characters, so that they will be better suited to the developing events of the plot. A character who begins as gentle and reserved winds up vindictive and violent, a supporting character turns protagonist, while the main character, to whom we have already grown attached, loses significance or actually completely disappears, much to our dismay.

The potential materialization of another season creates the necessity of open endings in which there is no way that mysterious things called catharsis can occur or resound fully – catharsis, formerly the experience of the internal transformation, the fulfilment and satisfaction of having participated in the action of the tale. Such complication, rather than conclusion – the constant postponement of the reward that is catharsis – renders the viewer dependent, hypnotizes her. The *fabula interrupta*, created long ago, and well known from the stories of Scheherazade, has now made its bold return in series, altering our subjectivity and having bizarre psychological effects, tearing us out of our own lives and hypnotizing us like a stimulant. At the same time, the series inscribes itself into the new, drawn-out and disordered rhythm of the world, into its chaotic communication, its instability and fluidity. This storytelling form is probably the one most creatively searching for a new formula today.

In that sense, there is serious work in the series on the narratives of the future, on reformatting the story so that it suits our new reality.

But above all, we live in a world of too many contradictory, mutually exclusive facts, all battling one another tooth and nail.

Our ancestors believed that access to knowledge would not only bring people happiness, well-being, health and wealth but would also create an equal and just society. What was missing in the world, to their minds, was the ubiquitous wisdom that would naturally arise from information.

John Amos Comenius, the great 17th-century pedagogue, coined the term 'pansophism', by which he meant the idea of potential omniscience, universal knowledge that would contain within it all possible cognition. This was also, and above all, a dream of information available to everyone. Would not access to facts about the world transform an illiterate peasant into a reflective individual conscious of himself and the world? Will not knowledge within easy reach mean that people will become sensible, that they will direct the progress of their lives with equanimity and wisdom?

When the Internet first came about, it seemed that this notion would finally be realized in a total way. Wikipedia, which I admire and support, might have seemed to Comenius, like many like-minded philosophers, the fulfilment of the dream of humanity – now we can create and receive an enormous store of facts being ceaselessly supplemented and updated that is democratically accessible to just about every place on Earth.

A dream fulfilled is often disappointing. It has turned out that we are not capable of bearing this enormity of information, which instead of uniting, generalizing and freeing has differentiated, divided, enclosed in individual little bubbles, creating a multitude of stories that are incompatible with one another or even openly hostile towards each other, mutually antagonizing.

Furthermore, the Internet, completely and unreflectively subject to market processes and dedicated to monopolists, controls gigantic quantities of data used not at all pansophically, for the broader access to information, but on the contrary, serving above all to program the behaviour of users, as we learnt after the Cambridge Analytica affair. Instead of hearing the harmony of the world, we have heard a cacophony of sounds, an unbearable static in which we try, in despair, to pick up on some quieter melody, even the weakest beat. The famous Shakespeare quote has never been a better fit than it is for this cacophonous new reality: more and more often, the Internet is a tale, told by an idiot, full of sound and fury.

Research by political scientists unfortunately also contradicts John Amos Comenius's intuitions, which were based on the conviction that the more universally available information was about the world, the more politicians would avail themselves of reason and make considered decisions. But it would appear that the matter is not at all as simple as that. Information can be overwhelming, and its complexity and ambiguity give rise to all sorts of defence mechanisms – from denial to repression, even to escape into the simple principles of simplifying, ideological, party-line thinking.

The category of fake news raises new questions about what fiction is. Readers who have been repeatedly deceived, misinformed or misled have begun to slowly acquire a specific neurotic idiosyncrasy. The reaction to such exhaustion with fiction could be the enormous success of non-fiction, which in this great informational chaos screams over our heads: 'I will tell you the truth, nothing but the truth', and 'My story is based on facts!'

Fiction has lost the readers' trust since lying has become a dangerous weapon of mass destruction, even if it is still a primitive tool. I am often asked this incredulous question: 'Is this thing you wrote really true?' And every time I feel this question bodes the end of literature.

This question, innocent from the reader's point of view, sounds to the writer's ear truly apocalyptic. What am I supposed to say? How am I to explain the ontological status of Hans Castorp, Anna Karenina or Winnie the Pooh?

I consider this type of readerly curiosity a regression of civilization. It is a major impairment of our multi-dimensional ability (concrete, historical, but also symbolic, mythic) to participate in the chain of events called our lives. Life is created by events, but it is only when we are able to interpret them, try to understand them and lend them meaning that they are transformed into experience. Events are facts, but experience is something inexpressibly different. It is experience, and not any event, that makes up the material of our lives. Experience is a fact that has been interpreted and situated in memory. It also refers to a certain foundation we have in our minds, to a deep structure of significations upon which we can unfurl our own lives and examine them fully and carefully. I believe that myth performs the function of that structure. Everyone knows that myths never really happened but are always going on. Now they not only go on through the adventures of ancient heroes but rather also make their way into the ubiquitous and most popular stories of contemporary film, games and literature. The lives of the inhabitants of Mount Olympus have been transferred to *Dynasty*, and the heroic acts of the heroes are attended to by Lara Croft.

In this ardent division into truth and falsehood, the tales of our experience that literature creates have their own dimension.

I have never been particularly excited about any straight distinction between fiction and non-fiction, unless we understand such a distinction to be declarative and discretionary. In a sea of many definitions of fiction, the one I like the best is also the oldest, and it comes from Aristotle. **Fiction is always a kind of truth.**

I am also convinced by the distinction between true story and plot made by the British writer and essayist E.M. Forster. He said that when we say, 'The king died and then the queen died', it's a story. But when we say, 'The king died, and then the queen died of grief', that is a plot. Every fictionalization involves a transition from the question 'What happened next?' to an attempt at understanding it based on our human experience: 'Why did it happen that way?'

Literature begins with that 'why', even if we were to answer that question over and over with an ordinary 'I don't know'.

Thus literature poses questions that cannot be answered with the help of Wikipedia, since it goes beyond just information and events, referring directly to our experience.

But it is possible that the novel and literature in general are becoming before our very eyes something actually quite marginal in comparison with other forms of narration. That the weight of the image and of new forms of directly transmitting experience – film, photography, virtual reality – will constitute a viable alternative to traditional reading. Reading is quite a complicated psychological and perceptual process. To put it simply: first the most elusive content is conceptualized and verbalized, transforming into signs and symbols, and then it is 'decoded' back from language into experience. That requires a certain intellectual competence. And above all, it demands attention and focus, abilities ever rarer in today's extremely distracting world.

Humanity has come a long way in its ways of communicating and sharing personal experience, from orality, relying on the living word and human memory, through the Gutenberg Revolution, when stories began to be widely mediated by writing and in this way fixed and codified as well as possible to reproduce without alteration. The major attainment of this change was that we came to identify thinking with language, with writing. Today we are facing a revolution on a similar scale, when experience can be transmitted directly, without recourse to the printed word.

There is no longer any need to keep a travel diary when you can simply take pictures and send those pictures via social networking sites straight into the world, at once and to all. There is no need to write letters, since it is easier to call. Why write fat novels, when you can just get into a television series instead? Instead of going out on the town with friends, it would be better to play a game. Reach for an autobiography? There's no point, since I am following the lives of celebrities on Instagram and know everything about them.

It is not even the image that is the greatest opponent of text today, as we thought back in the 20th century, worrying about the influence of television and film. It is instead a completely different dimension of the world, acting directly on our senses.

3.

I don't want to sketch an overall vision of crisis in telling stories about the world. But I'm often troubled by the feeling that there is something missing in the world, that by experiencing it through glass screens, and through apps, somehow it becomes unreal, distant, two-dimensional and strangely non-descript, even though finding any particular piece of information is astoundingly easy. These days the worrying words 'someone', 'something', 'somewhere', 'some time' can seem riskier than very specific, definite ideas uttered with complete certainty – such as 'the earth is flat', 'vaccinations kill', 'climate change is nonsense' or 'democracy is not under threat anywhere in the world'. 'Somewhere' some people are drowning as they try to cross the sea. 'Somewhere', for 'some time', 'some sort of' a war has been going on. In the deluge of information, individual messages lose their contours, dissipate in our memory, become unreal and vanish.

The flood of stupidity, cruelty, hate speech and images of violence are desperately counterbalanced by all sorts of 'good news', but it hasn't the capacity to rein in the painful impression, which I find hard to verbalize, that **there is something wrong with the world**. Nowadays this feeling, once the sole preserve of neurotic poets, is like an epidemic of lack of definition, a form of anxiety oozing from all directions.

Literature is one of the few spheres that try to keep us close to the hard facts of the world, because by its very nature it is always psychological, because it focuses on the internal reasoning and motives of the characters, reveals their otherwise inaccessible experience to another person or simply provokes the reader into a psychological interpretation of their conduct. Only literature is capable of letting us go deep into the life of another being, understand their reasons, share their emotions and experience their fate.

A story always turns circles around meaning. Even if it doesn't express it directly, even when it deliberately refuses to seek meaning and focuses on form, on experiment, when it stages a formal rebellion, looking for new means of expression. As we read even the most behaviouristically, sparingly written story, we cannot help asking the questions, 'Why is this happening?', 'What does it mean?', 'What is the point?', 'Where is this leading?' Quite possibly our minds have evolved towards the story as a process of giving meaning to millions of stimuli that surround us and that even when we're asleep keep on relentlessly devising their narratives. So the story is a way of organizing an infinite amount of information within time, establishing its relationship to the past, the present and the future, revealing its recurrence, and arranging it in categories of cause and effect. Both the mind and the emotions take part in this effort.

No wonder one of the earliest discoveries made by stories was Fate, which apart from always appearing to people as something terrifying and inhuman did in fact introduce order and immutability into everyday reality.

4.

Ladies and Gentlemen,
A few years later, the woman in the photograph, my mother, who missed me although I hadn't yet been born, was reading me fairy tales.

In one of them, by Hans Christian Andersen, a teapot that had been thrown on the trash heap complained about how cruelly it had been treated by people – as soon as its handle broke off, they had disposed of it. But if they weren't such demanding perfectionists, it could still have been of use to them. Other broken objects picked up his tune and told truly epic stories of their modest little lives as objects.

As a child, I listened to these fairy tales with flushed cheeks and tears in my eyes, because I believed deeply that objects have their own problems and emotions, as well as a sort of social life, entirely comparable to our human one. The plates in the dresser could talk to each other, and the spoons, knives and forks in the drawer formed a sort of family. Similarly, animals were mysterious, wise, self-aware creatures with whom we had always been connected by a spiritual bond and a deep-seated similarity. But rivers, forests and roads had their existence too – they were living beings that mapped our space and built a sense of belonging, an enigmatic *Raumgeist*. The landscape surrounding us was alive too, and so were the Sun and the Moon, and all the celestial bodies – the entire visible and invisible world.

When did I start to have doubts? I'm trying to find the moment in my life when at the flick of a switch everything became different, less nuanced, simpler. The world's whisper fell silent, to be replaced by the din of the city, the murmur of computers, the thunder of aeroplanes flying past overhead and the exhausting white noise of oceans of information.

At some point in our lives we start to see the world in pieces, everything separately, in little bits that are galaxies apart from one another, and the reality in which we live keeps affirming it: doctors treat us by specialty, taxes have no connection with snow-ploughing the road we drive to work along, our lunch has nothing to do with an enormous stock farm, or my new top with a shabby factory somewhere in Asia. Everything is separate from everything else; everything lives apart, without any connection.

To make it easier for us to cope with this, we are given numbers, name tags, cards, crude plastic identities that try to reduce us to using one small part of the whole that we have already ceased to perceive.

The world is dying, and we are failing to notice. We fail to see that the world is becoming a collection of things and incidents, a lifeless expanse in which we move around lost and lonely, tossed here and there by somebody else's decisions, constrained by an incomprehensible fate, a sense of being the plaything of the major forces of history or chance. Our spirituality is either vanishing or becoming superficial and ritualistic. Or else we are just becoming the followers of simple forces – physical, social and economic – that move us around as if we were zombies. And in such a world, we really are zombies.

This is why I long for that other world, the world of the teapot.

5.

All my life, I've been fascinated by the systems of mutual connections and influences of which we are generally unaware but which we discover by chance, as surprising coincidences or convergences of fate, all those bridges, nuts, bolts, welded joints and connectors that I followed in [the book] *Flights*. I'm fascinated by associating facts and by searching for order. At base – as I am convinced – the writer's mind is a synthetic mind that doggedly gathers up all the tiny pieces in an attempt to stick them together again to create a universal whole.

How are we to write, how are we to structure our story to make it capable of raising this great, constellation form of the world?

Naturally, I realize that it is impossible to return to the sort of story about the world that we know from myths, fables and legends, which, communicated orally, kept the world in existence. Nowadays, the story would have to be far more multidimensional and complicated. After all, we really do know much more; we're aware of the incredible connections between things that seem to be far apart.

Let us take a close look at a particular moment in the history of the world.

It is 3 August 1492, the day on which a small caravel named *Santa Maria* is to set sail from a quay at the port of Palos in Spain. The ship is commanded by Christopher Columbus. The sun is shining, there are sailors going to and fro on the quay, and there are stevedores loading the last crates of provisions on board. It is hot, but a light breeze from the west saves the families who have come to say farewell from fainting. Seagulls strut grandly up and down the loading ramp, closely observing the human activities.

The moment that we can now see across time led to the death of 56 million of the almost 60 million Native Americans. At the time, they represented about 10% of the world's entire population. The Europeans unwittingly brought them some lethal gifts – diseases and bacteria to which the indigenous inhabitants of America had no resistance. On top of that came ruthless oppression and killing. The extermination continued for years and changed the nature of the land. Where beans, corn, potatoes and tomatoes had once grown in cultivated fields that were irrigated in a sophisticated way, wild vegetation returned. In just a few years, almost 150 million acres of arable land changed into jungle. As it regenerated, the vegetation consumed vast quantities of carbon dioxide, thus weakening the greenhouse effect, and that in turn lowered the global temperature of the Earth.

This is one of many scientific hypotheses to explain the onset of the minor ice age that in the late 16th century brought a long-term cooling of the climate in Europe.

The minor ice age changed the economy of Europe. Over the decades that followed, the long, frozen winters, cool summers and intense precipitation reduced the yield of traditional forms of farming. In Western Europe, small family farms producing food for their own needs proved inefficient. Waves of famine ensued, and the need to specialize production. England and Holland were worst affected by the colder climate; as their economies could no longer rely on farming, they began to develop trade and industry. The threat of storms prompted the Dutch to dry out the polders and to convert marshy areas and shallow marine zones into land. The southward shift of the range where cod occur, though catastrophic for Scandinavia, proved advantageous for England and Holland: it allowed these countries to start developing into naval and commercial powers. The significant cooling was particularly acutely felt in the Scandinavian countries. Contact with Greenland and Iceland broke off, the severe winters reduced the harvests and years of famine and shortages set in. So Sweden turned its greedy gaze southward, embarking on a war against Poland (especially as the Baltic Sea had frozen, making it easy to march an army across it) and getting involved in the Thirty Years' War in Europe.

The efforts of scientists, trying to establish a better understanding of our reality, show it to be a mutually coherent, densely connected system of influences. This is no longer just the famous 'butterfly effect', which as we know involves the way that minimal changes at the start of a process can lead in the future to tremendous, unpredictable results, but here we have an infinite number of butterflies and their wings, in constant motion – a powerful wave of life that travels through time.

In my view, the discovery of the butterfly effect marks the end of the era of unswerving faith in our own capacity to be effective, our ability to control and, by the same token, our sense of supremacy in the world. This does not take away from mankind our power to be a builder, a conqueror and an inventor, yet it illustrates that reality is more complicated than mankind might ever have supposed. And that we are nothing but a tiny part of these processes.

We have more and more proof of the existence of some spectacular, sometimes highly surprising dependencies on a worldwide scale. We are all – people, plants, animals and objects – immersed in a single space, which is ruled by the laws of physics. This common space has its shape, and within it the laws of physics sculpt an infinite number of forms that are incessantly linked to one another. Our cardiovascular system is like the system of a river basin, the structure of a leaf is like a human transport system, the motion of the galaxies is like the whirl of water flowing down our washbasins. Societies develop in a similar way to colonies of bacteria. The micro and macro scale show an endless system of similarities.

Our speech, thinking and creativity are not something abstract, removed from the world, but a continuation on another level of its endless processes of transformation.

6.

I keep wondering if these days it's possible to find the foundations of a new story that's universal, comprehensive, all-inclusive, rooted in nature, full of contexts and at the same time understandable.

Could there be a story that would go beyond the uncommunicative prison of one's own self, revealing a greater range of reality and showing the mutual connections? That would be able to keep its distance from the well-trodden, obvious and unoriginal centre point of commonly shared opinions, and manage to look at things *ex*-centrically, away from the centre?

I am pleased that literature has miraculously preserved its right to all sorts of eccentricities, phantasmagoria, provocation, parody and lunacy. I dream of high viewing points and wide perspectives, where the context goes far beyond what we might have expected. I dream of a language that is capable of expressing the vaguest intuition; I dream of a metaphor that surpasses cultural differences, and finally of a genre that is capacious and transgressive but that at the same time the readers will love.

I also dream of a new kind of narrator – a 'fourth-person' one, who is not merely a grammatical construct of course but who manages to encompass the perspective of each of the characters, as well as having the capacity to step beyond the horizon of each of them, who sees more and has a wider view and who is able to ignore time. Oh yes, I think this narrator's existence is possible.

Have you ever wondered who the marvellous storyteller is in the Bible who calls out in a loud voice: 'In the beginning was the word'? Who is the narrator who describes the creation of the world, its first day, when chaos was separated from order, who follows the serial about the origin of the universe, who knows the thoughts of God, is aware of his doubts and with a steady hand sets down on paper the incredible sentence: 'And God saw that it was good'? Who is this, who knows what God thought?

Leaving aside all theological doubts, we can regard this figure of a mysterious, tender narrator as miraculous and significant. This is a point of view, a perspective from where everything can be seen. Seeing everything means recognizing the ultimate fact that all things that exist are mutually connected into a single whole, even if the connections between them are not yet known to us. Seeing everything also means a completely different kind of responsibility for the world, because it becomes obvious that every gesture 'here' is connected to a gesture 'there', that a decision taken in one part of the world will have an effect in another part of it and that differentiating between 'mine' and 'yours' starts to be debatable.

So it could be best to tell stories honestly in a way that activates a sense of the whole in the reader's mind, that sets off the reader's capacity to unite fragments into a single design and to discover entire constellations in the small particles of events. To tell a story that makes it clear that everyone and everything is steeped in one common notion, which we painstakingly produce in our minds with every turn of the planet.

Literature has the power to do this. We should drop the simplistic categories of highbrow and lowbrow literature, popular and niche, and take the division into genres very lightly. We should drop the definition of 'national literatures', knowing as we do that the universe of literature is a single thing, like the idea of *unus mundus*, a common psychological reality in which our human experience is united. The Author and the Reader perform equivalent roles, the former by dint of creating, the latter by making a constant interpretation.

Perhaps we should trust fragments, as it is fragments that create constellations capable of describing more, and in a more complex way, multidimensionally. Our stories could refer to one another in an infinite way, and their central characters could enter into relationships with each other.

I think we have a redefinition ahead of us of what we understand nowadays by the concept of realism, and a search for a new one that would allow us to go beyond the limits of our ego and penetrate the glass screen through which we see the world. Because these days the need for reality is served by the media, social networking sites and indirect relationships on the Internet. Perhaps what inevitably lies ahead of us is a sort of neo-surrealism, some rearranged points of view that won't be afraid to stand up to a paradox and will go against the grain when it comes to the simple order of cause and effect. Indeed, our reality has already become surreal. I am also sure that many stories require rewriting in our new intellectual contexts, taking their inspiration from new scientific theories. But I find it equally important to make constant reference to myth and to the entire human imaginarium. Returning to the compact structures of mythology could bring a sense of stability within the lack of specificity in which we are living nowadays. I believe that myths are the building material for our psyche, and we cannot possibly ignore them (at most we might be unaware of their influence).

No doubt a genius will soon appear, capable of constructing an entirely different, as yet unimaginable narrative in which everything essential will be accommodated. This method of storytelling is sure to change us; we will drop our old, constricting perspectives and we will open up to new ones that have in fact always existed somewhere here but we have been blind to them.

In *Doctor Faustus*, Thomas Mann wrote about a composer who devised a new form of absolute music capable of changing human thinking. But Mann did not describe what this music would depend on; he merely created the imaginary idea of how it might sound. Perhaps that is what the role of an artist relies on – giving a foretaste of something that could exist and thus causing it to become imaginable. And being imagined is the first stage of existence.

7.

I write fiction, but it is never pure fabrication. When I write, I have to feel everything inside myself. I have to let all the living beings and objects that appear in the book go through me, everything that is human and beyond human, everything that is living and not endowed with life. I have to take a close look at each thing and person, with the greatest solemnity, and personify them inside myself, personalize them.

That is what tenderness serves me for – because tenderness is the art of personifying, of sharing feelings and thus endlessly discovering similarities. Creating stories means constantly bringing things to life, giving an existence to all the tiny pieces of the world that are represented by human experiences, the situations people have endured and their memories. Tenderness personalizes everything to which it relates, making it possible to give it a voice, to give it the space and the time to come into existence, and to be expressed. It is thanks to tenderness that the teapot starts to talk.

Tenderness is the most modest form of love. It is the kind of love that does not appear in the scriptures or the Gospels; no one swears by it, no one cites it. It has no special emblems or symbols, nor does it lead to crime, or prompt envy.

It appears wherever we take a close and careful look at another being, at something that is not our 'self'.

Tenderness is spontaneous and disinterested; it goes far beyond empathetic fellow feeling. Instead it is the conscious, though perhaps slightly melancholy, common sharing of fate. Tenderness is deep emotional concern about another being, its fragility, its unique nature and its lack of immunity to suffering and the effects of time. Tenderness perceives the bonds that connect us, the similarities and sameness between us. It is a way of looking that shows the world as being alive, living, interconnected, cooperating with and co-dependent on itself.

Literature is built on tenderness toward any being other than ourselves. It is the basic psychological mechanism of the novel. Thanks to this miraculous tool, the most sophisticated means of human communication, our experience can travel through time, reaching those who have not yet been born but who will one day turn to what we have written, the stories we told about ourselves and our world.

I have no idea what their life will be like, or who they will be. I often think about them with a sense of guilt and shame.

The climate emergency and the political crisis in which we are now trying to find our way, and which we are anxious to oppose by saving the world, have not come out of nowhere. We often forget that they are not just the result of a twist of fate or destiny but of some very specific moves and decisions – economic, social and to do with world outlook (including religious ones). Greed, failure to respect nature, selfishness, lack of imagination, endless rivalry and lack of responsibility have reduced the world to the status of an object that can be cut into pieces, used up and destroyed.

That is why I believe I must tell stories as if the world were a living, single entity, constantly forming before our eyes, and as if we were a small and at the same time powerful part of it.

'Sensitivity' is a reproduction of the speech given by Olga Tokarczuk in 2019 when she received the Nobel Prize for Literature.

Soil

→ Agriculture | → Biodiversity | → Care | → Chthulucene | eco-apartheid | → Food | humus | Law of Exploitation | Law of Return | monocultures | → Resources | soil fertility

'Upon this handful of soil our survival depends. Take care of it and it will grow our food, our fuel and our shelter and surround us with beauty. Abuse it and the soil will collapse and die, taking humanity with it.'

Vedas Sanskrit Scripture, 1500 BCE

'Whatever, I dig of you, O Earth,
May that grow quickly upon you,
O pure One, may my thrust
never pierce thy
Vital points, Thy Heart.'

Prithvi Sukta, in a prayer to the Earth, in the ancient Indian text *Atharva Veda*

'To forget how to dig the earth and tend the soil is to forget ourselves.'

Gandhi

'The history of every nation is eventually written in the way in which it cares for its soil.'

Franklin D. Roosevelt

We are soil. We are the land. We are Earth. We are made of the same five elements – earth, water, fire, air and space – that constitute the Universe.

Dr **Vandana Shiva** (born 1952, located in Delhi, IN) is an Indian scholar and environmental thinker. She holds a PhD in quantum theory and later shifted to interdisciplinary research in science, technology and environmental policy. She has received many honorary doctorates and awards for her work and in 2010 was identified as one of the top Seven Most Powerful Women on the Globe by *Forbes* magazine.

What we do to soil we do to ourselves

Our future is inseparable from the future of the Earth. It is no accident that the word human has its roots in *humus*, 'soil' in Latin, and Adam the first human in Abrahamic traditions is derived from *Adamus*, 'soil' in Hebrew.

In taking care of the soil, we reclaim our humanity.
In living soil lies the prosperity and security of civilization. In the death of soil is the death of civilization and the extinction of our species.

This ecological truth is forgotten in the dominant paradigm because it is based on eco-apartheid, the false idea that we are separate and independent of the Earth, and also because it defines soil as dead matter. If soil is dead to begin with, human action cannot destroy its life, it can only 'improve' the soil with chemical fertilizers. And if we are masters and conquerors of the soil, we determine the fate of the soil; soil cannot determine our fate.

History, however, is witness to the fact that the fate of societies and civilizations is intimately connected to how we treat the soil – do we relate to soil through the Law of Return or through the Law of Exploitation and Extraction?

The Law of Return, of giving back, of gratitude to a living earth, has ensured that societies create and maintain fertile soil and can be supported by living soil over thousands of years. The Law of Exploitation, of taking without giving back, has led to the collapse of civilizations.

Agriculture is the culture of caring for the land

However, the dependence of fossil fuels has made us forget that we are soil. Fossil fuel-based industrial-chemical agriculture treats soil as inert and an empty container for chemical fertilizers. We have been mistakenly led to believe that soil fertility comes from factories that previously made explosives but now make synthetic fertilizers.

Industrial agriculture, based on a mechanistic paradigm, and the use of fossil fuels have created ignorance and blindness to the living processes that create a living soil. Instead of focusing on the soil food web, it has been obsessed with external inputs of chemical fertilizers – what Sir Albert Howard called the NPK mentality. Biology and life have been replaced with chemistry.

- External inputs and mechanization create the imperative for monocultures.

- By exposing the soil to wind, sun and rain, monocultures expose the soil to erosion by wind and water.

- Soils with low organic matter are also most easily eroded, since organic matter creates soil aggregates and binds the soil.

- Fertile soils contain 100 tonnes of organic matter per ha. Reduction of soil organic matter by 1.4–0.9% lowers yield potential by 50%.

- Chemical monocultures also make soils more vulnerable to drought and further contribute to food insecurity.

- 1 ha of corn or wheat will transpire more than five to seven million litres of water each season and lose an additional two million of water by evaporation from the exposed soil.

- Further, eroded soils and soils without organic matter absorb 10 to 300 mm less water per ha per year from rainfall. This represents a 7–44% decrease in water availability for food production, contributing to a decline in biological productivity of 10–25%.

No technology system can claim to feed the world while it destroys the life in the soil by failing to feed it on the basis of the Law of Return. This is why the claim that the Green Revolution or genetic engineering is feeding the world is false. Intrinsic to these technologies are monocultures based on chemical inputs, a recipe for killing the life of the soil and accelerating soil erosion and degradation. Degraded and dead soils, soils without organic matter, soils without soil organisms, soils with no water-holding capacity create famines and a food crisis; they do not create food security.

This is especially true in times of climate change. Industrial agriculture is not only responsible for 50% of the greenhouse gases contributing to climate change; it is also more vulnerable to it.[1]

Soils with organic matter are more resilient to drought and climate extremes. And increasing organic matter production through biodiversity intensive systems, which are in effect photosynthesis-intensive systems, is the most effective way to get the carbon dioxide out of the atmosphere, into the plants and then into the soil through the Law of Return.

Food security is soil security

Ecological agriculture is based on recycling organic matter, hence recycling nutrients. Organic matter is broken down by soil organisms to form humus.

The new paradigm recognizes the soil as living, in which billions of soil organisms create soil fertility. Their well-being is vital to human well-being. Looked at from this point of view, the immediate aim of fertilization is not to increase yields and fertilize plants but to build up soil fertility. This is exactly what the Austrian founder of the biodynamic movement, Rudolf Steiner, meant when he coined the famous phrase 'Fertilization means nurturing a living soil'.

Soil is a living system, with billions of soil organisms weaving an intricate soil food web to create, maintain and renew soil fertility, on which all food production rests. As Sir Albert Howard stated, 'The birthright of every crop is health', and he regarded 'health in soil, plant, animal, and man as one great subject'.[2]

Healthy and fertile soils make healthy plants, which make healthy people.

Sir Albert Howard defined fertile soil as 'a soil teeming with healthy life in the shape of abundant microflora and microfauna, will bear healthy plants, and these, when consumed by animals and man, will confer health on animals and man. But an infertile soil, that is, one lacking sufficient microbial, fungous, and other life, will pass on some form of deficiency to the plant, and such plant, in turn, will pass on some form of deficiency to animal and man'.[3]

'No one generation has the right to exhaust the soil from which humanity must draw its sustenance.'

Albert Howard, 1947, p. 13

Contemporary societies across the world stand on the verge of collapse as soils are eroded, degraded, poisoned, buried under concrete and deprived of their life.

Regenerating the soil is cultivating our future.

Works cited:

Howard, Albert. 1947. *Soil and Health: A Study of Organic Agriculture.* New York: Devin-Adair.

Howard, Louise E. 1953. *Sir Albert Howard in India.* London: Faber and Faber.

Shiva, Vandana. 2016. *Soil, not Oil: Climate Change, Peak Oil and Food Insecurity.* London: Zed Books.

Sun

→ Energy | → Fire | → Imagine | imagined community | natural powerhouse | → Resources | → The Sharing Economy

SPACE10 (founded 2015, located in Copenhagen, DK) is a research and design lab on a mission to enable a better everyday life for people and the planet. SPACE10 explores innovative solutions to some of the major societal changes expected to affect people and the planet in the years to come. SPACE10 is proudly supported by and entirely dedicated to IKEA – working as an independent and complementary centre for innovation and concept development.

SachsNottveit was founded by Carl Theodor Sachs (born 1985) and Anders Nottveit (born 1988) in 2017 in Copenhagen, DK. In 2020, after three years, the two architects decided to go in different directions. Sachs is an MAA Architect, graduated from the Royal Academy of Fine Arts in Copenhagen (DK) in 2016. He works in the field between architecture, design and installation art, with a strong focus on materials and how to repurpose them. Nottveit was educated at the Royal Danish Academy of Fine Arts, School of Architecture, Design and Conservation, in Copenhagen. After graduation, he established SANO, an architectural studio working within the field of architecture, craft and installation art. He is currently a partner of OK-Arkitekter, based in Bergen (NO).

Today, mankind faces an immense number of challenges, and while it would be overly simplistic to ever reduce these complex issues to one source, origin or theme, there seems to be certain trends within them – our relationship with our natural environment has been strained, artificiality has overtaken the natural, and anthropocentric needs have surpassed the limits of our planet.

To address the issues of our natural environment, we will likely have to reacquaint ourselves with the solutions it provides us naturally and pair them with our own imagination for what a better future could possibly look like.

Luckily, although the challenges we face are plentiful, so are their potential solutions. It is no longer a question of when new possibilities for a better way of living will arise but of how humanely, fairly and sustainably they are designed.

Now, meet SolarVille. SolarVille is, among other things, an imagined community. It is a model of a village that looks more like a children's toy than a prototype, but what lies at the foundation of its curved roads, carved cars and slanted roofs is this question: In a world where roughly two billion people have little to no access to clean and reliable electricity, how can we work towards democratizing clean energy, in a way that is efficient, sustainable and equitable for all?

Although there are many ways to explore this question, and most will have to be used in tandem to create the impact needed, we looked up to the sun for answers. This natural powerhouse provides on average 90,000 terawatts of energy to the Earth's surface, more than 4,000 times the energy we need to sustain a population of eight billion people. Even when taking into account clouds, seasonal changes and water-covered surfaces, the sun is still a leader for energy sources that work *with* nature, not against it.

Inspired by the sun, SolarVille imagines what could happen if every household was empowered to be their own maker and trader of solar energy – harnessing the power of the sun and then distributing it through blockchain-enabled microgrids, keeping all power and profit within the community itself.

This model community was made to embody solar research, an area we know is of immense importance to the future wellbeing of people across the world. With SolarVille's design, what could easily be complicated is now playful, and what could have been cold, abstract or removed is made warm, immediate and tangible. The hardwood material tells a story for a better future through the comforting lens of nostalgia, imbuing the project with a sense of childlike wonder so people feel compelled to touch, engage and play with the ideas central to SolarVille's conception.

Just as we once used the stars for navigation, we must now look to the one central in our orbit for a way towards a more sustainable future. It's time to find balance between ourselves and our environmental surroundings, between the artificially designed and the resourcefully natural, and to imagine communities like SolarVille that empower people to thrive with nature, not in spite of it.

Sustain-ability

→ Connectedness | → Development | → Future | future generations | imbalance | rethink growth

You know when it is not there.
The absence of sustainability can be seen, felt, sometimes smelt.
Just like you don't pay attention when things are in balance, while imbalance is felt instantly. Pollution is visible. Overexploitation puts its stamp on a landscape. As does the warming up of an ocean. For the eye that can actually *see*. For the human that has not been totally disconnected from nature.

Sustainability means meeting our own needs without compromising the ability of future generations to meet their own needs.

This most common definition of sustainability is as simple as it is complex for current generations to live according to this credo. The first part – 'meeting our own needs' – works more than well for most people in our part of the world. But to fully comprehend the implications of the second half, 'without compromising the ability of future generations to meet their own needs', that is the challenge.
How come? Most of us have children. No one is closer to our heart than they are. And yet we behave like a swarm of grasshoppers landing on a field, eating up everything and leaving nothing behind.

Connie Hedegaard (born 1960, located in Copenhagen, DK) has an MA in History and Literature and is Chair of the KR Foundation, of Berlingske Media and of Aarhus University, among others. From 2010 to 2014, she was EU Commissioner for Climate Action and in 2004–2009 Denmark's Minister for Environment and Climate and Energy.

In Delia Owens' bestseller novel *Where the Crawdads Sing*, young Tate gets the attention of the girl Kya by placing the most beautiful and rare bird feather visibly in a crack in a tree trunk.

A beautiful gesture in a world where connectedness to nature is intact, a beautiful feather represents huge value – a diametrical contradiction to our world disconnected from nature and materialistic, characterized by a Me, Me, SoMe culture, where consumption and immediate need for satisfaction seems to be the goal of everything.

SoMe is an abbreviation for social media commonly used in Denmark.

As the pendulum swung too far back to this one extreme, a fundamental balance was lost, as it is normally lost in systems where materialistic wealth is the one and only overriding value and where enough is never enough, because more and bigger is always better. On a planet with ever more people – and notably also with ever more people escaping poverty – growth is a condition. But our current growth model is not sustainable – to a degree where the absence of sustainability currently is the biggest threat and thus also the biggest challenge that mankind has faced.

In order to re-establish equilibrium, to make sustainability a reality and not just a nice word, we must rethink growth; the pendulum will have to swing back. Not from total individualism to the opposite total collective, where nobody is really responsible for anything. No, we have to re-establish the balance that we lost. To reinvent a sense of connectedness. With nature and with values that are not materialistic and with each other across generations, so that we live – not just in words but in our actions and daily practices – in a way that allows for future generations to have the same right as we do to a good, decent and rich life. It means we have to change focus in our economies, and we have to change our own behaviour. If we don't do that – and do it fast – sustainability for future generations will only be known as the thing that is not there.

T

~~technofossils~~ → Heritage
~~temporal becoming~~ → Bacteria
Tenderness Lundgaard & Tranberg Architects
Terraforming Emmy Laura Perez Fjalland
~~territorial positions~~ → Geo-Social Classes
~~the Age of Humans~~ → Anthropocene
~~the authorial self~~ → Sensitivity
~~the certain uncertainty~~ → Ecology
~~the city as a commons~~ → The Sharing Economy
~~The Edible Schoolyard Project~~ → Food
~~the freedom to affect and be affected by others~~ → Coexistence
~~the global inside the national~~ → Global
~~the multi-species many~~ → Air
~~the nature of the material world~~ → New Materialism
~~the other of the other~~ → Queer
~~the passport system~~ → Migration Flows
~~the power of sharing stories~~ → Description
~~the price of solidarity~~ → Moving Earths
~~the racist imagination of the West~~ → Plantationocene
~~the rivers of the atmosphere~~ → Air
The Sharing Economy Darren Sharp
~~the truth of past, present and future~~ → Earthlings
~~the world as fabric~~ → Sensitivity
~~theory of reality~~ → Object-Oriented Ontology
~~there is no away but there is still afar~~ → Wilderness
~~threat~~ → Xenophobia
~~tide~~ → Explicitation
Time Barbara Adam
~~timing~~ → Window of Opportunity
~~tipping points~~ → Power
~~to be vulnerable and powerful~~ → Connectedness
~~transversal vectors~~ → Global

Tenderness

→ Architecture | → Atmosphere | → Care | → Connectedness | → Future | → Imagine | keep listening | receptiveness | → Sensitivity | storytellers

Architecture is a love affair. And as with love between people, it is essential we give more than we take.

When we, as architects, begin a new project, we encounter a place for the first time. It may be in nature, it may be a plot in a well-established city or it may be a building that is destined for transformation. One always encounters something, never nothing. Every site has its own atmosphere and history. Often times, it is grand and overwhelming; other times it may initially prove elusive. But if one continues to listen, every site, sooner or later, begins to speak.

We like to imagine that we, as architects, make ourselves available as interpreters and storytellers. It requires a certain receptiveness to stand where a new building is to be planned and attempt to read a site's history while simultaneously imagining all possible futures and destinies that will flow through that particular site. Naturally, it is impossible to fathom the endless number of potential future scenarios, but that does not prevent us from trying, again and again. We have stood on the square in Denmark's oldest city, on the outskirts of small towns in the countryside, in open fields, in a bread factory, on a quay, next to a railway line.

When we engage with a place, our goal is to generate life. We do not see our own role as one of clearing and taking away, even though it may be necessary, in concrete terms, to remove something before we can build something new. The spirit of that which is removed can be woven into the new structure, perhaps in the way we interpret an architectural tradition, the scale and rhythm of a place, the placement of a window in a wall or the scintillating colour spectrum of a new roofing tile – materials and technical solutions that take on meaning when carefully placed in a context. This gives all of us, who are alive here and now, the ability to connect with something that is much greater than just a single moment in time. We can move through lively, unending spaces that awaken deep-rooted cultural traditions to life and illuminate how the future offers new ways of being present.

Not so long ago, we designed a school situated between urban Copenhagen and a large protected nature reserve. A structure of concrete rings defines a cluster of spaces that is occupied throughout the day by both children and adults. Constructions must be honed to perfection to last for centuries, but at a completely different level of understanding, it is necessary they constitute recognizable systems of meaning. Intuitively, the children may understand the circular structures of the atrium as trees encircling a clearing in a forest. Hopefully, they experience a sense of calm when they touch the columns, experiencing the cool, pleasant surface of concrete cast in smooth formwork. As they play over the course of the day, perhaps they follow the rays of sun traversing the spaces, reminding them of the way light falls in a natural landscape.

Although a school is a constructed space that provides more complete

Lundgaard & Tranberg Architects was founded in Copenhagen, DK, in 1985. Since then, the architecture firm has worked with buildings, urban and landscape planning, product design and renovation projects.

shelter from the elements than a woodland clearing, they both provide similar fundamental experiences of spaces and their interconnectedness. If children are allowed to realize a sense of self in relation to their physical surroundings, these experiences may stay with them and inform how they perceive the world for the rest of their lives. Hopefully, these primary understandings will in time result in new spaces that touch and affect future generations.

Kalvebod Fælled School, Copenhagen, Denmark, by Lundgaard & Tranberg Architects, 2018.

Terra-forming

→ Agency | → Borders | colonialism | curiosity | → Earth Ethics | → Earthlings | → Global | → Home | → Imagine | post-anthropogenic forming of terra

'Terraforming' means to modify the atmosphere, biosphere, ecology and topology of celestial others into Earth-like living environments so that they become habitable for humans (not that this is equal or inclusive). It seems to involve colonizations and territorialization as it is also mentioned as *extra*terrestial planeting, and Earth's companion planets, named Venus and Mars, have both been considered terraforming potentials. The concept has roots in both science fiction and technological and engineering sciences, and are lines of knowledge and imagining that significantly developed through the 1940s, 1950s and 1960s. With the looming environmental and climatic dooms, the thinking has gained renewed attraction – as escapism (we might have to leave this Earth), in search of resources, an ancient curiosity or to explore how life might be upheld on Earth under extreme conditions. Projects unfold in different ways: so-called high tech and low tech, spaceships and architectures, social and artistic explorations, speculative cosmologies and even agricultural explorations, to name just a few. Designing habitations and placing them within celestial others reflects and simulates what science and technologies are currently capable of; they can highlight mistakes, misinterpretations and gaps. Make us question questions, question sciences, question what makes Earth liveable, what it means to be human physically, biologically, spiritually, culturally. It is a practice that provokes fundamental ethical and political questions about what life is and what counts as life (what shall be upheld, whose lives shall be upheld), and they require the most humbleness, humility and delicacy.

While terraforming projects might be considered an extreme anthropogenic practice, the processes and explorations seem also to show how much we do not master, how small we are on a universal scale, how young we are in universal time and how dependent (as *made of*, *living from*, *becoming with*) humans are on other humans, on more-than-human organic worlds and non-human physical worlds. From every terraforming exploration, we might learn more about what it actually means to live here on Earth with Earth-Others among Celestial-Others. Despite this space for rethinking humanity and rethinking how this planet and humans relate to everything else in this universe, most projects are narrated and politicized with

Emmy Laura Perez Fjalland (born 1987, located in Copenhagen, DK) is a postdoctoral researcher at the Institute of Architecture, Urbanism and Landscape, at The Royal Danish Academy of Fine Arts in Copenhagen. She works with environmental humanities and explores the connections between critical thinking (feminist materialist and speculative realist traditions) and the current dialogues of environmental doom, more-than-human ontologies and ecological practices.

modernist values of Mastering, Progress, Control, Territory, Technology and Colonialism. Capitalization is used here as an attempt to express how these practices and concepts have Triumphed and are greatly praised throughout the 'Western' worlds that are so greatly defined by the 'linear temporalities of technoscientific productionism'.[1] Projects are labelled and marketed with hedonism, heroism, freedom. It might sound attractive, but it's not very new, or very Modern, actually. By now we might have learnt about the dangers of taking humans a bit too seriously, the dangers of weaponization, of slavery, of domination, of unjust and unequal rights (who gets through the walls? who gets to dine?). With the drama awaiting and the panic that might rise, we might be even more sceptical, more suspicious and maybe even more speculative about the terraforming 'inventions'.

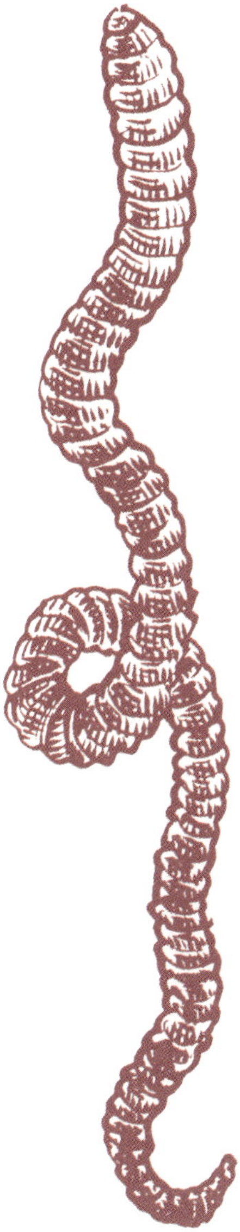

'Terra' comes from the Latin meaning 'earth, earthly' and has links to ground, land, dry land (as opposed to water, sea, lake), terrain, country, soil, region, territory. 'Forming' is an act of creating or making that might come via the Old French word *formacion* (formation, fashioning, creation), which seems to have appeared around the 12th century (on a Western, Christian timeline). It may also directly come from the Latin *formationem* (a forming of, shaping of). This is a noun of action or condition from the past-participle stem of *formare* (to form), from *forma* (form, shape). This forming as an active (as opposed to passive) human practice seems to be led by ideas, desires, politics, techniques and/or sciences about how life could or should be – yet as a relation to the material, matter, the form. Human formations might be Utopian, Dystopian or Ustopian (as Canadian writer Margaret Atwood suggests[2]). As science fiction (and speculative fiction) also plays a significant role in the development of the concept and practices of terraforming, 'utopia' might be another word, matter, place, practice that might assist the understanding of terraforming. The curious minds and speculative questions that nurture terraforming seem to be nurtured from a desire for creating, sharping an ideal, fleeing from the apocalypse or testing 'it'. *Forming*. Once upon a time, writers and scientists placed utopias on islands, but then most islands were discovered and colonized. Or utopias were found underground; think about how one could fall into a hole, through a tunnel and end up in utopia, but then an underground world was discovered. The utopian speculative minds moved up into the air, into space, and invented spaceships. But all together that might not be fairly put, as planetary as well as underground curiosity and connectedness most probably has been up for question and exploration since Ancient human days – and nights; Moons, stars, physics, spirituality, magic, maps, seasons, cosmologies, mythology, rhythms, meteors.

Observing the sky on a starry night, even in an over-lit urbanization, a planetary connectedness might appear – mundane speculations about how life might be in this deep dark unending bag and how particular Earthlings are, critters. With the planetary, material and speculative *turns* within humanities, arts and the social sciences, it might become clear that 'forming' – as in *making worlds* – is not only limited to humans. Spider webs, beaver dams, earthworm soils, stardust. Forming practices alone are not a social constructivist or a discursive practice. A human determinism. The soil of terra and the form of forming – both of terraforming – could be reminders of the diversity of temporalities, a darkness below our feet, collaborations of fungi, bacteria, mites, worms, atmospheric minerals, among others.[3] 'Composting Terra' – what a stirring, compassionate science-and-technology story we could tell. Thinking of 'terraforming' with these turns, the concept and practices could be a *terra* – as in soily, slow, dark, dirty, inconvenient, multi-temporal, fertile, cyclical – *landscape practice.* A practice that moves beyond the Anthropos into more-than-human world-making and planetary storytelling, it becomes a de-modernization project that rethinks how we study and conceptualize what makes the world world. A practice that could go beyond imperialism and decolonize sites, bodies, matters, meanings, knowledge, beings. We might start to be with the landscapes we live with. Un-naming 'it' – nature – and developing our languages and words about these beings and practices[4] and nuanced understandings, designs and practices with technologies. Especially because so-called hard or high technologies are so adored and valued and significant for many dominant terraforming projects. 'Anybody who ever lighted a fire without matches has probably gained some proper respect for "low" or "primitive" or "simple" technologies; anybody who ever lighted a fire *with* matches should have the wits to respect that notable hi-tech invention.'[5]

Terraforming could be a profound and ontological cultural rethinking of what it means to be and do in a non-anthropogenic world. Acknowledging the connectedness, and the vital dependency, between so-called cultures and natures might not be new, yet it is so undervalued, under-practiced among the Western Anthropos. Terraforming might yet hold dominant connections to colonial desires just as much as forming is considered a too human practice (e.g. engineering, design, architecture, agriculture).[6]

We ought to rethink the spatial terra and the forming practices, stories and techniques and meanwhile think with celestial-Others and Earth-Others, not to create another 'Othering' but to unsettle ideas about the centre of the world. For whom does the Moon turn around Earth around the Sun? Who drags what, holding each other in a peculiar, powerful relation? For whom do the stars shine? The trees grow? To whom does this unruly universal pouch belong? And to whom does this composting globe with plastic bags, critters, satellites and atomic bombs belong? How to belong in a post-anthropogenic world? How to belong to this composting-celestial? This cemetery-becoming.

This might be where our questions for post-anthropogenic terraforming might start.

Work cited:

Atwood, Margaret. 2011. 'Margaret Atwood: The Road to Ustopia'. *The Guardian*, 14 October. https://www.theguardian.com/books/2011/oct/14/margaret-atwood-road-to-ustopia. Accessed 21 January 2020.

Fjalland, Emmy Laura Perez, and Kristine Samson. 2019. 'Reparative Practices: Invitations from Mundane Urban Ecologies'. *Nordic Design Research Conference*, 8, May.

Griffith, Jay. 2019. *Dwelling on Earth. Emergence Magazine*, October.

Kimmerer, Robin Wall. 2015. *Braiding Sweetgrass: Indigenous Wisdom, Scientific Knowledge and the Teachings of Plants.* Minneapolis: Milkweed Editions.

Le Guin, Ursula K. 2004. 'A Rant about Technology'. http://www.ursulakleguinarchive.com/Note-Technology.html. Accessed 21 January 2020.

Puig de la Bellacasa, Maria. 2017. *Matters of Care: Speculative Ethics in More Than Human Worlds.* University of Minnesota Press. Minneapolis.

The Sharing Economy

access over ownership | → Agency | → Climate Risk Communities | → Geo-Social Classes | gig economy | → Local | platform cooperatives | → Resilience | → Resources | the city as a commons

---

The sharing economy is an emerging socioeconomic movement which facilitates the exchange of stuff, space and skills between networks of peers. It consists of a diverse mix of actors including for-profit, cooperative, community and public sector organizations that enable the sharing of surplus or idle assets. A common theme in the sharing economy is 'access over ownership', where people can rent, share or borrow physical items through car sharing services,[1] bike sharing programmes[2] and neighbour-based household goods exchanges.[3] New technologies have emerged over the last two decades that utilize digital platforms to reduce transaction costs at a peer-to-peer level using trust-based reputation systems. This has led to the rapid take-up of commercial platforms that facilitate ride-hailing (Uber), short-stay rentals (Airbnb), food delivery (Deliveroo) and online marketplaces for selling second-hand goods (eBay).

Community-based sharing predates many of the commercial platforms and encourages participation at the grassroots level by unlocking people's intangible assets like care, time and knowledge. Grassroots sharing creates social capital and stronger community connectedness through a range of initiatives, including meal sharing, community gardens, time banking, home sharing, tool libraries, repair cafés, carpooling, skill shares and food swaps. Community-based sharing groups are generally initiated and run by volunteers with support from local organizations that include municipal government, neighbourhood houses and associations. Community-based sharing builds resilience at the local level through self-provisioning of the production, consumption and exchange of useful resources. Such grassroots forms of sharing reframe idle stuff, space and skills as an opportunity to share, learn and connect with peers in local communities.

Dr **Darren Sharp** (born 1976, located in Melbourne, AU) is a sharing economy consultant and urban sustainability transitions researcher working at the intersection of grassroots innovation, sharing cities and collaborative governance. Darren is the founding director of strategy consultancy Social Surplus and is the Australian editor of Shareable.net. He co-authored the book *Sharing Cities: Activating the Urban Commons* (2018).

The sharing economy is not without its drawbacks, which include the enclosing influence of commercial platforms that monetize formally sacrosanct areas of private life. A ride to work, some help around the house or a spare room for an out-of-town guest have all become commodities to be bought and sold through a handful of platform monopolies.[4] The economic benefits of these services favour asset owners with a desirable car or home to share. There is also ongoing disagreement over what's considered the authentic sharing economy, which creates social, environmental and economic value, and the gig economy (aka 'on-demand' or 'platform economy'), characterized by platforms like Uber and Deliveroo, which critics argue is leading to the emergence of a new precariat or exploited underclass.[5] Related to this, Neal Gorenflo of Shareable makes the distinction between 'transactional sharing', which is primarily motivated by profit and resource efficiency, and 'transformational sharing', which involves a shift in power relations that builds social capital and community resilience through cooperation and strengthening of the civic commons.[6]

Many governments have been slow to respond to the shocks caused by Uber, Airbnb and Deliveroo and their disruptions to transportation, the housing market and the freelance sector.[7] These so-called 'gig economy' platforms provide convenience to their users but also raise serious concerns as this seemingly 'inevitable march of progress' creates winners and losers, enriching start-up founders and investors while making it hard for gig workers, who are mostly independent contractors, to make a living.[8] Revelations about the treatment of ridesharing drivers and the precarity of gig economy workers has led to much criticism,[9] including suggestions that the sharing economy is not about trust at all but just a guise for 'monetizing [...] stuff and [...] labor in creative ways'.[10] Janelle Orsi, co-founder of the Sustainable Economies Law Center, is critical of the 'business-as-usual' approach taken by the commercial platforms and argues that current ownership structures leave the door open to greater centralization through mergers and acquisitions that lock out users of sharing services and fail to create new jobs in the economy.[11] Lisa Gansky has called for commercial sharing economy platforms to 'share more value with the people who make them valuable'.[12]

Trebor Scholz, a digital labour scholar from the New School, developed the term 'platform cooperatives' to describe a new category of enterprises that are concerned with protecting the financial interests of people who create value in the sharing economy through collective ownership and democratic governance.[13] Emerging platform co-operatives address concerns for social equity and worker's rights via new digital platforms that promote solidarity through worker-owned structures.[14] Stocksy United, for example, is an artist-owned stock photography platform cooperative which shares 50% of standard license fees with its owner-photographers.[15] And Green Taxi Cooperative is a ride-hailing service which distributes profits back to its 800 driver-owners and leverages procurement from local anchor institutions in Denver, Colorado, to support community wealth building.[16]

The sharing economy is an interesting hybrid between the public, private and community sectors and relies on a range of public goods and urban commons to operate effectively. Cities themselves have become important platforms for sharing as hubs of disruptive innovation, knowledge transfer and creative communities. Commercial platforms have taken advantage of the agglomeration benefits of the urban commons, including everything from the taxpayer-funded public roads, which are quickly becoming congested by ride-hailing operators,[17] and the unique culture and quiet enjoyment of neighbourhoods, which is being threatened as long-term rental stock is removed from the housing market and converted into short-stay accommodation.[18] As activist and co-founder of the Commons Strategies Group David Bollier reminds us, the enclosure of the commons is a recurring threat and happens when private sector interests, often working with the support of government, privatize or convert shared resources into private resources and treat them as tradeable commodities.[19]

Sharing Cities proponents tell a new story of the sharing economy grounded in grassroots innovation, municipal provisioning of shared infrastructure and diverse forms of sharing that engender social justice, economic democracy and ecological sustainability.[20] The idea of the Sharing City was pioneered by Shareable,[21] a non-profit action hub and news site for the sharing economy that uses narratives of change and enabling tools like collaborative mapping to encourage urban experimentation that brings civil society, local government and alternative market actors together to create new forms of sharing for the common good. Shareable launched the Sharing Cities Network, a grassroots initiative, to mobilize, inspire and connect sharing advocates around the world. To date, over 50 cities have run MapJams and ShareFests to connect the dots and activate sharing within local communities using collaborative mapping to make shared resources more visible, convene local stakeholders and create new opportunities for partnerships to emerge.[22]

This movement has inspired local governments to formally declare themselves Sharing Cities and drive new institutional arrangements through policies and programmes to make their city assets like public buildings, vacant land and open data more amenable to sharing.[23] The Seoul Metropolitan Government, for example, has made over 800 of its public buildings available to the community for use during idle hours, runs a start-up school to support the next generation of sharing entrepreneurs and has invested millions of dollars through subsidies from taxes paid by citizens.[24] Seoul designates sharing enterprises and organizations as part of its Sharing City programme if they commit to solving urban problems through sharing via the economy, welfare, culture, environment and transportation sectors.[25] Amsterdam became Europe's first Sharing City and convened an Ambassador Group with local representatives from the corporate, government and knowledge sectors to develop a programme of activities to support the ecosystem and prototype sharing projects. The Amsterdam municipal government has also run a pilot programme to make its meeting rooms available to organizations with a social impact mission.[26]

The 'city as a commons' is another approach to urban sharing that creates post-neoliberal pathways for local governments to play a key enabling role in making services, programmes and staff available to the community through new modes of collaborative urban governance. One of the best examples can be found in the City of Bologna's 'Regulation on Collaboration between Citizens and the City for the Care and Regeneration of Urban Commons', which supports active citizens to co-lead city interventions through collaboration agreements, an instrument that aligns deliberative processes and intent with a legal contract between citizens and the municipality.[27] Since the regulation passed in 2014 with the support of researchers from LabGov, over 280 citizen-led projects have signed collaboration agreements with the city under the regulation to co-govern shared resources. Examples of Bologna's 'city as commons' in action include a women's association that converted an unused city-owned building into an 'ethical boutique' to support migrant women, and various projects to restore children's playgrounds, create public murals and redevelop green open space.[28]

The examples of community-based forms of grassroots sharing, Sharing Cities and the 'city as commons' movements demonstrate how transformational practices create new contexts outside of neoliberal market and policy logics to support authentic modes of the sharing economy in the era of the Anthropocene. These alternative sharing economy approaches provide a guiding vision for urban actors to develop new socioeconomic practices through commoning (the social production of value) and mobilize civic agency through collaborative urban governance. Cities and citizens can share resources and use digital platforms to strengthen local communities, but resisting enclosure and maintaining technological sovereignty will be an ongoing challenge that will define the future of the sharing economy.

Work cited:

Shareable. 2018. *Sharing Cities: Activating the Urban Commons.* San Francisco: Shareable.

Time

→ Connectedness | evolution siblings | → Future | potential futures | scale | → Sensitivity

Taking Anthropocene Seriously

368

Barbara Adam (born 1945, located in the UK) is Emerita Professor at Cardiff University and Affiliate Scholar at IASS Potsdam. Social time is her primary intellectual project, resulting in five social theory research monographs and a large number of articles, whose relevance transcends disciplines and is taught across the arts and humanities as well as the social and environmental sciences. She is founding editor of *Time & Society*.

Actions
In nature
Are changing
Transformed to
(Re)producing nature
Acts as evolution processes
Agents are responsible
For their deeds with
Eventual effects
Un/known
Scales
Increasing
To all of nature
And potential futures
Unlimited connectedness
Unbounded interdependencies
Of everything now and then
Creating in/determined
Realities rippling
Onwards
Selves
Expanding
The personal
Becoming global
Encompassing all of past
Exposing our relation to stars
Revealing algae and fish
As evolution siblings
And kinship to
All unborn
Ethics
Enfolding
Responsibility
For reach of actions
Personal covers all futures
Institutions challenged to embrace
Ecological span of *Timeprint*
With care and concern
As guardians of
Not Yet

Ū

~~UN~~ → Resources

~~undermining belief in the uniqueness of human species~~ → New Materialism

~~unequal interconnectedness~~ → Climate Risk Communities

~~unguided by human choices~~ → Wilderness

~~urban darkness~~ → City

~~urban metabolism~~ → Natureculture

~~us and them~~ → Xenophobia

~~using law~~ → Client: Earth

~~utopia~~ → Development

V

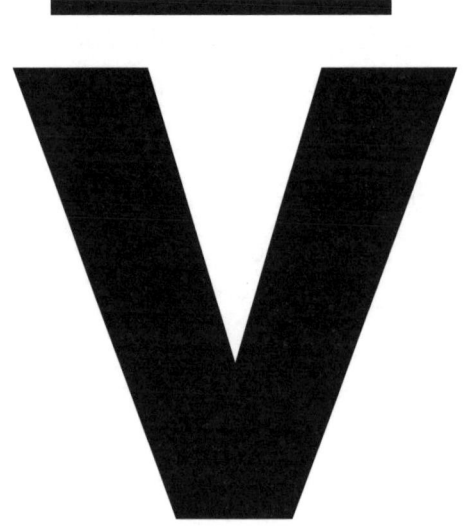

Violence

Niels Albertsen

~~violence against non-human nature~~ → Modernism

~~violence and power~~ → Violence

~~violent structures~~ → Violence

~~violent things~~ → Violence

~~voice of science~~ → Client: Earth

~~voice of the Earth~~ → Client: Earth

~~voice of the people~~ → Client: Earth

~~voluntary servitude~~ → Violence

~~vulnerability~~ → Pandemic

Violence

→ Anthropocene | → Body | → Connectedness | → Declaration of Rebellion | inclusive definitions of violence | → Power | pure violence | violence and power | violent structures | violent things | voluntary servitude

Violence and the Anthropocene. Why? Is the Anthropocene somehow violent? Does it challenge the concept of violence? The Anthropocene is about connectivity, so this text explores *violent connections*. Both violence and the Anthropocene are contested concepts, each of them calling for some clarification. Violence first.

Niels Albertsen (born 1945, located in Aarhus, DK) has an MSc in Political Science and from 2015 been Professor Emeritus at the Aarhus School of Architecture, which he joined in 1975. Since then, his research and teaching has evolved in an intersection between urban and social theory, architectural and design theory, the sociology of the architectural profession, and the sociology and philosophy of art.

Pure violence

The concept of violence is contested because violence comes in highly different forms. What counts as violence also varies with sociocultural and historical conditions. Violence is ambivalent too: violent actions may be immoral and illegal or moral and legal.[1] Hence, violence can be approached very differently and through mutually contested entries. Here, *pure violence* provides the entry following the intuition that whatever else violence may mean, most people will agree that pure violence is surely violence.

English political philosopher Thomas Hobbes's conception in *Leviathan* of a natural state among human beings is a convenient starting point. In the natural state, everyone is in a state of war of all against all. There is 'continual fear and danger of violent death', and the life of man is, in Hobbes's famous words, 'solitary, poor, nasty, brutish and short'. Only 'force and fraud' counts, and notions of right and wrong, just and unjust are (by definition) absent.[2] This is *pure violence* unfettered by any social or moral regulation. A similar idea of violence turns up in Prussian military theorist Carl von Clausewitz's classic *On War* as *pure or absolute violence*.[3] French contemporary sociologist Luc Boltanski theorizes along these lines too, relating to both Hobbes and Clausewitz. Violence is a regime of action that differs from other regimes of action: justification, fairness and love. Violence is conflict without any other 'rule' than force. 'To stop a force, it is necessary to relate to it in the mode of force and resist it'.[4]

In this conception, force becomes pure violence, because force in itself is unlimited. Unlimited force, however, encounters other limits. It is unbearable, insupportable. Human passion and reason confronts Hobbes's natural state. Passion: the fear of death and the desire for commodious living. Reason: reasonable rules for peace.[5] Clausewitz's absolute violence or *pure war* does not describe real war. Real war is always limited by politics. In his famous saying, war is the 'continuation of policy by other means'.[6] According to Boltanski, pure, absolute violence is 'an almost unthinkable limit for us'; it raises our 'indignation' at the interface of justice and violence.[7]

Legitimate violence

Pure violence, then, is first of all an abstract model. Pure violence certainly occurs in reality, but mostly limited, at least within the state, which in German sociologist Max Weber's famous formulation is 'a human community that (successfully) claims the *monopoly of the legitimate use of physical force* within a given territory'.[8] Hence, non-violent peaceful social intercourse is obtained not through the elimination of violence but through the legitimate use of some forms of violence and its monopolization in the state apparatus. Non-legitimate forms of violence are met by the counter-violence of the state. The state can 'keep the peace in the social body only if it is virtually at war with it'.[9] Violence is at the bottom of a non-violent society.

The scope of violence

What counts as violence? The most obvious image one gets from the above discussion is violence as 'bodily harm by physical use of force', which is an often used *restrictive* definition of violence.[10] But for Hobbes, also 'fraud' is violence, which gestures towards more *inclusive* definitions of violence. A very expansive one includes 'the use of power to harm another, whatever form it takes' be it physical, psychological, material, social or moral.[11] Such an expansion raises a lot of questions. One commentator worries that the concept of violence explodes into two separate concepts: violence as physical force and violence as *violation* of some limit or norm, for example of human rights.[12] Here, I shall comment on four other issues, first on British professor of criminal justice Stuart Henry's expansion of the concept of force into the concept of *power*.

Violence and power: In a late essay, French philosopher and social theorist Michel Foucault separated power and violence. Power presupposes the freedom of those acted upon, which means that power is acting upon other's actions rather than acting directly on bodies. Violence is understood restrictively as doing physical harm: 'violence acts upon a body or upon things; it forces, it bends, it breaks on the wheel, it destroys, or it closes the door on all possibilities; [...] slavery is not a power relationship when man is in chains'.[13] Violence is total domination; it annihilates freedom and the possibility that things could be otherwise. Power does not.

Voluntary servitude: Is there violence that is not recognized as such, violence that seems non-violent? French political philosopher Étienne de La Boétie thought so. He baptized it *voluntary servitude*, which 'does not proceed from an external constraint [as with Foucault's slave] but from the internal consent of the victim, himself becoming the accomplice of his tyrant'.[14] In the work of French sociologist Pierre Bourdieu, voluntary servitude re-emerges as *symbolic violence*. Symbolic violence 'is the violence which extorts submissions that are not even perceived as such by relying [...] on socially inculcated beliefs'.[15]

Violent structures: Human beings harming human beings physically or psychologically are clear incidents of violence. Bourdieu's symbolic violence cannot, however, be grasped at the level of individuals and groups in conflict; more structural or institutional forces are at work. In a seminal article, Norwegian peace researcher Johan Galtung defined two types of violence: *direct or personal*, where an actor (human) committing the violence can be identified, and *structural or indirect* violence, where none such actor exists. Violence is built into structures and occurs as unequal power and consequently as unequal life chances.[16] Later on, he added *cultural violence* as those aspects of the symbolic sphere of our existence that can justify or legitimize direct or structural violence.[17] Along similar lines, Slovenián Lacanian Marxist Slavoj Žižek distinguishes subjective violence performed by a clearly identifiable agent from objective violence, which comes in two forms: symbolic violence, which is embodied in language, and systemic violence, which concerns the often catastrophic consequences of our economic and political systems.[18]

Violent things: In Boltanski's regime of pure violence, human beings treat each other as things, as beings of nature, as forces of nature. This also means that there is no principal difference between a violent battle between (reified) humans and the battle of humans with 'a leaky oil well'.[19] Hence, if we follow Boltanski literally, our fight to survive a violent storm is a relation of violence just as much as a fight against a purely violent human being. While Foucault's concept of violence includes human violence against things (see above), Boltanski's concept includes the violence of things (non-human actors) against humans. Many will find this latter standpoint exaggerated; violence surely is a contested concept! But let one contested concept (violence) meet another (Anthropocene), and things may happen!

Anthropogenic violence

Anthropocene is a contested and contesting concept. The (hypo) thesis is that the Earth has entered a new geological epoch fundamentally marked by the impact of humanity entailing species extinctions, climate change and so on. The concept is *contested* for several reasons. Some geologists worry that the discipline is becoming improperly politicized, and some philosophers worry about outworn anthropocentrism. Hence: forget the concept. Marxists emphasize capitalism as the geological force, not humanity. Hence: Capitalocene. Disagreement rules the periodization, when did it start? Some say colonialism and slavery, hence: Plantationocene. Despite such contestability, the concept has shown useful as an umbrella for interdisciplinary dialogue between natural sciences and humanities and therefore also as a concept *contesting* received dualities such as nature versus culture, modernity versus tradition, global versus local. What does it imply for violence?

It provides backup to Boltanski's expansive, including, conception of physical violence. In the Anthropocene, physical violence is not limited to human beings. Violence is committed against the Earth, and the Earth strikes back, violently. Karl Marx understood the violence against the Earth. Capitalist agriculture is 'robbing the soil'; it ruins the lasting sources of fertility. Capitalist robbery (that is, violence) undermines 'the original sources of all wealth – the soil and the worker'.[20] In the Anthropocene context, this insight recurs as 'environmental violence', defined, for instance, as 'the use and extraction of natural resources in such a way as to preclude their sustainable use'.[21] Likewise, violence can take the form of direct physical violence against animals, as, for instance, in illegal 'shark finning', where sharks are caught at sea, their fins are cut off and the rest of the body is thrown back to the sea to slowly die. Purpose: shark-fin soup![22] Another form is 'slow violence', which occurs gradually and dispersed across time and space as climate change, deforestation, acidifying oceans 'and a host of other slowly unfolding environmental catastrophes'.[23] The Earth strikes violently back on humans through sudden as well as slow catastrophes: storms and floods, excessive rain, an increase of sea levels, the slow disappearance of island communities, the undermining of the living conditions of indigenous people, drought, crop failure, famine. The anthropocene Earth is connected in space and time. What happens violently to Amazonas may have violent climate repercussions on much larger spatial scales,[24] and irreversible anthropogenic changes in climate and biodiversity may slowly and violently affect future generations.

Anthropogenic violence occurs as violence among humans too. The abandonment by the United States of the 2016 Paris Agreement is a new kind of declaration of war. We Americans will continue our ways of producing and living whatever damages this may cost the rest of the world.[25] Direct physical violence has occurred as murder and the violent targeting of environmental defenders in Central America.[26] In France, direct physical violence has been used in the initially climate-generated conflicts between the Yellow Vests and the police forces, challenging the legitimacy and monopoly of state physical force. There are risks that future anthropogenic violence may include genocide[27] and that anthropogenic global warming will cause significant increases in premature deaths.[28]

Anthropogenic violence may be categorized and explained as structural-systemic violence, cultural-symbolic violence and direct, subjective violence. Fears of future developments may be dystopic. A global catastrophe cannot be avoided, it is said, and the result will be 'increased levels of malnutrition, starvation, disease, civil conflict and war'.[29] Life, it seems, will become 'solitary, poor, nasty, brutish and short', a Hobbesian war of all against all. Or it may be governed by an authoritarian state that turns the powers of potentialities into violent forces of total domination, relying as well on the symbolic violence of voluntary servitude legitimated by catastrophic narratives.[30] *Resistance* may take the form of anti-state and anti-capitalist struggles[31] in violent or non-violent forms. Étienne de La Boétie argued that voluntary servitude could and should be resisted by non-violent civil disobedience, precisely because servitude is voluntary. We can non-violently refuse to obey the tyrant. A movement like Extinction Rebellion seemingly performs such non-violent strategies against anthropogenic violence.

Works cited:

Abensour, Miguel. 2011. 'Is There a Proper Way to Use the Voluntary Servitude Hypothesis?' *Journal of Political Ideologies*, 16 (3), pp. 329–348.

Balibar, Étienne. 2015. *Violence and Civility: On the Limits of Political Philosophy*. New York: Columbia University Press.

Bendell, Jem. 2018. 'Deep Adaptation: A Map for Navigating Climate Tragedy'. *IFLAS Occasional Paper 2*. https://www.lifeworth.com/deepadaptation.pdf. Accessed 18 December 2019.

Bolt, Mikkel. 2019. 'Klimakampen blåstempler den autoritære stat'. *Politiken*, 24 November, part 2, p. 3.

Boltanski, Luc. 1990. *L'amour et la justice comme compétences: Trois essais de sociologie de l'action*. Paris: Éditions Métailié.

Bourdieu, Pierre. 1994. *Raisons pratiques: Sur la théorie de l'action*. Paris: Éditions du Seuil.

Bufacci, Vittorio. 2005. 'Two Concepts of Violence'. *Political Studies Review*, 3, pp. 193–204.

Clausewitz, Carl von. (1832) 2007. *On War*. Abridged with an introduction and notes by Beatrice Heuser. Oxford: Oxford University Press.

Foucault, Michel. 1983. 'The Subject and Power'. In Hubert L. Dreyfus and Paul Rabinow. *Michel Foucault: Beyond Structuralism and Hermeneutics: Second Edition with an afterword by and an interview with Michel Foucault*, pp. 208–226. Chicago: The University of Chicago Press.

Galtung, Johan. 1969. 'Violence, Peace, and Peace Research'. *Journal of Peace Research*, 6 (3), pp. 167–191.

Galtung, Johan. 1990. 'Cultural Violence'. *Journal of Peace Research*, 27 (3), pp. 291–305.

Haan, Willem de. 2008. 'Violence as an Essentially Contested Concept'. In Sophie Body-Gendrot and Pieter Spierenburg, eds. *Violence in Europe: Historical and Contemporary Perspectives*, pp. 27–40. New York: Springer.

Henry, Stuart. 2000. 'What Is School Violence? An Integrated Definition.' *Annals of the American Academy of Political and Social Science*, 567 (1), pp. 16–30.

Hobbes, Thomas. (1651) 1994. *Leviathan*. Edited by Edwin Curley. Indianapolis: Hackett Publishing Company, Inc.

La Boétie, Étienne de. (1576) 2002. *Discours de la servitude volontaire, suivi de les paradoxes de la servitude volontaire*. Paris: Vrin.

Marx, Karl. (1867) 1972. *Das Kapital: Kritik der politischen Ökonomie: Erster Band*. Berlin: Dietz Verlag.

Navas, Grettel, Sara Mingorria and Bernardo Aguilar-González. 2018. 'Violence in Environmental Conflicts: The Need for a Multidimensional Approach'. *Sustainability Science*, 13 (3), pp. 649–660.

Nixon, Rob. 2011. *Slow Violence and the Environmentalism of the Poor*. Cambridge, MA: Harvard University Press.

Parncutt, Richard. 2019. 'The Human Cost of Anthropogenic Global Warming: Semi-Quantitative Prediction and the 1,000-Tonne Rule'. *Frontiers in Psychology*, 10, article 2323.

Salcedo, Horacio de la Cueva. 2015. 'Environmental Violence and its Consequences'. *Latin American Perspectives*, 42 (5), pp. 19–26.

Stein Pedersen, Jakob Valentin, Bruno Latour and Nikolaj Schultz. 2019. 'A Conversation with Bruno Latour and Nikolaj Schultz: Reassembling the Geo-Social'. *Theory, Culture & Society*, 36 (7–8), pp. 215–230.

Weber, Max. 1946. 'Politics as a Vocation'. In H.H. Gerth and C. Wright Mills, eds. *From Max Weber: Essays in Sociology*, pp. 77–128. New York: Oxford University Press.

Zimmerer, Jürgen. 2014. 'Climate Change, Environmental Violence and Genocide'. *The International Journal of Human Rights*, 18 (3), pp. 265–280.

Žižek, Slavoj. 2008. *Violence*. New York: Picador.

W

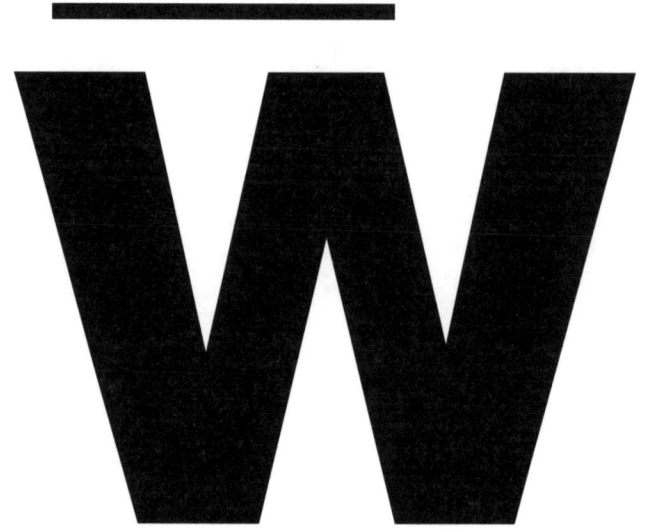

Waste Amanda Boetzkes
Water Astrida Neimanis
~~'we' are neither One, nor the Same~~ → Coexistence
Weather Astrida Neimanis and Jennifer Mae Hamilton
~~weather mapping~~ → Weather
~~weather measuring~~ → Weather
~~weathering~~ → Weather
~~wholes with holes~~ → Ecology
Wilderness Jason Mark
Window of Opportunity Mike Hulme
~~within species diversity~~ → Biodiversity
~~world risk society diagnosis~~ → Climate Risk Communities
World Scientists' Warning to Humanity
~~worlds of vibration~~ → Posthuman

Waste

aesthetic indifference | → Aesthetics | an inhabitor of life itself | → Environment | geochemical and geocultural agent | → Geology | → Plastic | → Pollution | quasi-life

Amanda Boetzkes (born 1976, located in Toronto, CA) is Professor of Contemporary Art History and Theory at the University of Guelph, Canada. She is the author of *Plastic Capitalism: Contemporary Art and the Drive to Waste* (2019) and *The Ethics of Earth Art* (2010) and co-editor of *Heidegger and the Work of Art History* (2014).

Waste is a geological agent that conditions land, water, climate and the future. Whereas in other historical eras waste was conceptualized and managed in a spatial paradigm by which it could be removed from human habitats and social visibility, today we are witnessing the collapse of the boundaries between interiority and exteriority along with the false binary of human/nature.

Plastic as geocultural agent

Take the case of plastic, an exemplary form of waste that is designed from its very production to be *disposable* – designed to be wasted – but which has now so permeated planetary ecosystems that microplastics can be found accumulating in Arctic sea ice and inducing genetic defects in animals. Australian cultural theorist Gay Hawkins argues that plastic must be understood through its patterns of emergent causation.[1] Rather than analyzing how external structures situate plastic in time and space, instead she reads the ways that plastic evolved through processes of chemical refinement, entrenching itself in social and material relations as it moved through global and planetary systems. Plastic generated a vital co-evolution of dense chemical programming, economic flexibility and the earth's material substrate, which exposed the limitations of waste management infrastructure. It now behaves as a geochemical agent and a geocultural schema.

At a key moment in the development of plastic, French philosopher Roland Barthes describes it in the following way: 'Whatever its final state, plastic keeps a flocculent appearance, something opaque, creamy and curdled, something powerless to ever achieve the triumphant smoothness of Nature.'[2] He wrote this in 1957, at a time when plastics were densely packed material monocultures; we might even say they were a mute waste by today's standards. But plastic became an increasingly informed material whose chemical make-up was thickened and enriched as it was designed to fulfil the demand to be cheap, available, sanitary, light, durable and expendable.[3] And it is exactly this informational richness that destines it to persist and become increasingly toxic as it accumulates in oceans, rivers, open-air landfills, in animal bodies, in the air. Plastic's force as a geocultural agent is fully revealed in the way it exposes the unthought of the economy – its total limitation as material intractability – in its recursion with the economy. In other words, plastic waste evolved in and through the paradoxical vectors of disposability and eternal return as pollution. As much as plastic has evolved to become more chemically complex, Barthes' fundamental analysis still holds, particularly in his reflection, 'It is impregnated throughout with this wonder: it is less a thing than the trace of a movement.'[4]

The economic criteria that dictated the chemical design of plastic destined it to a material reversal, whereby it became a virulent form of waste in its uselessness, persistence and recalcitrance. Its economic viability inverted, and it turned into its own economic antithesis. As it became an increasingly mobile and liquid medium that integrated into the biosphere on all possible levels, it transformed into a toxic element, an inhibitor of life itself. The spaces that once contained waste have collapsed entirely, and we now confront its return as a vital force that denaturalizes planetary ecologies and overturns the foundational concepts and material basis of biological life in its wake.

Waste as expressive medium

To describe plastic waste as a medium is also to suggest that it communicates and expresses. Inasmuch as plastic is an economic agent, it emerges in and through its interpenetration in social relations and subjectivities. It is in this sense that plastic can be thought of as an economic *expression*; its chemical refinement to market demands creates an ecological trajectory in much the same manner as the genetic expression of a DNA code. It shapes social parameters through its transposability across embodied registers of reaction while voiding itself as the cause or origin of any of them: the virtuosic chemical reactions that produce today's plastics induce allergic reactions (say asthma caused by carbon-based air pollutions), emotional reactions (oil addiction and its related climate change panic or denial), affective reactions (hollow affects, mimetic repetitions) or aesthetic reaction (a spontaneous replication of plastic as representation). Plastic reactions ultimately eliminate vitalities as they flatten scales, beings and objects into its common topology. The expressivity of waste lubricates the social pathways by which it travels as a geocultural agent.

Waste is the point at which economic expression can be understood through its systemic movement rather than merely the social relations it produces. The expressivity of plastic waste extends the logic and demands of the economy as an anarchical planetary wasting system. It would be fair to say, then, that it is an expression as we commonly think of it (a kind of spatial movement from the inner to the outer, from the economic system to its consumers, and outward to the planet at large as a communication of that very system). But it is also the dark antithesis of expression, pure reaction with no content and no defined spatio-temporal destination, only informational coordinates and force. As in the case of a chemical reaction, the catalytic movement is not so much intentional and directed as it is encompassing, and substantively irreversible. Whereas an expression might be subject to interpretation – 'what does this mean?' – a reaction is held to the basic mechanics of pure stimulus. But more pointedly, reaction becomes an indomitable material reality.

Waste not only embodies its economic value, its disposability; it developed this quality so thoroughly that it began to express the economy as a self-consuming vector. It not only stands for a new achievement of the capitalist drive that spurred its development; it has retroactively and quite uncontrollably informed that drive as a wasting operation. In other words, plastic is an economic expression of the self-eradication of that very economy. The return of plastic waste is the event of the self-voiding economy precisely *as* an ecological dilemma.

The *aesthesis* of waste

To consider the expressivity of waste is to address its aesthetic efficacy, how it moves through systems based on its appearance. Thus we can consider the expressivity and appearance of waste as an operation of *aesthesis*: a virulent movement across the planet in patterns of expression and reaction. But as part and parcel of this operation being an aesthetic movement per se, it may also raise the potential to be understood in and through its aesthetic *indifference*. While the analysis of waste from a socioeconomic perspective would lead us to understand the paradoxes of capitalism (its systemic drive toward its own collapse), if we were to interpret the aesthetic expression of plastic waste per se, we can see how its material form outstrips its economic expressivity and propels it into a future where its very usefulness – its disposability – has left it with no one to dispose of it. In its wasted form, plastic conjures a future in which it is the only species left. Plastic's reactivity propels it outside of the phenomenological experience of space and time and into a future in which it has supplemented life out of existence altogether. Once it has exited economic circulation, it wanders the planet, lonely for want of being used and disposed. Here is where plastic's recalcitrance betrays its dependency on social connection to ensure its circulation. It *wants* to insinuate itself into relations. Yet it also expresses environmental catastrophe: it is the harbinger of the catastrophe it brings. Waste is a material problem, the symptom of the problem and its ecological extension all in one. Its economic expressivity absorbs its social efficacy, leaving it behind as a quasi-life without a human society in which to dwell. In this recalcitrant state, its futural form, it becomes indifferent to humanity altogether.

In his unnerving series *Murmurations: Ephemeral Plastic Sculptures* (Fig. 1), French artist Alain Delorme constructs digitally manipulated photographs in which he shows multitudes of plastic bags that appear as a murmuration of starlings. The photographs produce an uncanny landscape dominated by a sense of the climate and atmosphere. The murmurations make their appearance against colourful skies, sunrises and sunsets, dawns and dusks. Yet the landscapes are dislocated from a ground in the human world. The perspective is noticeably suspended so that the tops of buildings, public monuments, wind turbines, factory smokestacks and power lines are suggested at the very bottom edge of the frame. The landscape is dominated by the sky and the murmuration that has taken flight from human infrastructure. Waste appears as a rhythmic but automated play of plastic bound up in fluxes of air.

The realization that the starlings are in fact plastic bags speaks to that material's invasion of natural life. The plastic bags are not the dense objects with the flocculent neon appearance of 1950s commercial plastics that Barthes describes. These objects are shadowy, nearly transparent, only becoming noticeable as they aggregate into black dots that mark the sky. The fluorescence of plastic has been redistributed from the objects to the pinks, peaches, yellows and bright blues of the sky itself. Plastic has been dispersed into a generalized ethos, released into the air to harmonize and synchronize with that element.

It is this mobilization of plastic in some kind of difference from its origin in human economy that is of interest. Here the photograph imagines the futural form of plastic waste as it projects across time and space as a geocultural agent. In putting plastic at odds with the social relations and economic ambitions it was designed for, it becomes possible to reconsider our reactivity to plastic and develop an alternative responsiveness to it. Art may offer the opportunity to resist the seemingly mandatory embrace of plastic precisely by bringing its inertia in planetary ecologies into visibility. At the very least, it shows us a condition in which this geocultural agent has become indifferent to the economy from which it originated.

Fig. 1. Alain Delorme Mumuration: *Ephemeral Plastic Sculptures #3*, 2012–2014
Courtesy of the artist and the Rutger Brandt Gallery

Works cited:

Barthes, Roland. 1972. 'Plastic'. In *Mythologies*. Translated by Annette Lavers. New York: Noonday Press.

Hawkins, Gay. 2013. 'Made to be Wasted: PET and Topologies of Disposability'. In *Accumulation: The Material Politics of Plastic*. Edited by Jennifer Gabrys, Gay Hawkins and Mike Michael. London: Routledge.

Water

→ Body | → Connectedness | → Creation | cycles | → Feminism | fluid | hydrosphere | → Imagine | life | → Natureculture | real

---

Except for perhaps some minute amounts of vapour that may enter our atmosphere from the cosmos, all the water that is here, on, in and hovering above our planet, has always been here. Each watery singularity has been somewhere, sometime before. Yet, while the water that moves through these cycles is always 'the same', it is by no means undifferentiated.

What repeats is always difference.[1]

384

Astrida Neimanis (born 1972, located in Sydney, AU) is a senior lecturer in gender and cultural studies at the University of Sydney. Her most recent book is *Bodies of Water: Posthuman Feminist Phenomenology* (2017).

water is
(a found poem)

Water is[2]
'water is siwlkw'[3]
water is thus in part to remind us of this still-pervasive ontological Old Boys' Club[4]
water is to stage a clubhouse break-and-enter[5]
water is a direct response[6]
'Water is siwlkw'[7]
Water Is What We Make It[8]
Water is to reimagine[9]
water is deterritorialized[10]
water is made known[11]
water is.[12]
'water is what we make it'[13]
'water' is our idea, our imaginary, our naming of matter in a way that corresponds to our worldviews[14]
water is also[15]
Water is thus also specifically[16]
water is always making us too[17]
water is not only fluid[18]
Water is one such 'experimental investigation'[19]
water is thus not only an experiment in human embodiment, but also a feminist commitment to following the flows of marginalization and injustice, as well as those of connection, empowerment, and joy that our watery corporealities collaboratively engender[20]
water is in fact engaged in a multiplicity of complex and co-implicated cycles[21]
water is in turn inaugurated into its own series of cycles – becoming plant breath, seed bath, muscle lubricant, protein folder, the fluid in your inner ear[22]
water is also the most restless[23]
water is evidently both finite and inexhaustible[24]
water is both exquisitely specific, yet also entirely mundane, and ubiquitous, and common[25]
Water is not only something we take in or use[26]
water is usually considered when[27]
Water is articulated as always both 'being' and a process of 'becoming' – gathering water from certain bodies and flowing back into others in return[28]
water is also both body and milieu[29]
water is what comprises bodies but also that which bathes bodies into being[30]
water is paradoxically[31]
Water is at once the originary condition of all possibility, but also its force of differentiation and wellspring of unknowability[32]
water is both common and intricately different[33]
Water is undoubtedly related to the fluid[34]
water is used in this text as a way of situating multiple 'feminines'[35]
water, is[36]
Water is necessary for maintaining our cell structure, for facilitating necessary chemical reactions in the body, for physically transporting nutrients and oxygen through the body, and for enabling waste elimination[37]
water is also productive of difference[38]
water is the element that crucially underpins these relations[39]
water) is never[40]
water is always becoming[41]
water is a unique iteration[42]

water is always an 'open system' as well[43]
water is needed for this[44]
water is in fact digging stealth channels through us all[45]
water, is not some amorphous matter[46]
water) is a permeable and regulating membrane[47]
water is contiguous with rather than analogous to these gestational species-seas[48]
water is often connected[49]
Water is life[50]
water is essential not only for the ongoing sustenance of any organism but also as a conduit for life-in-the-plural[51]
water is facilitative[52]
water is but one example of an impossible torsion[53]
water is also a limit at which a commonplace understanding of evolutionary temporality is torqued[54]
water is a situated knowledge[55]
water is also, somehow, mine[56]
water is also always beyond us[57]
water is never equally distributed across human bodies[58]
water is not simple, but[59]
water is inexhaustible – the things that it does and the bodies it proliferates[60]
water is deceptively strong, and persistent[61]
water is not quite clear but nonetheless iridescent[62]
water is also us[63]
water is life[64]
Water Is Life[65]
water is what we make it[66]
water is 'false'[67]

water is life[68]
water is is inextricable[69]
water is changeable[70]
water is thus[71]
water is what we[72]
water is also deterritorialized in a universalized and uniform cyclical schema, becoming 'placeless'[73]
water is the same as any other[74]
water is also 'operating on a global scale'[75]
water is directly conditioned by[76]
water is 'how much water is there in the world?'[77]
water is understood as the amalgamation of millions of smaller units[78]
water is are already[79]
Water is reinstated as something 'out there' that we can claim, and remains abstracted from our own implication in a hydrocommons with material contours and limits[80]
water is in our contemporary socio-historical moment spurs me[81]
water is thus, in the first place, a suggestion to pay more attention to the hydrosphere as the (again, oft-overlooked) fascia that lubricates and connects the Earth's lithosphere to its biosphere and atmosphere, those more popular players in this Anthropocene drama[82]
water is 'made'[83]
water is a giant tsunami[84]
water is the dominant kind of water[85]
water' is thus one alternative[86]
water is certainly[87]
Water is a living, spiritual being with its own responsibilities to fulfil'[88]
water is an integral part of spiritual life, but these questions are not separable from quotidian experiences of boil-water advisories[89]
water is, and always has been[90]
water is not a static 'thing'[91]

Water is also multiple[92]
Water is not, in this sense, a passive backdrop or 'resource'[93]
'Water is a relation'[94]
water is also kin[95]
(water is our literal kin)[96]
water, is a floating signifier, constantly realigning and resignifying in context[97]
water is understood as alive, rather than as mute matter[98]
water is life[99]
water is life[100]
water is life[101]
water is life[102]
water is life[103]
Water is life, water is life, water is life[104]
Water is Life?[105]
water' is both something we already are and a certain embodied orientation and potential we can amplify[106]
water is life[107]
water is abstracted[108]
water is life[109]
'water is life', too (so buy me!)[110]
'water is life' as an imaginary[111]
'water is life' into a commodity[112]
water is life[113]
water' is One Water[114]
'water is life' ethos[115]
water is life[116]
water is life[117]
'water is life' is not just a statement[118]
water is precious[119]
'water is life' – a phrase that repeats over and over again[120]
'water is life' in the context of a highly racialized imaginary[121]
'Water is life' morphs[122]
water is life on a terrain where 'life' has already been dangerously co-opted?[123]
'water is life' where life-fulfilment is drenched in heteronormativity and family values, saturated by straight time and a progress narrative of messianic future orientation?[124]
'water is life' is in the service of[125]
water, is made and unmade,[126]
'water is life' can be repeated, but to very different ends[127]
'water is life' is both an alibi, and a diversion[128]
water is water, one water is same as the next – [129]
'water is life' comes to support the very idea it hopes to challenge[130]
'water is life', despite the risks of co-optation that this involves[131]
'water is what we make of it'[132]
water is an idea, it is a material, embodied idea[133]
water is life[134]
water is life[135]
water is not an imposter that must be pushed aside so that the 'real' water can stand up[136]

Work cited:

Neimanis, Astrida. 2017. *Bodies of Water: Posthuman Feminist Phenomenology.* London: Bloomsbury.

Weather

→ Body | → Geo-Social Classes | human-weather relation | politics of privilege | → Resilience | situated knowledge | → Violence | weather mapping | weather measuring | weathering

---

Weather is the relation between socially, culturally, politically and materially differentiated bodies and the materiality of place, across a thickness of historical, geological and climatological time. Not all bodies weather the same; weathering names the situated, differentiated and durational embodied experience of living in political and ecological worlds. In the face of the current climate crisis, *weathering* thus means learning to live with the changing conditions of rainfall, drought, heat, thaw and storm *as never separable from* the 'total climate'[1] of the social, political and material existence of bodies. *We are always weathering.*[2]

In Western contexts, weather conditions are typically managed for us in a range of ways (for example, through architecture, technology, commodity culture, infrastructure, economic rationale). These forms of management produce a particular kind of human-weather relation. While such management is accompanied by discourses that encourage us to practice individual resilience and understand the weather as an entirely meteorological phenomenon, how can we insist that the need for a particular kind of relation with the more-than-human environment must also stake a claim for a different kind of sociality and politics? If weathering is never neutral, how might we learn to weather differently?

With its specific feminist, antiracist and decolonial intersectional attentiveness, such an understanding of weather, and weathering, would recommit to the need for an analysis of structural and systemic violence as essential to thinking through life in a changing climate. It would enable us to talk about the ethics of exposure, necessarily in relation to the political economies of place. It recognizes the need for shelter while remaining critically attentive to the politics of shelter, always textured by gender, race, class, accessibility, species and other embodied markers.

We know, however, that thinking and engaging the weather beyond dominant meteorological frames is tricky. What specific tactics might we adopt to pay better attention to the fact that weather, and weathering, is never neutral? How might we attune ourselves to the differentiated, durational and embodied experience of weather?

Astrida Neimanis (born 1972, located in Sydney, AU) is a senior lecturer in gender and cultural studies at the University of Sydney. Her most recent book is *Bodies of Water: Posthuman Feminist Phenomenology* (2017).

Jennifer Mae Hamilton (born 1982, located in Armidale, AU) is a lecturer in literary studies at the University of New England, on unceded Anaiwan Country. Her first book is *This Contentious Storm: An Ecocritical and Performance History of King Lear* (2017). Her current research examines the relationship between weather and housework. With Astrida Neimanis, she is co-founder of COMPOSTING Feminisms and Environmental Humanities.

Exercise 1
Gathering weathers

Begin by assembling your own weathering collective of two or more humans, in addition to who- or whatever else seems amenable to participating. Begin by discussing, what is climate change for you? Pay attention to the ambient weather conditions. Ask yourselves, is climate change here? How? Where? After reflecting on your responses, engage in the exercises below according to your bodily capacities, interests and time availability. We recommend undertaking all of the exercises outside, but if this isn't possible, bear in mind that all places in which we dwell make and are made by weather.

Exercise 2
Weather mapping through the body

Begin by asking, what is weather? How do we understand weather – according to bodily sensoria, cultural frames and temporal and spatial scales? How might our understanding of weather shift if we loosen and interrupt its quotidian frames of reference?

Gather index cards (or small pieces of paper), envelopes, a vessel for holding envelopes, a journal (or paper) and a writing implement for each participant. Then, copy statements such as the following onto a series of index cards (one per card), or think of your own:

- Notice what is around you and observe the relations, objects and infrastructures that define your situation. How do these mediate your relation to the weather?
- Is weather shared? How and by whom or what? Is weather individualized? In what ways?
- Move (either walking or rolling) your body slowly across a short distance. Can you notice the weather that you are passing through? Does it change?
- Stick out your tongue. What does the weather taste like? Can you bring the weather inside your mouth? Can you swallow it? What is the weather in your belly?
- If you can, put your hands in the air. What is the weather in the sky? If you can, put your hands on the ground. What is the weather on or in the ground?
- Lie down on the ground, or relax in a seated position. Can you make the weather a blanket? Can you make this blanket wrap more tightly, or loosely, around your body?
- Close your eyes. Inhale and exhale deeply through your nose. How does the weather smell?
- Extend your hand, palm facing up, out in front of you. Close your eyes. Can you hold the weather? What is the quality of that weather? Could you put the weather in your pocket?
- Close your eyes. Can you hear the weather? What are its sounds and rhythms?
- What was the weather on the day you were born?
- What will the weather be on the last day of Earth?

Place the index cards into small envelopes. You can write notes of encouragement on the envelopes such as, 'Be playful and take this seriously!' 'Enjoy and be rigorous!' 'Have fun and work hard!' Place the envelopes in a bowl. Invite participants to work individually or in pairs. Each participant or pair should choose an envelope and engage with the instruction. When finished, they should replace the instruction in the bowl. (Note: all bodies are different, with different capacities. Any of the instructions can be rejected or adapted to suit the needs of everybody.) Repeat as many times as you wish in the given time frame. Some activities can be completed in a few minutes; others may take 15 minutes or more, depending on the participant's depth of engagement.

Discuss and reflect: How did you respond to the instructions? Were some instructions easier, more difficult, more interesting, troubling? What did you learn about weather, your body and their relation?

Exercise 3
Do-it-yourself weathering meteorologist

Begin by asking, what is weather? Which meteorological elements do we assume can be measured and which ones can't (or shouldn't) be? What kinds of expertise are needed to measure weather? How are bodily and experiential knowledges relevant for weather measurement? How and to what extent is meteorology a form of situated knowledge?[3]

Gather up various materials and objects such as glue, fabric offcuts, pipe cleaners, scrap paper, pens, sticky tape, shoelaces, stones, a cup, plastic bag, phone charger, bike lock, sponge, butter knife, condoms or other random items.

Invite individuals or pairs to make a weather measurement device that responds to the location, using the items at hand. Encourage participants to be capacious in how they define the weather. Then, share the different devices and ask the makers to explain the logic of their device to the group.

Discuss and reflect: What new understandings of weather did these measurement devices engender? How might we rethink how and why weather is measured in certain ways, and by certain tools?

Exercise 4
Weathering without

Begin by asking, what is the difference between need and want in relation to shelter from weather? Who has power and authority to decide? How do politics of privilege, marginality and difference work to determine adequate or sufficient conditions for weathering well?

Read out the following instruction to the participants: If shelter is a necessity for living, what constitutes your 'shelter' (in the form of architecture, tools, devices, technologies, protection, props or aids)? What do you need in order to weather the world?

Ask each participant to catalogue all of the weather management devices and technologies they have in their life (from socks to windows to air conditioning) on a piece of paper. Then, going round in a circle, invite everyone to share their different devices and technologies. After hearing other inventories, participants can add items to their personal lists.

Instruct participants to pass their list to the person beside them clockwise. That person has to delete one of the items from the list they receive and then pass it again clockwise to the next person, who has to delete another item. Keep passing until your list returns to its original owner. What kinds of 'shelter' are left?

Invite participants to reflect out loud on life without the devices and technologies that have been struck from their list.

Discuss and reflect: What privileges and/or difficulties inform how you manage weather, or how it is managed on your behalf? How does it feel to possess the power to control the management of weather for others? How did you choose what to strike from others' lists? What was your emotional response to having certain items struck from your own list?

Works cited:

Haraway, Donna. 1988. 'Situated Knowledges: The Science Question in Feminism and the Privilege of Partial Perspective.' *Feminist Studies*, 14 (3), pp. 575–599.

Neimanis, Astrida, and Rachel Loewen-Walker. 2014. 'Weathering: Climate Change and the "Thick Time" of Transcorporeality.' *Hypatia: Journal of Feminist Philosophy*, 29 (3), pp. 558–575.

Neimanis, Astrida, and Jennifer M. Hamilton. 2018. 'Weathering.' *Feminist Review*, 118, pp. 80–84.

Sharpe, Christina. 2016. *In the Wake: On Blackness and Being*. Durham: Duke University Press.

Wilderness

→ Attention | beyond the human | → Chthulucene | → Description | → Dystopia | → Earth Ethics | → Earthlings | ethical guide | → Invisible | → New Materialism | → Plantationocene | → Posthuman | there is no away but there is still afar | unguided by human choices

What if we are all living in a computer simulation?

The idea would seem laughable, like some Hollywood scriptwriter's set-up for a dystopian melodrama. Yet one of the world's most influential futurists believes it just might true: our existence may be nothing more than the carefully crafted artefact of an advanced civilization.

That notion comes courtesy of Nick Bostrom, the Swedish philosopher at the University of Oxford who, in a turn-of-the-century paper for *Philosophical Quarterly*,[1] posited that, given the advances in computing power, it's logical to imagine that our universe has been conjured by the computers of the future. Maybe your consciousness, along with the whole of 'reality', is just an experiment being run by a future techno-civilization. Could it be that you're really just some bot's PhD project?

A group of American physicists, intrigued by the philosopher's parlour game, has proposed an empirical way to test Bostrom's hypothetical.[2] They say they can prove whether our universe is a computer simulation by looking at cosmic rays and examining whether they show the same kind of anomalies that are produced in today's computer recreations of cosmic phenomenon.

Jason Mark (born 1975, located in Oakland, US) is the editor-in-chief of the American environmental magazine *Sierra* and the author of *Satellites in the High Country: Searching for the Wild in the Age of Man* (2015). His writings have appeared in *The New York Times*, *Los Angeles Times*, *The Atlantic* and *The Nation*, among other publications. He is also a co-founder of the largest urban farm in San Francisco.

Here's a simpler, perhaps old-fashioned method for the physicists and futurists (and you, too) to test whether we are living inside a computer simulation. Drive out of the city, past the suburbs, through the farm fields and the orchards, and continue until the tarmac gives out. Keep going until you reach the end of gravel roads, and from there start walking. Continue walking until you reach one of those few remaining places where you are just a speck among the riot of other happenings. Look around. Listen. Smell. Get up close and touch something else that's alive. Pay close attention and try to spot wildness – that is, anything that is not dominated by human desires, imaginings or actions.

Now ask yourself whether the world is a computer simulation.

Run that kind of experiment in physical living and you're likely to discover proof of something important: here in the Anthropocene, Earth's last surviving wildernesses are an invaluable cultural asset. For in wilderness, we connect ourselves to the last refuge of the real.

As the evidences piles up that the activities of industrial civilization have become an evolutionary force – that we are on the verge of a new geologic age – it has become fashionable in some quarters to dismiss the value of wilderness. After all, if wild nature now rests inside of and is surrounded by civilization, doesn't that make wilderness obsolete? In the Human Age, perhaps wilderness has become little more than a vestigial biome.

Yet as we settle further into the Anthropocene – and especially as the technological advances of the information economy wrench our attention even tighter into all-human horizons – it is becoming clear that wilderness is actually more important than ever. Given that nearly 10% of the world's terrestrial wilderness has been lost in the last 25 years, the new importance of wilderness would seem to follow a basic axiom: like anything, wilderness becomes more valuable as it becomes scarcer.

'Wilderness' is a squirrely word (as those 25-year-old critiques pointed out), but here's a good working definition: wilderness is any place that is not controlled by human intentions or dominated by human actions. Pay special attention to that wording – wilderness doesn't mean pristine. Especially here in the Anthropocene, there is no place that is completely untouched by humanity. Civilization makes its impact felt everywhere, whether in the form of rising temperatures, disrupted weather, chemical pollution or the detritus of the atomic age. There is no *away*.

But there is still *afar* – which is to say, lands or waters that are beyond the reach of routine human control or intervention. Such places remain essentially still self-willed and sovereign. In the wilderness, the wishes and whims of human civilization count for little. There, life continues much as it has for millennia. Wilderness may be endangered, but it remains substantial; altogether, wilderness comprises about 23% of Earth's terrestrial surface outside of Antarctica.

It is imperative that we protect and defend these last wild places.

Preserving lands in their wild state is obviously a biological necessity. The untamed areas that remain will be essential refugia as climate chaos intensifies. (If anything, the overall area of wild lands should increase, ideally to around 50% of the planet, in order to maintain global biodiversity.) We need to preserve wilderness as a place where evolution can continue to unspool as it always has, unguided – if not unaffected – by human choices.

At the same time, wilderness is equally important as a cultural asset, as humanity's last link to the Holocene. This is especially true now that we have become an urban species entwined in (or is it *entombed* within?) our infrastructure. We are like the ants who labour always inside the anthill, oblivious to the fact that there is an entire forest outside; many, if not most, humans have never crossed the border into the non-human world. To preserve wilderness, then, is to preserve people's opportunity to, at the very least, glimpse something beyond the human. Wilderness is our final connection to the eons from which we arose.

On a humanized planet, wilderness provides perspective – our last, best chance of discovering an enduring ethics for human-nature relations. 'Nature's silence is its one remark,' American author Annie Dillard wrote

in her essay 'Teaching a Stone to Talk'. Spend some time in the backcountry, deep off-road and far from the grid, and one of the first things you'll notice is the unremitting silence. Nothing much happens in the woods, and what does happen would go on regardless of whether there's a human witness, much less a human hand to guide.

The pure disinterest of such quiet is 'awful' (Scottish–American naturalist John Muir's description, actually[3]), at once infinite and intimate. Among the most common observations people make when confronted with wild nature is that the landscape makes one feel small. Another way of describing this sensation would be to say that in the wild we are *right-sized*. The wild puts us in our place, a spot somewhere beneath the pinnacle of all existence.

The wild's indifference may be uncomfortable, but as a kind of ethical pedagogy it is essential, especially in this self-proclaimed age of human rule. Consider the songbirds. They still call to each other even as emails are piling up. They offer us nothing except the thrill of their song. Which is to say, their own selves. By resisting our entreaties and our flatteries, the songbird asserts its wildness, its sovereignty. In the wilderness – unlike in the domesticated landscapes of the Anthropocene – other critters are as autonomous as we are.

Solidarity begins with a recognition of equality. To be confronted by the inhuman of the wild is to remember that we are animals. When we are reminded of our animal condition, we return to a more equal plane with the other inhabitants of Earth. And with that recognition should come, hopefully, an acknowledgement of our responsibilities to the rest of life on Earth and our accountability to the human generations that will come after us. By forcing us to see – if only for a weekend visit – the other forms of life we share the globe with, wilderness can be a sort of ethical guide through the tests and challenges of the Anthropocene.

And what if those lessons are insufficient? What if civilization's steel glove keeps grasping more and more from the forests and the savannahs and the rivers and the mountains? Or what if Nick Bostrom's warnings come true, and a tyrannical Artificial Intelligence decides to rub out *Homo sapiens*? In that case, we're going to be glad to have had the foresight to keep some landscapes outside of the matrix and beyond the reach of omnipresent connectivity, if nothing else than to serve as the last redoubts to mount a final defence of the wild nature from which all of our artefacts spring.

Grandiose paranoia? Maybe.

Would you care to run the simulation?

Lucas Foglia
Kate in an EEG Study of Cognition in the Wild, Strayer Lab, University of Utah, 2015
Photo from the series *Human Nature*
Courtesy of Michael Hoppen Gallery, London, and Fredericks & Freiser Gallery, New York

Works cited:

Bostrom, Nick. 2003. 'Are You Living in a Computer Simulation?'. *Philosophical Quarterly*, 53 (211), pp. 243–255. https://www.simulation-argument.com/simulation.pdf. Accessed 15 January 2020.

Greene, Preston. 2019. 'Are We Living in a Computer Simulation? Let's Not Find Out'. *The New York Times*, 10 August. https://www.nytimes.com/2019/08/10/opinion/sunday/are-we-living-in-a-computer-simulation-lets-not-find-out.html. Accessed 15 January 2020.

Muir, John. 1987. *My First Summer in the Sierra*. New York: Penguin.

Window of Oppor-tunity

→ Anthropocene | appropriateness of action | → Attention | changing our 'minds-eye' | → Earth Ethics | imagination | → Time | timing

'We have a window of only 10–15 years to take the steps we need to avoid crossing catastrophic tipping points.' So said former UK Prime Minister Tony Blair in October 2006 in an open joint letter with his Dutch counterpart, Jan Peter Balkenende, to fellow EU leaders.[1] We are now nearly 15 years on from 2006, and many commentators might say Blair was prescient. The steps have *not* been taken, they would say, and the planet is indeed about to cross catastrophic tipping points.

On the other hand, whilst Blair's window has now virtually closed, other windows seem to have opened up. As reported in *National Geographic* in March 2019, 'A new scientific analysis of millions of possible climate futures found only a narrow window to keeping global warming to levels the international community has deemed safe.'[2] This 'narrow window' is in fact the forthcoming decade of the 2020s. Some public voices have used the IPCC's 2018 special report on 'Global Warming of 1.5 °C' to create a new 'window of opportunity' to limit global warming, one that will close in 2030 if global emissions of greenhouse gases are not halved by then.[3]

And this seems to be the problem with the metaphor of windows of opportunity as applied to climate change. They open and they close. And new ones are invented with different vistas, time frames and opportunities. I wonder what Blair would do today now that his 10–15 year 'window of opportunity' has closed? Look for a different window or give up on opportunities altogether? This too is the problem with the linked metaphor of ticking clocks. There are several climate clocks that are now ticking,[4] second by second, to some presumed end date after which it will be 'too late'.

Mike Hulme (born 1960, located in Norwich, UK) is Professor of Human Geography at the University of Cambridge and fellow of Pembroke College. His work illuminates the numerous ways in which the idea of climate change is deployed in public, political and scientific discourse. He is the author of nine books on climate change, including most recently *Contemporary Climate Change Debates* (2020).

Windows

A window is something one usually *looks through*, whether looking out or looking in. Windows create a separation between a here and a there but, at the same time, a transparency between these two created worlds. A window therefore offers up the imaginative possibility of being in a different place to where one currently is. The root meaning of the Old Norse word 'window' is, literally, a 'wind-eye' or an 'eye-hole'. One's eye, and hence one's mind and being, can be transported, tantalizingly, through the window into a different world.

So what then is a window of opportunity? Is it an open, shuttered or triple-glazed window? An opportunity to change one's actions or one's position in the world, or indeed to 'step-through' the window and change that world? Can we think of the Anthropocene as a window of opportunity? I want to explore briefly two ways in which we might frame this metaphor of a window of opportunity: acting within a definitive time frame versus acting in an appropriate way. I will suggest that whilst the idea of climate crisis might suggest the former, the idea of the Anthropocene points us much more towards the latter.

Acting in a definitive time frame

People often use the phrase 'window of opportunity', or 'critical window', to describe a period or unit of time during which an opportunity must be seized to achieve some desired outcome or else lost (perhaps forever). The association here is that of a window that opens for a while and then closes. It highlights the fleeting nature of opportunity, where timing is everything. Acting too early might be as bad as acting too late. Once this period is over, once the window has closed, the specified outcome is no longer possible. Thus there was a launch window for the Apollo space rockets, and the unsettled weather in the English Channel in early June 1944 gave General Eisenhower a fleeting window of opportunity to launch the Allies' invasion of Normandy.

Central to this reading is the urgency of some action. The 'time window' is limited; it will close, after which it will be too late. *Carpe diem* – seize the day. Act now. In the 1990s, the American political scientist John W. Kingdon introduced the term 'policy window'. In his thinking, three streams had to converge on a specific time in order for policymaking to happen: problems, proposals and politics. When these streams were propitiously aligned, and only when, then a policy window opened up, an opportune time to enact a specific policy. When a policy window is recognized and is open, there is a potential for policymaking to happen. The associated idea of the policy entrepreneur captures the notion of an action leader who then takes advantage of these open windows.

This framing of windows is all about timing – urgency, action, now is the time, before it is too late. One might say we are in such a discursive moment right now with respect to climate change.

Seeing a different world of actions
But there is another way of thinking about windows of opportunity. Rather than thinking temporally, we need to think imaginatively, windows not delineated by time but by an imagination. The window in this reading opens up a different world into which we can step. I suggest that we should think about the Anthropocene not as a temporally circumscribed opportunity – act now before it is too late; rather, it is an invitation to see the world, and our actions in the world, differently. The window is much more about framing a view than it is about defining a time. It is about changing our 'mind's eye'.

In political theory, the Overton Window refers to the *range of policies* that the public will accept at any one time. Its originator, in the 1990s, was American Joseph P. Overton, a former vice president of the Mackinac Center for Public Policy in Michigan. Policies falling outside the Overton Window are deemed to be out of step with public opinion and the current political climate. They are unimaginable. This is subtly different from Kingdon's policy windows. For Kingdon, the window is the limited time within which one can act, not the scope of those actions; for Overton, the window defines the range of imaginable actions, not their timing.

This second framing of windows is all about the appropriateness of the action – what is imaginable, virtuous, appropriate and feasible. One might say then that the idea of the Anthropocene is changing the Overton Window, changing the range and nature of how humans think imaginatively about their actions in the world. The Anthropocene invites us not to end a crisis within a limited window of time but to think differently about what virtuous human actions actually are.

Chronos* and *kairos
The ancient Greeks had two words to designate time: *chronos* and *kairos*. The former refers to chronological or sequential time, a unit of time which had a beginning and an end. The latter signifies a proper or an opportune action that takes place in an 'eternal now'. Early Christian theology developed a particular view of time as *kairos*. Discerning *kairos* for the Christian is a call for action – a conversion and transformation, a specific change of lifestyle and an orientation towards God. So acting releases God's moment of grace, *his* window of opportunity to bestow forgiveness.

Kairos implies a proper time to act or, rather, that there is always a proper action that we are called upon to make.

It is always possible to act improperly within the *chronos*, but with *kairos* it is never too late to act properly. The difference is between a quantity of time within which one acts and the opportuneness of the present time to act in particular ways in the world. With *kairos*, time is not rationed. The right actions are always opportune.

Aaron Hess, professor of rhetoric at Arizona State University, thinks of *kairos* as capturing both timeliness *and* appropriateness: what is said or done must be appropriate to the moment. Combining these two aspects of *kairos* offers a more extensive understanding of a window of opportunity. It turns our focus as much, if not more, towards the propriety of the action than on being preoccupied by the limited ration of time available to us in which to act. There is in fact no limit to the time within which we should act appropriately. As for the Christian, the call to repentance – the *kairos* – is always now.

Inspired by *kairos*, I contend that the Anthropocene encourages us to think carefully, ethically and creatively about the propriety of our actions in the world, about their virtue. It does not invite us to calculate the end point after which such actions are ineffective. The Anthropocene is not a crisis to be resolved through decisive action within a limited unit of time. The Anthropocene is offered to us as a description of a new condition of being human, an invitation to think differently about ourselves, the material world in which we are embedded, and about the conjoined future of the Anthropos and materiality.

The window of opportunity that is opened by the Anthropocene is captured much better by *kairos* than by *chronos*. The Anthropocene requires a commitment from us – a particular form of commitment – of being knowledgeable of and involved in the environment where the transformation is taking place. It is about seizing the opportune moment, appropriately. And, if one can do this, that moment is always now.

Works cited:

IPCC. 2018. 'Global Warming of 1.5 °C'. http://www.ipcc.ch/report/sr15/. Accessed 16 December 2019.

Leahy, Stephen. 2019. 'Climate Study Warns of Vanishing Safety Window – Here's Why'. *National Geographic*. https://www.nationalgeographic.com/environment/2019/03/climate-change-model-warns-of-difficult-future/, 12 March. Accessed 17 January 2020.

MCC. 2019. Mercator Research Institute on Global Commons and Climate Change. https://www.mcc-berlin.net/fileadmin/data/clock/carbon_clock.htm. Accessed 17 January 2020.

Watt, Nicholas. 2006. 'Blair Warns of Climate Change "Tipping Points"'. *The Guardian*, 20 October 2006. https://www.theguardian.com/world/2006/oct/20/greenpolitics.politics. Accessed 17 January 2020.

World Scientists' Warning to Humanity

→ Atmosphere | → Client: Earth | → Earth Ethics | → Environment | → Food | moral obligation | → Pollution | → Soil | → Water

At the time of this book's publication, the warning had 13,471 scientist signatories. The increasing number of signatories can be tracked on https://scientistswarning.forestry.oregonstate.edu/

Observations from the editor

'Scientists have a moral obligation to clearly warn humanity of any catastrophic threat and to "tell it like it is". On the basis of this obligation and the graphical indicators presented below, we declare, with 11,000 scientist signatories from around the world, clearly and unequivocally that planet Earth is facing a climate emergency.'

William J. Ripple et al., 2019.

In 1992, Henry W. Kendall, chair of the Union of Concerned Scientists, wrote 'World Scientists' Warning to Humanity'. In it, 1,700 of the world's leading scientists signed the warning, including 104 Nobel Prize winners in the sciences, a majority of the, at the time, living recipients.

'Human beings and the natural world are on a collision course.'
[...]
'A new ethic is required – a new attitude towards discharging our responsibility for caring for ourselves and for the earth. [...] This ethic must motivate a great movement, convincing reluctant leaders and reluctant governments and reluctant peoples themselves to effect the needed changes.'

Henry W. Kendal, 1992.

Twenty-five years later, in 2017, more than 15,000 scientists signed 'World Scientists' Warning to Humanity: A Second Notice', written by Professor of Ecology William J. Ripple at Oregon State University. This second notice featured graphs corresponding with the original points, illustrating the continuation of the environmental issues.

'This prescription was well articulated by the world's leading scientists 25 years ago, but in most respects, we have not heeded their warning. Soon it will be too late to shift course away from our failing trajectory, and time is running out.'
[...]
'We must recognize, in our day-to-day lives and in our governing institutions, that Earth with all its life is our only home.'

William J. Ripple et al., 2017.

In 2019, a third warning was signed and published in *BioScience* magazine: 'World Scientists' Warning of a Climate Emergency'. The warning includes six interrelated steps to mitigate climate change: energy, short-lived pollutants, nature, food, economy and population.

'Despite 40 years of global climate negotiations, with few exceptions, we have generally conducted business as usual and have largely failed to address this predicament.'
[...]
'The good news is that such transformative change, with social and economic justice for all, promises greater human wellbeing in the long-run than business as usual.'

William J. Ripple et al., 2019.

Works cited:

Kendall, Henry W. 1992. *World Scientists' Warning to Humanity*. https://www.ucsusa.org/resources/1992-world-scientists-warning-humanity. Accessed 10 December 2019.

Ripple, William J., Christopher Wolf, Thomas M. Newsome, Mauro Galetti, Mohammed Alamgir, Eileen Crist, Mahmoud I. Mahmoud and William F. Laurance. 2017. 'World Scientists' Warning to Humanity: A Second Notice'. *BioScience*, 67 (12), pp. 1026–1028. https://academic.oup.com/bioscience/article/67/12/1026/4605229. Accessed 21 August 2019.

Ripple, William J., Christopher Wolf, Thomas M. Newsome, Phoebe Barnard and William R. Moomaw. 2019. 'Worlds Scientists' Warning of a Climate Emergency'. *BioScience*. https://scientistswarning.forestry.oregonstate.edu/sites/sw/files/Ripple2019_Bioscience.pdf. Accessed 10 December 2019.

WORLD SCIENTISTS' WARNING TO HUMANITY

INTRODUCTION Human beings and the natural world are on a collision course. Human activities inflict harsh and often irreversible damage on the environment and on critical resources. If not checked, many of our current practices put at serious risk the future that we wish for human society and the plant and animal kingdoms, and may so alter the living world that it will be unable to sustain life in the manner that we know. Fundamental changes are urgent if we are to avoid the collision our present course will bring about.

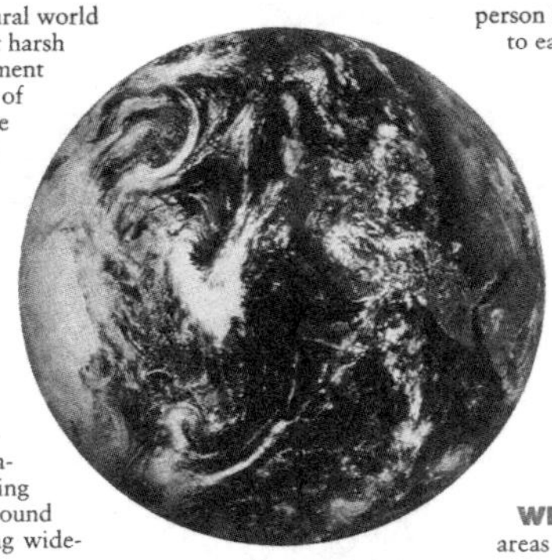

THE ENVIRONMENT The environment is suffering critical stress:

The Atmosphere Stratospheric ozone depletion threatens us with enhanced ultraviolet radiation at the earth's surface, which can be damaging or lethal to many life forms. Air pollution near ground level, and acid precipitation, are already causing widespread injury to humans, forests, and crops.

Water Resources Heedless exploitation of depletable groundwater supplies endangers food production and other essential human systems. Heavy demands on the world's surface waters have resulted in serious shortages in some 80 countries, containing 40 percent of the world's population. Pollution of rivers, lakes, and groundwater further limits the supply.

Oceans Destructive pressure on the oceans is severe, particularly in the coastal regions which produce most of the world's food fish. The total marine catch is now at or above the estimated maximum sustainable yield. Some fisheries have already shown signs of collapse. Rivers carrying heavy burdens of eroded soil into the seas also carry industrial, municipal, agricultural, and livestock waste—some of it toxic.

Soil Loss of soil productivity, which is causing extensive land abandonment, is a widespread by-product of current practices in agriculture and animal husbandry. Since 1945, 11 percent of the earth's vegetated surface has been degraded—an area larger than India and China combined—and per capita food production in many parts of the world is decreasing.

Forests Tropical rain forests, as well as tropical and temperate dry forests, are being destroyed rapidly. At present rates, some critical forest types will be gone in a few years, and most of the tropical rain forest will be gone before the end of the next century. With them will go large numbers of plant and animal species.

Living Species The irreversible loss of species, which by 2100 may reach one-third of all species now living, is especially serious. We are losing the potential they hold for providing medicinal and other benefits, and the contribution that genetic diversity of life forms gives to the robustness of the world's biological systems and to the astonishing beauty of the earth itself.

Much of this damage is irreversible on a scale of centuries, or permanent. Other processes appear to pose additional threats. Increasing levels of gases in the atmosphere from human activities, including carbon dioxide released from fossil fuel burning and from deforestation, may alter climate on a global scale. Predictions of global warming are still uncertain—with projected effects ranging from tolerable to very severe—but the potential risks are very great.

Our massive tampering with the world's interdependent web of life—coupled with the environmental damage inflicted by deforestation, species loss, and climate change—could trigger widespread adverse effects, including unpredictable collapses of critical biological systems whose interactions and dynamics we only imperfectly understand.

Uncertainty over the extent of these effects cannot excuse complacency or delay in facing the threats.

POPULATION The earth is finite. Its ability to absorb wastes and destructive effluent is finite. Its ability to provide food and energy is finite. Its ability to provide for growing numbers of people is finite. And we are fast approaching many of the earth's limits. Current economic practices which damage the environment, in both developed and underdeveloped nations, cannot be continued without the risk that vital global systems will be damaged beyond repair.

Pressures resulting from unrestrained population growth put demands on the natural world that can overwhelm any efforts to achieve a sustainable future. If we are to halt the destruction of our environment, we must accept limits to that growth. A World Bank estimate indicates that world population will not stabilize at less than 12.4 billion, while the United Nations concludes that the eventual total could reach 14 billion, a near tripling of today's 5.4 billion. But, even at this moment, one person in five lives in absolute poverty without enough to eat, and one in ten suffers serious malnutrition.

No more than one or a few decades remain before the chance to avert the threats we now confront will be lost and the prospects for humanity immeasurably diminished.

WARNING We the undersigned, senior members of the world's scientific community, hereby warn all humanity of what lies ahead. A great change in our stewardship of the earth and the life on it is required, if vast human misery is to be avoided and our global home on this planet is not to be irretrievably mutilated.

WHAT WE MUST DO Five inextricably linked areas must be addressed simultaneously:

1. We must bring environmentally damaging activities under control to restore and protect the integrity of the earth's systems we depend on. We must, for example, move away from fossil fuels to more benign, inexhaustible energy sources to cut greenhouse-gas emissions and the pollution of our air and water. Priority must be given to the development of energy sources matched to Third World needs—small-scale and relatively easy to implement.

We must halt deforestation, injury to and loss of agricultural land, and the loss of terrestrial and marine plant and animal species.

2. We must manage resources crucial to human welfare more effectively. We must give high priority to efficient use of energy, water, and other materials, including expansion of conservation and recycling.

3. We must stabilize population. This will be possible only if all nations recognize that it requires improved social and economic conditions, and the adoption of effective, voluntary family planning.

4. We must reduce and eventually eliminate poverty.

5. We must ensure sexual equality, and guarantee women control over their own reproductive decisions.

The developed nations are the largest polluters in the world today. They must greatly reduce their overconsumption, if we are to reduce pressures on resources and the global environment. The developed nations have the obligation to provide aid and support to developing nations, because only the developed nations have the financial resources and the technical skills for these tasks.

Acting on this recognition is not altruism, but enlightened self-interest: whether industrialized or not, we all have but one lifeboat. No nation can escape from injury when global biological systems are damaged. No nation can escape from conflicts over increasingly scarce resources. In addition, environmental and economic instabilities will cause mass migrations with incalculable consequences for developed and undeveloped nations alike.

Developing nations must realize that environmental damage is one of the gravest threats they face, and that attempts to blunt it will be overwhelmed if their populations go unchecked. The greatest peril is to become trapped in spirals of environmental decline, poverty, and unrest, leading to social, economic, and environmental collapse.

Success in this global endeavor will require a great reduction in violence and war. Resources now devoted to the preparation and conduct of war—amounting to over $1 trillion annually—will be badly needed in the new tasks and should be diverted to the new challenges.

A new ethic is required—a new attitude towards discharging our responsibility for caring for ourselves and for the earth. We must recognize the earth's limited capacity to provide for us. We must recognize its fragility. We must no longer allow it to be ravaged. This ethic must motivate a great movement, convincing reluctant leaders and reluctant governments and reluctant peoples themselves to effect the needed changes.

The scientists issuing this warning hope that our message will reach and affect people everywhere. We need the help of many.

We require the help of the world community of scientists—natural, social, economic, political;

We require the help of the world's business and industrial leaders;

We require the help of the world's religious leaders; and

We require the help of the world's peoples.

We call on all to join us in this task.

SPONSORED BY THE UNION OF CONCERNED SCIENTISTS, TWO BRATTLE SQUARE, CAMBRIDGE, MA 02238-9105

The first warning from 1992.

X

Xenophobia Georg Metz

Xeno-
phobia

→ Borders | → Care | dehumanization | → Denial | fatherland | international conventions | → Migration Flows | threat | us and them

Lexicon
Xenophobia:
From Greek: *xenos*, 'stranger'; *phobos*, 'fear or flight from'. Often used to mean hatred.

Credo
Strangers are a threat. They come to our country harbouring evil intentions, they are lazy and cannot be bothered to learn the language, although they know just enough to take advantage of our welfare services and game the system. They are cunning and calculating, carry dangerous diseases and bring with them contagion, primitive cultures and crappy religion.

Document
A politician warns against Romanies and their filthy Romany camps, he says.
A Speaker of Parliament will meet Muslims with unwavering opposition, she says.
A cabinet minister brings cake to work to celebrate the countless new restrictions in the laws and regulations targeting strangers. Strangers should not be allowed to cross the border. Rejected asylum seekers with so-called tolerated status will be treated intolerably, says the minister.
The strangers' religious beliefs and mindsets hang like a sword of Damocles over the vulnerable majority culture. Only the people whose ancestors have built this country over a millennium and who know and appreciate its culture and values will know how to manage and steward the country as it is and should be.

Georg Metz (born 1945, located in Copenhagen, DK) studied history at the University of Copenhagen. He was a former chief editor (at the newspaper *Information*), on Danish radio and TV, a journalist, executive consultant in the film industry, former chairman of the Danish Writers Association, columnist, writer and exhibiting visual artist. He has published several titles of fiction, novels and short stories as well as non-fiction on Danish history and literature.

The people is in tune with the land.
Earth to earth.
Those who are not of the earth are strangers. Strangers are not of the people but are invasive and undermine our cohesion.
Culture is like the *Volkskörper*, the national-ethnic body: fragile and overwhelmed by the influx of strangers, regardless how many or how few, since a few is always too many.
Thanks to their superior procreative capacity, the strangers will take over and dominate the country and ultimately drive out the people.
The strangers breed like rats. No, rabbits, says the Speaker.
Therefore it is necessary to try to ward them off by any and all means necessary, to stand up to the threat and to expel the ones who fail to assimilate one-to-one in faith and lifestyle, thought and words.
Alternatively: destroy the strangers if it has to come to that.

Liturgy
The true victim is the people and the community, as defined by origins and past. National exclusivity describes its natural right to the realm by means of these categories. The nation should define the values contained in history and faith, based on varying needs and with the goal of legitimizing the rejection of strangers or the expulsion of undesirables. Or xenophobia.
The country is divided into us and them. The differences are irreconcilable. When some speak up in the name of tolerance and co-existence and invite the strangers into the nation and community, their tolerance is viewed as the elite's betrayal of the country's inviolable national-ethnic body.

History lesson
Dislike of newcomers, fear of them, where fear turns to disgust or hatred, expressed in animal metaphors, is not traditionally limited to internal minorities in the present but has a long narrative stretching into the past and generally appears in national images of 'the other' with a clear xenophobic quality. The Nazis' use of the term 'racially alien' conveyed the threat using the metaphor of vermin and infestations. Rats and lice leech off the resources of the fatherland and must be neutralized. The end justifies the means, whether the means is DDT or Zyklon B.

The colonels in the Greek coup d'état in 1967 excised tumours from the diseased body of society, disinfected the fatherland and incarcerated political opponents in concentration camps. Danish post-war propaganda in the film *Danmark i Lænker* (Denmark in Chains) from 1945: two German soldiers in the frame are presented by the narrator as 'scab mites'. A view of a scab mite in a microscope moving diagonally across the screen dissolves into a shot of soldiers, viewed from an oblique overhead angle, making the same diagonal movement. The Germans are not persons but strangers; they are enemies, vermin: disease carriers to be eliminated like scab mites. Callousness is not the reserve of others.

Reflection

Strangers, and people who are defined as such, are marginalized in relation to an extreme nationally and religiously conditioned, alleged state of cohesion and normalcy in the original population.

'Us and them' defines right versus wrong, genuine versus imposters, good versus bad. Incompatibility rooted in the contrast between the truly human versus the opposite.

The latter is not only the stranger but the *enemy*, not like us, as being part of *we* is the condition for being true and good. Strangers are human, but only by species. Their emotions are not like ours; their pain is not deep, like the pain of those who are true, their suffering only superficial since they do not distinguish between good and evil. They are not human. Dehumanization is the condition for the ultimate consequence of xenophobia and contempt of strangers in the form of draconian measures of exclusion.

Nazi Germany did not begin to kill Jews on an industrial scale until the Jewish population had been dehumanized in social, physical and health terms.

The Nuremberg Race Laws (1935) stripped the Jewish population segment of all legal rights and incrementally limited and thus step by step, through thousands of ordinances and laws, rendered Jewish daily life and conditions impossible.

As this population group was visibly discriminated against and marked by imposed poverty, hunger and abuse, the final deportation process was facilitated by the loss of rights that preceded their ultimate destruction. Jews were not human and German but inferiors and, as victims of circumstance, filthy, tattered, unclean. Like Romanies.

Eventually, they had no tears left, no resistance before the destruction. They no longer had human feelings. They were not like us but merely rats and scab mites.

Warning

Since the genocide of the Armenians, since the Nazis' extermination of Jews, Gypsies, homosexuals and opponents of the regime, since the genocides in the former Yugoslavia and additional genocides in Africa, nations have made a concerted effort, using international law and justice and binding conventions, to prevent or hinder crimes against minorities and humanity in the form of genocide and other forms of general and specific abuse.

International conventions and courts are the tools.

Through legislation, the nations have surrendered judicial sovereignty to a specific degree with a view to enforcing the universal guarantees safeguarding human rights.

Driven by xenophobia, both before and after the refugee crises, angry people have attacked these conventions and the international agreements. Nationalist parties and opinion leaders argue that the legal protection is a threat against the nation state.

Moral

If the international order, arduously established after the demeaning experiences of the 20th century, is eroded, unrestrained xenophobia will celebrate new triumphs and add new crimes to a staggering account.

Without binding standards for the international community in formal treaties, the gateway is open to the next chapter of humanity's gloomy story.

MISSOURI
3610 Miles.
AMAZON
3130
IENESEI
3115
YANG-TSE
3237
NILE
2700
OBE
2179
VOLGA
2100
JOLIBA
QUORRA
2000
St LAWRENCE
2000
LA-PLATA
1830
DANUBE
1700
INDUS
1700
GANGES
1650
EUPHRA
1530
NEW ORLEANS
Natchez
St Louis
NANKIN
CAIRO
STRACHAN
QUEBEC
Montreal
BUENOS AYRES
Tatta
TOBOLSK
Kasan
Timbuktoo
Pest
Presburg
VIENNA
ATTOCK
Allahabad
El Bir
Ieneseisk
Tver
IRKOUTSK
Cape Horn
Cape Good Hope
Toluca

INE 37
ELBE 640
VISTULA 576
LOIRE 540
TAGUS 530
ODER 503
RHONE 442
SEINE 416
EBRO 400
SEVERN 350
PO 317
THAMES 204
SHANNON 192
FORTH 94
HAMBURG
Nantes
LISBON
Stettin
Havre
Tortosa
Bristol
Gloucester
LONDON
Limerick
Dunbar
EDINBURG
Rouen
Saragossa
PARIS
Frankfort
Orleans
LYONS
Turin
WARSAW
Breslau
Geneva
MADRID
DRESDEN
CRACOW
ASIA AND OCEANICA
AMERICA
Nevada de Sorata
Nevada d' Illimani
Gay-Lussac reached 23,100 ft in a balloon, in Sept 1804.
Chimborazo
Highest point reached by Humboldt
Highest growth of Lichens
HIMALAYA
Snow Line
Ararat
EUROPE
Heights of Assuay
AFRICA
Highest growth of Pines in the Torrid Zone
Lake of Titicaca
Snow
Etna
St. Bernard
Convent de St. Gothard
Grimsel Hospital
European Volcanoes
Briançon
San Ildefonso
Hecla
Stromboli
Vesuvius
BRITISH ISLANDS
Director's house at Leadhills
The highest inhabited place in Scotland
1280
Ailsa Craig
Bass

Notes

previous spread:
Ink-washed drawing from 1854 showing the comparative lengths of rivers and heights of mountains worldwide. Published in Adam & Charles Black, Sidney Hall and William Hughes, *General Atlas of the World: Containing Upwards Of Seventy Maps*, Edinburgh: A & C Black, 1854.

Aesthetics
1 Lewis and Maslin 2015. See also Lewis and Maslin 2018.
2 See Tsing 2015.
3 Norgaard 2011.

Agency
1 Schneider and Till 2009, pp. 97–111.
2 Brenner 2013, p. 44.
3 Giddens 1984, p. 14.

Architecture
1 Free Dictionary 2019.
2 UNESCO 2019.
3 Stengers 2015.
4 Haraway 2003.
5 Fisher and Tronto 1990, p. 3.
6 Ibid., p. 40.

Art
1 Dewey 2005, pp. 12–13.
2 Carson 1962.
3 Matilsky 1992, p. 36.
4 For example, Demos 2010.
5 For example, Thorsen 2019.
6 Demos 2010; Demos 2018, pp. 156–157.
7 For example, Demos 2018, p. 158.
8 For example, Malm et al. 2014; Haraway 2015; Haraway et al. 2016.
9 Latour 2014, p. 5.
10 Klingan et al. 2015.
11 For example, Gan et al. 2014; Vandsø et al. 2017.
12 Fukuoka 1993.
13 鶴見 (Tsurumi) 1967; Saito 2007; Saito 2017; Dewey 2005.

Atmosphere
1 Böhme 1999.
2 Böhme and Schramm 1985.

Attachment
1 Bennett 2001.
2 Latour 2014.
3 Gibson et al. 2015.
4 Bennett 2001.
5 Ibid., p. 12.
6 Haraway 2016.

Bacteria
1 Collated, e.g., in Margulis 1998.
2 MacFadden et al. 2018.
3 Haraway 2016, p. 61.

Capitalocene
1 Wilde 1892, p. 203.
2 Engels 1987.

Care
1 Haraway 2015.
2 Foucault 1984.
3 Heidegger 1996.
4 Whitehead 1920.
5 Latour 2013.
6 Tsing 2015.
7 Giraud et al. 2019.
8 Latour 2013.
9 Personal email communication, December 2019.
10 Dempster 2000, p. 5.
11 Ibid., p. 3.
12 Tsing 2015.
13 Harper 2019.
14 Stengers 2015.
15 Callén Moreu and López Goméz 2019.
16 Strathern 1988.
17 Strathern 1980.
18 See also Meulemans 2019; Puig de la Bellacasa 2019.
19 See also Munro 1996, drawing on Strathern 1991.
20 Latimer and López Goméz 2019.
21 Latimer 2013; Latimer 2019.

Chtuluscene
1 Bird Rose 2006, pp. 67–78.
2 For his first widely available Capitalocene argument, see Moore 2013 and Moore 2016.
3 See Haraway et al. 2015, pp. 1–30.
4 Refuge and resurgence are developed in Tsing 2015.
5 Detienne and Vernant 1974.
6 See Haraway 2014.
7 This glossary entry relies heavily on Haraway 2016.

Climate Risk Communities
1 Beck et al. 2013.
2 Beck 1999.
3 See Blok and Jensen 2019.
4 Latour 1993.
5 Haraway 1991.
6 Anderson 1983.
7 Beck et al. 2013, p. 2, italics added.
8 Blok 2015.
9 Beck 2010.
10 Blok 2019.
11 Data collection and visualization courtesy of issuecrawler. net, govcom.org Foundation, Amsterdam.
12 Blok and Jensen 2019.
13 Heise 2008.

Coexistence
1 Braidotti 2013; Braidotti 2017; Braidotti 2019a; Braidotti and Hlavajova 2018.
2 Hayles 1999.
3 Schwab 2015.
4 Kolbert 2014.
5 Guattari 2000.
6 Braidotti 2011.
7 Deleuze 2003.
8 Whyte 2016.
9 Viveiros de Castro 1998; Viveiros de Castro 2009; Descola 2009; Descola 2013; Braidotti and Bignall 2018.
10 Alaimo 2010.
11 Deleuze 1988.
12 Lloyd, 1994.
13 Guattari 2000.
14 Deleuze and Guattari 1994.
15 Moulier-Boutang 2012.
16 Shiva 1997.
17 Cooper 2008.
18 Gatens and Lloyd 1999.
19 Nixon 2011.
20 Braidotti 2013.

Connectedness
1 Woolf 1985, pp. 64–65.
2 Yeats and Arnold in Heaney 1980, p. 136.
3 Stein 1956.
4 Christensen 2000.
5 Haugland 2013.
6 Steffen 2017.
7 Jackson 2009, p. 6.
8 Hickel 2018.
9 Christensen 2000.
10 WEF 2019.

Declarations of Climate Emergency
1 Cedemia 2019.
2 Corbyn et al. 2019.

Description
1 Geertz 1773.
2 See https://www.snuneymuxw.ca/nation/culture.
3 Davis and Todd 2017, p. 763.

Development
1 Asafu-Adjaye et al. 2015, p. 6.
2 Berardi 2011, p. 18.
3 Ibid.
4 Stengers 2015, p. 23.
5 Welzer 2012, p. 6.
6 Snyder 2016, p. 327.
7 OHCHR 2019.

Earth Ethics
1 Darwin 1874.
2 Ibid., p. 120.
3 Ibid., p. 109.
4 Leopold 1949, p. 203.
5 Ibid., p. 204.
6 Darwin 1874, p. 127.

Energy
1 IPCC 2014.
2 IPCC 2018.
3 IEA 2019.
4 IPCC 2014.
5 IEA 2019.
6 World Bank 2019.
7 UN 2019.
8 IPCC 2018.

Environment
1 Luhmann 1995, p. 25.
2 Ibid.
3 Coleridge 1971, p. 472.
4 Clark 2015, p. 21.
5 Maturana and Varela 1992, p. 255.
6 Sloterdijk 2016, p. 230.
7 Maturana et al. 2004, p. 34.
8 Ibid.
9 Haraway 1991, p. 183.
10 Ibid., p. 193.

Facts
1 Wittgenstein 1922, p. 31.
2 Lombardus et al. 1989, p. 146.
3 Bacon 1858, p. 53.
4 Luhmann 2000, p. 1.
5 Festinger 1957.
6 Latour 2004, pp. 225–248.
7 Ibid., p. 227.
8 Rosling, Rönnl and Rosling 2018.

Feminism
1 hooks 2000, p. xi.
2 Grusin 2017.
3 Haraway 1988.
4 Glabau 2017.
5 TallBear 2019, p. 24.
6 Haraway 2015.
7 TallBear 2019, p. 38.
8 Söderbäck 2012.
9 hooks 2000, pp. x–xv.
10 Rendell 2011.
11 Gibson-Graham 2008.
12 TallBear 2019, p. 38.
13 Ibid., p. 25.
14 Tsing 2015.
15 Le Guin quoted in ibid., p. 287.
16 Petrescu 2007; Gibson-Graham 2008.
17 Lykke 2017.
18 Grosz 2001.
19 Ibid., p. 143.
20 Söderbäck 2012.
21 Grosz 2001.

Garden
1 Michelangelo Antonioni, Chung Kuo, Cina (1972).

Geo-Social Classes
1 Blok and Bruun Jensen 2019, pp. 1195–1211.
2 Marx 1987.
3 Marx 1992, p. 927.
4 Charbonnier 2018.
5 Steffen et al. 2015, pp. 1–18.

6 See, e.g., Moore 2015; Malm 2016; also the 'Capitalocene' entry in this encyclopedia, p. 92.
7 Latour 2017b; Latour 2017a.
8 Latour and Miranda 2019, pp. 60–73.
9 Charbonnier 2020.
10 See Latour, Stein Pedersen and Schultz 2019; Schultz 2020.

Global

1 Sassen 1991; Sassen 2014.

Heritage

1 Zalasiewicz et al. 2014, pp. 44–45.
2 Haff 2014.
3 Zalasiewicz et al. 2014.
4 Clark 2012, p. 260, italics added.
5 De Landa 1997, p. 103.
6 Szerszynski 2010; Szerszynski 2012.
7 Dibley 2018.
8 Westermann 2020.
9 Szerszynski 2012, p. 181.
10 Colebrook 2014, p. 40.
11 Yusoff 2013, p. 780.
12 Thacker 2011.
13 Ibid., pp. 5–6.

Local

1 Massey 1994, p. 154.
2 Le Guin 1986.
3 See also Ingold 1993; Ingold 2000.
4 Le Guin 1986.
5 Ibid.

Migration Flows

1 Castells 1996.

Moving Earths

1 Latour 2017b; Latour 2017a.

412

2 Latour 2017b.
3 Serres 1995, p. 86.
4 Koyré 1957.
5 Latour 2017a.
6 Charbonnier 2019.
7 Fichte 2012.
8 Schultz 2020b.
9 Osnos 2017.
10 Turkewitz 2019.
11 Haraway 2016.
12 Polanyi 2001.
13 Schultz 2020a.
14 Latour 2016.

Natureculture

1 UN 2018.

New Materialism

1 See, for example, Bennett 2010; Coole and Frost 2010.

Object-Oriented Ontology

1 Bogost 2012; Bryant 2011; Harman 2018a; Morton 2013.
2 Brassier et al. 2007, pp. 306–449.
3 Brentano 1995.
4 Twardowski 1977; Meinong 1988; Husserl 1993, pp. 345–387.
5 Russell 1905, pp. 479–493.
6 Norris 2013, pp. 38–47; Zahavi 2016, pp. 289–309.
7 Hume 1978.
8 Husserl 1970.
9 Harman 2007, pp. 21–30.
10 Kant 1987; Fried 1988.

Overpopulation

1 Malthus 1914.
2 United Nations 2019.
3 Hendrixson and Hartmann 2018.
4 United Nations 2019.
5 Ibid.
6 Wilson 2017, p. 441.
7 Sayre 2008.
8 Hynes 1999.
9 Hartmann 2017, pp. 174–175.
10 Sasser 2018.
11 Hartmann 2017.
12 Cited in Davis 2001, p. 32.
13 Connelly 2008; Hartmann 2016.
14 Hendrixson 2018.
15 Greenhalgh 2003.
16 Johnson 2016.
17 Dash 2019.
18 Kovensky 2019.
19 Ojeda, Sasser and Lunstrum 2019, p. 11.
20 Hartmann 2017.

Pollution

1 Carson 1962, p. 297.
2 See Davis 2014.
3 Ibid.
4 Carson 1962, pp. 32–33.
5 Ibid., p. 297.

Resilience

1 Lovell et al. 2016.
2 Alesso-Bendisch 2019.
3 Cicchetti and Blender 2004, p. 17325.
4 Bruneau and Reinhorn 2006, p. 1.
5 Rose 2004.
6 Gunderson and Holling 2001, p. 1.
7 Simonsen 2007.
8 Resilience Alliance 2018.
9 Gunderson and Holling 2001.
10 Walker and Salt 2006.
11 For this and the rest of the paragraph, ibid.
12 Gunderson and Holling 2001.
13 IPCC 2012, p. 563.
14 Simonsen et al. 2015.
15 Ibid.
16 Cutter et al. 2010; Adger 2000.
17 Simonsen et al. 2015.
18 For this and the following paragraph, ibid.
19 Ibid.
20 Norris et al. 2008; Ruth and Coelho 2007; Folke 2006.
21 Wilby and Dessai 2010.
22 Simonsen et al. 2015.
23 Moser 2008.
24 Norris et al. 2008; Osbahr 2007; Ostrom 2009.
25 Simonsen et al. 2015.
26 Ibid.
27 Osbahr 2007; Ostrom 2009.

Soil

1 Shiva 2016.
2 Howard 1947, pp. 4, 11.
3 Howard 1953, p. xv.

Terraforming

1 Puig de la Bellacasa 2017, p. 171.
2 Atwood 2011.
3 Puig del la Bellacasa 2017; Griffith 2019.
4 Kimmerer 2015.
5 Le Guin 2004.
6 Fjalland and Samson 2019.

The Sharing Economy

1 See https://theconversation.com/1-000-cars-and-no-garage-why-car-sharing-works-31179 (all links accessed 10 December 2019).
2 See http://www.melbournebikeshare.com.au/.
3 See http://www.streetbank.com/.
4 https://www.theguardian.com/commentisfree/2017/aug/30/nationalise-google-facebook-amazon-data-monopoly-platform-public-interest.
5 See http://www.washingtonindependentreviewofbooks.com/bookreview/raw-deal-how-the-uber-economy-and-runaway-capitalism-are-screwing-american.
6 See http://postgrowth.org/transactional-sharing-transformational-sharing-2/.
7 https://www.theguardian.com/technology/2015/jul/28/uber-lawlessness-sharing-economy-corporates-airbnb-google.
8 https://www.businessinsider.com.au/australia-uber-drivers-make-less-than-minimum-wage-2018-3?r=US&IR=T.
9 https://medium.com/the-nib/9ea5ba3d216d.
10 http://nymag.com/daily/intelligencer/2014/04/sharing-economy-is-about-desperation.html.
11 http://www.shareable.net/blog/the-sharing-economy-just-got-real.
12 https://www.fastcompany.com/3038476/collaborative-economy-companies-need-to-start-sharing-more-value-with-the-people-who-make-th.
13 http://www.rosalux-nyc.org/wp-content/files_mf/scholz_platformcoop_5.9.2016.pdf.
14 See http://www.shareable.net/blog/11-platform-cooperatives-creating-a-real-sharing-economy.
15 https://www.nytimes.com/2016/07/21/business/small-business/a-new-wrinkle-in-the-gig-economy-workers-get-most-of-the-money.html.
16 https://community-wealth.org/content/green-taxi-cooperative-building-alternative-corporate-sharing-economy.
17 https://www.apnews.com/e47ebfaa1b184130984e2f3501bd125d/Studies-are-increasingly-clear:-Uber,-Lyft-congest-cities.
18 https://theconversation.com/australian-governments-are-treading-lightly-around-airbnb-76389.
19 http://thinklikeacommoner.com/.
20 https://www.tandfonline.com/doi/full/10.1080/08111146.2017.1421533.
21 www.shareable.net.
22 http://www.shareable.net/blog/we-gathered-we-mapped-we-shared-a-mapjam-follow-up.
23 Shareable 2018.
24 https://www.shareable.net/blog/sharing-city-seoul-a-model-for-the-world.
25 http://sharehub.kr/sharestoryEn/resources_view.do?storySeq=83.
26 https://www.shareable.net/blog/amsterdam-to-launch-airbnb-style-rentals-of-municipal-buildings.
27 http://www.comune.bologna.it/media/files/bolognaregulation.pdf.
28 http://partecipa.comune.bologna.it/beni-comuni.

Violence

1 Haan 2008, pp. 28–29.
2 Hobbes 1994, pp. 76, 78.
3 Clausewitz 2007, p. 28.
4 Boltanski 1990, p. 116.
5 Hobbes 1994, p. 78.
6 Clausewitz 2007, pp. 16–17, 28.

7 Boltanski 1990, pp. 119–121.
8 Weber 1946, p. 78.
9 Balibar 2015, p. 32.
10 Haan 2008, pp. 30–31.
11 Henry 2000, p. 3, quoted in Haan 2008, p. 32.
12 Bufacci 2005.
13 Foucault 1983, pp. 220–221.
14 La Boétie 2002, p. 7, quoted in Abensour 2011, p. 332.
15 Bourdieu 1994, p. 190.
16 Galtung 1969, pp. 171–172.
17 Galtung 1990, p. 291.
18 Žižek 2008, pp. 2–3.
19 Boltanski 1990, pp. 115–116.
20 Marx 1972, pp. 529–530.
21 Salcedo 2015, p. 22.
22 Navas et al. 2018, p. 657.
23 Nixon 2011, p. 2.
24 Stein Petersen et al. 2019.
25 Ibid.
26 Navas et al. 2018, p. 656.
27 Zimmerer 2014.
28 Parncutt 2019.
29 Bendell 2018, p. 26.
30 Bolt 2019.
31 Ibid.

Waste

1 Hawkins 2013, pp. 49–67.
2 Barthes 1972, p. 98.
3 Hawkins 2013, p. 55.
4 Barthes 1972, p. 97.

Water

1 Neimanis 2017, p. 86.
2 Ibid., p. 1.
3 Ibid., p. 2.
4 Ibid., p. 3.
5 Ibid.
6 Ibid., p. 5.
7 Ibid., p. 9.
8 Ibid., p. 19.
9 Ibid.
10 Ibid., p. 20.
11 Ibid.
12 Ibid.
13 Ibid., p. 21.
14 Ibid.
15 Ibid.
16 Ibid.
17 Ibid., p. 22.
18 Ibid.
19 Ibid., p. 24.
20 Ibid., p. 64.
21 Ibid., p. 65.
22 Ibid., p. 66.
23 Ibid.
24 Ibid.
25 Ibid., p. 67.
26 Ibid.
27 Ibid.
28 Ibid., p. 68.
29 Ibid.
30 Ibid.
31 Ibid., p. 69.
32 Ibid.
33 Ibid., p. 78.
34 Ibid., p. 80.
35 Ibid.
36 Ibid., p. 81.
37 Ibid., p. 82.
38 Ibid.
39 Ibid., p. 85.
40 Ibid., p. 86.
41 Ibid., p. 89.
42 Ibid.
43 Ibid.
44 Ibid., p. 90.
45 Ibid., p. 94.
46 Ibid.
47 Ibid., p. 98.
48 Ibid., p. 106.
49 Ibid., p. 117.
50 Ibid.
51 Ibid., p. 124.
52 Ibid., p. 130.
53 Ibid., p. 131.
54 Ibid.
55 Ibid., p. 139.
56 Ibid., p. 143.
57 Ibid., p. 146.
58 Ibid.
59 Ibid.
60 Ibid., p. 147.
61 Ibid., p. 153.
62 Ibid., p. 154.
63 Ibid.
64 Ibid., p. 155.
65 Ibid.
66 Ibid.
67 Ibid., p. 156.
68 Ibid.
69 Ibid., p. 157.
70 Ibid.
71 Ibid.
72 Ibid.
73 Ibid., p. 158.
74 Ibid.
75 Ibid.
76 Ibid.
77 Ibid.
78 Ibid., p. 159.
79 Ibid.
80 Ibid., pp. 159–160.
81 Ibid., p. 160.
82 Ibid.
83 Ibid., p. 162.
84 Ibid., p. 168.
85 Ibid.
86 Ibid., p. 171.
87 Ibid.
88 Ibid., p. 172.
89 Ibid.
90 Ibid.
91 Ibid., p. 173.
92 Ibid.
93 Ibid.
94 Ibid.
95 Ibid.
96 Ibid.
97 Ibid., p. 174.
98 Ibid.
99 Ibid.
100 Ibid., p. 175.
101 Ibid.
102 Ibid.
103 Ibid.
104 Ibid.
105 Ibid.
106 Ibid., p. 176.
107 Ibid., p. 177.
108 Ibid.
109 Ibid.
110 Ibid.
111 Ibid., p. 178.
112 Ibid.
113 Ibid.
114 Ibid.
115 Ibid.
116 Ibid.
117 Ibid.
118 Ibid.
119 Ibid., p. 179.
120 Ibid.
121 Ibid., p. 180.
122 Ibid.
123 Ibid.
124 Ibid., p. 181.
125 Ibid.
126 Ibid.
127 Ibid., p. 182.
128 Ibid.
129 Ibid.
130 Ibid.
131 Ibid., p. 183.
132 Ibid., p. 184.
133 Ibid.
134 Ibid.
135 Ibid.
136 Ibid., p. 185.

Weather

1 Sharpe 2016.
2 Neimanis and Loewen-Walker 2014; Neimanis and Hamilton 2018.
3 Haraway 1988.

Wilderness

1 See Bostrom 2003.
2 See Greene 2019.
3 Muir 1987.

Window of Opportunity

1 Watt 2006.
2 Leahy 2019.
3 IPCC 2018.
4 MCC 2019.

Index

A
Adam, Barbara (1945–) 368
Addams, Charles (1912–1988) 306
Adolphsen, Peter (1972–) 282
Aerocene (2015-) 42, 43, 44, 45, 46, 47
Ahl, Sofie Isager (1988–) 40
Aït-Touati, Frédérique (1977–) 261
Albertsen, Niels (1945–) 374
Alston, Philip G. (1950–) 145
Anders, Günther (1902–1992) 175
Andersen, Gregers (1981–) 144
Andersen, Hans Christian (1805–1875) 345
Andersen, Kim Lenschow (1987–) 222
Anderson, Benedict (1936–2015) 114
Antonioni, Michelangelo (1912–2007) 198
Arendt, Hannah (1906–1975) 115
Arènes, Alexandra (1984–) 261
Aristotle (384–322 BC) 35, 126, 344
Arnold, Matthew (1822–1888) 123
Arrhenius, Svante (1859–1927) 201
Ashby, Ross (1903–1972) 166
Atwood, Margaret (1939–) 361

B
Bacon, Francis (1561–1626) 175
Bahadur, Aditya (1983–) 324
Baichwal, Jennifer (1965–) 58
Bakhtin, Mikhail Mikhailovich (1895–1975) 176
Balkenende, Jan Pieter (1956–) 396
Balkin, Amy (1967–) 57
Banerjee, Subhankar (1967–) 57
Bardi, Lina Bo (1914–1992) 53
Baring, Evelyn (1841–1917) 288
Barthes, Roland (1915–1980) 380, 383
Baudrillard, Jean (1929–2007) 175
Beck, Ulrich (1944–2015) 114, 115, 117
Bennett, Jane (1957–) 64, 65, 313
Berenthz, Marco (dates unknown) 170
Bergson, Henri–Louis (1859–1941) 313
Beuys, Joseph (1921–1986) 57
Biemann, Ursula (1955–) 57
Björk (Guðmundsdóttir) (1965–) 228
Blair, Anthony (Tony) Charles Lynton (1953–) 396
Blell, Mwenza (1979–) 82
Blok, Anders (1978–) 114
Boetzkes, Amanda (1976–) 380
Bogost, Ian (1976–) 280
Böhme, Gernot (1937–) 62
Bollier, David (1955–) 366
Boltanski, Luc (1940–) 375, 376
Bonpland, Aimé (1773–1858) 80, 81
Bosse, Rune (1987–) 230, 231
Bostrom, Nick (1973–) 392, 395
Bourdieu, Pierre (1930–2002) 375
Boyer, Dominic (dates unknown) 193
Braidotti, Rosi (1954–) 118
Branco, Miguel Rio (1946–) 96
Brecht Bertolt (1898–1956) 254
Brenner, Neil (1969–) 38
Brentano, Franz Clemens Honoratus Hermann (1838–1917) 280
Bricmont, Jean (1952–) 176
Bryant, Levi Reginald (dates unknown) 280
Bubandt, Nils (1964–) 126
Burtynsky, Edward (1955–) 58

C
Callicott, J. Baird (1941–) 152
Canguilhem, Georges (1904–1995) 313
Caple, Zachary (1979–) 300
Carson, Rachel (1907–1964) 178, 304, 305, 306, 307
Carus, Titus Lucretius (94–55 BC) 313
Castells, Manuel (1942–) 246
Charbonnier, Pierre (1983–) 205, 256, 258
Charrière, Julian (1987–) 291
Chebotareva, Polina (1989–) 66
Christiansen, Bjørnstjerne (1969–) 186
Christensen, Inger (1935–2009) 123, 124
Chung, Tiffany (1969–) 84, 86, 89
Clark, Timothy (1958–) 167
Colebrook, Claire (1965–) 220
Columbus, Christopher (1451–1506) 346
Comenius, John Amos (1592–1670) 343
Connolly, William Eugene (1938–) 313
Coole, Diana (1952–) 270
Crouch, Colin (1944–) 332
Crutzen, Paul J. (1933–) 53

D
da Vinci, Leonardo di ser Piero (1452–1519) 82
Dansgaard, Willi (1922–2011) 31
Darwin, Charles (1809–1882) 77, 153, 154, 155
Davis, Frederick Rowe (1965–) 304
Davis, Heather (1979–) 141, 302
de La Boétie, Étienne (1530–1563) 375, 377
de Pencier, Nicholas (dates unknown) 58
de Tracy, Antoine-Louis-Claude Destutt (1754–1836) 175
Debord, Guy (1931–1994) 175
Delorme, Alain (1979–) 381, 383
Demos, T. J. (1966–) 57
Dempster, Beth (dates unknown) 95
Derrida, Jacques (1930–2004) 168, 177
Despret, Vinciane (1959–) 97
Dewey, John (1959–1952) 56, 59
Dibley, Ben (1971–) 218
Dillard, Annie (1945–) 394
Dooren, Thom van (dates unknown) 97
Doyle, Kerry (dates unknown) 46

E
Ehrlich, Paul (1854–1915) 74
Eisenhower, Dwight David (1890–1969) 397
Ekins, Paul (1950–) 163
Eliasson, Olafur (1967–) 57
Elton, Charles (1900–1991) 305
Engel, Antke (1965–) 318
Engels, Friedrich (1820–1895) 93, 175
Eriksen, Thomas Hylland (1962–) 92
Extinction Rebellion (2008–) 38, 96, 98, 99, 113, 132, 377

F
Fang, Hu (1970–) 198
Faulkner, William (1897–1962) 123
Fenger, Jakob (1968–) 186
Ferriss, Hugh Macomber (1889–1962) 105
Festinger, Leon (1919–1989) 176
Fichte, Johann Gottlieb (1762–1814) 256
Fisher, Berenice (dates unknown) 54
Fjalland, Emmy Laura Perez (1987–) 64, 240, 360
Foglia, Lucas (1983–) 395
Forster, Edward Morgan (1879–1970) 344
Foucault, Léon (1819–1868) 175
Foucault, Michel (1926–1984) 94, 375, 376
Fried, Michael (1939–) 281

G
Galilei, Galileo (1564–1642) 175, 254, 255
Galtung, Johan (1930–) 375
Gammeltoft-Hansen, Thomas (1979–) 246
Gansky, Lisa (1961–) 365
Garnier, Charles (1825–1898) 105
Geertz, Clifford (1926–2006) 140
Giddens, Anthony (1938–) 39
Gilbert, Scott (1949–) 75, 101
Gilmour, David (1946–) 110
Gissen, David (1969–) 104
Gómez, Daniel López (dates unknown) 96
Gore, Albert Arnold (1948–) 266
Gorenflo, Neal (dates unknown) 365
Gormley, Antony (1950–) 63
Greenfort, Tue (1973–) 57
Greenhalgh, Susan (1949–) 288
Grégoire, Axelle (1986–) 261
Grosz, Elizabeth (1952–) 180, 181
Guin, Ursula Kroeber Le (1929–2018) 180, 240, 241
Guterres, António (1949–) 124

H

Haacke, Hans (1936–) 56
Hacking, Ian (1936–) 176
Haeckel, Ernst (1834–1919) 62, 77
Halsnæs, Kirsten (1956–) 162
Hamilton, Jennifer Mae (1982–) 388
Hannah, Dehlia (1978–) 34
Hansen, James (1941–) 123
Haraway, Donna (1944–) 54, 94, 95, 97, 100, 114, 127, 168, 178, 179, 180, 181, 257, 313
Hardin, Garrett James (1915–2003) 287
Harman, Graham (1968–) 280
Hartmann, Betsy (1951–) 286
Havsteen-Mikkelsen, Asmund (1977–) 250, 252
Hawkins, Gay (1954–) 380
Hedegaard, Connie (1960–) 354
Hegel, Georg Wilhelm Friedrich (1770–1831) 205, 206
Heidegger, Martin (1889–1976) 94
Hess, Aaron (1979–) 399
Hickel, Jason (dates unknown) 124
Hjortshøj, Rasmus (1979–) 66, 68
Hobbes, Thomas (1588–1679) 375
Hoffman, Steve (1953–) 257
Horn, Roni (1955–) 57
Howard, Sir Albert (1873–1947) 351
Howe, Cymene (dates unknown) 193
Hulme, Mike (1960–) 396
Hume, David (1711–1776) 280
Husserl, Edmund Gustav Albrecht (1859–1938) 280, 281
Høilund, Poul (1979–) 170
Håkansson, Henrik (1968–) 57

I

Iwatani, Yukiko (1958–) 58, 59, 60, 61

J

Jackson, Tim (1957–) 124
Jacobsen, Arne Emil (1902–1971) 268
Jeanneret, Charles-Édouard (Le Corbusier) (1887–1965) 105, 250, 251
Jencks, Charles Alexander (1939–2019) 251
Jensen, Carsten (1952–) 298
Jevons, William Stanley (1835–1882) 253
Johnsen, Sigfús (1940–) 31
Jones, Christine (dates unknown) 40
Just, Jesper (1974–) 146

K

Kant, Immanuel (1724–1804) 115, 281
Kendall, Henry Way (1926–1999) 400
Kingdon, John Wells (1940–) 397, 398
Klougart, Josefine (1985–) 122
Koyré, Alexandre (1892–1964) 255
Krasny, Elke (1965–) 52
Kristensen, Tom (1893–1974) 268
Kristiansson, Thérèse (1981–) 178
Krogh, Marianne (1965–) 13
Køppe, Simo (1951–) 138

L

La Frenais, Rob (1951–) 46
Lari, Yasmeen (1941–) 55
Latimer, Joanna (1954–) 94
Latour, Bruno (1947–) 14, 58, 65, 94, 95, 114, 177, 205, 254, 271
lenschow & pihlmann (2015-) 222
Leopold, Aldo (1887–1948) 154
Lessig, Lester Lawrence (1961–) 328
Lewis, Simon L. (dates unknown) 34
Lidegaard, Liv Sejrbo (1986–) 128
Lloyd, Genevieve (1941–) 119
Loos, Adolf Franz Karl Viktor Maria (1870–1933) 250
Louis XV (1710–1774) 187
Lovecraft, Howard Phillips (1890–1937) 103
Lovelock, James (1919–) 75, 254, 255, 259, 260
Luhmann, Niklas (1927–1998) 166, 176
Luther, Rikke (1970–) 328, 329, 330, 333, 334
Lundgaard og Tranberg Architects (1985-) 13, 17, 18, 19, 20, 22, 23, 24, 358, 359
Lykke, Nina (1949–) 180

M

Macron, Emmanuel Jean-Michel Frédéric (1977–) 259
Magnason, Andri Snær (1973–) 192, 193
Malm, Andreas (1977–) 101
Malthus, Thomas Robert (1766–1834) 286, 287
Mann, Paul Thomas (1875–1955) 348
Margulis, Lynn (1938–2011) 74, 75, 254, 255
Mark, Jason (1975–) 392
Marx, Karl (1818–1883) 92, 175, 188, 205, 206, 254, 258, 259, 376
Maslin, Mark A. (dates unknown) 34
Massey, Doreen (1944–2016) 241
Matilsky, Barbara (1953–) 56
Maturana, Humberto (1928–1958) 168
Mazé, Ramia (1974–) 178
McGlade, Christophe (dates unknown) 163
McKibben, Bill (1960–) 112
Meinong, Alexius (1853–1920) 280
Mendieta, Anna (1948–1985) 56
Metz, Georg (1945–) 404
Modi, Narendra (1950–) 288
Monteiro, Fabrice (1972–) 95, 96, 97
Montessori, Maria (1870–1952) 190
Moore, Jason W. (1971–) 54, 101
Moreu, Blanca Callén (dates unknown) 96
Morton, Timothy (1968–) 160, 280
Muir, John (1838–1914) 395
Musk, Elon Reeve (1971–) 257, 260

N

Neimanis, Astrida (1972–) 384, 388
Nielsen, Rasmus (1969–) 186
Nixon, Richard (1913–1994) 139
Nottveit, Anders (1988–) 352
NORRØN (2014-) 170

O

Orsi, Janelle (dates unknown) 365
Overton, Joseph P. (1960–2003) 398
Owens, Delia (1949–) 355

P

Pearl, Raymond (1879–1940) 287
Pihlmann, Søren Thirup (1987–) 222
Pompadour, Madame de (Poisson, Jeanne Antoinette) (1721–1764) 187
Polanyi, Karl Paul (1886–1964) 258

R

Rafn, Flemming (1976–) 266
Raleigh, Clionadh (dates unknown) 288
Rasmussen, Sidsel Kjærulff (1980–) 314
Rasmussen, Sune Olander (1974–) 30
Reed, Jim (1961–) 214
Rendell, Jane (1967–) 179
Ricardo, David (1772–1823) 93
Richardson, Katherine (1954–) 11
Rickert, Till (1976–) 314
Ripple, William J. (1952–) 400
Rohe, Ludwig Mies van der (1886–1969) 250
Romer, Paul Michael (1955–) 332
Roquet, Paul (1980–) 244
Rosing, Minik (1957–) 76, 200
Rosling, Hans (1948–2017) 177
Rottenberg, Mika (1976–) 270
Russell, Bertrand Arthur William (1872–1970) 280

S

Sachs, Carl Theodor (1985–) 352
SachsNottveit (2017-2020) 352
Saito, Yuriko (1950–) 59
Saraceno, Tomás (1973–) 42, 46, 47, 57, 308, 309, 310, 311
Sariola, Salla (1977–) 74
Sassen, Saskia (1947–) 210
Sayre, Nathan F. (dates unknown) 287
Schalk, Meike (1963–) 178
Schneider, Tatjana (1974–) 36
Scholz, Trebor (dates unknown) 365
Schrader, Gerhard (1903–1990) 304, 305
Schultz, Nikolaj (1990–) 204, 254
Serres, Michel (1930–2019) 255
Sharp, Darren (1976–) 364
Shiva, Vandana (1952–) 54, 350
Sigurðsson, Oddur (1959–) 193
Škart (dates unknown) 249
Skinnebach, Lars (1973–) 182
Skrydstrup, Martin (dates unknown) 33
Sloterdijk, Peter (1947–) 168
Snyder, Timothy David (1969–) 145
Söderbäck, Fanny (dates unknown) 179
Sokal, Alan (1955–) 176
Sonfist, Alan (1946–) 56
SPACE10 (2015-) 352
Spinoza, Baruch (1632–1677) 313
Stapleton, Jaime (1964–) 328
Steffen, Alex (1968–) 124
Steiner, Rudolf Joseph Lorenz (1861–1925) 351
Stengers, Isabelle (1949–) 53, 96
Stiglitz, Joseph (1943–) 333
Stoermer, Eugene F. (1934–2012) 53
Strathern, Marilyn (1941–) 97
SUPERFLEX (1993-) 186

T

TallBear, Kim (dates unknown) 178, 179
Taut, Bruno (1880–1938) 105
Thacker, Eugene (dates unknown) 221
Theilgaard, Jesper (1955–) 208
Thornton, James (1954–) 108
Thorsen, Line Marie (1985–) 56
Thunberg, Greta (2003–) 96, 99, 274
Todd, Zoe (1883–) 141
Tokarczuk, Olga (1962–) 340
Tredje Natur 266
Tronto, Joan (1952–) 54
Trump, Donald (1946–) 177, 257
Tsing, Anna (1952–) 23, 54, 180
Tsurumi, Shunsuke (1922–2015) 59
Twardowski, Kazimierz (1866–1938) 280
Tønder, Lars (1972–) 312

V

VanderMeer, Jeff (1968–) 156
Vannini, April (1976–) 140
Vannini, Phillip (1974–) 140
Venturi, Robert Charles (1925–2018) 251
Varela, Francisco (1946–2001) 168
Vince, Gaia (1974–) 48
von Bismarck, Julius (1983–) 290, 291
von Clausewitz, Carl (1780–1831) 375
von Hayek, Friedrich August (1899–1992) 328
von Humboldt, Alexander (1769–1859) 8, 76, 77, 78, 79, 260
von Uexküll, Jakob (1864–1944) 168

W

Wark, McKenzie (1961–) 54
Waters, Alice (1944–) 190
Weber, Max (1864–1920) 375
Weibel, Peter (1944–) 174
Weil, Simone (1909–1943) 40
Welzer, Harald (1958–) 145
Whitehead, Alfred North (1861–1947) 94
Wilde, Oscar (1854–1900) 92
Wittgenstein, Ludwig (1889–1851) 174
Wolfe, Cary (1959–) 166
Woolf, Adeline Virginia (1882–1941) 122, 123

Y

Yeats, William Butler (1865–1939) 123

Z

Zalasiewicz, Jan (1954–) 220
Žižek, Slavoj (1949–) 376
Zuboff, Shoshana (1951–) 333

Connectedness
An Incomplete Encyclopedia of the Anthropocene

Editing: Marianne Krogh
Copy editing: Sidsel Kjærulff Rasmussen
Project management: Sidsel Kjærulff Rasmussen
Translations:
'Con-nect-ed-ness: An Introduction', 'Agriculture', 'Connectedness', 'Denial', 'Explicitation', 'Fire', 'Natureculture', 'Pandemic', 'Production', 'Tenderness', 'Xenophobia': Translated from Danish by Dorte Herholdt Silver
'Garden': Translated from Chinese by Andrew Maerkle
'Oil': Translated from Danish by Charlotte Barslund
'Sensitivity': Translated from Polish by Jennifer Croft and Antonia Lloyd-Jones
'Chthulucene': First published in Rosi Braidotti and Maria Hlavajova, eds., *Posthuman Glossary*, London, 2018
Proofreading: Wendy Brouwer
Picture editing: Marianne Krogh, Claudia Rebecca Juul Kassentoft and Sidsel Kjærulff Rasmussen
Layout and cover design: Rasmus Koch Studio
The book is typeset in AG Book Pro and Adobe Caslon Pro
Paper: 115 g Munken Premium Cream, 240 g Munken Lynx
Prepress: Narayana Press
Printing: Livonia Press
Printed in Latvia 2021
2nd edition, 1st print run
ISBN 978-87-94102-30-8

Strandberg Publishing A/S
Gammel Mønt 14
1117 Copenhagen K
Denmark
www.strandbergpublishing.dk

DAC
Bryghuspladsen 10
1473 Copenhagen K
Denmark
www.dac.dk

MIX
Paper from responsible sources
FSC® C002795
FSC www.fsc.org

With thanks to Boris, Emmy, Polina, Rikke and Niels for helping to set this endeavour in motion.

The first edition of this book was published with the generous support of

New Carlsberg Foundation
The Danish Art Foundation
The Dreyer Foundation
Bestles Fond
The Ministry of Culture, Denmark

Photo credits

ABC 4 Utah – 293 m | Aerocene Foundation – 43, 47 | Alain Delorme – 382–383 | Andri Snær Magnason – 194–195 | Asmund Havsteen-Mikkelsen – 252 | Catherine Langer – 27 b l | CBS New York – 293 b | Courtesy Tomás Saraceno, with thanks to the Arachnophilia Archives – 309–311 | Creative Commons – 78–79, 80–81, 408–409 | Djordje Balmazovic – 248 | Extinction Rebellion – 132–135 | Fabrice Monteiro – 95–97 | FOX 13 – 293 t | © Frédérique Aït-Touati, Alexandra Arènes, Axelle Gérgoire – 262–263 | Galleri Nicolai Wallner and Jesper Just – 146–149 | Hampus Berndtson – 12, 15, 25 m t, 223–225 | Hans H. Bævholm – 269 | Henry W. Kendall, 1992 – 401 | Herbco – 27 m | IEA 2019, Total primary energy supply (TPES) by source, World 1990–2017, All rights reserved – 163 | Issuecrawler.net, govcom.org Foundation, Amsterdam – 116 | Jeff VanderMeer – 157–159 | Jim Reed – 214–217 | Julian Charrière and Julius von Bismarck; VG Bild-Kunst, Bonn, Germany – 290–292, 294–295 | Lars Skinnebach – 183–185 | Lucas Foglia – 394 | Lundgaard & Tranberg Architects – 18, 21–22, 25 m b | Mark Latimer – 98 | Martin Skydstrup – 33 | Miguel Medina / AFP / Ritzau Scanpix – 25 b | Minik Rosing – 201–203 | NAM BUI – 85, 88 | © National Maritime Museum, Greenwich, London – 63 t | Natural History Museum of Denmark – 27 t, 27 b r | NORRØN – 170–171 | Rasmus Hjortshøj – COAST – 66–71 | © Rikke Luther – 329–337 | Rune Bosse – 231–233 | Science History Images / Alamy Stock Photo – 6–7 | SPACE10 + Irina Boersma – 353 | Stephen White, London © Antony Gormley – 63 b | Steve Earle – 143 | Studio Tomás Saraceno – 44–46 | Superflex – 187–189 | Svetislava Isakov – 19, 24 b, 26 | Tiffany Chung – 86–87 | Till Rickert – 24 m l, 247, 301, 315, 361 | Torben Eskerod – 359 | Wikimedia Commons – 24 t (photo: Paolo Monti), 24 m r (photo: Wolfgang Moroder), 25 t, 77, 164 | Yale School of Architecture Students – 105–106 | Yasmeen Lari / Heritage Foundation of Pakistan © IOM 2014 – 55 | Yukiko Iwatani – 59–61

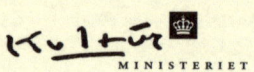